BEHAVIOR-BASED ROBOTICS

Intelligent Robots and Autonomous Agents
Ronald C. Arkin, editor

Behavior-Based Robotics
Ronald C. Arkin, 1998
Robot Shaping: An Experiment in Behavior Engineering
Marco Dorigo and Marco Colombetti, 1998

BEHAVIOR-BASED ROBOTICS

Ronald C. Arkin

The MIT Press
Cambridge, Massachusetts
London, England

Second printing, 1999

This book was set in Times Roman by Windfall Software using ZzTEX.

Printed and bound in the United States of America.

Library of Congress Cataloging-in-Publication Data

Arkin, Ronald C., 1949–
  Behavior-based robotics / Ronald C. Arkin.
    p.   cm. — (Intelligent robots and autonomous agents)
  Includes bibliographical references and index.
  ISBN 0-262-01165-4 (alk. paper)
  1. Autonomous robots.   2. Intelligent control systems. I. Title.
II. Series.
TJ211.A75   1998
629.8′92—dc21   97-18389
                                                     CIP

To Michaelle, Matthew, Rebekah, Sarah, and Hannah

Contents

x   Contents

Foreword

Michael Arbib

Had he turned from politics to robotics, John Fitzgerald Kennedy might well have said, "Ask not what robotics can do for you, ask what you can do for robotics." Ronald Arkin has a more balanced view, however, for his book makes us vividly aware that the interplay between robotics and a host of other disciplines proceeds richly and fruitfully in both directions.

The emphasis is on the "brains" of robots rather than on their "bodies"—thus the title "Behavior-Based robots," which moves the details of robot sensors and actuators firmly into the background, making them secondary to the main aim of the book: to understand what behaviors we should expect robots to exhibit, and which computational mechanisms can serve to achieve these behaviors. However, I should note two features of the book that contribute greatly to its liveliness: a fine selection of epigrams and a superb gallery of photographs of robots from all around the world. Thus even while the book focuses on robot brains, we have many opportunities to admire human wit and robot bodies.

Ronald Arkin has always been fascinated by parallels between animals (including humans) and robots. This is fully expressed here in his marshaling of data from biology and psychology to show that much of the behavior of animals and thus of robots can be understood in terms of patterns emerging from a basic set of reactive modules. However, Arkin also shows us that many behaviors can be achieved only by detailed analysis of representations of the world, and of the animal's place within it, built up from long-term experience. We are thus offered an insightful analysis of robot architectures that places them along a continuum from reactive to deliberative.

Schema theory provides a powerful framework exploited here to create behaviors that are distributed in their control structures, integrative of action and perception, and open to learning. These schemas can in turn be implemented using conventional computer programs, finite state acceptors, neural networks, or genetic algorithms. In building our appreciation of this frame-work, Arkin uses robotics to illuminate basic issues in computer science and artificial intelligence, and to feed new insights back into our reading of biology and psychology.

The book's chapter on social behavior presents what is itself a relatively recent chapter of robotics—sociorobotics. While in its infancy, we can see in the studies of robot teams, inter-robot communication, and social lerning the beginnings not only of a powerful new technology, but also of a new science of experimental sociology.

Finally, we are taken to that meeting place between science fiction, philos-ophy, and technology that attracted many of us to wonder about robots in the first place. The final chapter, "Fringe Robotics: Beyond Behavior" (a nod to the 1960s' British review "Beyond the Fringe"?), debates the issues of robot thought, consciousness, emotion, and imagination, returns to Arkin's long-standing concern with the possible utility to robots of analogs of hormones and homeostasis, and closes with an all too brief glimpse of nanotechnology.

In this way we are given a tour that impresses with the depth of its analysis of the schemas underlying robot behavior, while continually illustrating the deep reciprocity between robotics and biology, psychology, sociology, and philosophy, and the important connections between robotics and many other areas of computer science. This is a subject whose fascination can only increase in the decades ahead as many researchers build on the framework so ably presented here.

Preface

Unprovided with original learning, unformed in the habits of thinking, unskilled in the arts of composition, I resolved to write a book.
—Edward Gibbon

My motivation for writing this book grew out of a perceived need for an integrated explanatory text on the subject. This perception came from the difficulty I have had in finding a good book for a course in Autonomous Robots I have been teaching for the past ten years or so. Although an extensive body of literature has been produced on behavior-based robots, the lack of such a text made it hard to introduce students to this field without throwing them into fairly deep technical literature, generally making it accessible only to advanced graduate students. Though there are several good books of collected original papers, they proved to be only partially adequate as an introduction.

This book's intended audience includes upper-level undergraduates and graduate students studying artificial intellegence (AI) and robotics, as well as those interested in learning more about robotics in general. It assumes the ability to comprehend a course in college-level artificial intelligence. The text could be used to support a course in AI-based or autonomous robotics or to supplement a general AI course.

Acknowledgments, of course, are a necessity. Being a religious man, I'd first like to thank God and Jesus Christ for enabling me to complete this long and arduous task. Two biblical passages that have inspired me as a roboticist can be found in Matthew 3:9 and Luke 19:37–40.

My family has been most gracious in putting up with the hardships generated by authorship. My wife, to my amazement, proofread the entire work. She and my four children put up with the inevitable absences and strains caused by this time-sapping process. I love them dearly for their support.

Earlier tutorials on behavior-based robotics, presented initially by myself (at the 1991 IEEE International Conference on Systems, Man, and Cybernetics) and later with Rod Grupen (at the 1993 International Conference on Robotics and Automation, and the 1993 International Joint Conference on Artificial Intelligence) helped coalesce many of the ideas contained herein. I thank Rod for working with me on these.

A large number of students at Georgia Tech over many years have contributed in a wide range of invaluable ways. I'd expressly like to thank Robin Murphy, Doug MacKenzie, Tucker Balch, Khaled Ali, Zhong Chen, Russ Clark, Elizabeth Nitz, David Hobbs, Warren Gardner, William Carter, Gary Boone, Michael Pearce, Juan Carlos Santamaria, David Cardoze, Bill Wester, Keith Ward, David Vaughn, Mark Pearson, and others who have made this book possible. I'd also like to thank Brandon Rhodes for pointing out the short story that leads into chapter 10.

Interactions with many of my professional colleagues in residence at Georgia Tech, as well as visitors, have also helped to generate of the ideas found in this text. Among them are Prof. Chris Atkeson, Dr. Jonathan Cameron, Dr. Tom Collins, Prof. Ashok Goel, Prof. Jessica Hodgins, Dr. Daryl Lawton, Dr. John Pani, Prof. T. M. Rao, and Prof. Ashwin Ram. My thanks to y'all.

This book would never have been possible without the research funding support that came from a variety of sources. I'd like to acknowledge each of these agencies and the cognizant funding agent: the National Science Foundation (Howard Moraff), DARPA (Eric Mettala and Pradeep Khosla), the Office of Naval Research (Teresa McMullen), and the Westinghouse Savannah River Technology Center (Clyde Ward).

The folks at MIT Press have been great to work with from the book's inception, in particular the late Harry Stanton and Jerry Weinstein. I am also indebted to Prof. Michael Arbib for so graciously contributing the foreword to this book.

Special thanks go to Jim Hendler for piloting a draft version of the book for a course at the University of Maryland.

Finally, it is impossible to list all the people within the greater research community who have contributed with encouragement, support, and insight into this endeavor. To all of you I am deeply indebted and can only hope that this text serves in some way as compensation for those efforts.

Chapter 1

Whence Behavior?

<hr>

> **Chapter Objectives**
>
> 1. To understand what intelligent robots are.
> 2. To review the recent history that led to the development of behavior-based robotic systems.
> 3. To learn and appreciate the wide spectrum of robot control methods.

1.1 TOWARD INTELLIGENT ROBOTS

Perhaps the best way to begin our study is with a question: If we could create intelligent robots, what should they be like, and what should they be able to do? Answering the first part of this question—"What should they be like?"—requires a description of both the robot's physical structure (appearance) and its performance (behavior). However, the second part of the question—"What should they be able to do?"—frames the answer for the first part. Robots that need to move objects must be able to grasp them; robots that have to traverse rugged outdoor terrain need locomotion systems capable of moving in adverse conditions; robots that must function at night need sensors capable of operating under those conditions. A guiding principle in robotic design, whether structural or behavioral, involves understanding the environment within which the robot operates and the task(s) it is required to undertake. This ecological approach, in which the robot's goals and surroundings heavily influence its design, will be a recurring theme throughout this book.

But what is a robot? According to the Robotics Industry Association (RIA), "a robot is a re-programmable, multi-functional, manipulator designed to move material, parts, tools, or specialized devices through variable programmed motions for the performance of a variety of tasks" (Jablonski and Posey 1985).

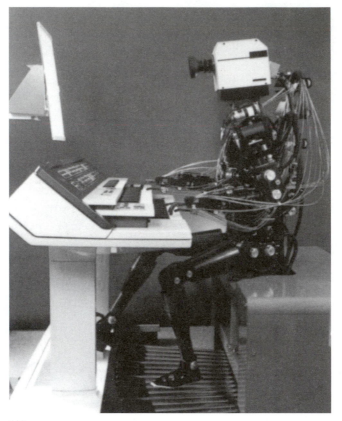

(A)

Figure 1.1
Anthropomorphic robots. (A) WASUBOT, a keyboard musician capable of reading music. (B) WHL-I, a robot that walked in excess of 65 km during one exhibition. (Photographs courtesy of Atsuo Takanishi of Waseda University.)

This definition is quite restrictive, excluding mobile robots, among other things. On the other extreme, another definition describes robotics as the intelligent connection of perception to action (Brady 1985). This seems overly inclusive but does acknowledge the necessary relationship between these essential ingredients of robotic systems.

In any case, our working definition will be: An intelligent robot is a machine able to extract information from its environment and use knowledge about its world to move safely in a meaningful and purposive manner. Hollywood has

(B)

Figure 1.1 *(continued)*

often depicted robots as anthropomorphic creatures fashioned in the image of man, having two legs, two arms, a torso, and a head. Indeed robots have actually been created that have a humanlike structure: Figure 1.1 illustrates two such robots. Robots have often been modeled after animals other than humans, however. Insectlike robots are now commonplace and are commercially available; others look more like horses, spiders, or octopi, as figure 1.2 shows.

Robots also often look like vehicles capable of operating on the ground, in the air, or underseas. The examples shown in figure 1.3 represent classes of robots generically referred to as unmanned vehicles: UAV (unmanned aerial vehicle), UGV (unmanned ground vehicle), and UUV (unmanned undersea vehicle).

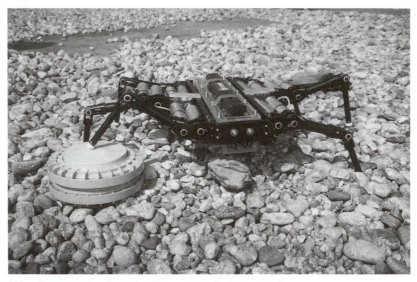

(A)

(B)

Figure 1.2

(C)

Figure 1.2 *(continued)*
Animal-like robots. (A) Ariel, a hexapod crablike robot. (Photograph courtesy of IS
Robotics, Somerville, MA.) (B) Quadruped robot that trots, paces and bounds, built at
the CMU leg laboratory in 1984. (Photograph by Jack Bingham. © 1992 Marc Raibert.
All rights reserved.) (C) HEG1060 Hexapod robot. (Photograph courtesy of California
Cybernetics Co., Tujunga, CA.)

Robots can be differentiated in terms of their size, the materials from which
they are made, the way they are joined together, the actuators they use (motors
and transmissions), the types of sensing systems they possess, their locomotion
system, and their onboard computer systems. But a physical structure is clearly
not enough. Robots must be animate, so they must have an underlying control
system to provide the ability to move in a coordinated way. This book focuses
on the performance and behavioral aspects of robotics and the design of control
systems that allow them to perform the way we would like. The physical design
of robots is not addressed: Many good sources already cover that material (e.g.,
Craig 1989, McKerrow 1991).

(A)

(B)

Figure 1.3

(C)

Figure 1.3 *(continued)*
Unmanned vehicles. (A) Unmanned undersea vehicle: the Advanced Unmanned Search System (AUSS). (B) Unmanned aerial vehicle: Multipurpose Surveillance and Security Mission Platform (MSSMP). (C) Unmanned Ground Vehicle: Ground Surveillance Robot (GSR). (Photographs courtesy of U.S. Navy.)

How do we realize the goal of intelligent robotic behavior? What basic science and technology is needed to achieve this goal? This book attempts to answer these questions by studying the basis and organization of behavior and the related roles of knowledge and perception, learning and adaptation, and teamwork.

1.2 PRECURSORS

People that are really weird can get into sensitive positions and have a tremendous impact on history.

—J. Danforth Quayle

To invent you need a good imagination and a pile of junk.
—Thomas Alva Edison

The significant history associated with the origins of modern behavior-based robotics is important in understanding and appreciating the current state of the art. We now review important historical developments in three related areas: cybernetics, artificial intelligence, and robotics.

1.2.1   Cybernetics

Norbert Wiener is generally credited with leading, in the late 1940s, the development of cybernetics: a marriage of control theory, information science, and biology that seeks to explain the common principles of control and communication in both animals and machines (Wiener 1948). Ashby (1952) and Wiener furthered this view of an organism as a machine by using the mathematics developed for feedback control systems to express natural behavior. This affirmed the notion of situatedness, that is, a strong two-way coupling between an organism and its environment.

In 1953, W. Grey Walter applied these principles in the creation of a precursor robotic design termed *Machina Speculatrix* which was subsequently transformed into hardware form as Grey Walter's tortoise. Some of the principles that were captured in his design include:

1. *Parsimony:* Simple is better. Simple reflexes can serve as the basis for behavior. "The variations of behavior patterns exhibited even with such economy of structure are complex and unpredictable" (Walter 1953, p. 126).

2. *Exploration* or *speculation:* The system never remains still except when feeding (recharging). This constant motion is adequate under normal circumstances to keep it from being trapped. "In its exploration of any ordinary room it inevitably encounters many obstacles; but apart from stairs and fur rugs, there are few situations from which it cannot extricate itself" (Walker 1953, p. 126).

3. *Attraction (positive tropism):* The system is motivated to move towards some environmental object. In the case of the tortoise, this is a light of moderate intensity.

4. *Aversion (negative tropism):* The system moves away from certain negative stimuli, for example, avoiding heavy obstacles and slopes.

5. *Discernment:* The system has the ability to distinguish between productive and unproductive behavior, adapting itself to the situation at hand.

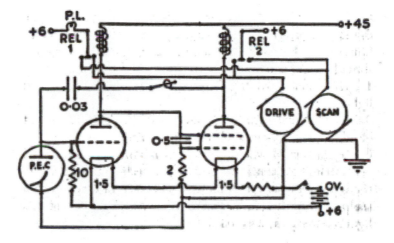

Figure 1.4
Circuit of *Machina Speculatrix*. (From *The Living Brain* by W. Grey Walter. Copyright 1953 © 1963 and renewed © 1981, 1991 by W. Grey Walter. Reprinted by permission of W. W. Norton and Company, Inc.)

The tortoise itself, constructed as an analog device (figure 1.4), consisted of two sensors, two actuators, and two "nerve cells" or vacuum tubes. A directional photocell for detecting light and a bump contact sensor provided the requisite environmental feedback. One motor steered the single front driving wheel. The photocell always pointed in the direction of this wheel and thus could scan the environment. The driving motor powered the wheel and provided locomotion.

The tortoise exhibited the following behaviors:

■ **Seeking light:** The sensor rotated until a weak light source was detected while the drive motor continuously moved the robot to explore the environment at the same time.

■ **Head toward weak light:** Once a weak light was detected, the tortoise moved in its direction.

■ **Back away from bright light:** An aversive behavior repelled the tortoise from bright light sources. This behavior was used to particular advantage when the tortoise was recharging.

■ **Turn and push:** Used to avoid obstacles, this behavior overrode the light response.

■ **Recharge battery:** When the onboard battery power was low, the tortoise perceived a strong light source as weak. Because the recharging station had a

Figure 1.5
Grey Walter's tortoise, recently restored to working order by Owen Holland. (Photograph courtesy of Owen Holland, The University of the West of England.)

strong light over it, the robot moved toward it and docked. After recharging, the light source was perceived as strong, and the robot was repelled from the recharging station.

The behaviors were prioritized from lowest to highest order: seeking light, move to/from light, and avoid obstacle. The tortoise always acted on the highest priority behavior applicable, for example choosing to avoid obstacles over moving toward a light. Behavior-based robotics still uses this basic principle, referred to as an arbitration coordination mechanism (section 3.4.3), widely. Walter's tortoise exhibited moderately complex behavior: moving safely about a room and recharging itself as needed (figure 1.5). One recent architecture (Agah and Bekey 1997), described in section 9.8.3, employs Walter's ideas on positive and negative tropisms as a basis for creating adaptive behavior-based robotic systems.

Valentino Braitenberg revived this tradition three decades after Walter (Braitenberg 1984). Taking the vantage point of a psychologist, he extended the principles of analog circuit behavior to a series of gedankenexperiments involving the design of a collection of vehicles. These systems used inhibitory

and excitatory influences, directly coupling the sensors to the motors. As before, seemingly complex behavior resulted from relatively simple sensorimotor
transformations. Braitenberg created a wide range of vehicles, including those
imagined to exhibit cowardice, aggression, and even love (figure 1.6). As with
Walter's tortoise, these systems are inflexible, custom machines and are not
reprogrammable. Nonetheless, the variability of their overt behavior is compelling.

Eventually, scientists created Braitenberg creatures that were true robots,
not merely thought experiments. In one such effort, scientists at MIT's Media
Lab (Hogg, Martin, and Resnick 1991) used specially modified LEGO bricks
to build twelve autonomous creature-vehicles using Braitenberg's principles,
including a timid shadow seeker, an indecisive shadow-edge finder, a paranoid
shadow-fearing robot, a dogged obstacle avoider, an insecure wall follower,
and a driven light seeker. Even more complex creatures have been assembled,

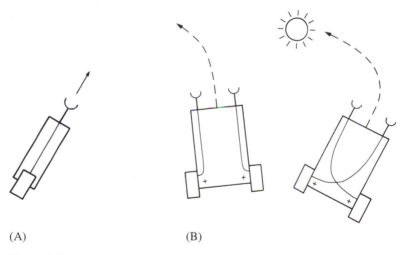

(A)   (B)

Figure 1.6
Braitenberg Vehicles
(A) Vehicle 1 (Single motor/single sensor): Motion is always forward in the direction of
the sensor stalk, with the speed controlled by the sensor. Environmental perturbations
(slippage, rough terrain) produce changes in direction.
(B) Vehicle 2 (Two sensors/two motors): The photophobe on the left is aversive to
light (exhibiting "fear" by fleeing) since the motor closest to the light source moves
faster than the one farther away. This results in a net motion away from the light. The
photovore on the left is attracted to light when the wires connecting sensors and motors
are merely reversed from the photophobe (exhibiting "aggression" by charging into the
attractor).

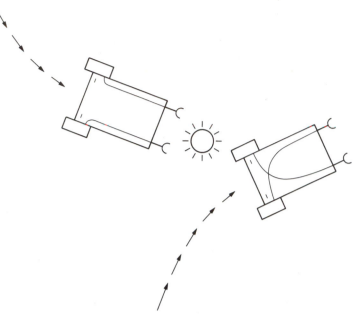

(C)

Figure 1.6 *(continued)*
(C) Vehicle 3: Same wiring as for Vehicle 2 but now with inhibitory connections. The vehicles slow down in the presence of a strong light source and go fast in the presence of weak light. In both cases, the vehicle approaches and stops by the light source (with one facing the light and one with the light source to the rear). The vehicle on the left is said to "love" the light source since it will stay there indefinitely, while the vehicle on the right explores the world, liking to be near its current attractor, but always on the lookout for something else.
(D) Vehicle 4: By adding various nonlinear speed dependencies to Vehicle 3, where the speed peaks somewhere between the maximum and minimum intensities, other interesting motor behaviors can be observed. This can result in oscillatory navigation between two different light sources (top) or by circular or other unusual patterns traced around a single source (bottom).
(Figures from Braitenberg 1984. Reprinted with permission.)

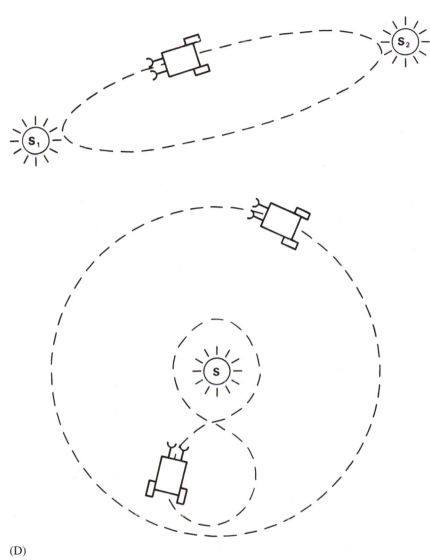

(D)

Figure 1.6 *(continued)*

attributed with personality traits such as persistence, consistency, inhumanity, or a frantic or observant nature. Granted, it is quite a leap to attribute these traits to robots built from such extremely simple circuits and plastic toy blocks, but the mere fact that an observer can perceive these qualities, even mildly, in such simple creatures is notable.

1.2.2 Artificial Intelligence

The birth of artificial intelligence (AI) as a distinct field is generally associated with the Dartmouth Summer Research Conference held in August 1955. This conference's goals involved the study of a wide range of topics including language use, neural nets, complexity theory, self-improvement, abstractions, and creativity. In the original proposal (McCarthy et al. 1955), Marvin Minsky indicates that an intelligent machine "would tend to build up within itself an abstract model of the environment in which it is placed. If it were given a problem it could first explore solutions within the internal abstract model of the environment and then attempt external experiments." This approach dominated robotics research for the next thirty years, during which time AI research developed a strong dependence upon the use of representational knowledge and deliberative reasoning methods for robotic planning. Hierarchical organization for planning was also mainstream: A plan is any hierarchical process in the organism that can control the order in which a sequence of operations is performed. (Miller, Galanter, and Pribram 1960, p.16).

Some of the better known examples of the AI planning tradition include:

- STRIPS: This theorem-proving system used first-order logic to develop a navigational plan (Fikes and Nilsson 1971).
- ABSTRIPS: This refinement of the STRIPS system used a hierarchy of abstraction spaces to improve the efficiency of a STRIPS-type planner, refining the details of a plan as they become important (Sacerdoti 1974).
- HACKER: This system searches through a library of procedures to propose a plan, which it later debugs. The blocks-world domain (toy blocks moved about by a simulated oversimplified robotic arm) served as a primary demonstration venue (Sussman 1975).
- NOAH: This hierarchical robotic assembly planner uses problem decomposition and then criticizes the potentially interacting subproblems, reordering their planned execution as necessary (Sacerdoti 1975).

The classical AI methodology has two important characteristics (Boden 1995): the ability to represent hierarchical structure by abstraction and the use of "strong" knowledge that employs explicit symbolic representational assertions about the world. AI's influence on robotics up to this point was in the idea that knowledge and knowledge representation are central to intelligence, and that robotics was no exception. Perhaps this was a consequence of AI's preoccupation with human-level intelligence. Considering lower life forms seemed uninteresting.

Behavior-based robotics systems reacted against these traditions. Perhaps Brooks (1987a) said it best: "Planning is just a way of avoiding figuring out what to do next." Although initially resisted, as paradigm shifts often are, the notion of sensing and acting within the environment started to take preeminence in AI-related robotics research over the previous focus on knowledge representation and planning. Enabling advances in robotic and sensor hardware had made it feasible to test the behavior-based robotics community's hypotheses. The results captured the imagination of AI researchers around the world.

The inception and growth of distributed artificial intelligence (DAI) paralleled these developments. Beginning as early as the Pandemonium system (Selfridge and Neisser 1960), the notion began to take root that multiple competing or cooperating processes (referred to initially as demons and later as agents) are capable of generating coherent behavior. Early blackboard-based speech understanding systems such as Hearsay II (Erman et al. 1980) referred to these asynchronous, independent agents as knowledge sources, communicating with each other through a global data structure called a blackboard. Minsky's Society of Mind Theory (Minsky 1986) forwarded multiagent systems as the basis for all intelligence, claiming that although each agent is as simple as it can be, through the coordinated and concerted interaction between these simple agents, highly complex intelligence can emerge. Individual behaviors can often be viewed as independent agents in behavior-based robotics, relating it closely to DAI.

1.2.3   Robotics

Mainstream roboticists have by necessity generally been more concerned with perception and action than their classical artificial intelligence counterparts. To conduct robotics research, robots are needed. Those who only work with simulations often ignore this seemingly obvious point. Robots can be complex to build and difficult to maintain. To position current research relative to them, it is worth briefly reviewing some of roboticists' earliest efforts, bearing in mind that technology in the 1960s and 1970s severely constrained these projects compared to the computational luxuries afforded researchers today.

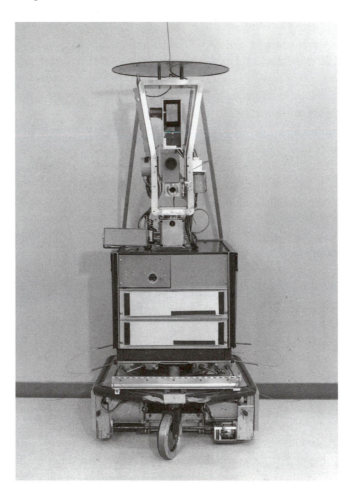

Figure 1.7
Shakey. (Photograph courtesy of SRI International.)

Many other robots will be discussed throughout this book, but these systems are notable as pioneers for those that followed.

■ **Shakey:** One of the first mobile robots, Shakey (figure 1.7), was constructed in the late 1960s at the Stanford Research Institute (Nilsson 1969). It inhabited an artificial world, an office area with objects specially colored and shaped to assist it in recognizing an object using vision. It planned an action such as pushing the recognized object from one place to another, and then executed the plan. The STRIPS planning system mentioned earlier was developed for use in this system. The robot itself was constructed of two independently controlled stepper motors and had a vidicon television camera and optical range finder mounted at the top. The camera had motor-controlled tilt, focus, and iris capabilities. Whiskerlike bump sensors were mounted at the periphery of the robot for protection. The planner used information stored within a symbolic world model to determine what actions to take to achieve the robot's goal at a given time. In this system, perception provided the information to maintain and modify the world model's representations.

■ **HILARE:** This project began around 1977 at Laboratoire d'Automatique et d'Analyse des Systèmes (LAAS) in Toulouse, France (Giralt, Chatila, and Vaisset 1984). The robot HILARE (figure 1.8) was equipped with three wheels: two drive and one caster. It was rather heavy, weighing in at 400 kg. Its world

Figure 1.8
HILARE. (Photograph courtesy of LAAS-CNRS, Toulouse, France.)

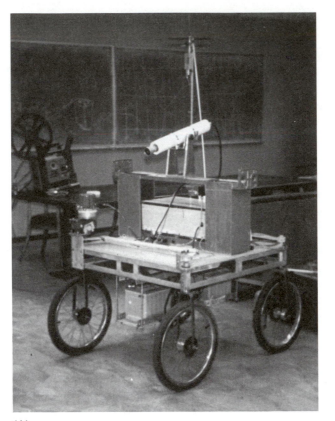

(A)

Figure 1.9

contained the smooth flat floors found in a typical office environment. For sensing, it used a video camera, fourteen ultrasonic sensors, and a laser range finder. Planning was conducted within a multilevel representational space: Geometric models represented the actual distances and measurements of the worlds, and a relational model expressed the connectivity of rooms and corridors. Of special note is HILARE's longevity. The robot was still being used for experimentation well over a decade after its initial construction (Noreils and Chatila 1989).

■ **Stanford Cart/CMU Rover:** The Stanford Cart (figure 1.9, A) was a minimal robotic platform used by Moravec to test stereo vision as a means for navigation (Moravec 1977). It was quite slow, lurching ahead about one meter every ten to fifteen minutes, with a full run lasting about five hours. The vi-

(B)

Figure 1.9 *(continued)*
(A) Stanford Cart. (B) CMU Rover. (Photographs courtesy of Hans Moravec and the Robotics Institute, Carnegie-Mellon University.)

sual processing was the most time-consuming aspect, but the cart successfully navigated fairly complex twenty meter courses, avoiding visually detected obstacles as it went. Obstacles were added to its internal world map as detected and were represented as enclosing spheres. The cart used a graph search algorithm to find the shortest path through this abstract model.

Around 1980, Moravec left for Carnegie-Mellon University (CMU) where he led the effort in constructing the CMU Rover (Moravec 1983), a smaller, cylindrical robot with three independently powered and steered wheel pairs capable of carrying a camera mounted on a pan/tilt mechanism as well as infrared and ultrasonic sensors (figure 1.9, B). This robot was followed by a

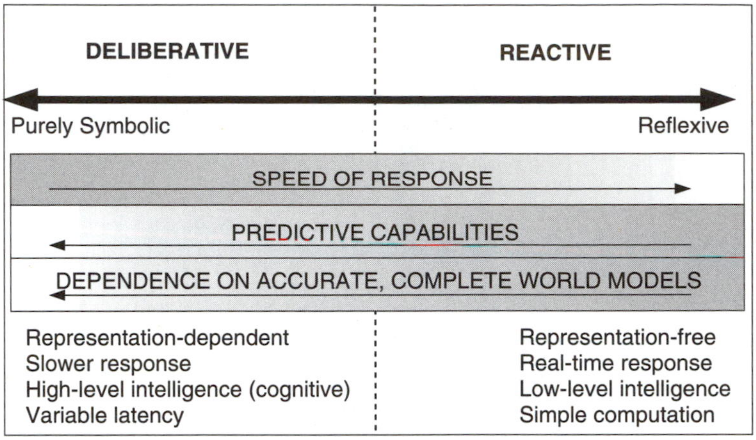

Figure 1.10
Robot control system spectrum.

long succession of other CMU robots, several of which are described in other portions of this book.

These and other robotic precursors set the stage for the advances and controversies to come as behavior-based robotic systems appeared in the mid-1980s.

1.3   THE SPECTRUM OF ROBOT CONTROL

Many different techniques and approaches for robotic control have been developed. Figure 1.10 depicts a spectrum of current robot control strategies. The left side represents methods that employ deliberative reasoning and the right represents reactive control. A robot employing deliberative reasoning requires relatively complete knowledge about the world and uses this knowledge to predict the outcome of its actions, an ability that enables it to optimize its performance relative to its model of the world. Deliberate reasoning often requires strong assumptions about this world model, primarily that the knowledge upon which reasoning is based is consistent, reliable, and certain. If the information the reasoner uses is inaccurate or has changed since obtained, the outcome of reasoning may err seriously. In a dynamic world, where objects may be moving arbitrarily (e.g., in a battlefield or a crowded corridor), it is potentially dangerous to rely on past information that may no longer be valid. Representational world models are therefore generally constructed from both prior knowledge about the environment and incoming sensor data in support of deliberation.

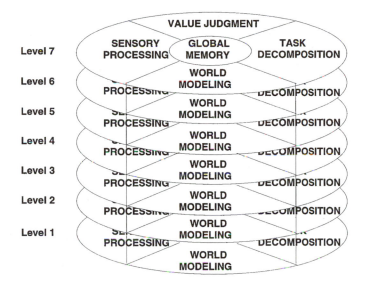

Figure 1.11
Albus's hierarchical intelligent control system.

Deliberative reasoning systems often have several common characteristics:

■ They are hierarchical in structure with a clearly identifiable subdivision of functionality, similar to the organization of commercial businesses or military command.

■ Communication and control occurs in a predictable and predetermined manner, flowing up and down the hierarchy, with little if any lateral movement.

■ Higher levels in the hierarchy provide subgoals for lower subordinate levels.

■ Planning scope, both spatial and temporal, changes during descent in the hierarchy. Time requirements are shorter and spatial considerations are more local at the lower levels.

■ They rely heavily on symbolic representation world models.

1.3.1   Deliberative/Hierarchical Control

The intelligent control robotics community, whose roots precede those of reactive behavior-based systems, uses deliberative reasoning methods as its principal paradigm. Albus, at the National Institute of Standards and Technology, is one of this philosophy's leading proponents. His methods attempt to integrate both natural and artificial reasoning (Albus 1991). Figure 1.11 depicts a jukebox-like hierarchical model, with each layer consisting of four components; as outlined in Albus's theory of intelligence: sensory processing, world modeling, task decomposition, and value judgment. All layers are joined by a global memory through which representational knowledge is shared. Perhaps the most telling assertion that represents the heavy reliance on world models is reflected in Albus's views regarding the role of perception: Perception is the establishment and maintenance of correspondence between the internal world model and the external real world. Consequently, action results from reasoning over the world model. Perception thus is not tied directly to action.

In the mid-1980s, this view so dominated robotics that the government developed a standard architecture that reflected this model. Figure 1.12 shows the NASA/NIST(NBS) standard reference model for Telerobot Control System Architecture or NASREM (Albus, McCain, and Lumia 1987). Despite the government's endorsement, NASREM has had only limited acceptance but is still being used for tasks such as creating a flight telerobotic servicer capable of performing maintenance and simple assembly tasks for NASA's space station Freedom (Lumia 1994). The six levels embodied on this system each capture a specific functionality. Simply put, from the lowest level to the highest:

1. Servo: provides servo control (position, velocity, and force management) for all the robot's actuators.
2. Primitive: determines motion primitives to generate smooth trajectories.
3. Elemental move: defines and plans for the robot paths free of collisions with environmental obstacles.
4. Task: converts desired actions on a single object in the world into sequences of elemental moves that can accomplish them.
5. Service bay: converts actions on groups of objects into tasks to be performed on individual objects, scheduling tasks within the service bay area.
6. Service mission: decomposes the overall high-level mission plan into service bay commands.

Higher levels in the hierarchy create subgoals for lower levels.

Another architectural embodiment of these same ideas, RCS (the Real-time Control System reference model architecture), has the same basic layering as NASREM but more faithfully embeds the components outlined in Albus's theory of intelligence. This approach was tested in simulation for an autonomous submarine (Huang 1996) but has not yet been fielded on the actual vehicle.

In other work along these same lines, researchers at Drexel University have focused on the theory of intelligent hierarchical control and created a control model possessing the following characteristics:

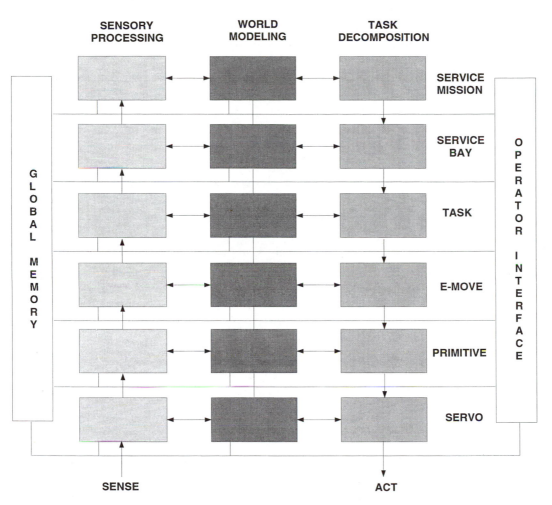

Figure 1.12
NASREM architecture.

- It correlates human teams and robotic control structures:
- A hierarchy of decision makers implements this idea.
- Autonomous control systems are organized as teams of decision makers.
- It assumes that the task is decomposable, that is, it can result in structured subtasks.
- Hierarchies are generated by recursion using a generalized controller.
- Preconditions are established at each level of recursion to ensure proper execution.

Figure 1.13 shows a mobile robot control system consisting of six levels. The set of nested hierarchical controllers consists of a high-level planner, navigator, pilot, path monitor, controller, and low-level control system.

In yet another representative of the intelligent controls community, research at the Rensselaer Polytechnic Institute (Lefebvre and Saridis 1992) restricted the hierarchy to three primary levels: organization level (conducts high-level planning and reasoning), coordination level (provides integration across various hardware subsystems), and execution level (supports basic control and hardware). This approach implements the principle of increasing precision with decreasing intelligence as one descends through the hierarchy. Figure 1.14 depicts a logical model of this architectural framework. Note the clear—and restrictive—flow of control and communication between levels within the hierarchy.

Hierarchical control is seemingly well suited for structured and highly predictable environments (e.g., manufacturing). Reactive systems, however, were developed in response to several of the apparent drawbacks associated with the hierarchical design paradigm including a perceived lack of responsiveness in unstructured and uncertain environments due both to the requirements of world modeling and the limited communication pathways; and the difficulty in engineering complete systems as incremental competency proved difficult to achieve, that is, virtually the entire system needed to be built before testing was feasible.

1.3.2   Reactive Systems

The right side of the spectrum depicted in figure 1.10 represents reactive systems. *Simply put, reactive control is a technique for tightly coupling perception and action, typically in the context of motor behaviors, to produce timely robotic response in dynamic and unstructured worlds.*

We further define the following:

■ *An individual behavior:* a stimulus/response pair for a given environmental setting that is modulated by attention and determined by intention.
■ *Attention:* prioritizes tasks and focuses sensory resources and is determined by the current environmental context.
■ *Intention:* determines which set of behaviors should be active based on the robotic agent's internal goals and objectives.
■ *Overt or emergent behavior:* the global behavior of the robot or organism as a consequence of the interaction of the active individual behaviors.

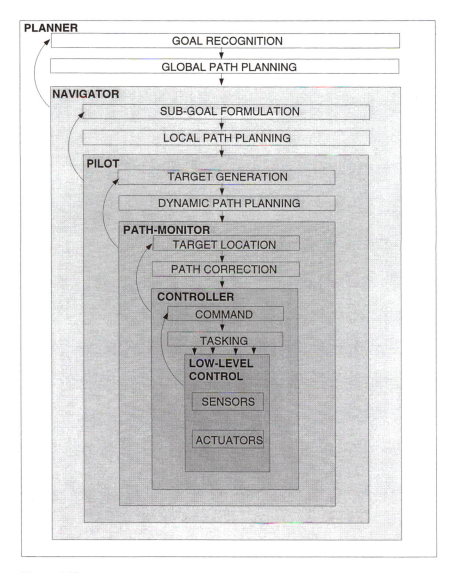

Figure 1.13
Nested hierarchical intelligent controller.

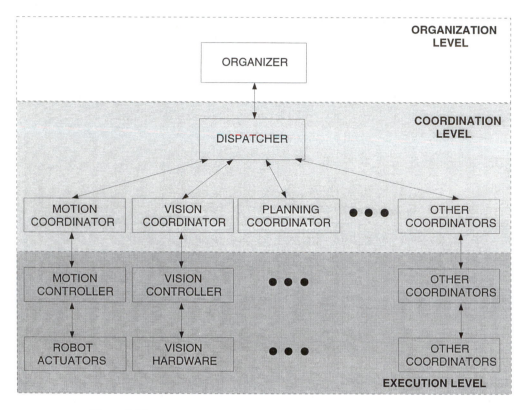

Figure 1.14
Logical model of hierarchical intelligent robot.

■ *Reflexive behavior* (alternatively, *purely reactive behavior*): behavior that is generated by hardwired reactive behaviors with tight sensor-effector arcs, where sensory information is not persistent and no world models are used whatsoever.

Several key aspects of this behavior-based methodology include (Brooks 1991b):

■ Situatedness: The robot is an entity situated and surrounded by the real world. It does not operate upon abstract representations of reality, but rather reality itself.
■ Embodiment: A robot has a physical presence (a body). This spatial reality has consequences in its dynamic interactions with the world that cannot be simulated faithfully.

■ Emergence: Intelligence arises from the interactions of the robotic agent with its environment. It is not a property of either the agent or the environment in isolation but is rather a result of the interplay between them.

This book focuses primarily on behavior-based reactive robotic systems, whose structure and organization chapters 3 and 4 describe in more detail. Hierarchical control, however, is also discussed further in the context of hybrid robotic architectures presented in chapter 6.

1.4   RELATED ISSUES

A few important issues central to understanding and appreciating the behavior-based paradigm warrant additional discussion before heading into the core of this book.

■ *Grounding in reality:* A chronic criticism of traditional artificial intelligence research is that it suffers from the *symbol grounding problem,* that is, the symbols with which the system reasons often have no physical correlation with reality; they are not grounded by perceptual or motor acts. In a sense ungrounded systems can be said to be delusional: Their world is an artifactual hallucination. Robotic simulations are often the most insidious examples of this problem, with "robots" purporting to be sensing and acting but instead just creating new symbols from old, none of which truly corresponds to actual events. Embodiment, as stated earlier, forces a robot to function within its environment: sensing, acting, and suffering directly from the consequences of its misperceptions and misconceptions. "Building robots that are situated in the world crystallizes the hard issues" (Flynn and Brooks 1989). For that reason this book focuses primarily on real robotic systems implemented in hardware as exemplars for robotic control.
■ *Ecological dynamics:* A physical agent does not reside in a vacuum but is typically immersed in a highly dynamic environment that varies significantly in both space and time. Further, these environmental dynamics, except for highly structured workplaces, are very difficult if not impossible to characterize. Nonetheless, if a situated robotic agent is to be designed properly, it must acknowledge within its design the opportunities and perils that the environment affords it. This is much easier said than done. In nature, evolutionary processes shape agents to fit their ecological niche; these time scales unfortunately are not available to the practicing roboticist. Adaptation, however can be crucially important; chapter 8 explores this further.

■ *Scalability:* Scalability of the behavior-based approach has been a major question from its inception. Although these methods are clearly well suited for low-level tasks requiring the competence of creatures such as insects, it has been unclear whether they would scale to conform to human-level intelligence. Tsotsos (1995), for example, argues that "the strict behaviorist position for the modeling of intelligence does not scale to human-like problems and performance." Section 7.1 considers this point further. Many of the strict behaviorists persist in their view that the approach has no limits; notably, Brooks (1990b) states that "we believe that in principle we have uncovered the fundamental foundation of intelligence." Others advocate a hybrid approach between symbolic reasoning and behavioral methods, arguing that these two approaches are fully compatible: "The false dichotomy that exists between hierarchical control and reactive systems should be dropped" (Arkin 1989d). (See also chapter 6.) Much current research focuses on testing the limits of behavior-based methods, and this theme will recur throughout this book.

1.5   WHAT'S AHEAD

This book consists of the following chapters:

1. **Introduction:** highlights the core issues of intelligent robotics and reviews the history of cybernetics, artificial intelligence, and robotics that led up to the development of behavior-based robotic systems.
2. **Animal behavior:** studies the basis for intelligence, biological systems, through the eyes of psychologists, neuroscientists, and ethologists and examines several representative robotic systems inspired by animal behavior.
3. **Robot behavior:** describes the basis for behavior-based robotics, including the notation, expression, encoding, assembling, and coordination of behaviors.
4. **Behavior-based architectures:** presents a range of robotic architectures employing the behavior-based paradigm.
5. **Representational issues for behavioral systems:** questions and explores the role of representational knowledge within the context of a behavior-based system.
6. **Hybrid deliberative/reactive architectures:** evaluates robotic architectures that couple more traditional artificial intelligence planning systems with reactive control systems in an effort to extend further the utility of behavior-based control.
7. **Perceptual basis for behavior-based control:** considers the issues concerning the connection of perception to action—sensor types, perceptual mod-

ules, expectations, attention, and so on—and presents perceptual design for a range of robotic tasks, including descriptions of specific applications.

8. **Adaptive behavior:** addresses how robots can cope with a changing world through a variety of learning and adaptation mechanisms, including reinforcement learning, neural networks, fuzzy logic, evolutionary methods, and others.

9. **Social behavior:** opens up behavior-based robotics to the consideration of how teams and societies of robots can function together effectively—raising new issues such as communication, interference, and multiagent competition, cooperation, and learning—and presents a case study illustrating many of these concepts.

10. **Open issues:** explores some open questions and philosophical issues regarding intelligence within artificial systems in general and behavior-based robots in particular.

Chapter 2
Animal Behavior

Animals, in their generation, are wiser than the sons of men; but their wisdom is confined to a few particulars, and lies in a very narrow compass.

—Joseph Addison

To create something in the image of nature is to create a machine, and it was by learning the inner workings of nature that man became a builder of machines.

—Eric Hoffer

Chapter Objectives

1. To develop an understanding of the possible relationships between animal behavior and robot control.
2. To provide a reasonable background in neuroscience, psychology, and ethology for the roboticist.
3. To examine a wide range of biologically motivated robotic systems.

2.1 WHAT DOES ANIMAL BEHAVIOR OFFER ROBOTICS?

The possibility of intelligent behavior is indicated by its manifestation in biological systems. It seems logical then that a suitable starting point for the study of behavior-based robotics should begin with an overview of biological behavior. First, animal behavior defines intelligence. Where intelligence begins and ends is an open-ended question, but we will concede in this text that intelligence can reside in subhuman animals. Our working definition will be that intelligence endows a system (biological or otherwise) with the ability to improve its likelihood of survival within the real world and where appropriate to compete or cooperate successfully with other agents to do so. Second, animal behavior provides an existence proof that intelligence is achievable. It is not a mystical concept, it is a concrete reality, although a poorly understood phenomena. Third, the study of animal behavior can provide models that a roboticist can operationalize within a robotic system. These models may be implemented with high fidelity to their animal counterparts or may serve only as an inspiration for the robotics researcher.

Roboticists have struggled to provide their machines with animals' simplest capabilities: the ability to perceive and act within the environment in a meaningful and purposive manner. Although a study of existing biological systems that already possess the ability to conduct these tasks successfully seems obviously a reasonable method to achieve that goal, the robotics community has historically resisted it for two principal reasons. First, the underlying hardware is fundamentally different. Biological systems bring a large amount of evolutionary baggage unnecessary to support intelligent behavior in their silicon-based counterparts. Second, our knowledge of the functioning of biological hardware is often inadequate to support its migration from one system to another. For these and other reasons, many roboticists ignore biological realities and seek purely engineering solutions.

Behavior-based roboticists argue that there is much that *can* be gained for robotics through the study of neuroscience, psychology, and ethology.

- **Neuroscience:** the study of the nervous system's anatomy, physiology, biochemistry, and molecular biology.
- **Psychology:** the study of mind and behavior
- **Ethology:** the study of animal behavior in natural conditions

---

The behavior-based roboticist needs to decide how to use results from these other disciplines. Some scientists attempt to implement these results as closely as possibly, concerning themselves primarily with testing the underlying hypotheses of the biological models in question. Others choose to abstract the underlying details and use these models for inspiration to create more intelligent robots, unconcerned with any impact within the disciplines from which the original models arose. We will see examples of both approaches within this book.

To appreciate behavior-based robotics, it is important to have some background in biological behavior, which this chapter attempts to provide. We first overview the important concepts of neuroscience, psychology, and ethology, in that order. The chapter concludes with several exemplar robotic systems whose goals have drawn heavily on biological models for robotic implementation, a theme that continues to varying degrees throughout the remainder of the book.

2.2 NEUROSCIENTIFIC BASIS FOR BEHAVIOR

The central nervous system (CNS) is a highly complex subject whose discussion warrants at least a separate textbook. This section attempts only a gross overview. First, it highlights the component technology of neural circuitry. Next, it introduces the reader to the most basic aspects of brain function and structure and the neurophysiological pathways that translate stimulus into response, that is, produce behavior. Last, it presents abstract computational models developed within brain theory that have served as a basis for behavior-based robotic systems.

2.2.1 Neural Circuitry

Each outcry of the hunted hare
A fibre from the brain does tear.
—William Blake

The nervous system's elemental cellular component is the neuron (figure 2.1). There is no single "canonical" neuron: They come in many different shapes and sizes, but they do possess a common structure. Emanating from the cell body at the axon hillock is the axon, which after a traversal of some length branches off into a collection of synaptic terminals or bulbs. This branching is referred to as axonal arborealization. The axon is often sheathed in myelin, which facilitates the transmission of the neural impulse along the fiber. The boundary between neural interconnections, referred to as a synapse, is where chemical neurotransmitters diffuse across the synaptic cleft when the cell "fires." At the neuron's receiving end, a collection of dendrites emanates from the cell body, continuing from the other side of the synapse.

Signal transmission occurs across the neuron by the conveyance of an electrical charge from the dendrites' input surfaces through the cell body. If the total amount of electricity impinging upon the cell is below a certain threshold, the current is passively propagated through the cell up the axon, becoming weaker as it progresses. If, however, it exceeds the threshold at the axon hillock, a spike is generated and actively propagated without significant loss

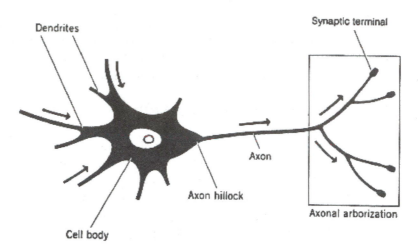

Figure 2.1
Stylized representation of a neuron. (From *The Metaphorical Brain* by M. Arbib. Copyright 1972 by Wiley-Interscience. Reprinted by permission of John Wiley and Sons, Inc.)

of current up the axon to the synaptic bulbs, causing the release of neurotransmitters across the synaptic cleft. The cell must then wait a finite amount of time (the refractory period) before it can generate another electrical spike. This spike is also referred to as the action potential. Basic neurotransmitters are of two principal types: *excitatory*, adding to the probability of the receiving cell's firing; and *inhibitory*, decreasing the likelihood of the receiving cell's firing.

Combinations of neurons give rise to ever-increasing complex neural circuitry. There are many examples of specialized small systems of neurons whose function neuroscientists have elucidated. These special purpose systems include (from Arbib 1995b):

- scratch reflexes in turtles
- bat sonar
- stomatogastric control in lobsters
- locomotion pattern generation in lampreys
- wiping reflex in frogs
- cockroach locomotion
- location of objects with electricity in electric fish
- visuomotor coordination in flies and frogs

Often roboticists can draw from these neural models to create similar forms of behavior in machines. In Section 2.5, we will study a few examples of this approach.

Neural tissue often consists of columnar structures (mini- or microcolumns), each dedicated to a specific function. These physically parallel columns also process information in parallel. This is of particular importance for space-preserving maps generated from sensory inputs. For example, in touch, space-preserving maps from the skin's embedded neural tactile sensors project to the brain's somatosensory cortex. This is also the case for visual input from the eyes' retinas that ultimately projects onto the visual cortex. Parallel pathways are naturally present for the processing of spatially distributed information.

One model related to the inherent parallelism in neural processing is referred to as lateral inhibition, where inhibition of a neuron's firing arises from the activity of its neural neighbors. Lateral inhibition can yield a single dominant pathway even when multiple concurrent active pathways are present. This results from amplification of the variations in activity between different neurons or neural pathways. Through strong lateral inhibition, one choice from many can be selected in a winner-take-all manner. This is of particular value in tasks such as competitive learning for pattern classification tasks, prey recognition, disambiguation of word sense in language, solving the correspondence problem in stereo vision (finding matching features in two or more separate images), or selecting one from among many possible behavioral responses.

2.2.2   Brain Structure and Function

It is said that the Limbic system of the brain controls the four F's: Feeding, Fighting, Fleeing, and Reproduction.
—Karl Pribram

Animal brains obviously come in a very wide range of sizes. Simple invertebrates have nervous systems consisting of 10^3–10^4 neurons, whereas the brain of a small vertebrate such as a mouse contains approximately 10^7 neurons. The human brain has been estimated to contain 10^{10}–10^{11} individual neurons. Despite a large variation in brain size, we can say several things generally about vertebrate brains. First, locality is a common feature. Brains are not a homogeneous mass of neurons; rather, they are structurally organized into different regions, each of which contains specialized functionality. Next, animal brains generally have three major subdivisions (figure 2.2). For mammalian brains, these generally consist of (1) the forebrain, which comprises the

- Neocortex: associated with higher level cognition.
- Limbic system (between the neocortex and cerebrum): providing basic behavioral survival responses.
- Thalamus: mediating incoming sensory information and outgoing motor responses.
- Hypothalamus: managing homeostasis, that is, maintaining a safe internal state (temperature, hunger, respiration, and the like).

(2) the brainstem, which comprises the

- Midbrain: concerned with the processing of incoming sensory information (sight, sound, touch, and so forth) and control of primitive motor response systems.
- Hindbrain, which consists of the
- Pons: projecting across the brain carrying information to the cortex.
- Cerebellum: maintaining the tone of muscle groups necessary for coordinated motion.
- Medulla oblongata: connecting the brain and the spinal cord.

and (3) the spinal cord, containing reflexive pathways for control of various motor systems. Finally, *afferent* inputs convey signals (typically sensory) toward the brain, whereas *efferent* signals convey commands from the brain to the body. Invertebrate neural structure is highly variable and thus fewer generalizations can be made.

Mammalian cortex has regions associated with specific sensory inputs and motor command outputs (figure 2.3). In humans, the visual cortex (sight) is toward the rear of the brain, the auditory cortex (sound) is to the side, and the somatosensory cortex (touch) is midbrain, adjacent to the motor cortex (locomotion). Space-preserving topographic mappings from the input sensory organs to the cortex are present within all these regions. It is interesting to note that these mappings are plastic in the sense that they can be reorganized after damage. This has been shown for both the somatosensory system (Florence and Kaas 1995) and for visual cortex (Kaas et al. 1990).

Subspecialization occurs within the brain as well. At this level neuroscientific models have often had an impact on behavior-based robot design. For example:

- In section 7.2.2 we encounter "what" and "where" cortical regions associated with visual processing.

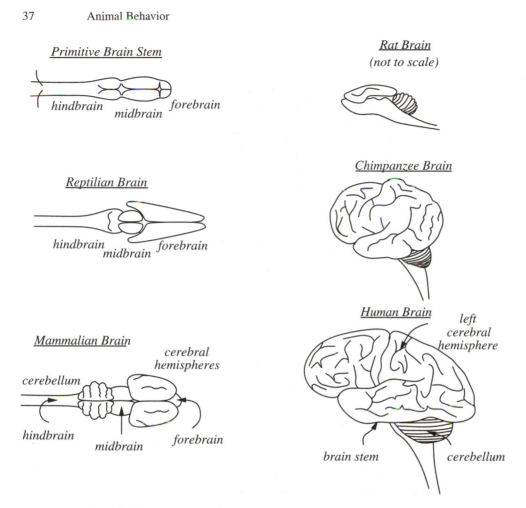

Figure 2.2
Animal brain structures. (Figure courtesy of Rod Grupen.)

■ Section 6.2 discusses distinctions between deliberative (willed) and automatic behavioral control systems for managing motor actions based upon neurophysiological evidence.

■ Evidence for parallel mechanisms associated with both long- and short-term memory has also been uncovered (Miller and Desimone 1994). For both cases, two distinct processing systems are seemingly present: one for facts and events, the other for learning motor and perceptual skills. Section 5.2 discusses the role of these two different types of memory for behavior-based robotic systems.

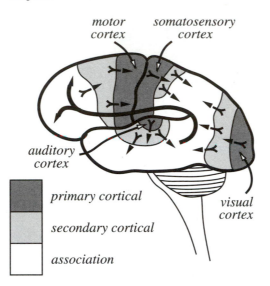

*motor
cortex*   *somatosensory
cortex*

*auditory
cortex*

primary cortical

secondary cortical

association

*visual
cortex*

Figure 2.3
Regions of sensory and motor process in the human cortex. The general flow of information within the brain is indicated by arrows. (Figure courtesy of Rod Grupen.)

Neurobiology often argues for the hypothesis of a vectorial basis for motor control, something that can be readily translated into robotic control systems (section 3.3.2). Research at MIT (Bizzi, Mussa-Ivaldi, and Giszter 1991) has shown that a neural encoding of potential limb motion encompassing direction, amplitude, and velocity exists within the spinal cord of the deafferented frog. Microstimulation of different regions of the spinal cord generates specific force fields directing the forelimb to specific locations. These convergent force fields move the limb towards an equilibrium point specified by the region stimulated (figure 2.4). The limb itself can be considered a set of tunable springs as it moves towards its rest position (equilibrium point). Thus the planning aspects of the CNS translate into establishing the equilibrium points that implicitly specify a desired motion. Of particular interest is the observation

Figure 2.4
(A) Force fields generated by microstimulation of lumbar regions (A-D) of frog spinal cord (shown at left).
(B) Superposition of multiple stimuli. C denotes simple vector summation of independent fields A and B. D represents actual field evoked by microstimulation of regions A and B concurrently. (Reprinted with permission from Bizzi, Mussa-Ivaldi, and Giszter 1991. Copyright 1991 by American Association for the Advancement of Science.)

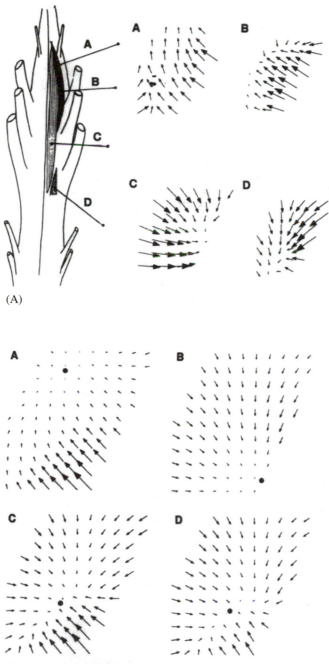

(A)

(B)

Box 2.1
Memory Types

- **Short-term memory** (STM): Short-term memory is a process, acting over an intermediate time scale, that involves "performing tasks requiring temporary storage and the manipulation of information to guide appropriate actions" (Guigon and Burnod 1995). STM is also referred to as "working" memory. Information stored in STM persists for periods of several seconds to minutes. STM is quite limited in its capacity for holding information, a significant distinction from long-term memory.
- **Long-term memory** (LTM): Long-term memory is what we usually refer to as memory in everyday conversation. The time scale for LTM is measured in hours, days or years. One working definition for LTM is information with "retention of longer than 24 hours" (McFarland 1981). Long-term memory is viewed by many as almost limitless in its capacity, but its recall accuracy is inferior to that of STM. The hippocampal region of the brain appears involved in the transfer process of information from STM to LTM.

that multiple stimulations give rise to new spatial equilibrium points generated by simple vector addition. This same principle is used in schema-based robotic control (section 4.4). New experiments in humans (intact fortunately), have been shown to be consistent with this force-field model when applied to reaching tasks (Shadmehr and Mussa-Ivaldi 1994).

Other compelling examples arguing that computations of motion within the brain should be considered as vectors include research from the New York University Medical Center (Pellionisz and Llinas 1980). The authors contend that activity within the brain is vectorial. Intended motion is generated as an activity vector within a three-dimensional space. Brain function is considered geometric where the "language of the brain is vectorial." The authors explain, however, that simple reflexes are not adequate to explain the entire range of complexity evidenced by the actions the brain generates.

Another example forwarding spatial vectors as an underlying representational medium for neural specification of motor behavior comes from the Johns Hopkins School of Medicine (Georgopoulos 1986). The "vector hypothesis" asserts that the changes in the activity of specific populations of neurons generates a neural coding in the form of a spatial vector for primate reaching. Experimental results have been shown to be consistent with this underlying hypothesis.

Finally, vector-based trajectory generation has served as an account for certain forms of animal navigation. Arbib and House's model (1987) explains detour behavior in toads (i.e., their circumnavigation of obstacles) by describing the animal's path planning in terms of the generation of divergence fields (directional vectors) based on the animal's perceived environment. In particular, repulsive fields surrounding obstacles, attractive forces leading to food sources, and directional vectors based on the frog's spatial orientation generate a computational model of path planning in toads consistent with observed experimental data. This model has been influential in the design of schema-based robot controllers (section 3.3.2).

2.2.3   Abstract Neuroscientific Models

Unfortunately, our knowledge of the brain's function is still largely superficial (literally). Progress in neuroscience is proceeding at a rapid pace as new tools for understanding brain function become available. Nonetheless, it has been said that even if we possessed a complete road map of the brain's neural structure (all of its neurons and their interconnections), our understanding would still be inadequate. Brain activity over the neural substrate is highly dynamic, and information regarding processing and control would still need to be elaborated.

What then should a brain theorist do? The key for many scientists lies in their first formulating an abstraction of brain function and then looking for neural confirmation. This top-down approach characterizes many researchers in neuroscience, and has potentially high payoff for roboticists, as abstract models of brain function hypothesized by these neuroscientists can potentially lead to robotic control systems useful in their own right.

Abstract computational models used to express brain behavior have two mainstream forms: schema theory and neural networks. These two approaches are fully compatible (figure 2.5). Schema theory is a higher-level abstraction by which behavior can be expressed modularly. Neural networks provide a basis for modeling at a finer granularity, where parallel processing occurs at a lower level. Schema theory is currently more adept at expressing brain function, whereas neural networks can more closely reflect brain structure. Schemas, once formulated, may be translated into neural network models if desired or deemed necessary. In this book we study both methods in the context of what they offer behavior-based robotic control systems.

2.2.3.1   Schema-Theoretic Methods

The use of schemas as a philosophical model for the explanation of behavior dates as far back as Immanuel Kant in the eighteenth century. Schemas

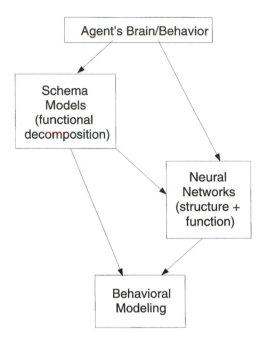

Figure 2.5
Abstract behavioral models. Schemas or neural networks by themselves can be used to represent overt agent behavior, or schemas can be used as a higher-level abstraction that is in turn decomposed into a collection of neural networks.

were defined as a means by which understanding is able to categorize sensory perception in the process of realizing knowledge or experience. Neurophysiological schema theory emerged early in the twentieth century. The first application was an effort to explain postural control mechanisms in humans (Head and Holmes 1911). Schema theory has influenced psychology as well, serving as a bridging abstraction between brain and mind. Work by Bartlett (1932) and Piaget (1971) used schema theory as a mechanism for expressing models of memory and learning. Neisser (1976) presented a cognitive model of interaction between motor behaviors in the form of schemas interlocking with perception in the context of the perceptual cycle. Norman and Shallice (1986) used schemas as a means for differentiating between two classes of behavior, willed and automatic, and proposed a cognitive model that uses contention-scheduling mechanisms as a means for cooperation and competition between behaviors. Sections 6.2 and 7.2.3 discuss these last two examples further. Arbib (1981) was the first to consider the applications of schema theory to robotic systems. Extensions of these principles have also been applied to computer vision systems (Riseman and Hanson 1987).

Many definitions exist for the term "schema", often strongly influenced by its application area (e.g., computational, neuroscientific, psychological). Some representative examples:

- a pattern *of* action as well as a pattern *for* action (Neisser 1976)
- an adaptive controller that uses an identification procedure to update its representation of the object being controlled (Arbib 1981)
- a functional unit receiving special information, anticipating a possible perceptual content, matching itself to the perceived information (Koy-Oberthur 1989)
- a perceptual whole corresponding to a mental entity (Piaget 1971)

Our working definition is as follows: A schema is the basic unit of behavior from which complex actions can be constructed; it consists of the knowledge of how to act or perceive as well as the computational process by which it is enacted. Schema theory provides a method for encoding robotic behavior at a coarser granularity than neural networks while retaining the aspects of concurrent cooperative-competitive control common to neuroscientific models.

Various neurocomputational architectures have been created that incorporate these ideas. For example, work at the University of Genova (Morasso and Sanguineti 1994) has led to the development of a model that encompasses the vector-based motion-planning strategies described earlier within the posterior parietal cortex. Here, multiple sensorimotor mappings are integrated into a unitary body schema, necessary for the generation of goal-oriented movements. Vector-based potential fields (section 3.3.2) provide the currency of task specification for this integration of task intentions. Later, section 4.4 explores other models and associated methods for operationalizing schema theory as a basis for behavior-based control.

2.2.3.2   Neural Networks

Computational models for neural networks, also referred to as connectionist systems, have a rich history paralleling the development of traditional symbolic AI. Some of the earliest work in the area can be traced to the McCulloch-Pitts model of neurons (1943). McCulloch and Pitts used a simple linear threshold unit with synaptic weights associated to each synaptic input. If a threshold was exceeded, the neuron fired, carrying its output to the next neuron. This

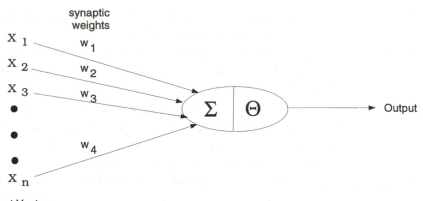

Figure 2.6
A perceptron. A vector of binary inputs x_i is multiplied by each component's associated synaptic weight w_i. The result is then summed together (Σ) and then subjected to a thresholding operation (Θ) to determine the unit's binary output. This output is then sent on to the next cell in the network.

simple model gave rise to networks capable of learning simple pattern recognition tasks. Rosenblatt (1958) later introduced a formal neural model called a perceptron (figure 2.6) and the associated perceptron convergence proof that established provable learning properties of these network systems. In the 1960s and 1970s, however, neural network research went into a decline for a variety of reasons, including the publication of the book *Perceptrons* (Minsky and Papert 1969), which proved the limitations of single-layer perceptron networks.

In the 1980s, however, the field resurged with the advent of multilayer neural networks and the use of backpropagation (Rumelhart, Hinton, and Williams 1986) as a means for training these systems. Many other notable efforts within connectionism during the last decade, far too numerous to review here, have yielded highly significant results. It should be remembered, however, that most neural networks are only inspired by actual biological neurons and provide poor fidelity regarding brain function. Nonetheless, these abstract computational models have relevance to the behavior-based roboticist and have been used widely in tasks ranging from visual road-following strategies (section 7.6.1) to adaptation and learning in behavioral control systems (section 8.4). Wasserman 1989 provides a more general treatment of neural networks.

2.3   PSYCHOLOGICAL BASIS FOR BEHAVIOR

Psychology is brainless, neuroscience is mindless.
—Les Karlovits

Psychology has traditionally focused on the functioning of the mind, less so the brain. It is not our intent to revisit the classical monist/dualist debate of mind and brain here but rather to look at what a psychologist's perspective can offer robotics.

Certainly psychology is preoccupied with behavior. Within that scope, we focus on perception and action, as these issues are of primary concern for the roboticist, and provide a brief history of the field, beginning with the twentieth century.

Sensory psychophysics was the first to relate stimulation intensity to perception. Weber and Fechner developed physical laws that described the relationships between a stimulus's physical intensity and its intensity as perceived by an observer (Pani 1996).

Behaviorism burst upon psychology in the early 1910s. Behaviorists discarded all mentalistic concepts: sensation, perception, image, desire, purpose, thinking, and emotion, among others (Watson 1925). Behavior was defined by observation only; data was obtained from observing what an organism did or said. Everything was cast in terms of stimulus and response. This approach's main benefit was making the field more scientifically objective, moving away from the use of introspection as the primary basis for the study of mind. Its main claim was "that there is a response to every effective stimulus and that response is immediate" (Watson 1925). As behaviorism progressed, psychology as a field became more and more scientific and less philosophical, sociological, and theological by relying heavily upon empirical data (Hull 1943). B.F. Skinner (1974) eventually became behaviorism's best known proponent.

Gestalt psychology (Kohler 1947) brought physics into the fray, drawing from the tradition of sensory psychophysics while broadening behaviorism's basis. This form of psychology inverted behaviorism somewhat, concerning itself heavily with sensory input (predominantly visual) and how behavior arises as a direct consequence of the structure of the physical environment interacting with the agent itself. The term "gestalt" was derived from the German where it referred to form or shape as an attribute. Certain gestalts enabled certain behaviors based upon the physics of retinal projection and the ability of the perceiver to organize the incoming stimuli. Gestalt psychology focused on perception whereas behaviorism principally concerned itself with action (Neumann and Prinz 1990). Gestalters, however, felt that behaviorism was limited, arguing that levels of organization exist above the sensation itself, which an organism could use to its advantage.

Ecological psychology, as advocated by J. J. Gibson (1979), demanded a deep understanding of the environment in which the organism was situated and how evolution affected its development. The notion of affordances (discussed further in section 7.2.3) provides a means for explaining perception's roots in behavior. This psychological theory says that things are perceived in terms of the opportunities they *afford* an agent to act. All actions are a direct consequence of sensory pickup. This results from the tuning by evolution of an organism situated in the world to its available stimuli. Significant assertions (Gibson 1979) include:

■ The environment is what organisms perceive. The physical world differs from the environment, that is, it is more than the world described by physics.
■ The observer and the environment complement each other.
■ Perception of surfaces is a powerful means of understanding the environment.
■ Information is inherent in the ambient light and is picked up by the agent's optic array.

Later, cognitive psychology emerged, paralleling the advent of computer science, defining cognition as "the activity of knowing: the acquisition, organization, and use of knowledge" (Neisser 1976). Information processing and computational models of the mind began to play an ever increasing role. Behaviorism was relegated to the role of explaining animal behavior and became far less influential in studying human intelligence. Unifying methods of explaining the relationship between action and perception (section 7.2.3) were developed under the banner of cognitive psychology (Neisser 1976). Mentalistic terms previously abandoned could now be considered using computational processes or metaphors. Some of the underlying assumptions of the information-processing approach (Eysenck 1993) include

■ A series of subsystems processes environmental information (e.g., stimulus → attention → perception → thought processes → decision → response).
■ The individual subsystems transform the data systematically.
■ Information processing in people strongly correlates with that in computers.
■ Bottom-up processing is initiated by stimuli, top-down processing by intentions and expectations (section 7.5.4).

Connectionism and the associated development of neural network technology (see Section 2.2.3) offer another alternative computational model to explain mental processing, available to be exploited by psychologists.

Although psychology has fluctuated significantly depending on the current school of thought, roboticists can derive considerable benefit from an understanding of these different perspectives. The roboticist's goals are generally different: Machine intelligence does not necessarily require a satisfactory explanation of human level intelligence. Indeed, even passé psychological theories can be of value as inspiration in building behavior-based automatons.

2.4   ETHOLOGICAL BASIS FOR BEHAVIOR

Animals are stylized characters in a kind of old saga—stylized because even the most acute of them have little leeway as they play out their parts.
—Edward Hoagland

Ethology is the study of animal behavior in its natural environment. To the strict ethologist, behavioral studies must be undertaken in the wild; animals' responses have no meaning outside their natural setting. The animal itself is only one component of the overall system, which must include the environment in which it resides.

Konrad Lorenz and Niko Tinbergen are widely acknowledged as the founders of the field. Tinbergen considered ethological studies to focus on four primary areas of behavior (McFarland 1981): causation, survival value, development, and evolution. Animal behavior itself can be roughly categorized into three major classes (Beer, Chiel, and Sterling 1990, McFarland 1981):

■ **Reflexes** are rapid, automatic involuntary responses triggered by a certain environmental stimuli. The reflexive response persists only as long as the duration of the stimulus. Further, the response intensity correlates with the stimulus's strength. Reflexes are used for locomotion and other highly coordinated activities. Certain escape behaviors, such as those found in snails and bristle worms, involve reflexive action that results in rapid contraction of specific muscles related to the flight response.

■ **Taxes** are behavioral responses that orient the animal toward or away from a stimulus (attractive or aversive). Taxes occur in response to visual, chemical, mechanical, and electromagnetic phenomena in a wide range of animals. Chemotaxis is evident in response to chemical stimuli as found in the trail following of ants. Klinotaxis occurs in fly maggots moving toward a light source by comparing the intensity of the light from each side of their bodies, resulting in a wavy course. Tropotaxis exhibited by wood louses results in their heading directly towards a light source through the use of their compound eyes.

■ **Fixed-action patterns** are time-extended response patterns triggered by a stimulus but persisting for longer than the stimulus itself. The intensity and duration of the response are not governed by the strength and duration of the stimulus, unlike a reflexive behavior. Fixed-action patterns may be motivated, unlike reflexes, and they may result from a much broader range of stimuli than those that govern a simple reflex. Examples include egg-retrieving behavior of the greyling goose, the song of crickets, locust flight patterns, and crayfish escape.

Motivated behaviors are governed not only by environmental stimuli but also by the internal state of the animal, being influenced by such things as appetite.

Ethologists such as Lorenz adopted the notion of schema as well. *Schemas* capture complicated combinations of reflexes, taxes, and patterns released in response to a suitable combination of stimuli. A sign stimulus is the particular external stimulus that releases the stereotypical response. Schemas, which were later renamed *innate releasing mechanisms* (IRMs) in an effort to clarify their meaning (Lorenz 1981), have the following traits (Lorenz and Leyhausen 1973):

■ An IRM is a simplified rendering of a combination of stimuli eliciting a specific, perhaps complex, response in a particular biological situation.
■ One IRM belongs to one reaction to a given situation, attuned to relatively few distinctive features of the environment and oblivious to the rest.
■ Every action dependent on its own releasing schema may be elicited completely independently of all other reactions intended for the same object.
■ The innate releasing mechanism provides the overall means for a specific sign stimulus to release a stereotypical response within a given environmental context.

For Lorenz and Tinbergen (Lorenz 1981), complex systems of behavioral mechanisms had a hierarchical component, although Tinbergen considered this a weak commitment useful principally only for organizational purposes. Figure 2.7 shows an example for the display behavior stickleback fish use in protecting territory. This notion of hierarchical grouping has parallels in schema theory as well, where assemblages serve as aggregates of component schemas (section 3.4.4).

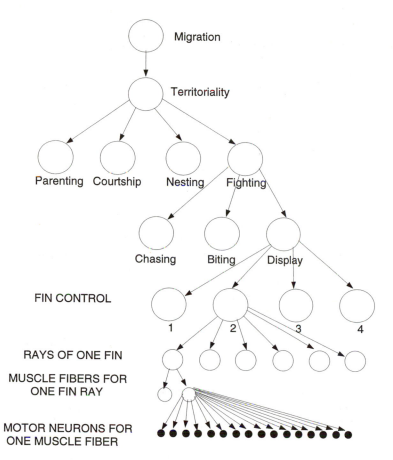

Figure 2.7
Partial hierarchical behavioral structure for the male stickleback fish. In particular, display behavior, a component of fighting, is shown with downward projections ultimately leading to their grounding in motor neuron signals within a single fin. After Lorenz 1981.

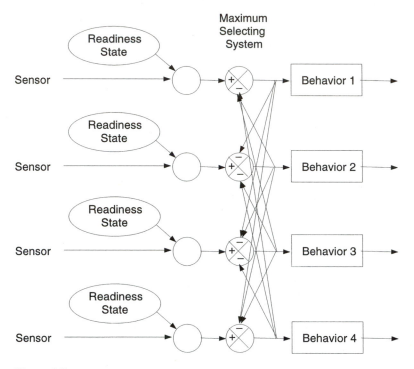

Figure 2.8
Model of maximum selection system providing lateral inhibition between behaviors.
Whenever a behavior is ready and its sensory stimulus present, it generates a positive
response while inhibiting other potentially active behaviors. After Lorenz 1981.

Reciprocal inhibition of parallel behaviors, a form of lateral inhibition, is
also available (figure 2.8). In one model, a *maximum selecting system* enables one of many behaviors to dominate based on its readiness and incoming
stimuli. This winner-take-all strategy is common with many of the arbitration
methods used in behavior-based robotics systems (section 3.4.3). All behaviors
not active at a particular moment are inhibited centrally. Supporting experimental evidence exists for this *locus of superior command* in animals ranging
from invertebrates to primates (Lorenz 1981). Hybrid behavior-based robotic
architectures, discussed at length in chapter 6, exploit the utility of this organizational concept.

Ethological studies in animal communication mechanisms are highly relevant for multiagent robotic systems (Arkin and Hobbs 1992). Display behavior,
in particular, involves the signaling of information by changes in posture or

activity. These stereotyped and often highly unusual displays are most often generated by fixed-action patterns (Smith 1977) and may be visible, audible, tactile, chemical, or even electrical, as in the case of the electric eel. The displays themselves include birdsong, raising of a dog's hackles, courting displays in ducks, color changes in fish, leg waving in spiders, etc. Such displays have evolutionary benefits for such activities as indirectly invoking escape behavior in the presence of predators, reducing the likelihood of fighting, and facilitating mating, among many others. The messages themselves may be behavioral selection messages that enable the recipient to respond appropriately for a given situation (i.e., "what" to do) such as flee, in the case of an alarm message. They may also be so-called nonbehavioral messages, such as "who messages" for kin or sex recognition or "where messages" providing location information from the sender. These nonbehavioral messages still may ultimately affect the recipient's behavior, but not so directly as behavioral messages. Ethologists have developed methods for analyzing and representing complex and ritualistic interactions such as courtship and greeting.

One of the most important concepts for behavior-based roboticists drawn from the field of ethology is the *ecological niche*. As defined by McFarland (1981, p. 411), "The status of an animal in its community, in terms of its relations to food and enemies, is generally called its niche." Animals survive in nature because they have found a reasonably stable niche: a place where they can coexist with their environment. Gibson (1979) strongly asserted this mutuality of animal and environment as a tenet of his school of ecological psychology (see section 2.3). Evolution has molded animals to fit their niche. Further, as the environment is always to some degree in flux, a successful animal must be capable of adapting to some degree to these changes or it will perish. Environmental pressures asserted by changes in habitat, climate, food sources, and the like, can profoundly influence the species' survivability.

This concept of niche is important to roboticists because of their goals. If the roboticist intends to build a system that is autonomous and can successfully compete with other environmental inhabitants, that system must find a stable niche or it (as an application) will be unsuccessful. This promulgates the view that robotic systems must find their place within the world as competitors with other ecological counterparts (e.g., people). For robots to be commonplace, they must find the ecological niches that allow them to survive and/or dominate their competitors, whether they be mechanical or biological. Often economic pressures are sufficient to prevent the fielding of a robotic system. If humans are willing to perform the same task as a robot (e.g., vacuuming) at a lower cost and/or with greater reliability, the robot will be unable to displace the human worker from the niche he already occupies. Thus, for a roboticist to design effective real world systems, he must be able to characterize the environment effectively. The system must be targeted towards some niche. Often this implies a high degree of specialization. These same arguments are often used in economics and marketing and are generalizable to behavior-based robotics (McFarland and Bosser 1993). Section 4.5.7 presents one example of a niche-based robotic architecture.

2.5 REPRESENTATIVE EXAMPLES OF BIO-ROBOTS

Let us begin our discussion of bio-robots by summarizing some important lessons animal behavior affords the roboticist:

- Complex behaviors can be constructed from simpler ones (e.g., through hierarchies or sequentially, as in fixed-action patterns).
- Perceptual strategies should be tuned to respond only to the specific environmental stimuli relevant for situation-specific responses.
- Competing behaviors must be coordinated by selection, arbitration, or some other means.
- Robotic behaviors should match their environment well, that is, fit a particular ecological niche.

We now turn to five representative examples of robotic systems heavily motivated by animal studies. The first two focus on perceptual aspects, that is, sensory devices mimicking chemotaxis in ants and the compound eye of the fly. A pair of examples then illustrates the problem of producing coordinated locomotion for a robotic cockroach and a primate swinging from trees. The last case concerns interagent communication for a robotic honeybee. These examples are but interesting pieces of the puzzle of building robots; subsequent chapters explore complete behavior-based robot design.

2.5.1 Ant Chemotaxis

Go to the ant, thou sluggard, consider her ways, and be wise.
—Proverbs 6:6

Ant behavior is of keen interest to roboticists because ants are relatively simple creatures capable of complex actions through their social behavior and biologists have studied them extensively. Excellent reference works are available on ant behavior (e.g., Holldobler and Wilson 1990). Much animal research significantly influenced multiagent robotic systems: We defer that discussion until chapter 9. For the moment we consider how chemical sensing, inspired by ants' behavior, can be used for path following in robots.

Ant communication is predominantly chemical. Visited paths are marked using a volatile trail pheromone. All ants traversing a useful path continually add this odor to the trail, strengthening and reinforcing it for future use. The variations in foraging strategies result in a wide range of species-specific collective patterns that have evolved to fit the ecological needs of the environment to which they are adapted. It could be useful for one interested in developing robots capable of foraging over long distances, to consider the models forwarded by ant entomologists.

Simulation studies conducted at the University of Brussels have shown the spontaneous development of biologically plausible trails using mathematical behavior models. Internest traffic for the Argentine ant has been simulated using pheromone models (Aron et al. 1990). Deneubourg and Goss (1989) have reproduced species-specific foraging patterns for three different army ant species. Goss et al. (1990) have likewise emulated computationally the rotation of foraging trails observed in the harvester ant. These simulation studies, although encouraging, still require implementation on real robots to gain widespread acceptance as useful models for robot foraging behavior.

Researchers in Australia have taken a step forward towards more directly emulating ant behavior by creating robotic systems capable of both laying down and detecting chemical trails (Russell, Thiel, and Mackay-Sim 1994). These systems exhibit chemotaxis: detecting and orienting themselves along a chemical trail. Camphor, a volatile chemical used in mothballs, serves as the chemical scent. The application method is straightforward: the robot drags a felt-tipped pen containing camphor across the floor as it moves, depositing a trail one centimeter wide (figure 2.9a). Sensing is more complex. The detection device contains two sensor heads separated by 50 mm (figure 2.9b). An inlet draws in air from immediately below the sensor across a gravimetric detector crystal. An air downflow surrounding the inlet insures that the inlet air is arriving from directly below the sensor. The detector crystal is treated with a coating that absorbs camphor, and as mass is added, the crystal's resonant frequency changes in proportion to the amount of camphor absorbed. When this chemotactic system has been attached to a tracked mobile robot provided with an algorithm that strives to keep the odor trail between the two sensor inlets, the robot has been able to follow the chemotactic trail successfully for up to one-half hour after the application of the camphor trail.

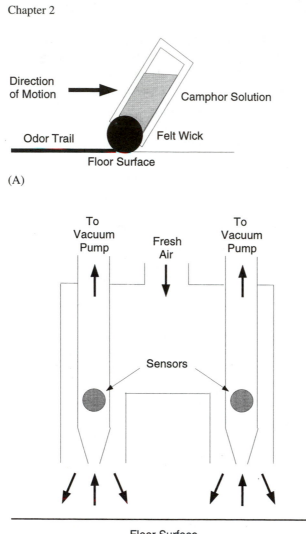

(A)

(B)

Figure 2.9
Chemotaxis hardware: (A) the camphor applicator; (B) the dual-head sensing device.

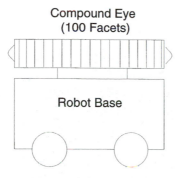

Compound Eye
(100 Facets)

Robot Base

Figure 2.10
Robot equipped with compound eye consisting of 100 facets providing a 360-degree panoramic view of the horizon.

2.5.2   Fly Vision

Research at France's Centre National de la Recherche Scientifique (C.N.R.S.) has considered the housefly's compound eye a useful way in which a robot can view the world (Franceshini, Pichon, and Blanes 1992). The housefly's visual navigation system consists of approximately one million neurons that constantly adjust the amplitude, frequency, and twist of the wings, which are controlled by seventeen different muscles. Visual motion is used for course control. The eye of the housefly is composed of 3,000 pixels each containing eight photoreceptors and operating in parallel. Several behavior-specific vision systems have been reported, including vision for sexual pursuit of mates and the detection of polarized light for use in navigation (Mazokhin-Porshnyakov 1969).

An in-depth study by the CNRS group has led to the development of a reactive mobile robot that uses an insect-like visual system (figure 2.10). This system's raison d'etre is simpler than that of the fly: it merely is to move safely about the world, avoiding obstacles by exploiting via vision the relative motion between itself and the environment. The biological principles exploited include

■ The use of a compound optic design, generating a panoramic view. The layout is nonuniform, with the visual space in the direction of motion more densely sampled than elsewhere.
■ Visuomotor control is conducted using optic flow induced by the robot's motion.

Figure 2.11
Robotic compound eye. (Reprinted with permission from Franceshini, Pichon, and Blanes 1992.)

■ Locomotion consisting of a succession of translational movements followed by abrupt rotations, typical of the fly's free-flight behavior.
■ Motion detection circuitry based on electrophysiological analysis of the housefly (Franceshini, Riehle, and Le Nestour 1989) using analog design.
■ The use of space-preserving topographic (retinotopic) mappings onto the control system.
■ Modeling from an invertebrate perspective, using an exoskeleton as opposed to a backbone.

This visual system was realized in specialized hardware. (figure 2.11). This small compound eye proved up to the task of supporting limited real-time navigation in a random obstacle field.

2.5.3   Cockroach Locomotion

Long after the bomb falls and you and your good deeds are gone, cockroaches will still be here, prowling the streets like armored cars.
—Tama Janowitz

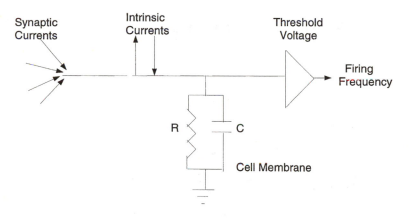

Figure 2.12
Neural model from the Artificial Insect Project. This model uses the intrinsic currents to capture the neuron's dynamic aspects by permitting time and voltage variation. The cell membrane uses a Resistor-Capacitor (RC) circuit that can temporally sum the synaptic and intrinsic inputs. A linear threshold function generates the firing frequency.

Interdisciplinary research conducted at Case Western Reserve University has studied the mechanisms of locomotor behavior in the American cockroach. In their Artificial Insect Project, Beer, Chiel, and Sterling (Beer 1990; Beer, Chiel, and Sterling 1990) developed a neural model more faithful to biology than most used in neural network research (figure 2.12). The model includes cell membrane properties, uses synaptic currents, and generates outputs in terms of the neuron's firing frequency. The individual leg neural control circuitry is composed of a small collection of these neurons based upon a biologically derived model for walking (Pearson 1976). In simulation studies, Beer and his colleagues created within the artificial insect the spontaneous generation of gaits (metachronal waves, tripod gaits) observed in the natural insect. The simulation model was endowed with higher-level behavioral controllers that used antennae and mouth sensors to extract information from the environment. The behaviors included wandering, edge following, appetitive orientation and attraction to food, and a fixed-action pattern representing food consumption (figure 2.13). These controllers were also modeled at the neural level. The overall insect was capable of exhibiting motivated behavior (exhibited through the buildup of arousal and satiation shown in feeding) and a variety of statically stable gaits, all "strikingly reminiscent" of the natural animal counterpart.

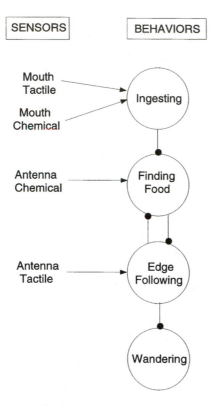

Figure 2.13
Simplified schematic of cockroach behavior. Lines with darkened circles show inhibition between behaviors.

Eventually Quinn and Espenschied (1993) implemented a portion of the neural simulation model on a hexapod robot about 50 centimeters in length with a mass of approximately one kilogram (figure 2.14 A). The aspects of the biological model concerning leg control were also implemented. The robot's performance confirmed the locomotion gaits observed in the simulation studies.

Espenscheid et al. (1994) later created a second biologically inspired hexapod robot with a mass of approximately 5 kilograms and about 50 centimeters long (figure 2.14 B), capable of a continuous range of insect-like gaits and of navigating irregular terrain. Whereas the earlier robot was capable only of straight-line motion, this newer version was generalized to handle both lateral and rotational movements.

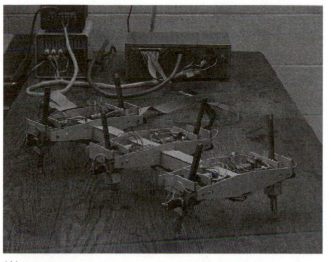

(A)

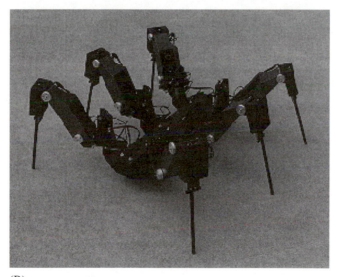

(B)

Figure 2.14
Robotic cockroaches: (A) shows the first version, which was later refined into the robot
shown in (B). (Photographs courtesy of R. Quinn, R. Beer, H. Chiel, and R. Ritzmann.)

2.5.4   Primate Brachiation

> Action is at bottom a swinging and flailing of the arms to regain one's balance and keep afloat.
>
> —Eric Hoffer

Another interesting aspect of animal behavior that influenced the design of robotic systems involves a mobile robot that travels by a rather unconventional means. Most mobile vehicles either have legs, wheels, or tracks, but researchers at Nagoya University in Japan have constructed a mobile system that swings from limb to limb (brachiates) in the style of a long-armed primate such as a gibbon (figure 2.15 A). The researchers designed a heuristic controller that enables the two-link brachiating robot (figure 2.15 B) to learn appropriate motion sequences by trial-and-error methods. It can, after learning, successfully catch a target bar from any initial state and continue locomotion along a series of spaced bars. It can also recover from a missed catch, using the initial state strategy to begin again.

The level of influence of the underlying animal behavioral studies for this research is markedly different than for the cockroach model we have just studied. In the insect work, an attempt was made to model closely the underlying neural control algorithms responsible for the animal's locomotor behavior. In the brachiation work, we see that no effort is made to be faithful to the neurophysiology of the primate that has motivated it. Instead, only the most outward aspects of locomotor behavior are involved, with the animal studies serving solely as inspiration for the creation of this type of robot.

2.5.5   Robotic Honeybee

> That which is not good for the bee-hive cannot be good for the bee.
>
> —Marcus Aurelius

Research involving communication via dance in the honeybee (Kirchner and Towne 1994) provides an interesting twist on the relationship between robotic and animal behavior. Honeybees have long been thought to convey information regarding the whereabouts of food source discoveries in their environs by a waggle dance in the hive. The question was whether bees used sound in addition to their dance to convey location information. The debate was resolved after the construction of a robotic honeybee capable of both singing and danc-

(A)

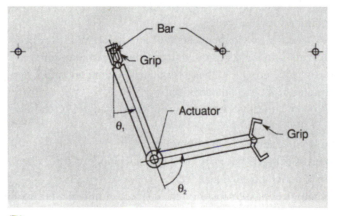

(B)

Figure 2.15
(A) Gibbon brachiation. (B) Brachiating robot. (Figures reprinted with permission from Saito, Fukuda, and Arai 1994. © 1994 IEEE.)

ing in a manner similar to that of a live bee. The bee's body was made from brass and covered with beeswax. The wings were constructed from pieces of razor blades capable of vibrating via an electromagnet. A long rod attached the body to motors capable of producing the waggle dance automatically when connected to computers.

The results indicated that the mechanical dancing bee was capable of recruiting bees to fly in the particular direction that the robot's dance indicated. This occurred only when the robot's wings were vibrating, indicating that sound played a role in the communication. Introducing variations in the robot's dance and observing the effect upon the foraging bees provided additional information about the nature of the communication contained in the dance itself. This research example illustrates that the relationship between robotics and the study of animal behavior is mutually beneficial rather than one-sided, as robotics can contribute to the study of animal behavior in addition to benefiting from it.

2.6   CHAPTER SUMMARY

- Animal behavior provides
- a definition for intelligence.
- an existence proof for the creation of intelligent mobile systems.
- models that roboticists can mimic or from which they can draw inspiration.
- Neuroscience provides a basis for understanding and modeling the underlying circuitry of biological behavior.
- The roboticist can view neuroscience from many different levels:
- at the cellular level of neurons
- at the organizational level of brain structure
- at the abstract level based on computational models (e.g., schemas and neural networks) derived from the above.
- Psychological models focus on the concept of mind and behavior rather than the brain itself.
- Various (often opposing) psychological schools of thought have inspired roboticists:
- Behaviorism: using stimulus-response mechanisms for the expression of behaviors
- Ecological psychology: capturing the relationship an agent has with its environment
- Cognitive psychology: using computational models to describe an agent's behavior within the world

■ Ethology is concerned with the behavior of animals within their natural world.

• The definition of behavioral classes, including reflexes, taxes and fixed-action patterns, provides a useful language for operationalizing robotic behavior.

• Innate releasing mechanisms (referred to earlier as schemas) provide a means for coordinating multiple competing behaviors, especially when coupled with lateral inhibition.

• The concept of an ecological niche enables the roboticist to consider how a robot is positioned within its overall environment and how it can be a success-ful competitor within the world.

■ Many robotic systems have been heavily influenced, at various levels, by biological studies. Examples include ant chemotaxis, fly vision, cockroach locomotion, primate brachiation, and robotic honeybees.

Chapter 3
Robot Behavior

The great end of life is not knowledge, but action.
—Thomas Henry Huxley

We really only know, when we don't know; with knowledge, doubt increases.
—Johann Wolfgang von Goethe

For in much wisdom is much grief, and he that increaseth knowledge increaseth sorrow.
—Ecclesiastes 1:18

Chapter Objectives

1. To learn what robotic behaviors are.
2. To understand the methods that can be used to express and encode these behaviors.
3. To learn methods for composing and coordinating multiple behaviors.
4. To obtain a basic understanding of the design choices related to behavior-based robotic systems.

3.1 WHAT ARE ROBOTIC BEHAVIORS?

After developing an understanding of behavior's biological basis in chapter 2, we now study how to express the concepts and formalisms of behavior-based robotic systems. It is important to remember that biological studies are not necessarily viewed as constraining for robots, but nonetheless serve as inspirations for design.

Perhaps the easiest way to view simple robotic behaviors is by adopting the concept advocated by the behaviorist school of psychology. A behavior, simply put, is a reaction to a stimulus. This pragmatic view enables us to express how a robot should interact with its environment. By so doing, we are confining ourselves in this chapter to the study of *purely* reactive robotic systems.

3.1.1   Reactive Systems

If we had more time for discussion we would probably have made a great many more mistakes.
—Leon Trotsky

> A **reactive** robotic system tightly couples perception to action without the use of intervening abstract representations or time history.

Reactive robotic systems have the following characteristics:

■ *Behaviors serve as the basic building blocks for robotic actions.* A behavior in these systems typically consists of a simple sensorimotor pair, with the sensory activity providing the necessary information to satisfy the applicability of a particular low-level motor reflex response.

■ *Use of explicit abstract representational knowledge is avoided in the generation of a response.* Purely reactive systems react directly to the world as it is sensed, avoiding the need for intervening abstract representational knowledge. In essence, what you see is what you get. This is of particular value in highly dynamic and hazardous worlds, where unpredictability and potential hostility are inherent. Constructing abstract world models is a time-consuming and error-prone process and thus reduces the potential correctness of a robot's action in all but the most predictable worlds.

■ *Animal models of behavior often serve as a basis for these systems.* We have seen in chapter 2 that biology has provided an existence proof that many of the tasks we would like our robots to undertake are indeed doable. Additionally, the biological sciences, such as neuroscience, ethology, and psychology, have elucidated various mechanisms and models that may be useful in operationalizing our robots.

■ *These systems are inherently modular from a software design perspective.* This enables a reactive robotic system designer to expand his robot's competency by adding new behaviors without redesigning or discarding the old. This accretion of capabilities over time and resultant reusability is very useful for constructing increasingly more complex robotic systems.

Purely reactive systems are at one extreme of the robotic systems spectrum (section 1.3). In subsequent chapters, we will see that it may be useful to add additional capabilities to reactive systems, but for now we focus on these simpler systems.

3.1.2   A Navigational Example

Let us construct an example with which we can frame the discussion to come. Consider a student going from one classroom to another. A seemingly simple task, at least for a human. Let's examine it more closely and see the kinds of things that are actually involved. These include

1. getting to your destination from your current location
2. not bumping into anything along the way
3. skillfully negotiating your way around other students who may have the same or different intentions
4. observing cultural idiosyncrasies (e.g., deferring to someone of higher priority if in conflict with priority determined by age or gender, in the United States passing on the right, etc.)
5. coping with change and doing whatever else is necessary

So what sounds simple (getting from point A to point B) can actually be quite complex (figure 3.1), especially in a situation where the environment is not controllable or well predicted.

Behavior-based robotics grew out of the recognition that planning, no matter how well intentioned, is often a waste of time. Paraphrasing Burns: The best laid plans of mice and men oft go astray. *Oft* is the keyword here. Behavior-based robotic systems provide a means for a robot to navigate in an uncertain and unpredictable world without planning, by endowing the robot with behaviors that deal with specific goals independently and coordinating them in a purposeful way.

3.1.3   Basis for Robotic Behavior

Where do robotic behaviors come from? This primary question leads to a series of subsidiary questions that must be answered to provide a robot with behavioral control:

THE FAR SIDE   By GARY LARSON

"Well, lemme think. ... You've stumped me, son. Most folks only wanna know how to go the other way."

Figure 3.1
Things may be harder than they seem. (The Far Side © 1993 Farworks, Inc. Distributed by Universal Press Syndicate. Reprinted with permission. All rights reserved.)

- What are the right behavioral building blocks for robotic systems?
- What really is a primitive behavior?
- How are these behaviors effectively coordinated?
- How are these behaviors grounded to sensors and actuators?

Unfortunately there are currently no universally agreed-upon answers to these questions. A variety of approaches for behavioral choice and design have arisen. The ultimate judge is the appropriateness of the robotic response to a given task and environment. Some methods currently used for specifying and designing robotic behaviors are described below.

1. Ethologically guided/constrained design. As previously mentioned, studies of animal behavior can provide powerful insights into the ways in which behaviors can be constructed. Roboticists can put models generated by biological scientists to good use. One such example comes from Arbib and House's (1987) studies of the navigational behavior of the toad and its relationship to Arkin's (1989a) schema-based robotic navigational system (section 4.4). In this instance, motion divergence fields are specified for a toad navigating amid a collection of poles toward a can of worms. This model provides an analogous means for representing robot behaviors using a modified potential (force) field method (figure 3.2). The key phrase for the design process here is "ethologically guided": consulting the biological literature for classifications, decompositions, and specifications of behaviors that would be useful for robotic systems, but not necessarily being constrained by them.

Other researchers, epitomized by Beer (Beer, Chiel, and Sterling 1990) (discussed earlier in section 2.5.3), look toward high-fidelity models of the neurological substrate of an animal (in Beer's case, the cockroach) in their attempt to emulate an appropriate behavioral response by a robot. These scientists choose to deliberately constrain their behavioral models to match those of the animal under study. In many ways this overconstrains the problem of producing intelligent behavior in a robot, but as a side effect this research can potentially answer interesting questions regarding actual biological behavior, for example in terms of predictive modeling.

The methodology for designing ethologically guided/constrained behaviors is illustrated schematically in figure 3.3. A model is provided from a scientific study, preferably with an active biological researcher in tow. The animal model is then modified as necessary to realize it computationally, and is then grounded within the robot's sensorimotor capabilities. The results from the robotic experiments are then compared to the results from the original biological studies, and either the biological model or its robotic alter ego are

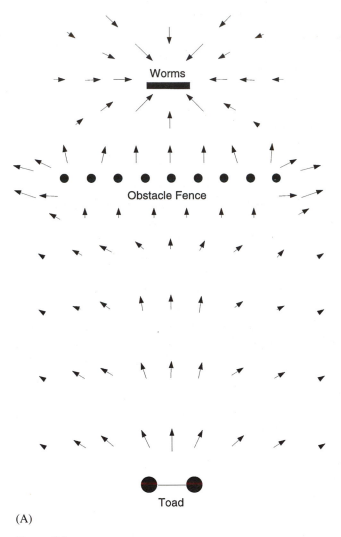

(A)

Figure 3.2

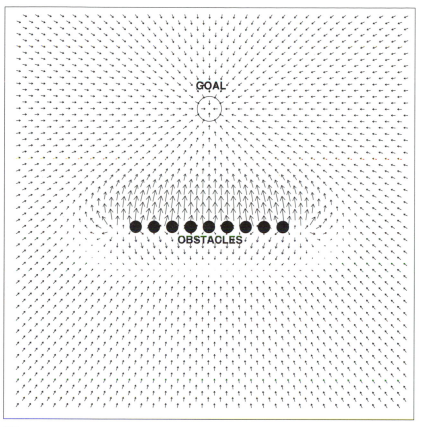

(B)

Figure 3.2 *(continued)*
Toad/robot navigational model (A) Represents a model of a toad's attraction to a can
of worms, avoidance from a pole fence, and an egocentric animal potential for motion.
The vectors represent the most likely direction of motion for the animal at each point
in space. This model was shown to be consistent with experimentally observed animal
data (after Arbib and House 1987). (B) Represents a set of robotic behaviors for similar
circumstances: avoid-static-obstacles and move-to-goal. An egocentric potential is not
needed in this similar, yet different, representation.

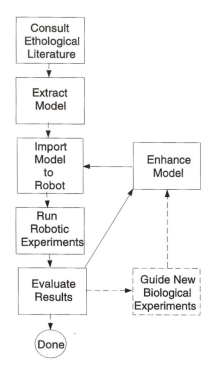

Figure 3.3
Design methodology for ethologically guided systems (dotted lines indicate optional pathway).

modified or enhanced in an attempt to produce results more in agreement with the original animal data. The results of these experiments have two customers: roboticists, who can use these insights to produce even more-intelligent machines, and experimental biologists, who can use them to develop and test their theories of animal behavior.

2. Situated activity–based design. Situated activity means that a robot's actions are predicated upon the situations in which it finds itself. Hence the perception problem is reduced to recognizing what situation(s) the robot is in and then choosing one action (out of perhaps many) to undertake. As soon as the robot finds itself in a new situation, it selects a new and more appropriate action. These manifold situations can be viewed as microbehaviors, that is, behaviors specified and useful only in very limited circumstances. Designing a robot based on this methodology requires a solid understanding of the relationship between the robotic agent and its environment. The design strategy typifying this method appears in figure 3.4.

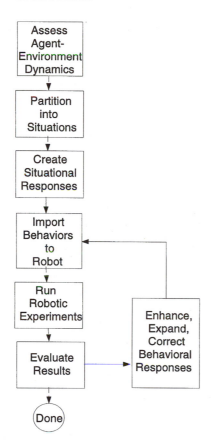

Figure 3.4
Situated activity design methodology.

Arbitrarily complex situations can be created and specified that may have no biological basis. Pengi (Agre and Chapman 1987) is a system that characterizes situations by their *indexical-functional* aspects. *Indexical* refers to what makes the circumstances unique, *functional* refers to a robotic agent's intended outcome or purpose in a given situation. This system uses lengthy phrases to characterize particular situations that demand certain responses. For example (paraphrasing the situations from the original Pengi somewhat), the-block-I-need-to-kick-at-the-enemy-is-behind-me is a situation that requires the agent to backtrack to obtain the object in question. I've-run-into-the-edge-of-the-wall requires that the robot turn and move along the edge. These situations can be highly artificial and arbitrarily large in number. Coordination in Pengi is handled by an arbitration mechanism, where one of the candidate actions is chosen (there may be many applicable) and executed. Indeed, one candidate action may be in conflict with another. Hopefully the best action is chosen, but there is no guarantee, as no planning is conducted, nor does the mechanism project the consequences of undertaking any action.

Assuming that there is no limit to the number of situational conditions that can be enumerated leads us to a more expansive version of this theory of situated activity: universal plans. Universal plans, as developed by Schoppers (1987), require the robotic agent to have the ability of recognizing each unique situation for what it is and then selecting an appropriate action for each possible world state. These universal plans cover the entire domain of interaction, use sensing to conduct the classification, and presuppose no ordering on the situations or even the type of situations that might arise for that matter (Schoppers 1989). Sensing is conducted continuously, so situational assessment, and thus appropriate response, is continuously reevaluated.

To deal with the issue of the sheer bulk regarding the vast number of possible situations, the idea of caching plans is forwarded. Despite this technique, universal plans have encountered significant criticism (e.g., Ginsberg 1989) predominantly due to the immensity of the numbers of plans required and the potential irrelevancy of most. Even the harshest critics acknowledge that more limited versions of the situated activity paradigm have utility, even when it is designed to include not only routine situations but a wide range of contingent ones. The argument, however, that an enumeration of *every* possible situation (i.e., universal plans) is impractical at best and mathematically intractable at worst is a valid one.

Reactive action packages (RAPs) (Firby 1989) constitute an unusual variant on situation-driven execution. As with the other methods, the current situation provides an index into a set of actions regarding how to act in that environment. RAPs, however, operate at a coarser granularity than the other situated-action approaches and provide multiple methods of acting within a given context. RAPs consist of a set of methods specific to a task-situation, and for each of those methods, a sequence of steps to accomplish the task is provided (a kind of "sketchy" plan). RAPs differ from most reactive systems, however, in that they are not truly behavior based (but rather task based) and in that the system relies heavily on a strong explicit internal world model.

3. Experimentally driven design. Experimentally driven behaviors are invariably created in a bottom-up manner. The basic operating premise is to endow a robot with a limited set of capabilities (or competences), run experiments in the real world, see what works and what does not, debug imperfect behaviors, and

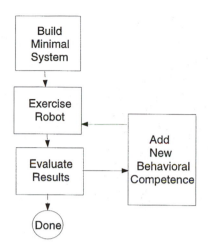

Figure 3.5
Experimentally driven methodology for behavioral design.

then add new behaviors iteratively until the overall system exhibits satisfactory performance (figure 3.5).

An excellent example of this design paradigm appears in Brooks' (1989a) work on the design of a behavior-based controller for a legged walking robot. Initially the robot (panel (A) in figure 3.6) was provided with the ability to stand up and conduct a simple walk. This worked adequately for smooth terrain but posed problems as the robot attempted to walk over irregular surfaces. Based on the requirements of this extended capability, force balancing was added to modify the leg controllers and help the robot maintain a steady posture. Whiskers (protruding sensors in the front of the robot) were then added to provide more warning to the control system to deal with larger objects that the robot needed to climb over. A final problem was noted involving balance in situations where the robot was heavily tilted fore or aft (pitching). To compensate, an inclinometer coupled with new pitch stabilization code was added to provide even better performance as the robot maneuvered over highly irregular terrain. It was then decided to allow the robot to track warm objects such as people, so infrared sensors were added, coupled with a new behavior to provide prowling. Each of these competencies was added incrementally, based upon the results of previous experiments and the goal of providing greater utility for the robotic system. Section 4.3 details the development of this system.

In Payton et al. 1992, fault tolerance is introduced into reactive robotic systems through the design of suitable behaviors that can handle unanticipated

(A)

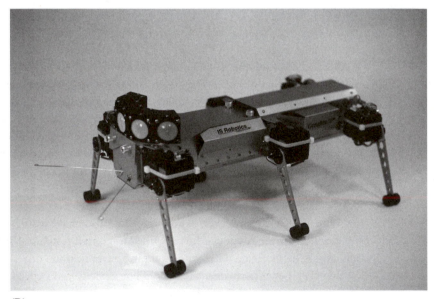

(B)

Figure 3.6
(A) Original Genghis. (Photograph courtesy of Rodney Brooks.) (B) Genghis II—a
robotic hexapod, commercial successor to the original Genghis. (Photograph courtesy
of IS Robotics, Somerville, MA.)

contingencies as they arise. This design methodology, dubbed "Do whatever works," has a goal of generating a sufficiently general set of low-level behaviors that when activated can cope with events beyond the initial designer's vision. Redundancy is the key feature, that is, allowing things to be accomplished in more than one way and then designing a controller capable of selecting the most successful behavior for the current situation. In a sense, this feature is also embodied in the RAPs system described previously, in which multiple methods are used to accomplish a task.

Ferrell (1994) developed a complex control system for another walking hexapod potentially suitable as a lunar or Mars rover using this bottom-up strategy. In this implementation, 1,500 concurrent processes supported locomotion over rough terrain and provided the requisite sensing with a significant level of fault tolerance. The entire system was constructed without any reliance on simulation technology. Earlier, Connell (1989a) demonstrated the efficacy of this experimental method with the design of a mobile manipulator (figure 3.7). In particular, the arm controller for this system consisted of fifteen independent behaviors capable of finding a soda can, then grabbing, transporting, and depositing it at another location.

Whatever the design basis, a generic classification of robot behaviors can be used to categorize the different ways in which a robotic agent can interact with its world:

```
Exploration/directional behaviors (move in a general direction)
   heading based
   wandering
Goal-oriented appetitive behaviors (move towards an attractor)
   discrete object attractor
   area attractor
Aversive/protective behaviors (prevent collisions)
   avoid stationary objects
   elude moving objects  (dodge, escape)
   aggression
Path following behaviors (move on a designated path)
   road following
   hallway navigation
   stripe following
Postural behaviors
   balance
   stability
```

Figure 3.7
Herbert—a mobile manipulator. (Photograph courtesy of Jon Connell.)

```
Social/cooperative behaviors
   sharing
   foraging
   flocking/herding
Teleautonomous behaviors (coordinate with human operator)
   influence
   behavioral modification
Perceptual behaviors
   saccades
   visual search
   ocular reflexes
```

```
Walking behaviors (for legged robots)
  gait control
Manipulator-specific behaviors (for arm control)
  reaching
Gripper/dextrous hand behaviors (for object acquisition)
  grasping
  enveloping
```

Perceptual support is required to implement any of these behaviors. Chapter 7 describes how perception can be tailored to behavioral need.

3.2   EXPRESSION OF BEHAVIORS

Several methods are available for expressing robotic behavior. This book employs three: Stimulus-response (SR) diagrams, functional notation, and finite state acceptor (FSA) diagrams. These methods will be used throughout the text in representing various behavior-based systems. SR diagrams will be used for graphic representations of specific behavioral configurations, functional notation for clarity in design of the systems, and FSAs whenever temporal sequencing of behaviors is required.

3.2.1   Stimulus-Response Diagrams

Stimulus-response (SR) diagrams are the most intuitive and the least formal method of expression. Any behavior can be represented as a generated response to a given stimulus computed by a specific behavior. Figure 3.8 shows a simple SR diagram.

Figure 3.9 presents an appropriate SR diagram for our navigational example (section 3.1.2). Here five different behaviors are employed in the task of getting to the classroom. The outputs of each behavior is channeled into a co-ordination mechanism (schematized here) that produces an appropriate overall motor response for the robot at any point in time given the current existing environmental stimuli. Section 3.4 discusses further the problem and methods of coordinating behaviors.

Figure 3.8
SR diagram of a simple behavior.

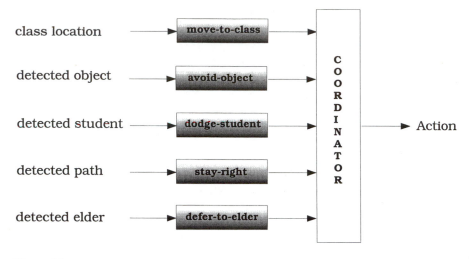

Figure 3.9
SR diagram for classroom navigation robot.

3.2.2   Functional Notation

Mathematical methods can be used to describe the same relationships using a functional notation,

$$b(s) = r,$$

meaning behavior b when given stimulus s yields response r. In a purely reactive system, time is not an argument of b, as the behavioral response is instantaneous and independent of the system's time history.

A functional expression of the behaviors necessary to carry out our example navigational task of getting to the classroom would appear as:

```
coordinate-behaviors[
            move-to-classroom(detect-classroom-location),
            avoid-objects(detect-objects),
            dodge-students(detect-students),
            stay-to-right-on-path(detect-path),
            defer-to-elders(detect-elders)
] = motor-response
```

The = motor-response is usually implicit and is generally not written when using this notation.

Each of the five behaviors listed can produce an output depending on the current environmental stimuli. A coordination function determines what to do with those outputs (e.g., selecting one of them or combining them in some meaningful way). It is not a trivial problem to ensure that the outputs of each behavioral function are in a form that can be coordinated, as section 3.4 will detail.

Coordinated functions can also be the arguments for other coordinating functions. For example

```
coordinate-behaviors[
          coordinate-behaviors(behavioral-set-1)
          coordinate-behaviors(behavioral-set-2)
          coordinate-behaviors(behavioral-set-3)
]
```

where each of the behavioral sets is a set of primitive behaviors. Clearly this notation readily permits a recursive formulation of behavior, ultimately grounded in physical robotic hardware but able to move upward into arbitrary levels of abstraction.

Functional notation has an interesting side effect in that it is fairly straightforward to convert this representation into a computer program. Often a functional programming language such as LISP is used, although the C language also enjoys widespread usage.

3.2.3 Finite State Acceptor Diagrams

Finite state acceptors (Arbib, Kfoury, and Moll 1981) have very useful properties when describing aggregations and sequences of behaviors (section 3.4.4). They make explicit the behaviors active at any given time and the transitions between them. They are less useful for encoding a single behavior, which results in a trivial FSA (figure 3.10).

In figure 3.10, the circle b denotes the state where behavior b is active and is accepting any stimulus input. The symbol a denotes *all* input in this case.

A finite state acceptor M can be specified by a quadruple (Q, δ, q_0, F) with Q representing the set of allowable behavioral states; δ being a transition function mapping the input and the current state to another, or even the same, state; q_0 denoting the starting behavioral configuration; and F representing a set of accepting states, a subset of Q, indicating completion of the sensorimotor task. δ can be represented in a tabular form where the arcs represent state transitions in the FSA and are invoked by arriving stimuli.

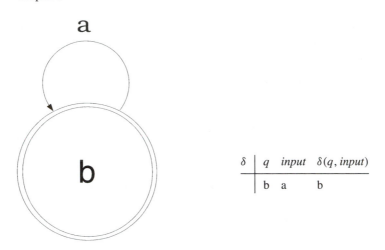

δ	q	$input$	$\delta(q, input)$
	b	a	b

Figure 3.10
FSA for a simple behavior. The table shows the allowable states, the inputs that induce a transition from one state to another, and the resulting state. For this trivial FSA, all inputs result in the same state.

For the trivial example shown in figure 3.10:

$$M = \{\{b\}, \delta, b, \{b\}\}.$$

FSAs are best used to specify complex behavioral control systems where entire sets of primitive behaviors are swapped in and out of execution during the accomplishment of some high-level goal (Arkin and MacKenzie 1994). Gat and Dorais (1994) have also expressed the need for sequencing behaviors. FSAs provide a ready mechanism to express these relationships between various behavioral sets and have been widely used within robotics to express control systems. In their MELDOG system, Tachi and Komoriya (1985) use an automaton map to capture actions that should be executed at various places within the world. Similar examples exist of FSA usage for guiding vision-based robots (Fok and Kabuka 1991; Tsai and Chen 1986). Brooks (1986) has also used a variation, augmented finite state machines (AFSMs), to express behaviors within his subsumption architecture (section 4.3). In this text, however, we use the notation developed in Arkin and MacKenzie 1994 based on the formalisms described in Arbib, Kfoury, and Moll 1981.

The classroom navigation example can also be expressed with FSAs, although the result is of a decidedly different character (figure 3.11). This example has four different states: start, journey, lost, and at-class. The last two

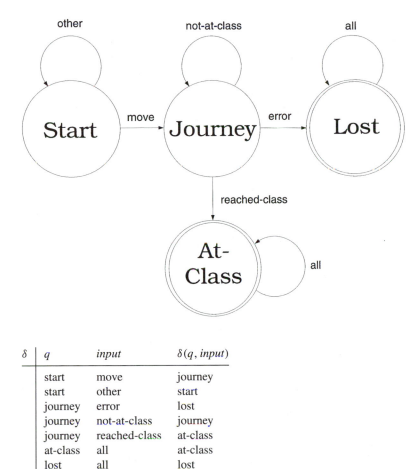

δ	q	input	$\delta(q, input)$
	start	move	journey
	start	other	start
	journey	error	lost
	journey	not-at-class	journey
	journey	reached-class	at-class
	at-class	all	at-class
	lost	all	lost

Figure 3.11
FSA representing classroom navigation example.

are terminal states: lost is abnormal, at-class normal. Journey, the main behavioral state, actually consists of an assemblage (a coordinated collection) of the five other low-level behaviors mentioned earlier (move-to-classroom, avoid-objects, dodge-students, stay-to-right-on-path, and defer-to-elders). Specifically,

$$M = \{\{start, journey, lost, at\text{-}class\}, \delta, start, \{lost, at\text{-}class\}\}.$$

The FSA provides us with a higher level of abstraction by which we can express the relationships between sets of behaviors.

To further illustrate this, let's look at an even more complex example. Figure 3.12 depicts an FSA constructed for a robot used in a competition conducted by the American Association for Artificial Intelligence. Here, a collection of high-level behaviors, each represented schematically as a state, encodes the robot's goal of moving about an arena looking for ten distinct poles, then moving to each of those poles in sequence. This robot has three major behavioral states, wander, move-to-pole, and return-to-start. Move-to-pole consists of a subset of actions for selecting a pole, orienting the robot so it points toward the pole, moving to the pole, and tracking the pole visually during motion until it is reached. In this case,

$$M = \{\{start, \text{find-next-pole}, \text{move-to-pole}, wander,$$
$$\text{return-to-start}, halt\}, \delta, start, \{halt\}\},$$

where δ contains the transition information depicted in figure 3.12. The FSA shows the sequencing between behaviors as the robot carries out its mission (figure 3.13). More details on this task and robot can be found in Arkin et al. 1993. Incidentally, the use of finite state descriptions in the University of Southern California's Phony Pony project on quadruped locomotion (McGhee 1967) is probably the first example of their application for specifying a robot control system.

3.2.4   Formal Methods

Formal models for behavior-based robotics can potentially provide a set of very useful properties to the robot programmer:

- They can be used to verify designer intentions.
- They can facilitate the automatic generation of robotic control systems.
- They provide a complete common language for the expression of robot behavior.
- They provide a framework for conducting formal analysis of a specific program's properties, adequacy, and/or completeness.
- They provide support for high-level programming language design.

Several formal methods have been developed for specifying and designing behavior-based robotic systems. A brief review of two representative strategies is presented below.

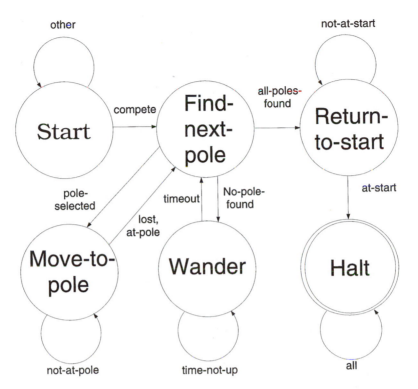

Figure 3.12
FSA representing robot competition example.

δ	q	input	δ(q, input)
	start	compete	find-next-pole
	start	other	start
	find-next-pole	all-poles-found	return-to-start
	find-next-pole	no-pole-found	wander
	find-next-pole	pole-selected	move-to-pole
	return-to-start	not-at-start	return-to-start
	return-to-start	at-start	halt
	move-to-pole	lost	find-next-pole
	move-to-pole	at-pole	find-next-pole
	move-to-pole	not-at-pole	move-to-pole
	wander	time-not-up	wander
	wander	timeout	find-next-pole
	halt	all	halt

Figure 3.13
Robot executing behaviors at competition arena.

3.2.4.1   *RS*

Lyons and Arbib (1989) developed the *RS* (robot schema) model as a method for expressing distributed sensor-driven robot control programs. A process algebra is used that permits the composition of a network of processes called *schemas* (behaviors). Process composition operators have been defined as a basis for creating these networks, which include methods for conditional, sequential, parallel, and iterative structures. Preconditions are established for coordination operators to ensure a smooth flow of control during execution.

In particular, a port automata model has been adopted as the underpinning for expressing the relationships between schemas. Port automata can be viewed as an extension of FSAs with supplemental formal methods for specifying the interconnections between states. Schemas communicate with each other via predefined input-output ports using synchronous message passing techniques. A schema's behavioral description, which encodes its response to any input messages, fully determines its action. Schemas are aggregated via a nesting mechanism termed an assemblage. Each assemblage recursively encodes a unique network of schemas or other assemblages.

A high-level algebraic *RS* encoding for the navigational example used throughout this chapter would be:

```
Class-going-robot = (Start-up ; (done? , Journey) : At-classroom)
Journey = (move-to-classroom , avoid-objects, dodge-students,
            stay-to-right-on-path, defer-to-elders)
```

Translating, the `Class-going-robot` consists of a robot that, beginning from an initial start-up state, sequentially transitions to the `Journey` state (the sequential operator is denoted ;) and which then remains in the `Journey` state with a concurrent monitor process checking for arrival at the classroom (the concurrency operator is denoted with a ,). If the robot is at the classroom it transitions to the `At-classroom` state (denoted by the conditional operator :). `Journey` consists of the concurrent execution of the behaviors specified during travel from one location to the next. This method combines advantages of both the functional and FSA methods into a single syntax.

There is far more to the *RS* model than what is presented here. The interested reader is referred to Lyons and Arbib 1989, Lyons and Hendriks 1994, and Lyons 1992 for more details.

3.2.4.2 Situated Automata

The situated automata model, developed by Kaelbling and Rosenschein (1991), recognizes the fundamental relationship an agent has as a participant within its environment. The model employs logical formalisms as underpinnings for the design of circuitry that corresponds to a robot's goals and intentions. The use of logic enables reasoning over the system, which can lead to the establishment of provable properties (Rosenschein and Kaelbling 1987), an important goal for the designer of any type of system. Rex (Kaelbling 1986), a LISP-based system, was the first language to embody the basic tools to generate specifications for synchronous digital circuitry embodying a reactive control program. Gapps is a more recently developed language that enables goals to be specified more directly and is inherently easier to use, akin to a higher generation language in conventional programming. Goals are either achieved, executed or maintained: Achieved goals are those that should be eventually realized; executed goals are those that should be done now; and maintained goals are those that should be preserved, as they have already been attained. Operators are defined in a LISP-like format that correspond to these three goal states: `(ach goal)` for achieve, `(do goal)` for execute, and `(maint goal)` for maintain. The logical boolean operators and, or, not, if are used to create higher-level goals.

Circuits are generated from these high-level goal expressions. Standard logical methods can be used to compile the high-level circuitry into a collection of digital logic gates. This type of formalism provides a very concrete grounding onto actual digital hardware for creating situated automata robots.

A simplified Gapps specification for our ongoing classroom navigation example would be:

```
(defgoalr (ach in-classroom)
         (if (not start-up)
             (maint (and (maint move-to-classroom)
                         (maint avoid-objects)
                         (maint dodge-students)
                         (maint stay-to-right-on-path)
                         (maint defer-to-elders)
                     )
                 )
             )
)
```

This encoding states that the robot is to achieve the goal of being in the classroom. If the robot is not in start-up state, then it is to journey to the location by maintaining the concurrent goals of moving to the classroom, avoiding objects, dodging students, staying to the right, and deferring to elders. Methods also exist to prioritize goals within the Gapps language should the need arise. As in the case with *RS,* there is far more to the Gapps language than can be discussed here, so the interested reader is referred to Kaelbling and Rosenschein 1991 for additional information.

Gapps circuitry was used for an unmanned underwater vehicle (UUV), described in Bonasso 1992. The basic goals established for this system were

- (maint not-crashed) which established the subgoal of (ach avoid nearest obstacle) along with other behaviors such as avoiding collision with the ocean bottom.
- (ach wander) endowed the robot with exploration capabilities.
- (ach joystick goal-point) allowed user directed input to control the direction of the robot.

The first two of these behaviors provided the UUV with the ability to navigate safely in a water tank. Additional behavioral goals were described using Gapps and tested in simulation, including (maint best-heading) and mission-specific tasks such as (ach record-thermal-vent-event) and (ach quiescence).

3.3   BEHAVIORAL ENCODING

To encode the behavioral response that the stimulus should evoke, we must create a functional mapping from the stimulus plane to the motor plane. We will not concern ourselves at this point as to whether a behavioral response is appropriate to a given stimulus, only how to encode it.

An understanding of the dimensionality of a robotic motor response is necessary in order to map the stimulus onto it. It will serve us well to factor the robot's motor response into two orthogonal components: strength and orientation.

■ *Strength* denotes the magnitude of the response, which may or may not be related to the strength of a given stimulus. For example, it may manifest itself in terms of speed or force. Indeed the strength may be entirely independent of the strength of the stimulus yet modulated by exogenous factors such as intention (what the robot's internal goals are) and habituation (how often the stimulus has been previously presented). We will later see that by controlling the strength of the response to a given stimulus, inroads are created for integrating goal-oriented planning into behavioral systems (chapter 6) as well as introducing the opportunity for adaptive learning methods (chapter 8).

■ *Orientation* denotes the direction of action for the response, (e.g., moving away from an aversive stimulus, moving towards an attractor). The realization of this directional component of the response requires knowledge of the robot's kinematics. It may or may not be dependent on the stimulus's strength.

In general, *kinematics* is the science of objects in motion, including aspects of position, velocity, and acceleration. This includes, in particular, all of the robot's geometric and time-based physical properties. *Dynamics* extends kinematics to include the study of the forces that produce motion in objects.

A behavior can be expressed as a triple (S, R, β) where S denotes the domain of all interpretable stimuli, R denotes the range of possible responses, and β denotes the mapping $\beta: S \rightarrow R$.

R—Range of Responses

Refining this further, the *instantaneous* response **r** (where $\mathbf{r} \in R$) of a behavior-based reactive system can be expressed as a six-dimensional vector consisting of six subcomponent vectors. Each of the subcomponent vectors encodes the magnitude of the translational and orientational responses for each of the six degrees of freedom of motion of a general mobile robot.

A *degree of freedom* (DOF) refers to one of the set of independent position variables, with respect to a frame of reference, necessary to specify an object's position within the world.

An unconstrained rigid object has six DOFs,

$$\mathbf{r} = [\mathbf{x}, \mathbf{y}, \mathbf{z}, \theta, \phi, \psi],$$

where the first three components of **r** represent the three translational degrees of freedom (x, y, z in three-dimensional cartesian coordinates), and the last three components encode the three rotational degrees of freedom (θ for roll, ϕ for pitch, ψ for yaw). Often pitch is alternatively referred to as tilt, and yaw as pan, as in a pan-tilt device. This is especially true in the context of controlling the pointing of sensors such as cameras.

For ground-based mobile robots, the dimensionality is often considerably less than six DOFs. For example, a robot that moves on flat ground and can rotate only about its central axis has only three degrees of freedom, $\mathbf{r} = [x, y, \theta]$, representing translation in the cartesian ground plane $[x, y]$ and the one degree of rotation θ (yaw, or alternatively pan).

Another factor that can limit the realization of a generated behavioral response is the robot's non-holonomicity.

A *non-holonomic* robot has restrictions in the way it can move, typically because of kinematic or dynamic constraints on the robot, such as limited turning abilities or momentum at high velocities.

A truly holonomic robot can be treated as a massless point capable of moving in any direction instantaneously. Obviously this is a very strong assumption and does not hold for any real robot (although it is easy to make this assumption in simulation, potentially generating misleading results regarding a control algorithm's utility on an actual robot). Omnidirectional robots moving at slow translational velocities, however, (that is, robots that can essentially turn on a dime and head in any direction), can often pragmatically be considered to be holonomic, but they are not in the strictest sense. Non-holonomicity is generally of great significance when there are steering angle constraints, such as in a car attempting to park parallel. If the wheels were capable of turning perpendicular to the curb, parking would be much easier, but as they cannot, a sequence of more complex motions is required to move the vehicle to its desired location.

The constraints imposed by non-holonomic systems can be dealt with either during the generation of the response, by including them within the function β, or after $\mathbf{r}$ has been computed, translating the desired response to be within the limitations of the robot itself.

S—The Stimulus Domain

S consists of the domain of all perceivable stimuli. Each individual stimulus or percept $\mathbf{s}$ (where $\mathbf{s} \in S$) is represented as a binary tuple (p, λ) having both a particular type or perceptual class p and a property of strength λ. The complete set of all p over the domain S defines all the perceptual entities a robot can distinguish, that is, those things it was designed to perceive. This concept is loosely related to affordances as discussed in section 2.3. The stimulus strength λ can be defined in a variety of ways: discrete (e.g., binary: absent or present; categorical: absent, weak, medium, strong) or real valued and continuous.

In other words, it is not required that the mere presence of a given stimulus be sufficient to produce an action by the robot.

> The presence of a stimulus is necessary but not sufficient to evoke a motor response in a behavior-based robot.

We define τ as a threshold value, for a given perceptual class p, above which a response is generated.

Often the strength of the input stimulus (λ) will determine whether or not to respond and the magnitude of the response, although other exogenous factors can influence this (e.g., habituation, inhibition, etc.), possibly by altering the value of τ. In any case, if λ is nonzero, the stimulus specified by p is present to some degree.

Certain stimuli may be important to a behavior-based system in ways other than provoking a motor response. In particular, they may have useful side effects on the robot, such as inducing a change in a behavioral configuration even if they do not necessarily induce motion. Stimuli with this property are referred to as *perceptual triggers* and are specified in the same manner as previously described (p, λ). Here, however, when p is sufficiently strong, the desired behavioral side effect is produced rather than motion. We return to our discussion of stimuli in the context of perception in chapter 7.

β—The Behavioral Mapping

Finally, for each individual active behavior we can formally establish the mapping between the stimulus domain and response range that defines a behavioral function β where

$$\beta(\mathbf{s}) \mapsto \mathbf{r}.$$

β can be defined arbitrarily, but it must be defined over all relevant p in S. Where a specific stimulus threshold, τ, must be exceeded before a response is produced for a specific $\mathbf{s} = (p, \lambda)$:

$$\beta: (p, \lambda) \mapsto \{\text{for all } \lambda < \tau \text{ then } \mathbf{r} = [0, 0, 0, 0, 0, 0] \qquad \text{\\* no response *\\}$$

$$\text{else } \mathbf{r} = \text{arbitrary function}\} \qquad \text{\\* response *\\}$$

where $[0, 0, 0, 0, 0, 0]$ indicates that no response is required given the current stimuli $\mathbf{s}$.

Examples

Consider the example of collision avoidance behavior. If an obstacle stimulus is sufficiently far away (hence weak), no actual action may be taken despite its presence. Once the stimulus is sufficiently strong (in this case measured by proximity), evasive action will be taken. To illustrate intuitively, imagine you are walking on a long sidewalk and you see someone approaching far ahead of you. In general, you would not immediately alter your path to avoid a collision, but rather you would not react to the stimulus until action is truly warranted. This makes sense, as the situation may change significantly by the time the oncoming walker reaches you. She may have moved out of the way or even turned by herself off the path, requiring no action whatsoever on your part.

The functional mapping between the strength of stimulus and the magnitude (strength) and direction of robotic motor response defines the design space for a particular robotic behavior. Figure 3.14 depicts two possible stimulus strength-response strength plots for the situation described above. One is a step function in which, once the distance threshold is exceeded, the action is taken at maximum strength. The other formulation involves increasing the response strength linearly over some range of stimulus strength (measured by distance here). Other functions are of course possible. The response's orientation may also vary depending on how the behavior has been constructed. For example, the motor response may be directly away from the detected object (strict repulsion—move away), or alternatively tangential to it (circumnavigation— go left or right) (figure 3.15).

Associated with a particular behavior, β, may be a scalar gain value g (strength multiplier) further modifying the magnitude of the overall response $\mathbf{r}$ for a given $\mathbf{s}$:

$$\mathbf{r}' = g\mathbf{r}$$

These gain values are used to compose multiple behaviors by specifying their strengths relative to one another (section 3.4). In the extreme case, g can be used to turn off a behavior by setting it to 0, thus reducing $\mathbf{r}'$ to 0.

The behavioral mappings, β, of stimuli onto responses fall into three general categories:

- Null: The stimulus produces no motor response.
- Discrete: The stimulus produces a response from an enumerable set of prescribed choices (all possible responses consist of a predefined cardinal set of actions that the robot can enact, e.g., turn-right, go-straight, stop, travel-at-speed-5). R consists of a bounded set of *stereotypical* responses enumerated for the stimulus domain S and specified by β.
- Continuous: The stimulus domain produces a motor response that is continuous over R's range. (Specific stimuli $\mathbf{s}$ are mapped into an infinite set of response encodings by β.)

Obviously it is easy to handle the null case as discussed earlier: For all $\mathbf{s}$, β: $\mathbf{s} \mapsto \mathbf{0}$. Although this is trivial, there are instances (perceptual triggers) where this response is wholly appropriate and useful, enabling us to define perceptual processes independent of direct motor action.

The methods for encoding discrete and continuous responses are discussed in turn.

3.3.1 Discrete Encoding

We have already seen one instance of discrete encodings, in section 3.1.3: situated action. For these cases, β consists of a finite set of (situation, response)

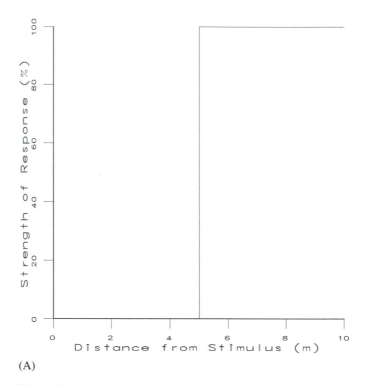

(A)

Figure 3.14

pairs. Sensing provides the index for finding the appropriate situation. The responses generated for a situation can be very simple, such as halt, or more complex, potentially generating a sequence of actions akin to the fixed-action patterns described in chapter 2.

Another strategy using discrete encodings involves the use of rule-based systems. Here β is represented as a collection of If-then rules. These rules take the general form:

IF *antecedent* **THEN** *consequent*

where the antecedent consists of a list of preconditions that must be satisfied in order for the rule to be applicable and the consequent contains the motor response. The discrete set of possible responses corresponds to the set of rules in the system. More than one rule may be applicable for any given situation. The strategy used to deal with *conflict resolution* typically selects one of the potentially many rules to use based on some evaluation function. Many rule-

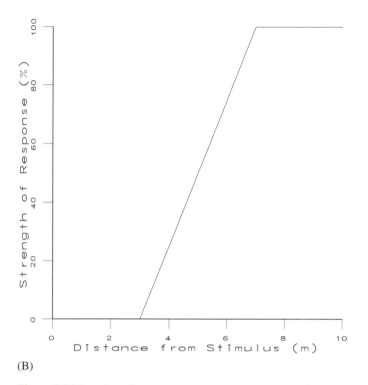

(B)

Figure 3.14 *(continued)*
Stimulus distance/response strength plot: (A) step function, and (B) linear increase.

based behavioral systems encode their behaviors using fuzzy rules; we will study these systems in more detail in chapter 8.

Gapps (section 3.2.4.2) uses goal-reduction rules to encode the actions required to accomplish a task. Here the antecedent specifies a higher-level goal that if necessary will require that certain subgoals be achieved. Eventually these subgoals translate into specific motor commands (or action vectors, to use their terminology). One example for an underwater robot (Bonasso 1992) used the following Gapps rule:

```
(defgoalr (ach wander)
    (if (not (RPV-at-wander-angle))
        (ach turn to wander angle)
        (ach wander set point)))
```

Here the wander behavior requires that the robot turn to a new wander angle and then move to a newly established set point.

(A)

Figure 3.15

In Nilsson 1994, condition-action production rules control the robot. The condition (antecedent) is based partially on sensory information, whereas the consequent encodes a response for the robot to enact. The resulting actions are themselves *durative* instead of discrete, here meaning that the action resulting from the invocation of the rule persists indefinitely. (Contrast the durative response of "Move at a speed of five meters/second" with the discrete response "Move fifteen meters.") This *teleo-reactive* method is somewhat related to the circuitry models epitomized by Gapps, yet uses distinguishing formalisms that can potentially facilitate analysis.

Another example of discrete encoding involves rules encoded for use within the subsumption architecture (Brooks 1986). To facilitate the use of this partic-

(B)

Figure 3.15 *(continued)*
Two directional encodings for collision avoidance: (A) repulsive, and (B) circumnavigation, with approach from the bottom of the figure.

ular approach to reactive systems, the Behavior Language was created (Brooks 1990a). This language embodies a real-time, rule-based approach for specifying and encoding behavior. Using a LISP-like syntax, rules are specified with the whenever clause:

(**whenever** *condition &rest body-forms*)

where the *condition* portion of the rule corresponds to the antecedent and the *&rest* to the consequent. Behaviors are constructed by collecting a set of these real-time rules into a group typically using the **defbehavior** clause:

(**defbehavior** *name &key inputs outputs declarations processes*)

where the list of rules appears in the *processes* location.

Similar rules were used for the control of a wheelchair in Connell and Viola 1990. A loose translation of a few of these behavioral rules include

- Approach: IF an object is detected beyond specified sonar range, THEN go forward.
- Retreat: IF an object is nearby according to sonar, THEN move backward.
- Stymie: IF all the front infrared sensors indicate an object immediately in front, THEN turn left.

The entire robotic system consisted of fifteen such behaviors encoding a mapping of direct sensing to motor activity. (These behaviors still require coordination, which is discussed in section 3.4).

3.3.2   Continuous Functional Encoding

Continuous response allows a robot to have an infinite space of potential reactions to its world. Instead of having an enumerated set of responses that discretizes the way in which the robot can move (e.g., {*forward*, *backward*, *left*, *right*, *speedup*, *slowdown*, . . . , *etc.*}), a mathematical function transforms the sensory input into a behavioral reaction. One of the most common methods for implementing continuous response is *based* on a technique referred to as the potential fields method. (We will revisit why the word *based* is italicized in the previous sentence after we understand the potential fields method in more detail.)

Khatib (1985) and Krogh (1984) developed the potential fields methodology as a basis for generating smooth trajectories for both mobile and manipulator robotic systems. This method generates a field representing a navigational space based on an arbitrary potential function. The classic function used is that of Coulomb's electrostatic attraction, or analogously, the law of universal gravitation, where the potential force drops off with the square of the distance between the robot and objects within its environment. Goals are treated as attractors and obstacles are treated as repulsors. Separate fields are constructed, based upon potential functions, to represent the relationship between the robot and each of the objects within the robot's sensory range. These fields are then combined, typically through superpositioning, to yield a single global field. For path planning, a smooth trajectory can then be computed based upon the gradient within the globally computed field. A detailed presentation of the potential fields method appears in Latombe 1991.

Using the inverse-square law expressing the relationship between force and distance,

$$Force \propto \frac{1}{Distance^2}$$

we construct a field for a repulsive obstacle, shown in (A) in figure 3.16. A ballistic goal attraction field, where the magnitude of attraction is constant throughout space, is depicted for an attractor located in the lower right of (B) in figure 3.16. In figure 3.17, (A) shows the linear superposition of these two fields, with (B) illustrating an example trajectory for a robot moving within this simple world.

Because potential fields encode a continuous navigational space through the sensed world (i.e., the force can be computed at any location), they provide an infinite set of possibilities for reaction. Potential fields are not without their problems, however, (Koren and Borenstein 1991). In particular, they are vulnerable to local minima (locations where the robot may get stuck) or cyclic-oscillatory behavior. Numerous methods have been developed to address these problems, including the use of harmonic potential fields (Kim and Khosla 1992; Connolly and Grupen 1993), time-varying potential fields (Tianmiao and Bo 1992), random noise injected into the field (Arkin 1987a) and adaptive methods (Clark, Arkin, and Ram 1992), among others. We will examine more closely the methods for combining potential fields in section 3.4.

Another seemingly significant problem with the use of the potential fields method is the amount of time required to compute the entire field. Reactive robotic systems eliminate this problem by computing each field's contribution at the instantaneous position merely where the robot is currently located (Arkin 1989b). This is why we said earlier that these techniques are only *based* on the potential fields method: no field is computed at all. No path planning is conducted at all: Rather, the robot's reaction to its environment is recomputed as fast as sensory processing will permit. One of the major misconceptions in understanding reactive methods based on potential fields is a failure to recognize the fact that the only computation needed is that required to assess the forces from the robot's current position within the world. This method is thus inherently very fast to compute as well as highly parallelizable. When the entire field is represented in a figure, it is only for the reader's edification. Reiterating, behavior-based reactive systems using potential fields do not generate plans based on the entire field but instead react only to the robot's egocentric perceptions of the world. This is of particular importance when the world is dynamic (i.e., there are moving objects, thus invalidating static planning tech-

(A)

Figure 3.16

niques) or sensor readings are noisy or unreliable (as a plan generated on bad data is likely to be defective itself). Frequent resampling of the world helps overcome many of these deficiencies.

Slack (1990) developed another method for describing continuous pathways through navigational space. Navigational templates (NATs) are defined as arbitrary functions to characterize navigational space that do not necessarily have any correlation with typical potential fields methods. These NAT primitives rather characterize space on a task-oriented approach and are defined on an as-needed basis. An example of this method involves the use of spin-based techniques for obstacle treatment, circumventing the problem of local min-

(B)

Figure 3.16 *(continued)*
Potential fields for (A) an obstacle and (B) a goal located in the lower right side of the figure.

ima found in traditional potential fields methods. In figure 3.18, (A) shows a spin-based version for obstacle avoidance for the situation depicted in (B) in figure 3.16. The results of superpositioning this new template (as opposed to field) with (A) in Figure 3.16 are shown in (B) in Figure 3.18. By using knowledge of the goal's location relative to the detected obstacle, a spin direction is chosen, either clockwise (when the obstacle is to the right of the goal, viewed from above) or counterclockwise (when it is to the left). Unfortunately, the modularity of the behavior is somewhat compromised with this technique, for

(A)

Figure 3.17

the correct choice for the obstacle's spin direction requires knowledge of the goal location, which normally is used only within the goal attraction behavior.

One other novel representation uses a technique called deformation zones for collision avoidance (Zapata et al. 1991). This technique defines two manifolds: the information-boundary manifold, which represents the maximum extent of sensing, and the range manifold, constructed from the readings of all active sensors, which can be viewed as a deformed version of the information-boundary manifold because of the presence of obstacles (figure 3.19). Perception produces deformation of the information-boundary manifold, and control strategies are generated in response to remove the deformation. In the example

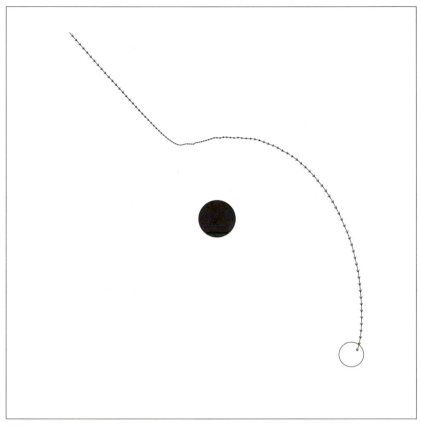

(B)

Figure 3.17 *(continued)*
(A) Linear superposition of fields in figure 3.16. (B) An example trajectory through this navigational space.

shown, the robot would steer to the left. In this approach, reactive behaviors are defined, including emergency stop, dynamic collision avoidance, displacement (orientation), and target following. One interesting aspect of this work allows for the definition of a variable collision avoidance zone dependent on the robot's velocity (i.e., when the robot is moving faster it projects further into the information-boundary manifold, and when it moves more slowly the information-boundary manifold shrinks). This enables effective control of the robot's speed by recognizing that if the deformation zone cannot be restored by steering, it can be restored by slowing the vehicle down.

(A)

Figure 3.18

3.4   ASSEMBLING BEHAVIORS

Having discussed methods to describe individual behaviors, we now study methods for constructing systems consisting of multiple behaviors. This study requires the introduction of notational formalisms that we will use throughout this book and an understanding of the different methods for combining and coordinating multiple behavioral activity streams. We first examine, however, the somewhat controversial notion of emergent behavior.

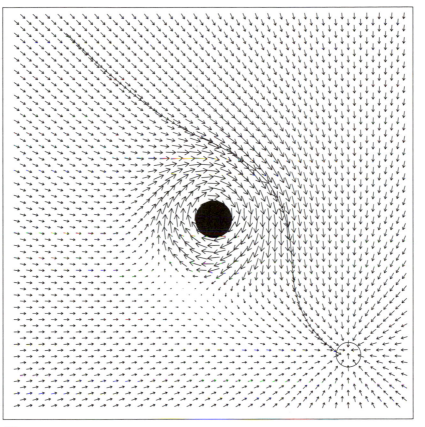

(B)

Figure 3.18 *(continued)*
(A) NAT spin field for the obstacle in (B) in figure 3.16. (B) Superposition of fields (A) in this figure and figure 3.16b. Also superimposed on this figure is the path for a robot using this combined field for the same start and goal as shown in (B) in figure 3.17.

3.4.1   Emergent Behavior

Emergence is often invoked in an almost mystical sense regarding the capabilities of behavior-based systems. Emergent behavior implies a holistic capability where the sum is considerably greater than its parts. It is true that what occurs in a behavior-based system is often a surprise to the system's designer, but does the surprise come because of a shortcoming of the analysis of the constituent behavioral building blocks and their coordination, or because of something else?

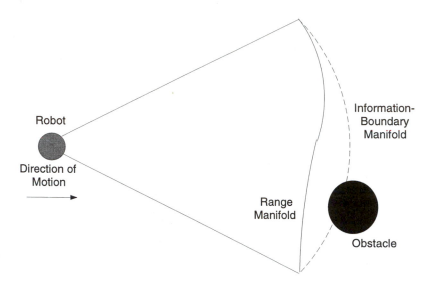

Figure 3.19
The use of manifolds for reactive collision avoidance.

The notion of emergence as a mystical phenomenon needs to be dispelled, but the concept in a well-defined sense can still be useful. Numerous researchers have discussed emergence in its various aspects:

■ Emergence is "the appearance of novel properties in whole systems" (Moravec 1988).
■ "Global functionality emerges from the parallel interaction of local behaviors" (Steels 1990).
■ "Intelligence emerges from the interaction of the components of the system" (where the system's functionality, i.e., planning, perception, mobility, etc., results from the behavior-generating components) (Brooks 1991a).
■ "Emergent functionality arises by virtue of interaction between components not themselves designed with the particular function in mind." (McFarland and Bosser 1993).

The common thread through all these statements is that emergence is a property of a collection of interacting components, in our case behaviors. The question arises however: Individual behaviors are well defined functionally, so why should a coordinated collection of them produce novel or unanticipated results?

Coordination functions as defined in this chapter are algorithms and hence contain no surprises and possess no magical perspective. In some cases, they are straightforward, such as choosing the highest ranked or most dominant behavior; in others they may be more complex, involving fusion of multiple active behaviors. Nonetheless, they are generally deterministic functions and certainly computable. Why then does the ineffable quality of emergence arise when these behavior-based robotic systems are released in the world? Why can we not predict their behavior exactly?

The answer to this question lies not within the robot itself but rather in the relationship the robot has with its environment. For most situations in which the behavior-based paradigm is applied, the world itself resists analytical modeling. Nondeterminism is rampant. The real world is filled with uncertainty and dynamic properties. Further, the perception process itself is also poorly characterized: Precise sensor models for open worlds do not exist. If a world model could be created that accurately captured *all* of its properties then emergence would not exist: Accurate predictions could be made. But it is the nature of the world to resist just such characterization, hence we cannot predict a priori, with any degree of confidence, in all but the simplest of worlds, how the world will present itself. Probabilistic models can provide guidance but not certainty.

For example, simply consider all the things involved in something as simple as your attending a class. Lighting conditions and weather will affect perceptual processing, the traffic on the road and sidewalks can be characterized only weakly (i.e., you do not know ahead of time the location and speeds of all people and cars that you meet). The complexities of the world resist modeling, leading to the aphorism espoused by Brooks (1989b): "The world is its own best model." Since the world cannot be faithfully modeled and is full of surprises itself, it is small wonder that behavior-based systems, which are tightly grounded to the world, reflect these surprises to their designers and observers by performing unexpected or unanticipated actions (or by definition actions not explicitly captured in the designer's intentions).

Summarizing, emergent properties are a common phenomena in behavior-based systems, but there is nothing mystical about them. They are a consequence underlying the complexity of the world in which the robotic agent resides and the additional complexity of perceiving that world. Let us now move on to methods for expressing the coordination of behavior within these robotic systems.

3.4.2 Notation

We now consider the case where multiple behaviors may be concurrently active within a robotic system. Defining additional notation, let

- **S** denote a vector of all stimuli s_i relevant for each behavior β_i detectable at time t.
- **B** denote a vector of all active behaviors β_i at a given time t.
- **G** denote a vector encoding the relative strength or gain g_i of each active behavior β_i.
- **R** denote a vector of all responses r_i generated by the set of active behaviors.

A new behavioral coordination function, **C**, is now defined such that

$$\rho = \mathbf{C}(\mathbf{G} * \mathbf{B}(\mathbf{S})),$$

or alternatively

$$\rho = \mathbf{C}(\mathbf{G} * \mathbf{R})$$

where

$$\mathbf{R} = \begin{bmatrix} \mathbf{r}_1 \\ \mathbf{r}_2 \\ \vdots \\ \mathbf{r}_n \end{bmatrix}, \quad \mathbf{S} = \begin{bmatrix} \mathbf{s}_1 \\ \mathbf{s}_2 \\ \vdots \\ \mathbf{s}_n \end{bmatrix}, \quad \mathbf{G} = \begin{bmatrix} g_1 \\ g_2 \\ \vdots \\ g_n \end{bmatrix}, \text{ and } \mathbf{B} = \begin{bmatrix} \beta_1 \\ \beta_2 \\ \vdots \\ \beta_n \end{bmatrix},$$

and where $*$ denotes the special scaling operation for multiplication of each scalar component (g_i) by the corresponding magnitude of the component vector ($\mathbf{r}_i$), resulting in a column vector $\mathbf{r}'_i$ of the same dimension as $\mathbf{r}_i$. In other words, $\mathbf{r}'_i$ represents a response reaction in the same direction as $\mathbf{r}_i$ with its magnitude scaled by g_i. (Alternatively, **G** can be represented as a diagonal matrix).

Restating, the coordination function **C**, operating over all active behaviors **B**, modulated by the relative strengths of each behavior specified by the gain vector **G**, for a given set of detected stimuli at time t, **S**, produces the overall robotic response ρ, where ρ is the vector encoding the global response that the robot will undertake, represented in the same form as r (e.g., [$\mathbf{x}, \mathbf{y}, \mathbf{z}, \theta, \phi, \psi$]).

C can be arbitrarily defined, but several strategies are commonly used to encode this function. They are split across two dimensions: competitive and cooperative. The simplest competitive method is pure arbitration, where only one behavior's output ($\mathbf{r}_i$) is selected from **R** and assigned to ρ, that is, arbitrarily choosing only one response from the many available. Several methods have been used to implement this particular technique, including behavioral prioritization (subsumption) or action selection. Cooperative methods, on the other hand, blend the outputs of multiple behaviors in some way consistent with the agent's overall goals. The most common method of this type is vector addition. Competitive and cooperative methods can be composed as well. Section 3.4.3 examines these methods in more detail.

First, however, let us revisit the classroom example. Given the robot's current perceptions at time t:

$$\mathbf{S} = \begin{bmatrix} (class - location, 1.0) \\ (detected - object, 0.2) \\ (detected - student, 0.8) \\ (detected - path, 1.0) \\ (detected - elder, 0.0) \end{bmatrix},$$

for each $\mathbf{s}_i = (p, \lambda)$, where λ is the stimulus p's percentage of maximum strength. The situation above indicates that the robot knows exactly where the classroom is, has detected an object a good distance away, sees a student approaching nearby, sees the sidewalk (path) with certainty, and senses that there are no elders nearby.

We can then represent the behavioral response as:

$$\mathbf{B(S)} = \begin{bmatrix} \beta_{move-to-class}(\mathbf{s}_1) \\ \beta_{avoid-object}(\mathbf{s}_2) \\ \beta_{dodge-student}(\mathbf{s}_3) \\ \beta_{stay-right}(\mathbf{s}_4) \\ \beta_{defer-to-elder}(\mathbf{s}_5) \end{bmatrix}.$$

$\mathbf{R}$ then is computed using each β,

$$\mathbf{R} = \begin{bmatrix} \mathbf{r}_{move-to-class} \\ \mathbf{r}_{avoid-object} \\ \mathbf{r}_{dodge-student} \\ \mathbf{r}_{stay-right} \\ \mathbf{r}_{defer-to-elder} \end{bmatrix},$$

with component vector magnitudes equal to (arbitrarily for this case)

$$\mathbf{R}_{magnitude} = \begin{bmatrix} 1.0 \\ 0 \\ 0.8 \\ 1.0 \\ 0 \end{bmatrix},$$

where each $\mathbf{r}_i$ encodes an $[x, y, \theta]$ for this particular robot expressing the desired directional response for each independent behavior. In the example, *avoid-object* and *defer-to-elder* are below threshold and generate no response, whereas *move-to-class* and *stay-right* are at maximum strength (defined as 1.0 here). Remember that the response is computed from $\beta: S \to R$.

Before the coordination function $\mathbf{C}$ is applied, $\mathbf{R}$ is multiplied by the gain vector $\mathbf{G}$. For the numbers used in the example for $\mathbf{G}$, *stay-right* is least important ($g_{stay-right} = 0.4$), *dodge-student* is deemed the most important behavior ($g_{dodge-student} = 1.5$), while *move-to-class* and *defer-to-elder* are of equal intermediate priority ($g_{move-to-class} = g_{defer-to-elder} = 0.8$) and the *avoid-object* behavior ranks second overall ($g_{avoid-object} = 1.2$).

$$\mathbf{R'} = \mathbf{G} * \mathbf{R},$$

where:

$$\mathbf{G} = \begin{bmatrix} g_{move-to-class} \\ g_{avoid-object} \\ g_{dodge-student} \\ g_{stay-right} \\ g_{defer-elder} \end{bmatrix} = \begin{bmatrix} 0.8 \\ 1.2 \\ 1.5 \\ 0.4 \\ 0.8 \end{bmatrix},$$

yielding:

$$\rho = \mathbf{C}(\mathbf{R'}) = \mathbf{C} \left(\begin{bmatrix} g_1 * \mathbf{r}_1 \\ g_2 * \mathbf{r}_2 \\ g_3 * \mathbf{r}_3 \\ g_4 * \mathbf{r}_4 \\ g_5 * \mathbf{r}_5 \end{bmatrix} \right),$$

with scaled component vector magnitudes

$$\mathbf{R'}_{magnitude} = \begin{bmatrix} 0.8 \\ 0 \\ 1.2 \\ 0.4 \\ 0 \end{bmatrix}.$$

$\mathbf{G}$ is of value only when multiple behaviors are being coordinated, as it enables the robot to set priorities through establishing the relative importance of each of its constituent behaviors.

If a simple winner-take-all coordination strategy is in place (action-selection), a single component vector $g_i\mathbf{r}_i$ (based on some metric such as greatest magnitude) is chosen by **C**, assigned to ρ and executed. In the example above, this is the component with a value of 1.2, associated with the *dodge-student* behavior. Thus the response undertaken using this simple arbitration function is the action required to dodge an oncoming student. Note that this behavior dominates only given the current perceptual readings at time t and that the behavioral response will change as the robot's perceptions of the world also change. For a priority-based arbitration system, the highest-ranked component behavior encoded in **G** (above threshold) would be chosen and executed, independent of the individual components' relative magnitudes. In our example, *dodge-student* would also be chosen using this method, assuming the stimulus is above threshold, since $g_{dodge-student}(1.5)$ is the highest-ranked behavior.

Finally, coordination functions are recursively defined to operate not only on low-level behavioral responses but also on the output of other coordination operators (which also are behavioral responses).

$$\rho' = \mathbf{C'} \left(\begin{bmatrix} \rho_1 \\ \rho_2 \\ \vdots \\ \rho_n \end{bmatrix} \right),$$

where ρ' coordinates the output of lower-level coordinative functions. One benefit of this definition is the ability to sequence sets of behavioral activities for a robot temporally.

3.4.3   Behavioral Coordination

We now turn to examine the nature of **C**, the coordination function for behaviors. This function has two predominant classes, competitive and cooperative, each of which has several different strategies for realization. The different classes may be composed together, although frequently in the behavior-based architectures described in chapter 4, a commitment is made to one type of coordination function specific to a particular approach.

3.4.3.1   Competitive Methods

Conflict can result when two or more behaviors are active, each with its own independent response. Competitive methods provide a means of coordinating behavioral response for conflict resolution. The coordinator can often be viewed

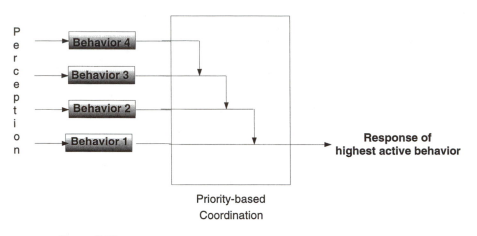

Figure 3.20
Arbitration via suppression network.

as a winner-take-all network in which the single response for the winning behavior out-muscles all the others and is directed to the robot for execution. This
type of competitive strategy can be enacted in a variety of ways.

Arbitration requires that a coordination function serving as an arbiter select
a single behavioral response. The arbitration function can take the form of a
fixed prioritization network in which a strict behavioral dominance hierarchy
exists, typically through the use of suppression and inhibition in a descending
manner. This is a hallmark of subsumption-based methods (Brooks 1986), the
particulars of which are described in chapter 4. Figure 3.20 shows an example
illustrated as a dominance hierarchy.

Action-selection methods (Maes 1990) arbitrarily select the output of a single behavior, but this is done in a less autocratic manner. Here the behaviors
actively compete with each other through the use of activation levels driven
by both the agent's goals (or intentionality) and incoming sensory information. No fixed hierarchy is established; rather the behavioral processes compete
with each other for control at a given time. Run time arbitration occurs by the
selection of the most active behavior, but no predefined hierarchy is present.
Figure 3.21 captures this notionally. The concept of lateral inhibition (section 2.2.1) can easily be implemented using this method where one behavior's
strong output negatively affects another's output.

Another even more democratic competitive method involves behaviors' generating votes for actions, with the action that receives the most votes being the single behavior chosen (Rosenblatt and Payton 1989). This technique

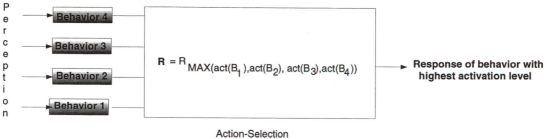

Figure 3.21
Arbitration via action-selection.

is embodied in the Distributed Architecture for Mobile Navigation (DAMN) (Rosenblatt 1995). Here instead of each behavior's being encoded as a set of rule-based responses, each behavior casts a number of votes toward a predefined set of discrete motor responses. For navigation of an unmanned ground vehicle, the behavioral response set for steering consists of

{*hard-left*, *soft-left*, *straight-ahead*, *soft-right*, *hard-right*}.

Each active behavior (e.g., *goal-seeking, obstacle-avoidance, road-following, cross-country, teleoperation, map-based navigation*) has a certain number of votes (g_i) and a user-provided distribution for allocating those votes. Arbitration takes place through a winner-take-all strategy in which the single response with the most votes is enacted. In a sense, this allows a level of behavioral cooperation, but the method is still arbitrary in its choice of a single response. Figure 3.22 depicts this type of arbitration method.

3.4.3.2 Cooperative Methods

Cooperative methods provide an alternative to competitive methods such as arbitration. Behavioral fusion provides the ability to use concurrently the output of more than one behavior at a time.

The central issue in combining the outputs of behaviors is finding a representation amenable to fusion. The potential-fields method, as described in section 3.3.2, provides one useful formalism. As shown earlier, the most straightforward method is through vector addition or superpositioning. Each behavior's relative strength or gain, g_i, is used as a multiplier of the vectors before addition. Figure 3.23 illustrates how this is accomplished.

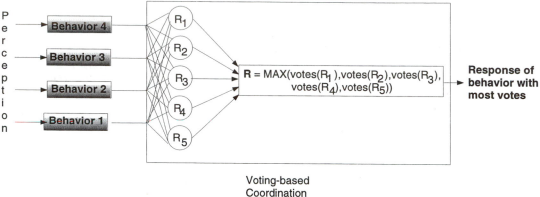

Voting-based
Coordination

Figure 3.22
Arbitration via voting.

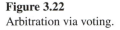

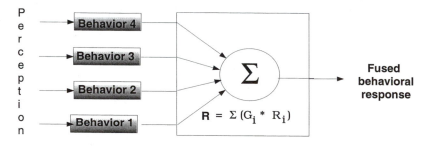

Figure 3.23
Behavioral fusion via vector summation.

Figure 3.24 shows a field with three active obstacles and a goal located in the lower right corner. In (A), the goal attractor behavior has twice the obstacle avoidance behavior's relative strength. The path the robot takes through this field cuts fairly close to the obstacles themselves, resulting in a shorter although more perilous path. In (B), the obstacle avoidance has twice the strength of the goal attraction. The path taken is considerably longer but also further from the obstacles themselves. Vector addition provides a continuum for combining these fields controllable through the gain vector **G**.

In work at Hughes Artificial Intelligence Center (Payton et al. 1992), the issue of combining multiple disparate behavioral outputs is handled by avoiding the sole use of single discrete response values. Instead, the responses of each behavior constrain the control variables as follows:

- Zone: establishment of upper and lower bounds for a control variable
- Spike: single value designation resulting in standard priority-based arbitration
- Clamp: establishment of upper or lower bound on a control variable

In essence, the system provides constraints within which the control system must operate to satisfy its behavioral requirements. The algorithm for fusing the behaviors is as follows:

```
Generate a profile by summing each active behavior's zones and
spikes
If maximum is a spike
     choose that command
else (maximum is in zone)
     choose command requiring minimal change from current
     control setting
If command chosen beyond a clamped value
     choose most dominant clamp from all clamps
     If that clamp dominates profile
          move command value to just within clamped region
```

In this manner, commands can be described in the control variables for each actuator (e.g., speed of a motor, angles of a control surface, etc). Clamps limit the acceptable ranges for each actuator. This particular system has been applied to the control of an underwater robot using high-level behaviors such as stealth, safety, urgency, and efficiency, which are mapped onto low-level behaviors that control the vehicle's speed, the angle of the dive plane, proximity to the ocean bottom, and so forth, which in turn control the vehicle actuators, such as the ballast pumps and dive plane motor.

Formal methods for expressing behavioral blending are discussed in Saffiotti, Konolige, and Ruspini 1995. In this approach, each behavior is assigned a desirability function that can be combined using specialized logical operators called t-norms, a form of multivalued logic. A single action is chosen from a set of actions created by blending the weighted primitive action behaviors. As this is essentially a variation of fuzzy control, where blending is the fuzzification operation and selection is the defuzzification process, the method for generating these results is deferred until chapter 8.

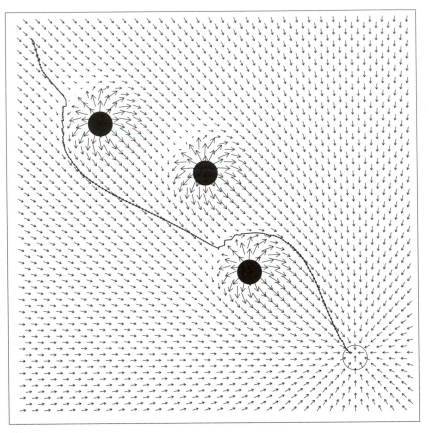

(A)

Figure 3.24

It is also possible that the deformation manifolds approach described for obstacle avoidance in section 3.3.2 could be extended to behavioral fusion as the approach potentially can provide a common representation for robotic action. So far, however, it has been limited to arbitration.

3.4.4   Behavioral Assemblages

Behavioral assemblages are the packages from which behavior-based robotic systems are constructed. An assemblage is recursively defined as a coordinated collection of primitive behaviors or assemblages. Each individual assemblage consists of a coordination operator and any number of behavioral components

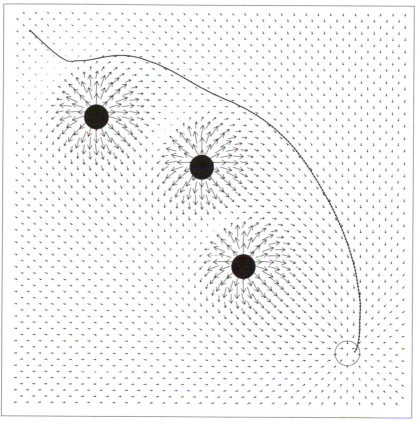

(B)

Figure 3.24 *(continued)*
Behavioral fusion: (A) goal attraction dominates; (B) obstacle avoidance dominates.

(primitives or assemblages). The power of assemblage use arises from the notion of abstraction, in which we can create higher-level behaviors from simpler
ones and refer to them henceforward independent of their constituent elements.
Abstraction has traditionally been a powerful concept in AI (Sacerdoti 1974),
and it is no less so here. Abstraction enables us to reuse assemblages in an
easy, modular manner to construct behavior-based systems; provides the ability to reason over them for use in hybrid architectures (chapter 6); and provides
coarser levels of granularity for adaptation and learning methods to be applied
(chapter 8).

We have previously used the notation $\mathbf{C}(\mathbf{G} * \mathbf{B}(\mathbf{S})) = \rho$, in section 3.4.2. We denote an assemblage q_i such that q_i symbolizes $\mathbf{C}(\mathbf{G} * \mathbf{B}(\mathbf{S}))$, hence $q_i = \rho$. For convenience, we will generally omit the ρ in assemblage expression, leaving q_i, which maps conveniently onto a state within an FSA diagram. Although assemblages can be expressed in any of the notational formats section 3.4.2 describes, whenever there is a temporal component (i.e., the behavioral structure of the system changes over time), FSA notation is used most often.

Figure 3.12 has already shown an assemblage of assemblages in FSA form for a competition robot. The constituent behaviors for two of that robot's assemblage states are

- move-to-pole
- move-to-goal(detect-pole)
- avoid-static-obstacle(detect-obstacles)
- noise(generate-direction) low gain
- wander
- probe(detect-open-area)
- avoid-static-obstacle(detect-obstacles)
- noise(generate-direction) high gain
- avoid-past(detect-visited-areas)

Each of these FSA states can be equivalently depicted as an SR diagram, an example of which appears in figure 3.25.

All of these assemblages can, in turn, be bundled together in a high-level SR diagram if desired (figure 3.26). Using this alternate representation, which has merely a sequencer label for the coordination function, the explicit temporal dependencies between states (i.e., the state transition function q associated with the perceptual triggers) are lost when compared to the earlier FSA version (figure 3.12).

Another form of assemblage construction, referred to rather as "hierarchically mediated behaviors," appears in Kaelbling 1986. A similar hierarchical abstraction capability also appears in teleo-reactive systems (Nilsson 1994). In RS (Lyons and Arbib 1989), an assemblage is defined as a network of schemas that can be viewed as a schema itself. In all these cases, behavioral aggregations (or assemblages) can be viewed recursively (or alternatively, hierarchically) as behaviors themselves.

Assemblages, defined as hierarchical recursive behavioral abstractions, constitute the primary building blocks of behavior-based robotic systems and are ultimately grounded in primitive behaviors attached to sensors and actuators.

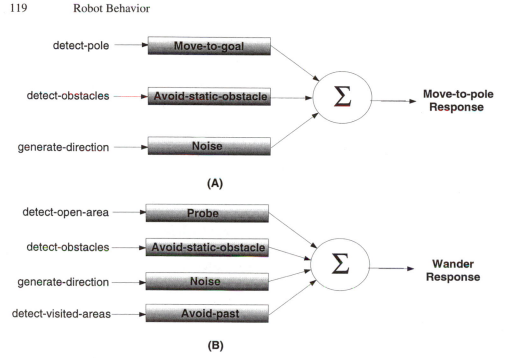

Figure 3.25
SR diagram for the move-to-pole and wander assemblages.

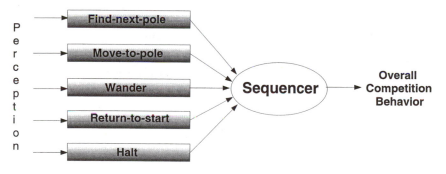

Figure 3.26
Competition SR diagram.

3.5   CHAPTER SUMMARY

- Robotic behaviors generate a motor response from a given perceptual stimulus.
- Purely reactive systems avoid the use of explicit representational knowledge.
- Behavior-based systems are inherently modular in design and provide the ability for software reuse.
- Biological models often serve as the basis for the design of behavior-based robotic systems.
- Three design paradigms for building behavior-based systems have been presented: ethologically guided/constrained design, using biological models as the basis for behavioral selection, design and validation; situated activity, which creates behaviors that fit specific situational contexts in which the robot will need to respond; and experimentally driven design, which uses a bottom-up design strategy based on the need for additional competency as the system is being built.
- The expression of behaviors can be accomplished in several different ways: SR diagrams, which intuitively convey the flow of control within a behavior-based system; functional notation, which is amenable to the generation of code for implementation; and FSA diagrams, which are particularly well suited for representing behavioral assemblages' time-varying composition.
- Other, more formal methods have been developed for expressing behaviors, such as RS and situated automata as epitomized by the Gapps language.
- Behaviors can be represented as triples (S, R, β), with S being the stimulus domain, R the range of response, and β the behavioral mapping between them.
- The presence of a stimulus is necessary but not sufficient to evoke a motor response in a behavior-based robot. Only when the stimulus exceeds some threshold value τ will it produce a response.
- g_i, a strength multiplier or gain value, can be used to turn off behaviors or increase the response's relative strength.
- Responses are encoded in two forms: discrete encoding, in which an enumerable set of responses exists; or continuous functional encoding, in which an infinite space of responses is possible for a behavior.
- Rule-based methods are often used for discrete encoding strategies.
- Approaches based on the potential-fields method are often used for the continuous functional encoding of robotic response.
- There is nothing magical about emergent behavior; it is a product of the complexity of the relationship between a robotic agent and the real world that resists analytical modeling.

■ Notational methods for describing assemblages and coordination functions used throughout the text have been presented.

■ The two primary mechanisms for behavioral coordination are competitive or cooperative, but they can be combined if desired.

• Competitive methods result in the selection of the output of a single behavior, typically either by arbitration or action-selection.

• Cooperative methods often use superpositioning of forces or gradients generated from field–based methods, including potential field-based approaches or navigational templates.

■ Assemblages are recursively defined aggregations of behaviors or other assemblages.

■ Assemblages serve as important abstractions useful for constructing behavior-based robots.

Chapter 4

Behavior-Based Architectures

One can expect the human race to continue attempting systems just within or just beyond our reach; and software systems are perhaps the most intricate and complex of man's handiworks. The management of this complex craft will demand our best use of new languages and systems, our best adaptation of proven engineering management methods, liberal doses of common sense, and a God-given humility to recognize our fallibility and limitations.

–Frederick P. Brooks, Jr.

There are two ways of constructing a software design. One way is to make it so simple that there are obviously no deficiencies. And the other way is to make it so complicated that there are no obvious deficiencies.

—C.A.R. Hoare

Chapter Objectives

1. To characterize what a robot architecture is.
2. To understand the requirements for the design of a behavior-based robotic architecture.
3. To understand, in depth, two different reactive robotic architectures: subsumption and motor schema.
4. To review many of the other behavior-based architectural choices available to the robot system builder.
5. To develop design principles for the construction of a behavior-based robotic architecture.

4.1   WHAT IS A ROBOTIC ARCHITECTURE?

In chapter 3, we learned about robotic behaviors, including methods for expressing, encoding, and coordinating them. To design and build behavior-based
robotic systems, commitments need to be made to the actual, specific methods
to be used during this process. This need leads us to the study of robotic architectures: software systems and specifications that provide languages and tools
for the construction of behavior-based systems.

All of the architectures described in this chapter are concerned with behavioral control. As described in chapter 1, several non–behavior-based robotic
architectures appeared before the advent of reactive control, for example,
NASREM (section 1.3.1). Here, however, we focus on behavior-based systems. Though considerably varied, these architectures share many common
features:

- emphasis on the importance of coupling sensing and action tightly
- avoidance of representational symbolic knowledge
- decomposition into contextually meaningful units (behaviors or situation-
action pairs)

Although these architectures share a common philosophy on the surface,
there are many deep distinctions between them, including

- the granularity of behavioral decomposition
- the basis for behavior specification (ethological, situated activity, or experimental)
- the response encoding method (e.g., discrete or continuous)
- the coordination methods used (e.g., competitive versus cooperative)
- the programming methods, language support available, and the extent of
software reusability.

In this chapter we study several common robotic architectures used to build
behavior-based systems. Tables appear throughout summarizing the characteristics for each of the behavior-based architectures discussed. Two of the
architectures have been singled out for closer scrutiny than the others: the
subsumption architecture using rule-based encodings and priority-based arbitration; and motor schemas using continuous encoding and cooperative combination of vectors.

4.1.1 Definitions

Perhaps a good place to begin searching for our definition of robotic architectures would be with the definition of computer architectures. Stone (1980,
p. 3), one of the best-known computer architects, uses the following definition: "Computer architecture is the discipline devoted to the design of
highly specific and individual computers from a collection of common building
blocks."

Robotic architectures are essentially the same. In our robotic control context,
however, architecture usually refers to a software architecture, rather than the
hardware side of the system. So if we modify Stone's definition accordingly,
we get:

> Robotic architecture is the discipline devoted to the design of highly specific and
> individual robots from a collection of common software building blocks.

How does this definition coincide with other working definitions by practicing robotic architects? According to Hayes-Roth (1995, p. 330), an architecture
refers to " . . . the abstract design of a class of agents: the set of structural
components in which perception, reasoning, and action occur; the specific
functionality and interface of each component, and the interconnection topology between components." Although her discussion of agent architectures is
targeted for artificially intelligent systems in general, it also holds for the sub-
class with which we are concerned, namely, behavior-based robotic systems.
Indeed, a surveillance mobile robot system (figure 4.1) has been developed that
embodies her architectural design principles (Hayes-Roth et al. 1995). She argues that architectures must be produced to fit specific operating environments,
a concept closely related to our earlier discussion of ecological niches in chapter 2 and related to the claim in McFarland and Bosser 1993 that robots should
be tailored to fit particular niches.

Mataric (1992a) provides another definition, stating, "An architecture provides a principled way of organizing a control system. However, in addition
to providing structure, it imposes constraints on the way the control problem
can be solved." One final straightforward definition is from Dean and Wellman
(1991, p. 462): "An architecture describes a set of architectural components
and how they interact."

Figure 4.1
Nomad 200 robot, of the type used for surveillance at Stanford. (Photograph courtesy
of Nomadic Technologies Inc., Mountain View, California.)

4.1.2   Computability

Existing robotic architectures are diverse, from the hierarchical NASREM
architecture to purely reactive systems such as subsumption (section 4.3) to
hybrid architectures (chapter 6). In what ways can instances chosen from the
diversity of architectural solutions be said to differ from one another? In what
ways can they be said to be the same?

The answer to these questions is related to the distinction between computability and organizing principles. Architectures are constructed from components, with each specific architecture having its own peculiar set of building
blocks. The ways in which these building blocks can be connected facilitate
certain types of robotic design in given circumstances. Organizing principles
underlie a particular architecture's commitment to its component structure,
granularity, and connectivity.

From a computational perspective, however, we may see that the various
architectures are all equivalent in their computational expressiveness. Consider, for instance, the differences between programming languages. Different

choices are available to the programmer ranging from machine language to assembler to various high-level languages (such as Fortran, Cobol, C, Pascal, and LISP) to very high–level languages such as those used in visual programming. Is there any fundamental incompatibility in the idea that one language can do something that another cannot?

Consider the results that Bohm and Jacopini (1966) derived concerning computability in programming languages. They proved that if any language contains the three basic constructs of sequencing, conditional branching, and iteration, it can compute the entire class of computable functions (i.e., it is Turing equivalent). This essentially states that from a computational perspective the common programming languages have no differences.

The logical extension is that since all robotic architectures provide the capability to perform tasks sequentially, allow conditional branching, and provide the ability for iterative constructs, these architectures are computationally equivalent. All behavior-based robotic architectures are essentially software languages or frameworks for specifying and controlling robots. The level of abstraction they offer may differ, but not the computability.

This does not mean, of course that we will start writing AI programs in Cobol. It does mean that each current programming language has in turn found a niche in which it serves well and thus has survived (i.e., remained in usage) because it is well suited for that particular task. Some argue that the same holds for robotic architectures as well: each serves a particular domain (or niche) and will be subjected to the same environmental stresses for survival as are computer architectures or software languages.

Behavior-based robotic systems serve best when the real world cannot be accurately characterized or modeled. Whenever engineering can remove uncertainty from the environment, purely behavior-based systems may not necessarily afford the best solution for the task involved and hierarchical architectures (chapter 1) may prove more suitable, as, for example, in factory floor operations where the environment can be altered to fit the robot's needs. More often than not, however, much as we try, we cannot remove uncertainty, unpredictability, and noise from the world. Behavior-based robotic architectures were developed in response to this difficulty and choose instead to deal with these issues from the onset, relying heavily on sensing without constructing potentially erroneous global world models. The more the world changes during execution, the more the resulting value of any plan generated a priori decreases, and the more unstable any representational knowledge stored ahead of time or gathered during execution and remembered becomes.

At a finer level, we will see that behavior-based architectures, because of their different means of expressing behaviors and the sets of coordination functions they afford, provide significant diversity to a robotic system's designer. Each approach has its own strengths and weaknesses in terms of what it is best at doing or where it is most appropriately applied. The remainder of this chapter discusses a variety of behavior-based robot architectural solutions. Not all are expected to withstand the test of time, and many will likely suffer a fate similar to that of early programming languages (e.g., ALGOL, SNOBOL) and fade off into obscurity. Ecological pressure from sources ranging from ease of use for the designer to generalizability to public opinion to exogenous factors (political, economic, etc.) will ultimately serve as the fundamental selection mechanism, not merely an academic's perspective on their elegance, simplicity, or utility.

As an aside, we note the recent controversy Penrose (1989, 1994) stirred up by claiming that no computer program can ever exhibit intelligence as according to Penrose, intelligence must incorporate solutions to noncomputable problems as well as those that are computable. Interestingly, he does not dismiss the attainment of intelligence as utterly impossible in a device and presents a novel, but rather speculative, approach based on quantum mechanics (a microtubule architecture if you will), rather than a computational approach, to achieve this goal. To say the least, his position has been strongly rebutted by many within the AI community and is often cursorily dismissed as rubbish. In the book's final chapter, we will revisit this issue of what intelligence means within the context of a robotic system and what we can or should expect from these systems. Suffice it to say, for now, that all the behavior-based architectures considered in this book are computational.

4.1.3   Evaluation Criteria

How can we measure an architecture's utility for a particular problem? A list of desiderata for behavior-based architectures is compiled below.

■ **Support for parallelism**: Behavior-based systems are inherently parallel in nature. What kind of support does the architecture provide for this capability?

■ **Hardware targetability**: Hardware targetability really refers to two different things. The first regards how well an architecture can be mapped onto real robotic systems, that is, physical sensors and actuators. The second is concerned with the computational processing. Chip-level hardware implementations are often preferred over software from a performance perspective. What type of support is available to realize the architectural design in silicon (e.g., compilers for programmable logic arrays [Brooks 1987b])?

■ **Niche targetabilty**: How well can the robot be tailored to fit its operating environment (Hayes-Roth 1995)? How can the relationships between robot and environment be expressed to ensure successful niche occupation?

■ **Support for modularity**: What methods does an architecture provide for encapsulating behavioral abstractions? Modularity can be found at a variety of levels. By providing abstractions for use over a wide range of behavioral levels (primitives, assemblages, agents), an architecture makes a developer's task easier and facilates software reuse (Mataric 1992a).

■ **Robustness**: A strength of behavior-based systems is their ability to perform in the face of failing components (e.g., sensors, actuators, etc.) (Payton et al. 1992; Horswill 1993a; Ferrell 1994). What types of mechanisms does the architecture provide for such fault tolerance?

■ **Timeliness in development**: What types of tools and development environments are available to work within the architectural framework? Is the architecture more of a philosophical approach, or does it provide specific tools and methods for generating real robotic systems?

■ **Run time flexibility**: How can the control system be adjusted or reconfigured during execution? How easily is adaptation and learning introduced?

■ **Performance effectiveness**: How well does the constructed robot perform its intended task(s)? This aspect also encompasses the notion of timeliness of execution, or how well the system can meet established real-time deadlines. In other instances, specific quantitative metrics can be applied for evaluation purposes within a specific task context (Balch and Arkin 1994). These may include such things as time to task completion, energy consumption, minimum travel, and so forth, or combinations thereof.

These widely ranging criteria can be used for evaluating the relative merits of many of the architectures described in the remainder of this chapter.

4.1.4   Organizing Principles

From the discussion in chapter 3, several different dimensions for distinguishing robotic architectures become apparent, including

■ Different coordination strategies, of particular note, competitive (e.g., arbitration, action-selection, voting) versus cooperative (e.g., superpositioning)
■ Granularity of behavior: microbehaviors such as those found in situated activity-based systems (e.g., Pengi) or more general purpose task descriptions (e.g., RAPs).

▪ Encoding of behavioral response: discrete, that is, a prespecified set of possible responses (e.g., rule-based systems or DAMN), or continuous (e.g., potential field–based methods).

The remainder of this chapter first discusses two architectures in some detail: the subsumption architecture and motor schema–based systems (the reactive component of the Autonomous Robot Architecture (AuRA). Next it reviews several other significant behavior-based architectures, although at a higher level. Finally it presents design principles for constructing a behavior-based robotic system, in an architecture-independent manner as much as possible.

4.2   A FORAGING EXAMPLE

To ground the following architectural discussions, let us consider a well-studied problem in robotic navigation: foraging. This task consists of a robot's moving away from a home base area looking for attractor objects. Typical applications might include looking for something lost or gathering items of value. Upon detecting the attractor, the robot moves toward it, picks it up and then returns it to the home base. It repeats this sequence of actions until it has returned all the attractors in the environment. This test domain has provided the basis for a wide range of results on both real robots (Balch et al. 1995; Mataric 1993a) and in simulation. Foraging also correlates well with ethological studies, especially in the case of ants (e.g., Goss et al. 1990).

Several high-level behavioral requirements to accomplish this task include:

1. *Wander*: move through the world in search of an attractor
2. *Acquire*: move toward the attractor when detected
3. *Retrieve:* return the attractor to the home base once acquired

Figure 4.2 represents these higher-level assemblages. Each assemblage shown is manifested with different primitive behaviors and coordinated in different ways as we move from one architectural example to the next.

4.3   SUBSUMPTION ARCHITECTURE

Rodney Brooks developed the subsumption architecture in the mid-1980s at the Massachusetts Institute of Technology. His approach, a purely reactive behavior-based method, flew in the face of traditional AI research at the time. Brooks argued that the *sense-plan-act* paradigm used in some of the first autonomous robots such as Shakey (Nilsson 1984) was in fact detrimental to

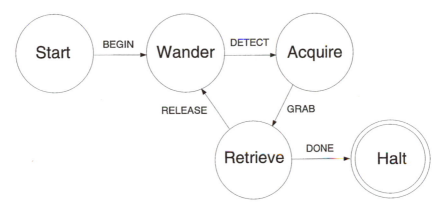

Figure 4.2
FSA diagram for foraging.

the construction of real working robots. He further argued that building world models and reasoning using explicit symbolic representational knowledge at best was an impediment to timely robotic response and at worst actually led robotics researchers in the wrong direction.

In his seminal paper, Brooks (1986) advocated the use of a layered control system, embodied by the subsumption architecture but layered along a different dimension than what traditional research was pursuing. Figure 4.3 shows the distinction, with the conventional *sense-plan-act* vertical model illustrated in (A) and the new horizontal decomposition in (B). (The orientation of the lines that separate the components determines vertical and horizontal.)

Much of the presentation and style of the subsumption approach is dogmatic. Tenets of this viewpoint include

- Complex behavior need not necessarily be the product of a complex control system.
- Intelligence is in the eye of the observer (Brooks 1991a).
- The world is its own best model (Brooks 1991a).
- Simplicity is a virtue.
- Robots should be cheap.
- Robustness in the presence of noisy or failing sensors is a design goal.
- Planning is just a way of avoiding figuring out what to do next (Brooks 1987a).
- All onboard computation is important.
- Systems should be built incrementally.
- No representation. No calibration. No complex computers. No high-bandwidth communication (Brooks 1989b).

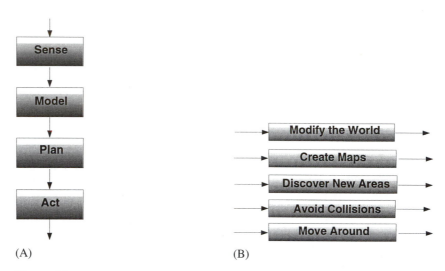

Figure 4.3
(A) Sense-plan-act model. (B) Subsumption (reactive) model.

This was hard to swallow for many in the AI community (and in many cases, still is). Brooks lobbied long and hard for rethinking the way intelligent robots in particular, and intelligent systems in general, should be constructed. This stance changed the direction of autonomous robotics research. Although currently many in the AI community take a more tempered position regarding the role of deliberation and symbolic reasoning (chapter 6), Brooks has not to date disavowed in print any of these principles (1991a).

Let us now move to the specifics of the subsumption architecture. Table 4.1 is the first of many tables throughout this chapter that provide a snapshot view of the design characteristics of a particular architecture in light of the material discussed in chapter 3.

4.3.1   Behaviors in Subsumption

Task-achieving behaviors in the subsumption architecture are represented as separate layers. Individual layers work on individual goals concurrently and asynchronously. At the lowest level, each behavior is represented using an augmented finite state machine (AFSM) model (figure 4.4). The AFSM encapsulates a particular behavioral transformation function β_i. Stimulus or response signals can be suppressed or inhibited by other active behaviors. A reset input is also used to return the behavior to its start conditions. Each AFSM performs

Table 4.1
Subsumption Architecture

Name	Subsumption architecture
Background	Well-known early reactive architecture
Precursors	Braitenberg 1984; Walter 1953; Ashby 1952
Principal design method	Experimental
Developer	Rodney Brooks (MIT)
Response encoding	Predominantly discrete (rule based)
Coordination method	Competitive (priority-based arbitration via inhibition and suppression)
Programming method	Old method uses AFSMs; new method uses Behavior Language
Robots fielded	Allen, Genghis (hexapod), Squirt (very small), Toto, Seymour, Polly (tour guide), several others
References	Brooks 1986; Brooks 1990b; Horswill 1993a

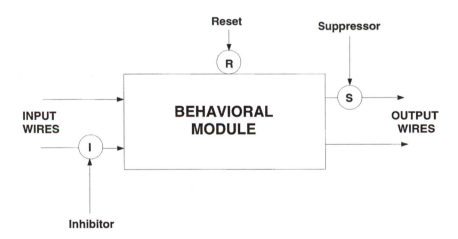

Figure 4.4
Original AFSM as used within the subsumption architecture.

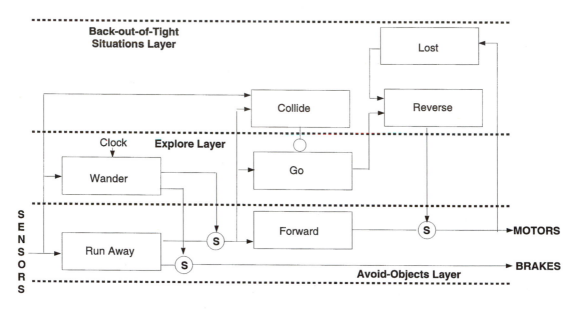

Figure 4.5
AFSMs for a simple three-layered robot (Brooks 1987b).

an action and is responsible for its own perception of the world. There is no global memory, bus, or clock. With this design, each behavioral layer can be mapped onto its own processor (Brooks 1987b). There are no central world models or global sensor representations. Required sensor inputs are channeled to the consuming behavior.

Figure 4.5 shows a simple robot with three behavioral layers. The system was implemented on a radio-controlled toy car (Brooks 1987b). The lowest behavior layer, *avoid-objects,* either halts or turns away from an obstacle, depending upon the input from the robot's infrared proximity sensors. The *explore* layer permits the robot to move in the absence of obstacles and cover large areas. The highest layer, *back-out-of-tight-situations*, enables the robot to reverse direction in particularly tight quarters where simpler avoidance and exploration behaviors fail to extricate the robot.

As can be seen, the initial subsumption language, requiring the specification of low-level AFSMs, was unwieldy for those not thoroughly schooled in its usage. Recognizing this problem, Brooks (1990a) developed the Behavior Language, which provides a new abstraction independent of the AFSMs themselves using a single rule set to encode each behavior. This high-level language is then compiled to the intermediate AFSM representation, which can then be further compiled to run on a range of target processors.

4.3.2   Coordination in Subsumption

The name subsumption arises from the coordination process used between the layered behaviors within the architecture. Complex actions subsume simpler behaviors. A priority hierarchy fixes the topology. The lower levels in the architecture have no awareness of higher levels. This provides the basis for incremental design. Higher-level competencies are added on top of an already working control system without any modification of those lower levels.

The older version of subsumption specified the behavioral layers as collections of AFSMs, whereas the newer version uses behavioral abstractions (in the form of rules) to encapsulate a robot's response to incoming sensor data. These abstractions are then compiled into the older AFSM form, but this step is transparent to the developer.

Coordination in subsumption has two primary mechanisms:

- Inhibition: used to prevent a signal being transmitted along an AFSM wire from reaching the actuators.
- Suppression: prevents the current signal from being transmitted and replaces that signal with the suppressing message.

Through these mechanisms, priority-based arbitration is enforced.

Subsumption permits communication between layers but restricts it heavily. The allowable mechanisms have the following characteristics:

- low baud rate, no handshaking
- message passing via machine registers
- output of lower layer accessible for reading by higher level
- inhibition prevents transmission
- suppression replaces message with suppressing message
- reset signal restores behavior to original state

The world itself serves as the primary medium of communication. Actions taken by one behavior result in changes within the world and the robot's relationship to it. New perceptions of those changes communicate those results to the other behaviors.

4.3.3   Design in Subsumption-Based Reactive Systems

The key aspects for design of subsumption-style robots are situatedness and embodiment (Brooks 1991b). Situatedness refers to the robot's ability to sense its current surroundings and avoid the use of abstract representations, and embodiment insists that the robots be physical creatures and thus experience the world directly rather than through simulation. Mataric 1992a presents heuristics for the design and development of this type of robot for a specific task. The basic procedure outlined is as follows:

1. Qualitatively specify the behavior needed for the task, that is, describe the overall way the robot responds to the world.
2. Decompose and specify the robot's independent behaviors as a set of observable disjoint actions by decomposing the qualitative behavior specified in step 1.
3. Determine the behavioral granularity (i.e., bound the decomposition process) and ground the resulting low-level behaviors onto sensors and actuators.

An additional guideline regarding response encoding recommends the use of small motions rather than large ballistic ones by resorting to frequent sensing. Finally, coordination is imposed by initially establishing tentative priorities for the behaviors and then modifying and verifying them experimentally.

Let us now review the example of experimentally driven subsumption-style design (Brooks 1989a) previously mentioned in section 3.1.3. The target robot is a six-legged walking machine named Genghis (figure 3.6). Its high-level behavioral performance is to be capable of walking over rough terrain and to have the ability to follow a human. This constitutes the qualitative description of task-level performance mentioned in step 1 above.

The next step, involving behavioral decomposition, must now be performed. Each of the following behavioral layers was implemented, tested, and debugged in turn:

1. Standup: Clearly, before the robot can walk, it needs to lift its body off of the ground. Further decomposition leads to the development of two AFSMs, one to control the leg's swing position and the other its lift. When all six legs operate under the standup behavior, the robot assumes a stance from which it can begin walking.
2. Simple walk: This requires that the leg be lifted off the ground and swung forward (advance). A variety of sensor data is used to coordinate the motion between legs, including encoders returning the position of each leg's joints. When appropriately coordinated, a simple walk over smooth terrain (tripod gait) is achieved.
3. Force balancing: Now the issues concerning rough terrain are confronted. Force sensors are added to the legs, providing active compliance to changes in the ground's contour.

4. Leg lifting: This helps with stepping over obstacles. When required, the leg can lift itself much higher than normal to step over obstacles.

5. Whiskers: These sensors are added to anticipate the presence of an obstacle rather than waiting for a collision. This capability emerges as important through experiments with the previous behaviors.

6. Pitch stabilization: Further experiments show that the robot tends to bump into the ground either fore or aft (pitching). An inclinometer is added to measure the robot's pitch and use it to compensate and prevent bumping. Now the robot's walking capabilities are complete.

7. Prowling: The walking robot is now concerned with moving toward a detected human. The infrared sensors are tied in. When no person is present, walking is suppressed. As soon as someone steps in front of the robot, the suppression stops and walking begins.

8. Steered prowling: The final behavior allows the robot to turn toward the person in front of it and follow him. The difference in readings between two IR sensors is used to provide the stimulus, and the swing end points for the legs on each side of the robot are determined by the difference in strength.

The completed robot, satisfying the task criteria established for it, consists of fifty-seven AFSMs built in an incremental manner. Each layer has been tested experimentally before moving onto the next, and the results of those tests have established the need for additional layers (e.g., whiskers and pitch stabilization).

4.3.4 Foraging Example

The foraging example presented earlier also illustrates subsumption-based design. In particular, the robots Mataric (1993a) constructed for several tasks including foraging provide the basis for this discussion. The robots are programmed in the Behavior Language. The target hardware is an IS Robotics system (figure 4.6).

Each behavior in the system is encoded as a set of rules (standard for the Behavior Language). The overall system has actually been developed as a multiagent robotic system (chapter 9), but for now we will restrict this discussion to a single robot foraging. The following behaviors are involved:

- Wandering: move in a random direction for some time.
- Avoiding:
  - turn to the right if the obstacle is on the left, then go.
  - turn to the left if the obstacle is on the right, then go.

138   Chapter 4

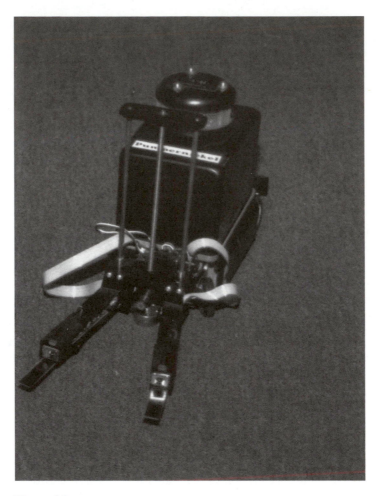

Figure 4.6
Subsumption-based foraging robot: R1. (Photograph courtesy of IS Robotics, Somerville, MA.)

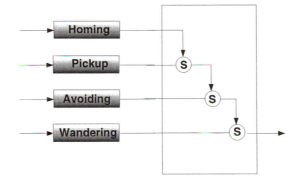

Figure 4.7
SR diagram for subsumption-based foraging robot.

• after three attempts, back up and turn.
• if an obstacle is present on both sides, randomly turn and back up.
■ Pickup: Turn toward the sensed attractor and go forward. If at the attractor, close gripper.
■ Homing: Turn toward the home base and go forward, otherwise if at home, stop.

Figure 4.7 illustrates the SR diagram for this set of behaviors. Priority-based arbitration is the coordination mechanism, and the robot is executing only one behavioral rule at any time. Note in particular that when the robot senses the attractor, wandering is suppressed and when the attractor is grabbed, homing then suppresses pickup (allowing the robot to ignore the potential distraction of other attractors it might encounter along the way).

4.3.5   Evaluation

When the criteria presented in section 4.1.3, are applied to evaluate the subsumption architecture, they identify the following strengths:

■ Hardware retargetability: Subsumption can compile down directly onto programmable-array logic circuitry (Brooks 1987b).
■ Support for parallelism: Each behavioral layer can run independently and asynchronously.
■ Niche targetability: Custom behaviors can be created for specific task-environment pairs.

The following characteristics emerge as neither strength nor weaknesses:

- Robustness: This can be successfully engineered into these systems but is often hard-wired (Ferrell 1994) and hence hard to implement.
- Timeliness for development: Some support tools exist for these systems, but a significant learning curve is still associated with custom behavioral design. Experimental design, involving trial-and-error development, can slow development. Also, consistent with Brooks' philosophy, simulators are not used to pretest behavioral efficiency.

Under the criteria, the following show up as weaknesses:

- Run time flexibility: The priority-based coordination mechanism, the ad hoc flavor of behavior generation, and the architecture's hard-wired aspects limit the ways the system can be adapted during execution.
- Support for modularity: Although behavioral reuse is possible through the Behavior Language, it is not widely evidenced in constructed robots. Subsumption has also been criticized on the basis that since upper layers interfere with lower ones, they cannot be designed completely independently (Hartley and Pipitone 1991). Also behaviors cannot always be prioritized (nor should they be), leading to artificial arbitration schemes (Hartley and Pipitone 1991). Commitment to subsumption as the sole coordination mechanism is restrictive.

4.3.6   Subsumption Robots

Many different robots (figure 4.8) have been constructed using the subsumption architecture. Brooks 1990b reviews many of them. They include

- Allen: the first subsumption-based robot, which used sonar for navigation based on the ideas in Brooks 1986.
- Tom and Jerry: two small toy cars equipped with infrared proximity sensors (Brooks 1990b).
- Genghis and Attila: six-legged hexapods capable of autonomous walking (Brooks 1989a).
- Squirt: a two-ounce robot that responds to light (Flynn et al. 1989).
- Toto: the first map-constructing, subsumption-based robot and the first to use the Behavior Language (Mataric 1992b).
- Seymour: a visual motion-tracking robot (Brooks and Flynn 1989).
- Tito: a robot with stereo navigational capabilities (Sarachik 1989).
- Polly: a robotic tour guide for the MIT AI lab (Horswill 1993b).
- Cog: a robot modeled as a humanoid from the waist up, and used to test theories of robot-human interaction and computer vision (Brooks and Stein 1994).

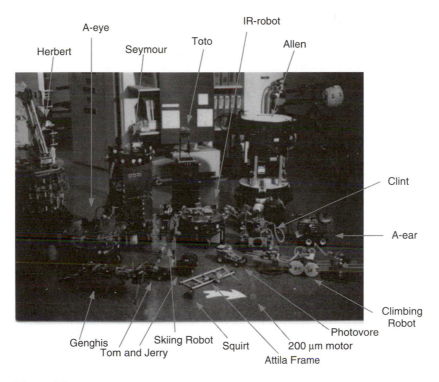

Figure 4.8
Robots of the MIT Mobile Robot Laboratory. (Photograph courtesy of Rodney Brooks.)

4.4   MOTOR SCHEMAS

Another approach, more strongly motivated by the biological sciences, appeared on the heels of the subsumption architecture. This behavior-based method used schema theory, which we reviewed in chapter 2. We recall from that review that schema theory provides the following capabilities for specifying and designing behavior-based systems (adapted from Arbib 1992):

■ Schema theory explains motor behavior in terms of the concurrent control of many different activities.
■ A schema stores both how to react and the way that reaction can be realized.
■ Schema theory is a distributed model of computation.
■ Schema theory provides a language for connecting action and perception.
■ Activation levels are associated with schemas that determine their readiness or applicability for acting.

■ Schema theory provides a theory of learning through both schema acquisition and schema tuning.

■ Schema theory is useful for explaining the brain's functioning as well as distributed AI applications (such as behavior-based robotics).

Schema theory is an attempt to account for the commonalities in both neurobiological and artificial behavior, and Arkin chose it as a suitable vehicle to implement robotic behavior.

Arkin (1989a, 1990a, 1993) addressed the implications of schema theory for autonomous robotics:

1. Schemas provide large grain modularity, in contrast to neural network models, for expressing the relationships between motor control and perception.
2. Schemas act concurrently as individual distributed agents in a cooperative yet competing manner and thus are readily mappable onto distributed processing architectures.
3. Schemas provide a set of behavioral primitives by which more complex behaviors (assemblages) can be constructed.
4. Cognitive and neuroscientific support exists for the underpinnings of this approach. These can be modified, if appropriate, as additional neuroscientific or cognitive models become available.

The overall method of schema-based robotics is to provide behavioral primitives that can act in a distributed, parallel manner to yield intelligent robotic action in response to environmental stimuli. Lyons has also used schema theory in his research (sections 3.2.4.1 and 6.6.3), but here we focus on the methodology Arkin adopted.

The motor schema method differs from other behavioral approaches in several significant ways:

■ Behavioral responses are all represented in a single uniform format: vectors generated using a potential fields approach (a continuous response encoding).

■ Coordination is achieved through cooperative means by vector addition.

■ No predefined hierarchy exists for coordination; instead, the behaviors are configured at run-time based on the robot's intentions, capabilities, and environmental constraints. Schemas can be instantiated or deinstantiated at any time based on perceptual events, hence the structure is more of a dynamically changing network than a layered architecture.

■ Pure arbitration is not used; instead, each behavior can contribute in varying degrees to the robot's overall response. The relative strengths of the behaviors (**G**) determine the robot's overall response.

Table 4.2
Motor schemas

Name	Motor Schemas
Background	Reactive component of AuRA Architecture
Precursors	Arbib 1981; Khatib 1985
Principal design method	Ethologically guided
Developer	Ronald Arkin (Georgia Tech)
Response encoding	Continuous using potential field analog
Coordination method	Cooperative via vector summation and normalization
Programming method	Parameterized behavioral libraries
Robots fielded	HARV, George, Ren and Stimpy, Buzz, blizzards, mobile manipulator, others
References	Arkin 1987a; Arkin 1989b; Arkin 1992a

■ Perceptual uncertainty can be reflected in the behavior's response by allowing it to serve as an input within the behavioral computation.

Table 4.2 summarizes the important aspects of this architecture. The remainder of this section studies the details of its implementation.

4.4.1 Schema-Based Behaviors

Motor schema behaviors are relatively large grain abstractions reusable over a wide range of circumstances. Many of the behaviors have internal parameters that provide additional flexibility in their deployment. The behaviors generally are analogous to animal behaviors (section 2.4), at least those useful for navigational tasks.

A perceptual schema is embedded within each motor schema. These perceptual schemas provide the environmental information specific for that particular behavior. Perception is conducted on a need-to-know basis: individual perceptual algorithms provide the information necessary for a particular behavior to react. Chapter 7 details this sensing paradigm, referred to as *action-oriented perception*. Suffice it to say for now that attached to each motor schema is a perceptual process capable of providing suitable stimuli, if present, as rapidly as possible. Perceptual schemas are recursively defined, that is, perceptual sub-schemas can extract pieces of information that are subsequently processed by another perceptual schema into a more behaviorally meaningful unit. An example might involve recognition of a person with more than one sensor: Infrared

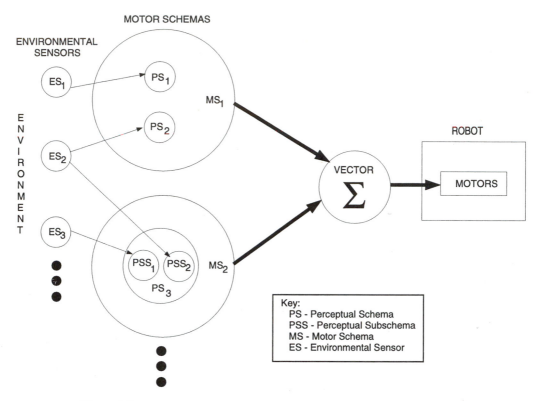

Figure 4.9
Perception-action schema relationships.

sensors can provide a heat signature, whereas computer vision may provide a human shape. The information generated from each of these lower-level perceptual processes would be merged into a higher-level interpretation before passing it on to the motor behavior. This enables the use of multiple sensors within the context of a single sensorimotor behavior. Figure 4.9 illustrates this relationship.

   Each motor schema has as output an action vector (consisting of both orientation and magnitude components) that defines the way the robot should move in response to the perceived stimuli. This approach has been used for ground-based navigation where each vector is two dimensional (Arkin 1989b), for generating three-dimensional vectors for use in flying or underwater navigation (Arkin 1992a), and for use in mobile manipulators with many additional degrees of freedom (Cameron et al. 1993).

Many different motor schemas have been defined, including

- Move-ahead: move in a particular compass direction.
- Move-to-goal: move towards a detected goal object. Two versions exist of this schema: ballistic and controlled.
- Avoid-static-obstacle: move away from passive or nonthreatening navigational barriers.
- Dodge: sidestep an approaching ballistic projectile.
- Escape: move away from the projected intercept point between the robot and an approaching predator.
- Stay-on-path: move toward the center of a path, road, or hallway. For three-dimensional navigation, this becomes the stay-in-channel schema.
- Noise: move in a random direction for a certain amount of time.
- Follow-the-leader: move to a particular location displaced somewhat from a possibly moving object. (The robot acts as if it is leashed invisibly to the moving object.)
- Probe: move toward open areas.
- Dock: approach an object from a particular direction.
- Avoid-past: move away from areas recently visited.
- Move-up, move-down, maintain-altitude: move upward or downward or follow an isocontour in rough terrain.
- Teleautonomy: allows human operator to provide internal bias to the control system at the same level as another schema.

These are the basic building blocks for autonomous navigation within this architecture. Figure 4.10 depicts several of the schemas. Remember that although the entire field is illustrated, only a single vector needs to be computed at the robot's current location. This ensures extremely fast computation.

The actual encodings for several schemas appear below, where $V_{magnitude}$ denotes the magnitude of the resultant response vector and $V_{direction}$ represents its orientation:

- move-to-goal (ballistic):

$V_{magnitude}$ = fixed gain value.

$V_{direction}$ = towards perceived goal.

- avoid-static-obstacle:

$$V_{magnitude} = \begin{cases} 0 & \text{for } d > S \\ \frac{S-d}{S-R} * G & \text{for } R < d \leq S \ , \\ \infty & \text{for } d \leq R \end{cases}$$

(A)

Figure 4.10
Representative schemas: (A) avoid-static-obstacle, (B) move-ahead (toward east), (C) move-to-goal, guarded (compare to ballistic version in figure 3.16 (B)), (D) noise, (E) stay-on-path, and (F) dodge.

where

$S =$ sphere of influence (radial extent of force from the center of the obstacle),

$R =$ radius of obstacle,

$G =$ gain, and

$d =$ distance of robot to center of obstacle.

$V_{direction} =$ radially along a line from robot to center of obstacle, directed away from the obstacle.

(B)

Figure 4.10 *(continued)*

■ stay-on-path

$$V_{magnitude} = \begin{cases} P & \text{for } d > (W/2) \\ \frac{d}{W/2} * G & \text{for } d \leq (W/2) \end{cases},$$

where

W = width of path,

P = off-path gain,

G = on-path gain, and

d = distance of robot to center of path.

$V_{direction}$ = along a line from robot to center of path, heading toward centerline.

(C)

Figure 4.10 *(continued)*

- move-ahead

$V_{magnitude}$ = fixed gain value.

$V_{direction}$ = specified compass direction.

- noise

$V_{magnitude}$ = fixed gain value.

$V_{direction}$ = random direction changed every p time steps (p denotes persistence).

It can be seen that the actual response computations are very simple and fast.

(D)

Figure 4.10 *(continued)*

4.4.2   Schema-Based Coordination

The next issue is how coordination is accomplished with motor schemas. The answer is straightforward: vector summation. All active behaviors contribute to some degree to the robot's global motion. **G**, the gain vector, determines the relative composition for each behavior. The notion of schema gains is loosely aligned with the concept of activation levels mentioned previously. In a system where no learning or adaptation is permitted, the gain levels remain constant throughout the run. We will see in chapter 8 that this can be modified during execution to permit learning. Action-selection techniques, soon to be described in more detail, also reflect the notion of activation levels.

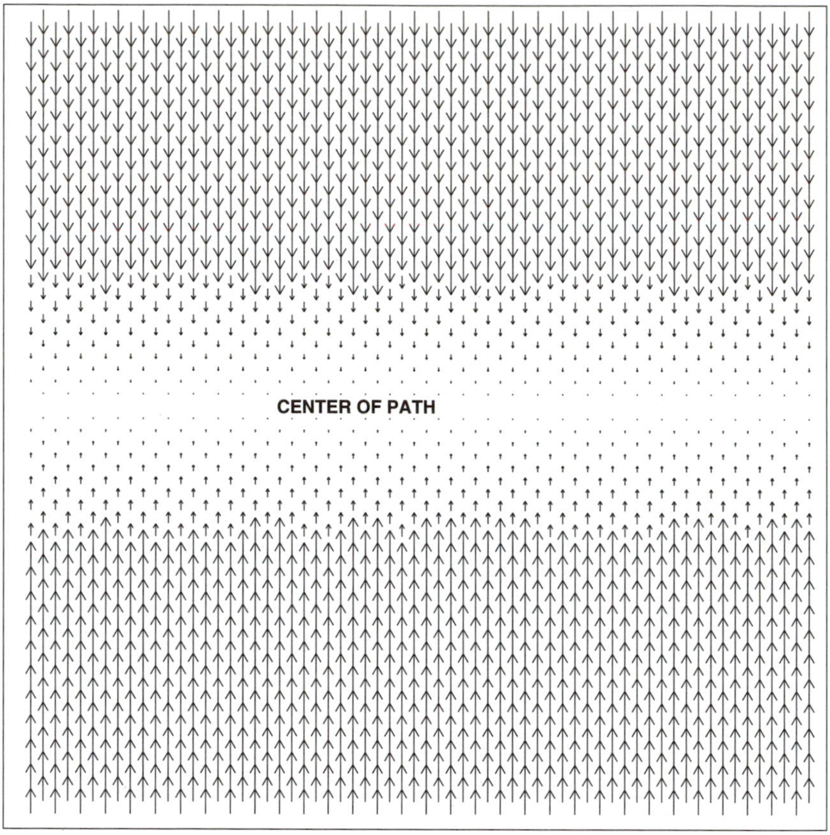

(E)

Figure 4.10 *(continued)*

Returning to coordination, each schema output vector is multiplied by its associated gain value and added to all other output vectors. The result is a single global vector. That vector must be normalized in some manner (often merely by clipping the magnitude) to ensure that it is executable on the robot. The resulting normalized global vector is sent to the robot for execution. This sense-react process is repeated as rapidly as possible. The schemas can operate asynchronously, each delivering its data as quickly as it can. Perceptual performance generally limits overall processing speed since the simple and distributed motor response computation is extremely rapid. Some care must be taken to ensure that the reaction produced is based on information still relevant (i.e., the perceptual data is not too old). Normally, the perceptual algorithms'

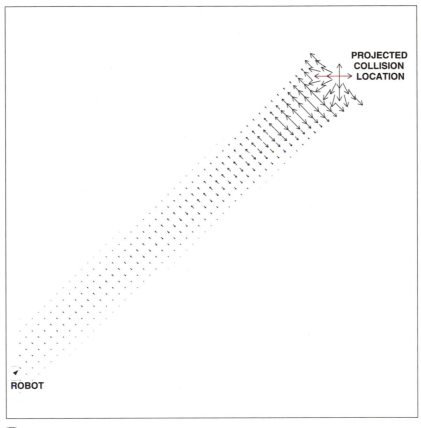

(F)

Figure 4.10 *(continued)*

action-oriented design ensures relatively prompt processing independent of the data source.

Figure 4.11 shows several different types of robot paths resulting from these methods. It is interesting to observe some of the biological parallels for these type of systems (figure 4.12).

Section 3.3.2 described certain problems endemic to the use of potential fields, in particular local minima and cyclic behavior. Schema-based systems are not immune to these problems, nor have they been ignored. One of the simplest methods to address these problems is through noise, injecting randomness into the behavioral system through the noise schema. Noise is a common technique used to deal with local minima in many gradient descent methods, for

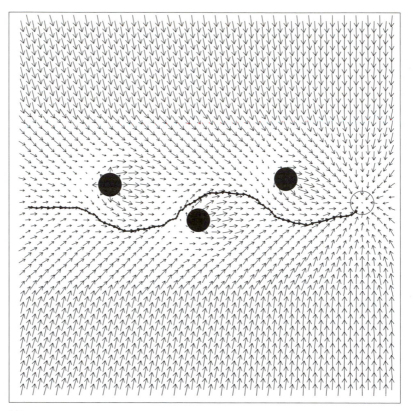

(A)

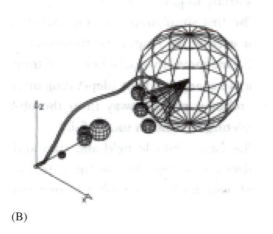

(B)

Figure 4.11

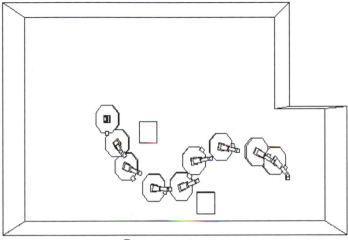

Top room view

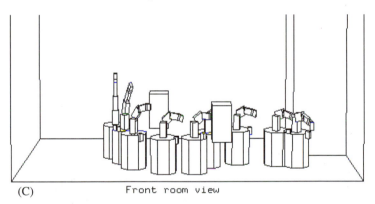

(C)   Front room view

Figure 4.11 *(continued)*
Representative simulated robot paths: (A) stay-on-path, move-to-goal, 3 avoid-static-obstacle, and noise schemas; (B) three-dimensional docking and avoid-static-obstacles; and (C) mobile manipulator moving to target object through obstacles.

(A)

(B)

Figure 4.12

example, simulated annealing (Hinton and Sejnowski 1986) and mutation in genetic algorithms (Goldberg 1989), to name a few. In schema-based control, randomness works in several ways: in some cases it prevents the entry into local minima, acting as a sort of "reactive grease" (figure 4.13). In general, it is always useful to inject a small amount of noise into a schema-based system to help ensure progress.

Balch and Arkin (1993) developed another schema, avoid-past, to ensure progress is made even if the robot tends to stall. Avoid-past uses a short-term representation as it retains a timewindow into the past indicating where the robot has been recently. It is still reactive, however, since no path planning for the robot is ever conducted, and the output of this behavior is a vector of the same form as all the other behaviors and is combined in the same way. Repulsive forces are generated from recently visited areas that prevent the robot from stalling when not at its goal. This approach has proven very effective in even degenerate cases (figure 4.14).

Additionally chapter 8 will discuss several adaptive and learning techniques that have been applied to improve navigational performance.

4.4.3   Design in Motor Schema–Based Systems

The design process for building a schema-based robotic system is typically as follows:

1. Characterize the problem domain in terms of the motor behaviors necessary to accomplish the task.
2. Decompose the motor behaviors to their most primitive level, using biological studies whenever feasible for guidelines.
3. Develop formulas to express the robot's reaction to perceived environmental events.
4. Conduct simple simulation studies assessing the desired behaviors' approximate performance in the proposed environment.
5. Determine the perceptual requirements needed to satisfy the inputs for each motor schema.

Figure 4.12 *(continued)*
Biological parallels: (A) A school of anchovies being attacked by diving birds. (Photograph courtesy of Gary Bell). (B) A herd of sheep in flight from their handlers. (Photograph courtesy of Temple Grandin, Colorado State University.)

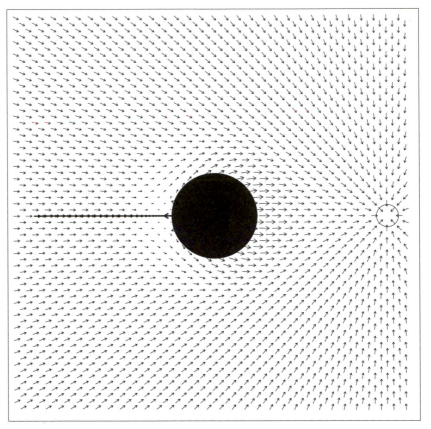

(A)

Figure 4.13
Effect of noise on schema-based navigation (A) Exact counterbalancing of forces causes robot to stall; (B) With noise added, the problem is prevented.

6. Design specific perceptual algorithms that extract the required data for each behavior, utilizing action-oriented perception, expectations, and focus-of-attention techniques to ensure computational efficiency (chapter 7).

7. Integrate the resulting control system onto the target robot.

8. Test and evaluate the system's performance.

9. Iterate and expand behavioral repertoire as necessary.

Behavioral software reuse greatly simplifies this process, because schemas developed using biological guidelines often have extensive utility in many different circumstances.

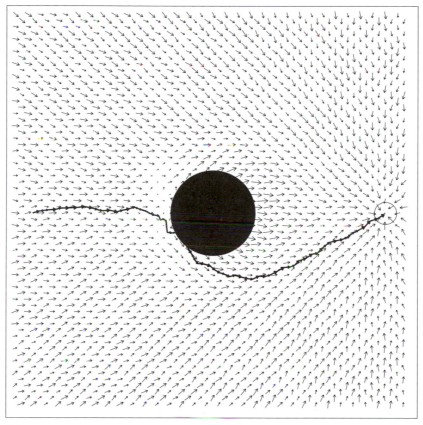

(B)

Figure 4.13 *(continued)*

4.4.4   Foraging Example

Motor schemas have been used in several implementations of foraging systems. The first example, mirroring the FSA shown in figure 4.2, consists of three assemblages, each consisting of up to four behaviors (Arkin 1992b). The primitive behaviors are

■ Avoid-static-obstacle: instantiated differently for either environmental obstacles or other robots.
■ Move-to-goal: changes its attention from the attractor to the home base depending upon the state in which the robot finds itself.

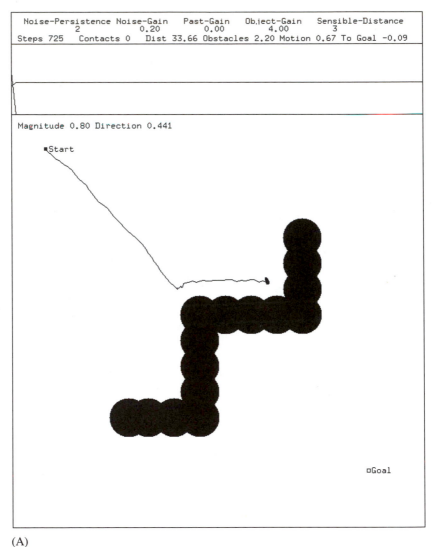

Noise-Persistence	Noise-Gain	Past-Gain	Object-Gain	Sensible-Distance
2	0.20	0.00	4.00	3

Steps 725   Contacts 0   Dist 33.66 Obstacles 2.20 Motion 0.67 To Goal −0.09

Magnitude 0.80 Direction 0.441

▪Start

▫Goal

(A)

Figure 4.14
Avoid-past schema usage for overcoming local minima. Repulsive forces are generated at recently visited areas, preventing the robot from stalling: (A) without and (B) with *avoid-past* behavior; (C) deep box with *avoid-past*; (D) maze with *avoid-past*.

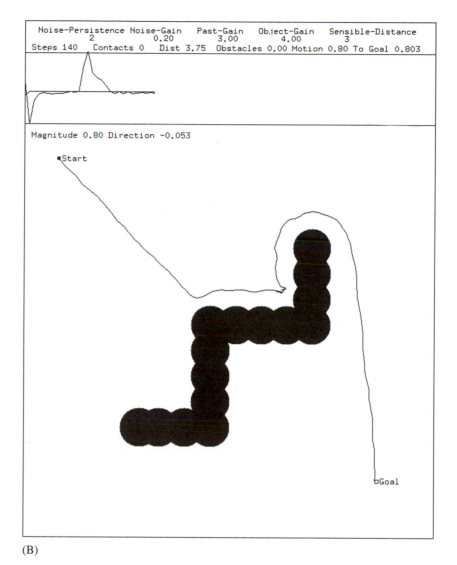

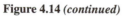
(B)

Figure 4.14 *(continued)*

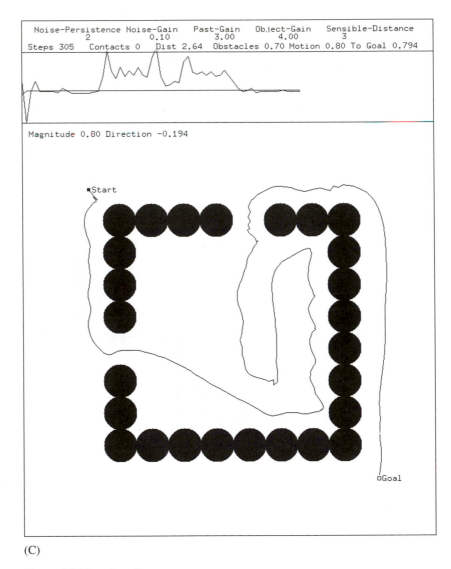

(C)

Figure 4.14 *(continued)*

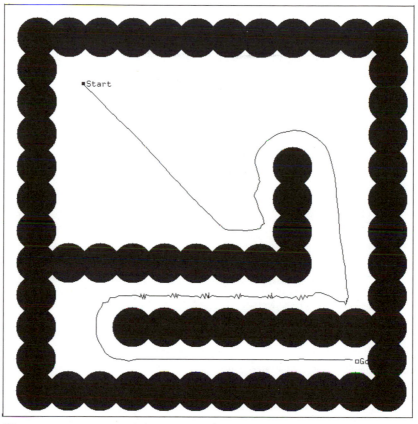

(D)

Figure 4.14 *(continued)*

■ Noise: Initially set at a high gain to ensure broad exploration of the area, then reduced greatly upon encountering an attractor.

Figure 4.15 depicts the behavioral configuration using an SR diagram.

Subsequently, Balch et al. (1995) created more-complex foraging robots (figure 4.16) using a similar methodology for use in a robot competition. Chapter 9 discusses this multirobot implementation in more detail.

4.4.5   Evaluation

When evaluated using the criteria presented in section 4.1, motor schema–based robotic systems are found to have the following strengths:

FORAGE

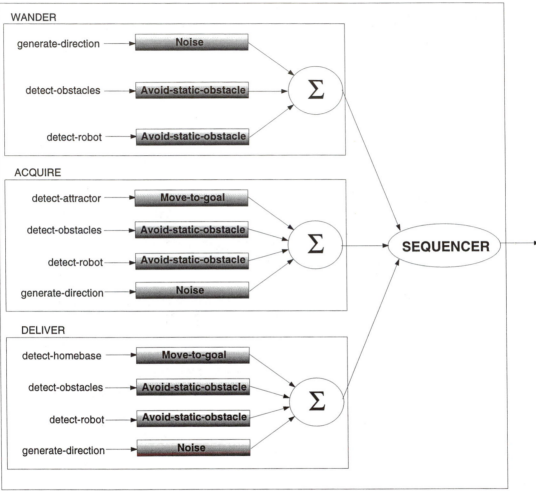

Figure 4.15
SR diagram for schema-based foraging robot.

Figure 4.16
Callisto, a foraging schema-based robot.

- Support for parallelism: Schema theory is a distributed theory of computation involving multiple parallel processes. Motor schemas are naturally parallelizable.
- Run time flexibility: As schemas are software agents, instantiated at run time as processes and are not hard-wired into the architecture, it is simple to reconfigure the behavioral control system at any time.
- Timeliness for development and support for modularity: Schemas are essentially software objects and are by definition modular. They can be stored in behavioral libraries and are easily reused (Mackenzie, Cameron, and Arkin 1995).

The following is found to be neither a strength nor a weakness:

- Robustness: As with any reactive system, schemas can well cope with change in the environment. One deficiency lies in the use of potential field analogs for behavioral combination, which has several well-known problems. Specific methods, however, such as the introduction of noise and the *avoid-past* behavior, have been developed to circumvent this difficulty.

The following weaknesses are identified under the evaluation criteria:

Figure 4.17
Several motor schema-based robots. First row (left to right): Io, Callisto, and Ganymede. Second row: Shannon and Sally. Third row: George, Ren, and Stimpy. Rear: GT Hummer.

- Niche targetability: Although it is feasible to design niche robots, the generic modular nature of the primitive schemas somewhat discourages the design of very narrowly focused components.
- Hardware retargetability: Schema-based systems are essentially software architectures mappable onto hardware multiprocessor systems. They do not provide the hardware compilers that either subsumption or Gapps does. Hardware mappings are feasible, however (Collins, Arkin, and Henshaw 1993), just not as convenient as with some other systems.

4.4.6   Schema-Based Robots

The incremental development of the library of motor schemas can be traced through a series of fielded mobile robots (figure 4.17). Schemas from earlier robots were easily reused for newer machines as they became available.

- HARV: An early Denning mobile robot, named after the cocktail Harvey Wallbanger, which reflected its early behavior. This early robot was capable of a wide range of complex behaviors including:

• Exploration: a combination of avoid-static-obstacle and noise.

• Hall following: move-ahead in the direction of the hall coupled with avoid-static-obstacle; enabled safe navigation down a corridor.

• Wall following or "drunken sailor" behavior: useful for going through doorways. A move-ahead schema pointing at an angle into the wall coupled with avoid-static-obstacle produced a behavior where the robot followed the wall and then passed through the first opening it found. This enabled the robot to complete nonspecific tasks such as "go down the hall and enter the first door on your right."

• Impatient waiting: occurred while the robot waited for a door to open. It consisted of a small amount of noise and a move-to-goal behavior targeted immediately beyond a closed door, coupled with the avoid-static-obstacle schema. The robot would oscillate in its local minima until the door opened. When the obstacle stimulus was no longer present because of the new opening, the robot moved through the doorway. This behavior is potentially useful for entering elevators, among other things. The behavior is also referred to as the fly-at-a-window behavior since a fly is attracted towards the light yet repelled by the glass at the window, and the behavior has a noisy component (panic?) that is actually helpful to the fly in finding openings that it may not initially sense.

• Indoor and outdoor navigation: demonstrated in several ways, including various combinations of the stay-on-path, avoid-static-obstacle, noise, move-ahead, and move-to-goal schemas.

■ George: This Denning DRV-3, named after a fictitious Georgia Tech student, was the first robot to exhibit behavior-based docking (Arkin and Murphy 1990), teleautonomy (Arkin 1991), and avoid-past behaviors (Balch and Arkin 1993).

■ Ren and Stimpy: A pair of Denning MRV-2 robots used for dodge, escape, forage, and multiagent behavioral research.

■ Buzz: Used in the AAAI competition described in section 3.4.4 (Arkin et al. 1993).

■ Io, Callisto, Ganymede: Three student-constructed small mobile robots for multiagent research and winners in a robot competition (Balch et al. 1995).

■ Mobile manipulator: One of the MRV-2s fitted with a CRS+ robot arm (Cameron et al. 1993).

4.5   OTHER ARCHITECTURES

We now survey a representative sampling of the wide range of other behavior-based architectures that exist, highlighting each one's approach and contribution. All share a philosophy of commitment to sensing and action, elimination

Table 4.3
Circuit architecture

Name	Circuit Architecture
Background	Early reactive architecture
Precursors	Brooks 1986; Nilsson 1984; Barbera et al. 1984; Johnson 1983
Principal design method	Situated activity
Developers	L. Kaelbling and S. Rosenschein (SRI)
Response encoding	Discrete (rule based)
Coordination method	Hierarchical mediation (arbitration with abstraction)
Programming method	Rex and Gapps
Robots fielded	Flakey
References	Kaelbling 1986; Kaelbling and Rosenschein 1991

or reduction of symbolic representational knowledge, and the use of behavioral units as their primary building blocks. Each one's uniqueness arises from its choice of coordination mechanisms, the response encoding methods used, the behavioral granularity, and the design methodology employed.

4.5.1   Circuit Architecture

The circuit architecture is a hybridization of the principles of reactivity as typified by the subsumption architecture, the abstractions used in RCS (Barbera et al. 1984) and Shakey (Nilsson 1984), and the use of logical formalisms (Johnson 1983). Table 4.3 summarizes this approach. We discussed aspects of this architecture in section 3.2.4.2, in particular the role of logical formalisms and situated automata. One strength this approach provides involves the use of abstraction through the bundling of reactive behaviors into assemblages and by allowing arbitration to occur within each level of abstraction, that is, what the designers refer to as hierarchical mediation. Another advantage is the use of formal logic as a means for expressing the behaviors, permitting compilation into hardware and assisting with the verification of the performance of the resulting robotic system (Rosenschein and Kaelbling 1987).

The motivations for this architecture, according to its designers, are typical for behavior-based systems in general: *modularity*, permitting incremental development; *awareness*, tightly coupling sensing to action; and *robustness*, being able to perform despite unanticipated circumstances or sensor failure.

4.5.2   Action-Selection

Action-selection is an architectural approach developed by Pattie Maes in the late 1980s. It uses a dynamic mechanism for behavior selection. Instead of employing a predefined priority-based strategy typified by the subsumption approach, individual behaviors (competence modules) have associated activation levels that ultimately provide the basis for run-time arbitration. A competence module resembles a traditional AI robotic operator with preconditions, add lists and delete lists. Additionally, an activation level is associated with the module that ultimately governs its applicability at any particular time by being above some threshold. The activation level for any particular module is affected by the current situation, higher level goals, spreading activation due to previous or potentially succeeding events in time, or inhibition from conflicting modules. Activation levels also decay over time. The module with the highest activation level is chosen for execution from the set of all modules whose preconditions are satisfied. The selection process is repeated as rapidly as possible as the world's circumstances change about the agent.

Because there is no predefined layering of behaviors as in subsumption, it is harder in action-selection to predict the agent's global performance in a dynamic environment, and thus action-selection has a greater emergent quality. Several global parameters are used to tune the control system, all of which are related to the activation levels (e.g., activation threshold, amount of activation energy injected). An advantage of this strategy is flexibility and openness, as the system's responses are not hard-wired. As an agent's intentions can influence the activation parameters, higher level goals can also induce performance changes (see Norman-Shallice model from chapter 6). The action-selection approach also shares much in philosophy with schema theory (Arbib 1992), especially regarding the use of activation levels for controlling behavioral performance. Its primary perceived limitation is the lack of real implementations on actual robots and thus no evidence exists of how easily the current competence module formats would perform in real world robotic tasks. Table 4.4 summarizes this architecture's characteristics.

4.5.3   Colony Architecture

The colony architecture (Connell 1989b) is a direct descendent of the subsumption architecture that uses simpler coordination strategies (i.e., suppression only) and permits a more flexible specification of behavioral relations. The

Table 4.4
Action-selection architecture

Name	Action-selection
Background	Dynamic competition system
Precursors	Minsky 1986; Hillis 1988
Principal design method	Experimental
Developer	Pattie Maes (MIT)
Response encoding	Discrete
Coordination method	Arbitration via action-selection
Programming method	Competence modules
Robots fielded	Simulations only
References	Maes 1990; Maes 1989

Table 4.5
Colony architecture

Name	Colony architecture
Background	Descendent of subsumption architecture
Precursors	Minsky 1986; Brooks 1986
Principal design method	Ethologically guided/experimental
Developer	John Connell (IBM)
Response encoding	Discrete rule based
Coordination method	Priority-based arbitration with suppression only
Programming method	Similar to subsumption
Robots fielded	Herbert (mobile manipulator), wheelchair
References	Connell 1989; Connell 1989b

colony architecture permits a treelike ordering for behavioral priority as opposed to the total ordering of layered behaviors found in subsumption. A closer relationship to ethology was also developed, using models derived from animals such as the coastal snail to justify the use of pure suppression networks. The pinnacle of this architecture was Herbert, a robot designed to wander about the corridors of the MIT laboratory and retrieve soda cans for recycling using vision, ultrasound, and infrared proximity sensors. Table 4.5 summarizes the colony architecture's characteristics.

Table 4.6
Animate Agent Architecture

Name	Animate agent architecture
Background	RAP-based situated activity system
Precursors	Miller, Galanter, and Pribram 1960; Georgeff et al. 1986; Agre and Chapman 1987; Ullman 1985
Principal design method	Situated activity
Developer	R. James Firby (University of Chicago)
Response encoding	NAT based (continuous)
Coordination method	Sequencing
Programming method	RAP language
Robots fielded	Chip (trash-cleaning robot)
References	Firby 1989, 1995; Firby and Slack 1995

4.5.4   Animate Agent Architecture

The animate agent architecture adds two components to the RAPs discussed in section 3.1.3: a skills system and special-purpose problem solving modules (Firby 1995). The skills provide continuous environmental response, typically using a NAT encoding (Slack 1990) (section 3.3.2), whereas RAPs provide an assemblage mechanism for bundling skills useful in particular situations. In a sense, RAPs are related to FSA states and can be used to sequence through a collection of skills over time (Firby and Slack 1995). Situations, however, are used to define the states (or context) and provide the overall design basis. Table 4.6 summarizes this architecture's key points.

4.5.5   DAMN

The Distributed Architecture for Mobile Navigation (DAMN) boasts a rather provocative name. Developed by Rosenblatt (1995), initially at the Hughes AI Center and subsequently at Carnegie-Mellon University, this behavior-based system has a unique coordination mechanism. The behaviors in DAMN, which was initially touted as a fine-grained alternative to the subsumption architecture (Rosenblatt and Payton 1989), are themselves asynchronous processes each generating outputs as a collection of votes cast over a range of responses. The votes for each behavior can be cast in a variety of ways, including differing statistical distributions over a range of responses. The behavioral arbitration

Table 4.7
DAMN Architecture

Name	DAMN (Distributed Architecture for Mobile Navigation)
Background	Fine-grained subsumption-style architecture
Precursors	Brooks 1986; Zadeh 1973
Principal design method	Experimental
Developer	Julio Rosenblatt (CMU)
Response encoding	Discrete vote sets
Coordination method	multiple winner-take-all arbiters
Programming method	Custom
Robots fielded	DARPA ALV and UGV vehicles
References	Rosenblatt and Payton 1989; Rosenblatt 1995

method, discussed in section 3.4.3, is a winner-take-all strategy in which the response with the largest number of votes is selected for enactment. Table 4.7 highlights its characteristics.

Also unique to the DAMN architecture are the multiple parallel arbiters for both speed and turning control. Arbitration for each of these activities occurs completely independently. Chapter 9 revisits the DAMN architecture in examining the Defense Advanced Research Project Agency's (DARPA's) Unmanned Ground Vehicle Demo II Program.

4.5.6   Skill Network Architecture

The skill network architecture is a behavior-based system developed for graphical animation rather than robotics. Indeed, the use of behavior-based techniques within animation is becoming widespread. Pioneering work by Craig Reynolds (1987) on his Boids system provided a compelling set of visual behaviors for flocks of birds and schools of fish. Recent work by Hodgins and Brogan (1994) has extended these techniques to model not only graphical creatures' responses to their fictional environments but also their dynamics. Zeltzer and Johnson (1991), however, developed the skill network architecture in a more general way, providing for a variety of computing agents: sensing agents that provide information regarding the environment, skill agents that encode behaviors, and goal agents that monitor whether certain conditions have been met. A modification of Maes' action-selection mechanism serves as the basis

Table 4.8
Skill network architecture

Name	Skill network architecture
Background	Behavior-based animation architecture
Precursors	Maes 1989; Badler and Webber 1991
Principal design method	Ethological/Experimental
Developer	David Zeltzer (MIT)
Response encoding	Discrete
Coordination method	Action-selection
Programming method	Agent libraries
Robots fielded	Graphical animations only
References	Zeltzer and Johnson 1991

for coordination. Of particular note in this architecture is the designer's concern for mapping the multiple concurrent processes over a network of Unix workstations to minimize computation time, an essential aspect of computer-generated animation. The general characteristics of the skill network architecture appear in table 4.8.

4.5.7   Other Efforts

Several other behavioral approaches warrant mentioning.

- BART: The Behavioral Architecture for Robot Tasks, was an early approach (Kahn 1991) that defined task behaviors arbitrarily and provided support for military robotic missions. Of note was its use of a focus-of-attention manager to provide situational context for the selection of relevant behaviors. A BART language was developed for specifying behavioral tasks.
- Autochthonous behaviors: Developed by Grupen and Henderson (1990), this behavioral approach uses logical impedance controllers as the basis for specifying behavioral response. Of particular interest is its focus on grasping and manipulation tasks as opposed to robot navigation. Grupen and Henderson's method also relies far more heavily on representational knowledge (3D models generated by sensor data) than typical reactive systems.
- Anderson and Donath: A behavioral approach strongly influenced by ethological studies and fielded on Scarecrow, a 400-pound robot (Anderson and Donath 1991). The system, similar in spirit to the schema-based approach, uses

potential fields methods for the response encoding and vector summation for the coordination mechanism.

■ SmartyCat: Defined in the SmartyCat Agent Language (Lim 1994), similar in flavor to the Behavior Language (Brooks 1990a), this behavior specification approach has been tested on a Cybermotion K2A robot.

■ Dynamic Reaction: A behavior-based system capable of using goal-based constraints in dynamic or rapidly changing worlds (Sanborn 1988). This system was tested in simulation in trafficworld, a driving simulator.

■ ARC (Artificial Reflex Control): In this model for robot control systems, actual biological reflexes serve as a basis for their design in robots. The model has particular relevance for rehabilitative robotics, in which a prosthetic device such as an artificial hand or limb must coordinate with an active human. This control model has been applied to hand, knee, and leg controllers for potential use within human-assistive technology (Bekey and Tomovic 1986, 1990).

■ Niche Robot Architecture: This architecture, developed by Miller (1995), draws on the notion of ecological niches as espoused by MacFarland (McFarland and Bosser 1993) and presented in chapter 2. It focuses more on the philosophical issues of creating robots for specific tasks rather than on rigid commitments to specific behavioral encodings or coordination strategies. Several real world robots fit into this paradigm, including Rocky III, a prototype Mars microrover; Fuddbot, a simplistic vacuum cleaning robot; and a robotic wheelchair tasked with assisting the handicapped.

4.6   ARCHITECTURAL DESIGN ISSUES

We can extract a number of common threads from this diversity of architectural approaches as well as some themes driving the development of these systems.

■ Analysis versus synthesis. This methodological difference relates to the underlying assumptions regarding just what intelligence is. In some instances, intelligence is perceived as something that can be reduced to an atomic unit that when appropriately organized and replicated can yield high-level intelligent action. In other approaches, abstract pieces of intelligent systems, often extracted from or motivated by biological counterparts, can be used to construct the required robotic performance.

■ Top-down (knowledge-driven) versus bottom-up (data-driven) design. This aspect relates more closely to experimentation and discovery as a design driver versus a formal analysis and characterization of the requisite knowledge a system needs to possess to manifest intelligent robotic performance. These differences perhaps parallel to a degree the "scruffy versus neat" dichotomy in AI.

■ Domain relevance versus domain independence. To some extent this characteristic captures the view that there either is or is not a single form of intelligence. Here the AI parallel is "weak versus strong" methods.

■ Understanding intelligence versus intelligent machines. The fundamental difference here lies in the designer's goals. Biological constraints can be applied in the development of a robotic architecture in an effort to understand the nature of animal intelligence. This approach may compromise the utility of the resulting machine intelligence. Often robot architects who follow this path have an underlying assumption that intelligence is fundamentally independent of the underlying substrate in which it is embedded. This is merely a working hypothesis, as there is yet no strong evidence to support it (nor to contradict it). Other architects are concerned with the more direct goal of building useful and productive machines with sufficient intelligence to function within the world in which they are situated. Whether these machines relate to biological systems is not their concern.

These competing goals and methods result in a wide range of architectural approaches, as we have seen throughout this chapter. Many roboticists feel that although behavior-based methods provide excellent responsiveness in dynamic environments, much is lost in their eliminating the use of representational knowledge. These researchers have considered how representational knowledge in various forms can be integrated into these behavioral architectures. In chapter 5, we will encounter various methods that can introduce representational knowledge into reactive robotic architectures while maintaining most, if not all, of their desirable properties. In chapter 6 we will study hybrid architectures that attempt to supplement behavior-based architectures with not only representational knowledge but additional deliberative planning capabilities. Chapter 8 discusses how learning and adaptation can be introduced into these systems, another very important research area.

4.7   CHAPTER SUMMARY

■ A wide range of architectural solutions exist under the behavior-based paradigm.
• These architectures, in general, share an aversion to the use of representational knowledge, emphasis on a tight coupling between sensing and action, and decomposition into behavioral units.

• These architectures differ in the granularity of behavioral decomposition, co-ordination methods used, response encoding technique, basis for development, and other factors.

■ Our working definition is that robotic architecture is the discipline devoted to the design of highly specific and individual robots from a collection of common software building blocks.

■ Robotic architectures are similar in the sense that they are all Turing computable but indeed differ significantly in terms of their organizational components and structure.

■ Behavior-based architectures can be evaluated in terms of their support for parallelism, hardware retargetability, ecological niche fitting, modularity support, robustness, flexibility, ease of development, and performance.

■ The subsumption architecture is a layered architecture that uses arbitration strategies and augmented finite state machines as its basis. It has been implemented on many robotic systems using rule-based encodings and an experimental design methodology.

■ Motor schemas are a software-oriented dynamic reactive architecture that is non-layered and cooperative (as opposed to competitive). Vectors serve as the continuous response encoding mechanism with summation as the fundamental coordination strategy. Several robotic systems have been implemented, and the architecture has had significant influence from biological considerations.

■ Circuit architectures predominantly use logical expressions for behavioral encoding, use abstraction coupled with arbitration, and typically follow the situated activity design paradigm.

■ Action-selection architectures are dynamic rather than fixed competition systems, and they also use arbitration.

■ The colony architecture is a simplified version of subsumption, more straightforward in its implementation.

■ The animate agent architecture uses reactive action packages (RAPs) and sequencing methods to unfold situational responses over time.

■ The DAMN architecture provides voting mechanisms for behavioral response encodings, with a winner-take-all arbitration mechanism in the style of subsumption.

■ The skill network architecture is particularly well suited for graphical animation and uses action-selection techniques.

■ Many other behavior-based architectures also exist, varying at some level from the other architectural systems.

■ Design choices for robotic architects involve issues such as whether to use analysis or synthesis, take a top-down or bottom-up design stance, design for specific domains or be more general, and whether to consider the abstract role of intelligence in general or simply be concerned with building smarter machines.

Chapter 5

Representational Issues for Behavioral Systems

Knowledge is to embark on a journey which . . . will always be incomplete, cannot be charted on a map, will never halt, cannot be described.
—Douglas R. Hofstadter

The only justification for our concepts and systems of concepts is that they serve to represent the complex of our experiences; beyond this they have not legitimacy.
—Albert Einstein

There is no knowledge that is not power.
—Ralph Waldo Emerson

Is knowledge knowable? If not, how do we know this?
—Woody Allen

Chapter Objectives

1. To develop working definitions for knowledge and knowledge use.
2. To explore the qualities of knowledge representation.
3. To understand what types of knowledge may be representable for use within robotic systems.
4. To determine the appropriate role of world and self-knowledge within behavior-based robotic systems.
5. To study several representational strategies developed for use within behavior-based systems.

5.1   REPRESENTATIONAL KNOWLEDGE

A significant controversy exists regarding the appropriate role of knowledge within robotic systems. Oversimplifying this conflict somewhat, we can say that behavior-based roboticists generally view the use of symbolic representational knowledge as an impediment to efficient and effective robotic control, whereas others argue that strong forms of representational knowledge are needed to have a robot perform at anything above the level of a lower life form.

In this chapter, we attempt to defuse this argument by first providing some definitions and characteristics of knowledge and knowledge representations and then showing successful examples where knowledge representations of various forms have been introduced into reactive robotic systems at the behavioral level. We emphasize the appropriate use of knowledge, not merely using knowledge for knowledge's sake. Later, in chapter 6, we describe how it is possible to exploit multiple robotic control paradigms within a single architecture, with different components of the system employing knowledge representations in different ways.

5.1.1   What Is Knowledge?

Knowledge, much like intelligence, is a word notoriously difficult to define. Information arises from data, and knowledge can be said to emanate from information (figure 5.1). Tanimoto's (1990, p. 111) definition for knowledge seems particularly to the point: "information in context, organized so that it can be readily applied to solving problems, perception, and learning."

Turban's (1992, p. 792) definition is also useful: "Understanding, awareness, or familiarity acquired through education or experience. The ability to use information." Knowledge involves using information intelligently. To do this effectively, knowledge must be efficiently organized, otherwise it becomes burdensome.

Of course, if we intend to use knowledge to guide robotic behavior, it must somehow be represented within the robotic system. Much of the debate regarding knowledge's role within behavior-based systems centers on how it is represented within the context of the control system. Steels (1995) considers knowledge representations to involve "physical structures (for example electro-chemical states) which have correlations with aspects of the environment and thus have a predictive power for the system." Although this definition is broader than most, it does capture two very important characteristics:

Volume

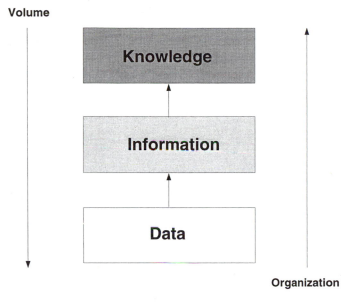

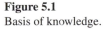

Organization

Figure 5.1
Basis of knowledge.

1. **Environmental correlation.** To be useful, a representation must have some relationship with the external world. The nature of that relationship will serve as a defining characteristic for many of the knowledge representations that we consider. In particular, the temporal durability or persistence of the represented knowledge (e.g., short term, long term) and the nature of the correlational mapping itself (e.g., metric, relational) will serve as defining factors.
2. **Predictive power.** This predictive ability is central to the value of knowledge representation. If there is no need to predict, we can rely entirely on what is sensed, resulting in a purely reactive approach. However, if there is useful information beyond the robot's sensing capabilities that is accurate, durable, and reliable, then it can be worthwhile in providing knowledge representations that encode this information to the robot. As we all know, however, the future is notoriously difficult to predict in the real world, even in the best of circumstances. Here lies the controversy: in the utility of knowledge at a given time within a given environment, since it has an ability not only to predict, but also to deceive should that information be inaccurate or untimely.

Figure 5.2 captures some of the trade-offs regarding sensing versus representing in various task environments. Whenever the world changes rapidly,

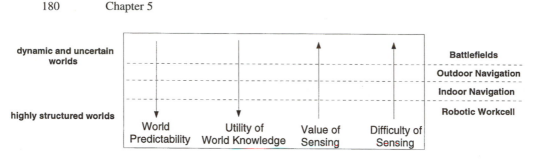

Figure 5.2
Trade-offs for knowledge use. An increase is denoted by the arrow's direction.

stored knowledge becomes potentially obsolete quickly. On the other hand, continuous sensing is not free, and from a computational perspective it is better to conduct that process as few times as necessary. If the world is unlikely to change, it can be advantageous to retain previously sensed information instead of unnecessarily oversampling the environment.

A related problem is maintaining an accurate correlation between the robot's position within the world and its representational point of view. This is not a trivial problem. When this involves the spatial location of a mobile robot it is referred to as *localization*. If maps of any form are maintained, the problem of resolving the robot's egocentric frame of reference and the representational frame of reference must be addressed. In other words, the question that must be answered is "Where am I?" Purely reactive systems do not address this question at all, for they are concerned only with the robot's immediate sensations. There is no projection into the future, nor any reasoning over past experience.

This chapter delves into various approaches for addressing these trade-offs, maximizing robotic utility in differing circumstances. We must keep in mind as we study these methods that they depend strongly on the environment in which the robotic agent resides and not merely on the architectural choice itself.

5.1.2   Characteristics of Knowledge

Early psychologists such as Hull and Sherrington, who preceded behaviorists, took the stance that "knowledge is embedded in the structure of the reflex units that generate action" (Gallistel 1980, p. 336). There were neither discrete knowledge structures nor translational processes to complete the mapping from knowledge store to action. In subsequent years, behaviorists (epitomized by B.F. Skinner), eschewed mentalistic terms such as "knowledge" or "mental representations," which have no place within the behaviorist point of view and are viewed merely as artifacts derived from complex stimulus-response couplings.

Cognitive psychologists (e.g., Neisser 1976) have recently forwarded compelling evidence and theories of knowledge representation that have displaced much of the earlier behaviorist stance. Knowledge structures are conceived as manipulable units of information involved in various ways with action generation. *Cognitive maps* (Gallistel 1990) are often referred to as the means for both storage of previous experience and its translation into action. Neurobiological evidence now exists for "what and where" centers within the brain (Mishkin, Ungergleieder, and Macko 1983), providing a compelling basis for the importance of localization and object recognition and categorization. These maps may be as simple as collections of action vectors that maintain a spatial correlation with sensory events arriving from the outside world and appropriate actions by the agent (Bizzi, Mussa-Ivaldi, and Giszter 1991; Gallistel 1990).

Learning is often inextricably bound up with the issues of knowledge representation: for example, how are these cognitive maps created and stored in the first place? We defer most of these learning issues until chapter 8, but inevitably some aspects seep into our discussion here.

This perspective on psychology clearly relates to behavior-based robotic systems in that we would like our robots to act intelligently or knowledgeably. The debate over knowledge's role resides not in whether it is useful but rather in how it appears within a robotic system.

Traditional AI is often distinguished from behavior-based systems along the knowledge representation front. Let us consider a taxonomy of knowledge representations (Dennett 1982; Malcolm and Smithers 1990):

- **Explicit**: symbolic, discrete, manipulable knowledge representations typical of traditional AI.
- **Implicit**: Knowledge that is non-explicit but reconstructable and can be made explicit through procedural usage.
- **Tacit**: Knowledge embedded within the system that existing processes cannot reconstruct.

Symbolic systems use explicit knowledge as defined above, *subsymbolic* systems involve either implicit or tacit knowledge use.

It can be said that all intelligent systems must use knowledge to accomplish their goals. To be truly intelligent, the knowledge usage must be efficient and effective. Those within the behavior-based robotics community resist the use of explicit knowledge, as we have noted, because of another difficulty: the *symbol grounding problem*. Succinctly stated, the symbol grounding problem refers to the difficulty in connecting the meaning (semantics) of an arbitrary symbol to a real world entity or event. It is easy to create a symbol with the intention of representing something. It is difficult, however, to attach the full meaning and implications of that real world object or event to the symbol. The degeneracy is often recursive or circular. Other symbols are used to define the symbol that one is trying to anchor. This only compounds the problem by leading to a proliferation of symbols that still have no true meaning. We, as humans, are capable of grounding our symbols (or language) and extracting meaning from them partly because of our ability to perceive and manipulate the environment. Meaning arises from our interactions with objects within the world and is not intrinsic to the objects themselves. Fortunately robotics, unlike much of AI, provides us a means by which our agent can interact with the world, that is, the robot's sensors and actuators.

If we want our robots to act knowledgeably, various types of knowledge are necessary. Listed below are several possibilities:

- Spatial world knowledge: an understanding of the navigable space and structure surrounding the robot.
- Object knowledge: categories or instances of particular types of things within the world.
- Perceptual knowledge: information regarding how to sense the environment under various circumstances.
- Behavioral knowledge: an understanding of how to react in different situations.
- Ego knowledge: limits on the abilities of the robot's actions within the world (e.g., speed, fuel, etc.) and on what the robot itself can perceive (e.g., sensor models).
- Intentional knowledge: information regarding the agent's goals and intended actions within the environment–a plan of action.

Spatial world knowledge can take several forms: quantitative or metric, where some absolute measure is used to establish the robot's relationship to the world; and qualitative or relational, where information about the world is described in relative terms (e.g., the goal is just to the right of the second door on the left).

Another way in which knowledge can be characterized is in regard to its durability: how long it will be useful. Two basic forms of knowledge, persistent and transitory, can be distinguished. *Persistent* knowledge involves a priori information about the robot's environment that can be considered relatively static for the mission's or task's duration. These data typically arise from object models of things the robot might expect to see within its world, models of the free space where it moves, and an ego model of the robot itself. The knowledge base within which this information resides is termed long-term memory (LTM), indicative of this data's persistence.

The robot acquires *transitory* knowledge dynamically as it moves through the world and stores it in short-term memory (STM). World models constructed from sensory data typically fall into this category. Although STM is rarely used directly for reactive control, it can be applied when purely reactive techniques encounter difficulties. In behavior-based robotic systems, dynamically acquired world models should be used only when the control regime fails to cope with difficult situations. Even then, STM is best used to reconfigure the control system rather than to supplant it. Transitory knowledge is typically forgotten (fades) as the robot moves away from the locale where that information was gathered.

For both persistent and transitory knowledge, the choice of representational structure and format is less important than merely the availability of the knowledge itself. Persistent knowledge allows for the use of preconceived ideas of the robot's relationship to the world, enabling more efficient use of its resources than would be accomplished otherwise. Either form of knowledge, if misused, could interfere with the simplicity and efficiency of reactive control. Nonetheless, when difficulties with a behavioral control regime arise, it is useful to provide a bigger picture to help resolve them. This can result in solutions to problems such as the fly-at-the-window situation in reactive control, when an insect strives to go toward sunlight entering from an outside window, is rebuffed by the glassy barrier, expends all of its energy trying to solve the problem with its fixed set of behaviors, and ultimately dies. If transitory environmental models are constructed under these conditions (STM), a robot could use the information to circumnavigate the barrier.

We previously discussed STM and LTM in box 2.1. STM performs over an intermediate time scale, in contrast to LTM, which is more durative, and reflexive memory, which is quasi-instantaneous. Strong neuroscientific evidence exists that STM processes are distinct from LTM (Guigon and Burnod 1995). LTM is persistent and is generally viewed as the basis for learning. Figure 5.3 illustrates these relationships.

Associative memory is another form of knowledge representation, often linked with neural network models (Anderson 1995). Here input patterns, often only partially complete, evoke responses or memories encoded in a network model. Various mappings are found within the nervous system. Primary

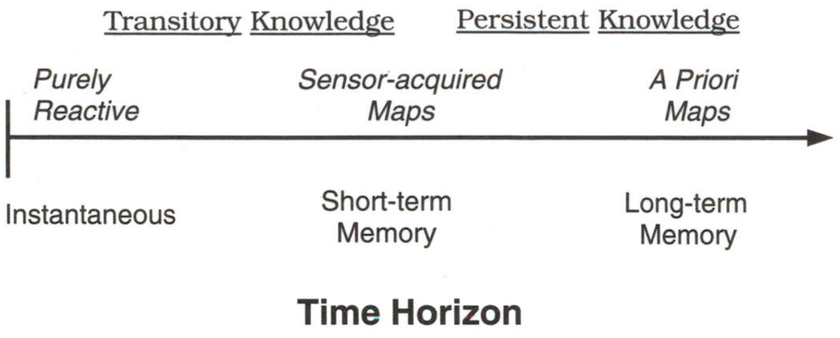

Transitory Knowledge   Persistent Knowledge

| Purely | Sensor-acquired | A Priori |
| Reactive | Maps | Maps |

Instantaneous   Short-term   Long-term
              Memory   Memory

Time Horizon

Figure 5.3
Time horizon for knowledge.

examples include retinotopic maps, space-preserving mappings of the retina onto the visual cortex; and somatotopic maps, topographic representations of the body surface projecting onto the brain (Florence and Kaas 1995). Chapter 8 revisits neural network models for behavior-based robotic systems.

The philosophies regarding knowledge use itself form two subdivisions of metaphysics. As defined by Webster 1984, epistemology is "the study or a theory of the nature and grounds of knowledge especially with reference to its limits and validity." Ontology, on the other hand, is defined as "a particular theory about the nature of being or the kinds of existents."

Epistemological considerations, in our context, concern the use and validity of knowledge within behavior-based robotic systems. Ontological considerations are more specific to the representational choices and determine what kinds of things exist (or are understandable) within the framework of our robotic system. In the remainder of this chapter, we primarily address the ontological factors in our examples of knowledge use: what knowledge is available to the system and the representational choices (i.e., vocabularies) made.

5.2   REPRESENTATIONAL KNOWLEDGE FOR BEHAVIOR-BASED SYSTEMS

A little knowledge that acts is worth infinitely more than much knowledge which is idle.
—Khalil Gibran

Any number of animals use cognitive maps. Foraging animals, such as insects and birds, are believed to use polar vector representations near their homesites (Waterman 1989). These vectors are imposed over a polar grid coordinate system created by a mosaic of recognizable landmarks. Gallistel (1990) presents compelling evidence for the use of cognitive maps in animal systems, including the following:

- Evidence for vector spaces in animals capable of spatial encoding includes tectal maps for angular deviation in birds and auditory cortex maps for encoding distance and velocity in the bat, among others.
- Many animals are capable of distance triangulation from known landmarks, including many insects, such as locusts, wasps, and bees, and other animals, such as the gerbil.
- Cognitive maps in nature have found uses in foraging, homing, puddle jumping (gobies), resource location (e.g., refinding calcium depots for the desert tortoise), avoiding nearly undetectable obstacles by remembering their location (bats), orienting towards hidden goals (rats swimming for platforms), route selection based on relative distance (chameleons), remembering places passed en route to another location (maze finding in rats), and route selection between places encountered in the past (chimpanzees).
- Of particular interest is the localization of a geometric module within the hippocampus of the rat brain, believed capable of encoding metric relations and compass sense and performing the necessary transformations to make the information useful to the rat. Below we discuss an example of a robotic representation system inspired by the rat's hippocampus (Mataric 1990).

Of course, animals' use of cognitive maps is not a sufficiently compelling argument for including them within robotic systems. At the very least, however, it should certainly give the reactive roboticist pause to consider their potential use and impact upon performance. Indeed, the principle of biological economy argues that systems are generally not included within biological systems unless they provide some utility or advantage to the animal.

Knowledge representations can be made available in several ways to the control system for behavior-based robotic systems. Each compromises the purely reactive philosophy (chapter 3) to varying degrees but provides benefits difficult to realize within the strictest view of behavior-based robotics. These representational approaches correlate closely to our notions of transitory and persistent knowledge manifested in various forms of STM and LTM.

- Short-term behavioral memory: Isolating representational knowledge to a specific behavior provides knowledge on a need-to-know basis, in a manner similar to action-oriented perception (section 4.4.1). Analogously we can refer to this use as action-oriented knowledge representation. Only that information necessary for the performance of a specific behavior is represented. This preserves the behavioral modularity and opportunity for incremental development that is so valuable from the behavior-based design perspective.

■ Sensor-derived long-term cognitive maps: Information that is directly perceived from the environment and gathered only during the lifetime of the robot's experience in a particular environment is used to construct a stand-alone world model. This model is plastic in the sense that as new sensor data arrives the model is continuously updated and modified attempting to maintain a close correlation with the actual world. These representations are constructed in a behavior-independent manner and may provide information to the overall behavioral control system in a variety of ways. The greatest difficulties lie in maintaining a high fidelity correspondence with the world, especially when it is dynamic and unpredictable.

■ A priori map-derived representations: With these methods, information is introduced beyond the robot's sensing capabilities. It may be compiled from floorplans or external maps of the world, but it was gathered independently of the robotic agent. The strength of these representations lies in their ability to provide expectations regarding the environment even before the robot has entered it. Significant problems arise from the fact that the initial knowledge source may be inaccurate, untimely, or just plain wrong, and that the form of the initial representation may not be easily or conveniently translated into a useful robotic format.

We now review specific instances of behavior-based robotic systems capable of taking advantage of knowledge in these various forms.

5.2.1   Short-Term Behavioral Memory

Knowledge is soon changed, then lost in the mist, an echo half-heard.
—Gene Wolfe

Behavioral memory provides certain advantages to a robot: It reduces the need for frequent sensor sampling in reasonably stable environments, and it provides recent information to guide the robot that is outside of its sensory range. Representations that fit this particular category have three general characteristics. First, they are used in support of a single behavior in a behavioral control system, most often obstacle avoidance. Second, the representation directly feeds the behavior rather than directly tying it to a sensor. In essence, the memory serves as a buffer and translator for a limited number of previous sensings (figure 5.4). Third, they are transitory: the representations are constructed, used while the robot is in the environment, and then discarded. They must be reconstructed if the robot reenters the environment. Although initially this might

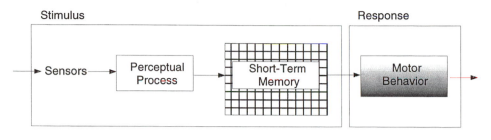

Figure 5.4
Behavioral memory.

appear to penalize the robot by making it somewhat absentminded, it is actually valuable as it eliminates much of the difficulty associated with long-term localization (i.e., having the robot maintain its bearings relative to a map) and is well suited for somewhat dynamic environments where the position of obstacles may change over time. In general, purely reactive systems still have an advantage in very dynamic worlds (e.g., navigating along a crowded sidewalk), but some behavioral STM techniques can deal quite well even with these situations.

Both behavioral memory and cognitive mapping commonly use grids to represent the navigable space around the robot. Grid representations are arbitrarily tessellated regions surrounding the robot. They can vary in the following ways:

- Resolution: the amount of area each grid unit covers (e.g., an inch, a meter, or more).
- Shape: most frequently square, but also in other forms such as radial sectors (Malkin and Addanki 1990).
- Uniformity: the grid cells may all be the same size, or they may vary. The most common variable-sized grid methodology involves the use of quadtrees (Andresen et al. 1985), which are formed through the recursive decomposition of free space.

Figure 5.5 depicts a few variations of grids. Implementations of grid-based representations most often use preallocated two-dimensional arrays, but occasionally (especially for quadtrees) involve linked lists as the central data structure.

We discussed in section 4.4.2 one example of behavioral memory used for navigation: the avoid-past behavior. This behavior prevented stagnation during navigation by adding repulsion from places the robot has recently visited. A regular grid stored sensory information concerning where the robot had

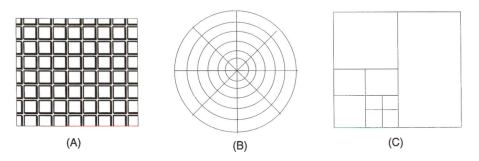

Figure 5.5
Grid representations: (A) regular grid, (B) sector grid, and (C) quadtree.

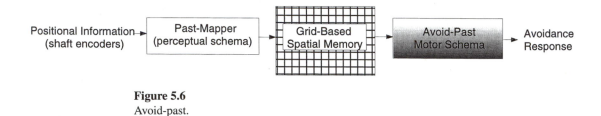

Figure 5.6
Avoid-past.

recently been (figure 5.6). The original work (Balch and Arkin 1993) used dead reckoning information based on shaft encoder readings for incrementing counter values within the grid. Other, more effective sensors, could also be readily used, however, such as global positioning systems (GPS), infrared bar code readers, or inertial navigation systems (INS) with no impact on the behavior or the representation itself (assuming the sensor could provide the necessary resolution). The avoid-past behavior was fully self-contained in that it was constructed with the intent of using a representation from the onset, and was completely modular and integrable with all of the other behaviors within the control system.

Yamauchi (1990) developed two different forms of behavioral memory. The first, referred to as *wall memory*, uses an array of elements, corresponding to the number of ultrasonic sensors, to increase confidence over time that the robot is near a wall. The memory readings are then used to support a wall-following behavior (figure 5.7).

Yamauchi further extends the notion of behavioral memory by storing in an *action memory* information not only about the world (e.g., walls) but also about the robot's most recent responses. This memory permits the robot to favor

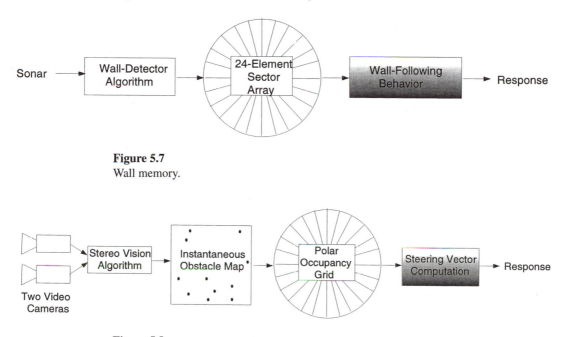

Figure 5.7
Wall memory.

Figure 5.8
Real-time obstacle avoidance using stereo vision.

the direction in which it is currently moving by using a weighted average of past responses to bias the immediate reactive response. This tends to remove noise and reduce the possibility of premature reflexive action due to a single reading.

Badal et al. (1994) developed an example of real-time obstacle avoidance using stereo vision with a form of behavioral memory. An *instantaneous obstacle map* stores detected obstacle points projected onto the ground plane. To produce the steering behavior for a high-mobility multipurpose wheeled vehicle (HMMWV), these points are mapped onto a polar occupancy grid (sector based) using a coarse configuration space approach, which then generates a steering vector in the direction of the least hindrance (i.e., the direction with the farthest possible avoidance distance). This behavior is depicted schematically in Figure 5.8.

Borenstein and Koren (1989) patented a method for conducting obstacle avoidance in real time using sonar data and a grid-based representation. Their work centers on the use of a certainty grid, an outgrowth of earlier work by Moravec and Elfes (1985). Moravec's work focused on constructing a world

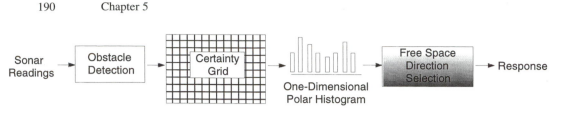

Figure 5.9
Vector field histogram usage for obstacle avoidance.

model using sonar data coupled with probabilistic sensor models that, when given multiple readings of the world, could create a grid-based map. Traditional path planning was then conducted within this representational framework to produce a route for the robot, which would then move through the world in a nonreactive manner. Matthies and Elfes (1988) later extended this work to provide sensor fusion of both sonar and visual stereo data.

Borenstein and Koren (1989) modified this method so that many more sensor readings could be taken by greatly simplifying the world map updating process. Information could be added continuously from the incoming data. Further, they added decay processes to decrement cell values over time, ensuring currency of the data. Initially the grid took the traditional two-dimensional square format in their vector force field concept. A repulsive vector, generated in a manner analogous to that of the potential fields method (section 3.3.2), produced the steering direction and velocity for the robot. In later work (1991), Borenstein and Koren altered the representational format to include a one-dimensional polar form, the vector field histogram, further decreasing the processing time by collapsing the two-dimensional grid directly into a directional representation centered on the robot's current location. Each sector stores the polar obstacle density. The steering computation becomes trivial, simply selecting the most suitable direction in the histogram consistent with the robot's overall goal. Figure 5.9 depicts this approach.

All of the examples discussed thus far have been concerned with short-term data that is used, then discarded, and that is channeled directly to a particular behavior. We now look at representational methods that are more persistent and potentially have broader use for a variety of behavioral responses.

5.2.2   Long-Term Memory Maps

Under some circumstances, persistent information regarding the environment may be useful for behavior-based robotic systems. In general, these long-term representations are best used to advise a behavioral control regime rather than dictate to it.

The origin of the map data itself provides a useful way to classify these maps. Some are derived directly from sensors onboard the robot, as the robot moves about the world storing information in a particular representational format for later use. Others are constructed from information gathered independently of the robot but transformed into some useful format. These a priori maps are not as timely as sensor-derived maps but can be obtained from a broader range of resources, even including remote sensing devices such as satellites.

The map representational knowledge itself is typically encoded in one of two forms:

- Metric: in which absolute measurements and coordinate systems are used to represent information regarding the world. Latitude and longitude measurements are typical of this format.
- Qualitative: in which salient features and their relationships within the world are represented. This may support behavioral descriptions such as "turn left at the second door on the right," or "continue moving until you see the sign." There is little or no notion of any quantitative measurement within the world, only spatial or temporal relationships.

The use of any form of map knowledge is dangerous primarily in the fact that it may be untimely (i.e., the world has changed since the map was constructed) and hence inaccurate. Additionally, localization, a nontrivial perceptual activity providing environmental correlation of the robot's position within the mapped world, needs to be conducted. Map knowledge is advantageous primarily in that maps can provide guidance beyond the horizon of immediate sensing. These trade-offs need to be weighed very carefully when considering map usage for particular task environments. The behavior-based roboticist who chooses to use maps strives to permit immediate sensory activity to override any potentially erroneous map information.

5.2.2.1   Sensor-Derived Cognitive Maps

Sensor-derived maps provide information directly gleaned from the robot's experiences within the world. How long the information is retained will determine its timeliness. As the world is sampled from the robot's egocentric point of view, it is often advantageous to use qualitative representations instead of metric ones because of the inherent inaccuracies in robot motion and the sensor

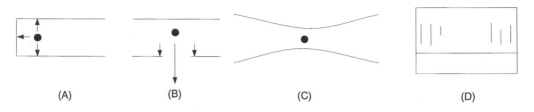

(A)   (B)   (C)   (D)

Figure 5.10
Distinctive regions: (A) end of hall—three-way symmetry; (B) doorway—abrupt depth discontinuity; (C) hallway constriction—depth minimum; (D) visual constellations—unique feature patterns (in this case, two triplets of vertical lines).

readings themselves. In behavior-based systems, since the information is intended only to supplement the reactive control system rather than to replace it, which is not the case with traditional robotic motion planning (Latombe 1991), inaccuracies in the sensor data are tolerated in a much more forgiving manner.

One of the hallmarks of qualitative navigational techniques is the notion of *distinctive places,* regions in the world that have characteristics that distinguish them from their surroundings (Kuipers and Byun 1988). A distinctive place is defined as "the local maximum found by a hill-climbing control strategy given an appropriate distinctiveness measure" (Kuipers and Byun 1991). Higher-level topological and geometric representations are always derived in this system from these semantically grounded sensory observations. In robotic systems, these characteristics are most often derived from the sensor readings themselves. Locales that exhibit symmetry in some manner, abrupt discontinuities in sensor readings, unusual constellations of sensor readings, or a point where a maximum or minimum sensor reading occurs are typical examples (figure 5.10). After the robot determines these observable and ultimately recognizable landmarks, they can later be used for lower-level control, such as moving to a particular point in this observation space.

As these map features are often directly tied to sensing, integration into a behavior is fairly easy. For example, the robot can readily be instructed to move ahead until an abrupt depth discontinuity occurs on the right and then switch to a move-through-door behavior. The sensor-derived qualitative map serves as the basis for behavioral configuration and action. Of course, obvious problems arise should the door happen to be closed, but that is typical of reliance on map data of any sort. The world is assumed to exist as it is modeled, which may or may not be the case.

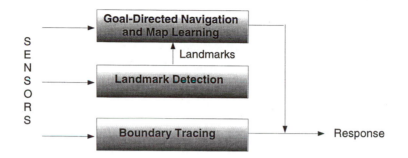

Figure 5.11
Integration of representation in subsumption-style architecture.

Qualitative representations' primary advantage is their relative immunity to errors in motion, especially when the robot relies heavily upon dead reckoning as its basis for localization. An example system used for outdoor navigation uses *viewframes,* representations constructed from visual input that possess the qualities of distinctiveness discussed earlier (Levitt and Lawton 1990). As such they constitute a visual memory of where the robot has been and provide landmarks regarding its position within the world. Path transformations link aggregations of viewframes together and describe how the robotic agent moved from one place to the other. The resulting network constitutes a sensor-derived map useful in instructing the robot in how to navigate. This form of qualitative navigation can be readily tied to behavior-based systems (Arkin and Lawton 1990; Lawton, Arkin, and Cameron 1990). In particular, reactive control can provide a safe basis for exploring unknown areas during the qualitative mapping process. Behaviors can be developed that are capable of attracting the robotic agent to areas that it has not yet surveyed; they can provide the ability to track relative to qualitative landmarks and permit recovery from disorientation by allowing the robot to search for specific perceptual events.

Mataric (1992b) demonstrated the integration of qualitative maps and behavior-based robotic systems in a subsumption-based system. Figure 5.11 depicts the subsumption-style controller. Landmarks are derived from sonar data, using features that are stable and consistent over time. In particular, right walls, left walls, and corridors are the landmark features derived from the sensors. Spatial relationships are added connecting the various landmarks through constructing a graph. Map navigation consists of following the boundaries of wall or corridor regions. When the robot, Toto, determines that it is in a particular region, it can move to different locales by traversing the graph representation that connects different regions, effectively conducting path planning. Nonetheless, the advantages of reactive navigation are not lost, as the robot is not required to follow its path blindly through the world when other overriding sensor data indicate that it is more important to detour (e.g., for obstacle avoidance). Of additional interest is the claim that this mode of navigational behavior is a possible interpretation of the manner in which the rat's brain (specifically the hippocampus) conducts navigation (Mataric 1990).

Several other variations of qualitative maps suitable for behavior-based navigation have been developed, including

■ A behavior-based controller capable of such actions as hallway following and corner turning is coupled with a finite state automata representation of the world (Basye 1992). The navigational task then becomes a depth-first search through the state transition graph (Dean et al. 1995). This system has been developed predominantly for officelike environments and to date has had only limited experimental testing.

■ A model derived from panoramic visual sensing (a 360-degree field of view) based on depth recovery from the motion of a robot (Ishiguro et al. 1994). Though not specifically focused on reactive robotic systems, it is potentially useful in that regard. A two-and-a-half–dimensional outline structure of the environment (contour depth along a line) is recovered using visual depth from motion techniques and broken into consistent visual features. The resulting panoramic representation is converted into a qualitative form by segmenting the outline model into objects based on abrupt depth discontinuities. This qualitative model can be used for visual event prediction along the robot's intended navigational path or for localization purposes.

Map knowledge need not be derived solely from sensory data. Let us now investigate some other methods of map construction of potential use in behavior-based robotics.

5.2.2.2   A Priori Map-Derived Representations

A priori maps are constructed from data obtained independently from the robotic agent itself. The most compelling arguments for using this type of map knowledge arise from convenience and greater scope:

■ It may be easier to compile these data directly without forcing the robot to travel through the entire world ahead of time.

■ These data may be available from standard sources such as the Defense Mapping Agency or the U.S. Geographical Survey, among others.
■ Precompiled sources of information may be used, such as blueprints, floor-plans, and roadmaps, that need only to be encoded for the robot's use.

Of course, the perils to the accuracy of this data are different since it comes from other sources:

■ Errors may be introduced in the process of encoding the new data.
■ The data may be relatively old compared to recent robotic sensor readings.
■ The frame of reference for the observations may be somewhat incompatible with the robot's point of view.

These are just some of the trade-offs that must be considered when using a priori map knowledge. Clearly, a behavior-based roboticist's goal would be to include this information in a manner that does not impede the robot's reactive performance, but that allows for guidance from knowledge outside the robot's direct experience.

Payton (1991) provides one of the most compelling examples of use of a priori map knowledge within the behavior-based robotics paradigm. In Payton's research, fielded in DARPA's Autonomous Land Vehicle Program, a map of the environment containing known obstacles, terrain information, and a goal location is provided in a grid-based format derived from a digital terrain map. A cost is associated with each grid cell based on mission criteria; the cost can take into account such factors as traversability, visibility to the enemy, ease of finding landmarks, and impact on fuel consumption, among others. A gradient field is computed over the entire map from start point to goal point with the minimum cost direction represented within each cell to get to the goal. Figure 5.12 depicts an example map. The gradient field represents what is referred to as an *internalized plan*, since it contains the preferred direction of motion to accomplish the mission's goals.

The key to this approach's success is its integration with the other behaviors within the overall control system. The internalized plan acts like another behavior sitting atop a subsumption-style architecture (figure 5.13). The lower-level behaviors guide the vehicle when the situation warrants, but if the vehicle is proceeding normally, the highest-level action that corresponds to the internalized plan representing the overall mission is enacted. This method of injecting map knowledge into reactive control is also readily applicable to other behavior-based architectures.

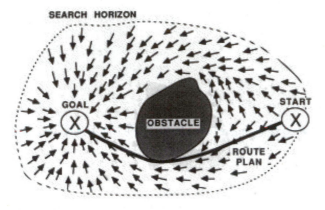

Figure 5.12
Gradient field representing an internalized plan. (Reprinted from Payton, D., "Internalized Plans: A Representation for Action Resources", 1991, pp. 94, with kind permission from Elsevier Science—NL, Sara Burgerhartstraat 24, 1055 KV, Amsterdam, The Netherlands.)

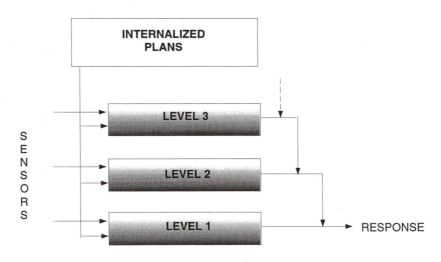

Figure 5.13
Behavioral control using internalized plans.

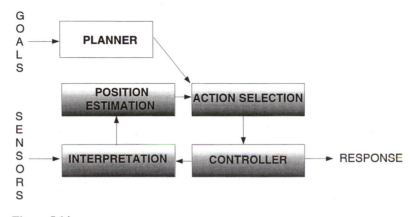

Figure 5.14
Action-selection control architecture (Simmons and Koenig 1995).

Simmons and Koenig (1995) present a different approach to encoding both topological and metric information from maps obtained from floorplans. The base representation is constructed from topological (connectivity) models of the environment, common knowledge about office structure (e.g., corridors are straight), and approximate measurement of the environment regarding width of passageways and distances between turning (decision) points. The resulting graph represents the world. Markov models (specialized probabilistic models) encode the actions that a robot can take at different locations within the model. As the layout of the office chosen is simple, the allowable actions are simply turning right or left 90 degrees or proceeding straight ahead for one meter. Obstacle avoidance is handled using the same approach as in Arkin 1987a, and supplemented with planned actions based on where the robot needs to proceed according to its mission. The planner itself uses an A* search algorithm to specify the actions to be taken at each point within the topological model. The Markov model–based planner issues directives to the robot for turning left or right, moving forward or stopping. The navigational architecture uses an action-selection mechanism (figure 5.14). The specific arbitration mechanism used is a best-action strategy, based on the highest probability for each possible directive. The probability for a directive depends on the probabilities derived from sensing that assesses the location of the robot within the map. This system has been fielded on a mobile robot named XAVIER (built on a RWI B24 base) (figure 5.15) and is reported to have successfully completed 88 percent of its missions using this strategy in more than a kilometer of total distance traveled.

Figure 5.15
XAVIER. (Photograph courtesy of Reid Simmons, The Robotics Institute, Carnegie-Mellon University.)

Figure 5.16
Navlab II. (Photograph courtesy of The Robotics Institute, Carnegie-Mellon
University.)

Another system capable of integrating a priori map knowledge into a
behavior-based control system was fielded on the Navlab II robot testbed
(Stentz and Hebert 1995) (figure 5.16). An eight-connected cartesian grid-
based representation capable of storing complete, partially complete, or no
knowledge of the world is available to a *Dynamic A** or D* planner (Stentz
1994). D* has the special ability to replan very efficiently should sensor data
update the stored map representation. This in essence provides a variant on
Payton's work, discussed earlier, that can provide rapid updates to the map
based on incoming sensory data. In the overall system, an obstacle avoidance behavior based on range data provides local navigation abilities. The
DAMN steering arbiter (section 4.5.5) chooses the correct behavioral action

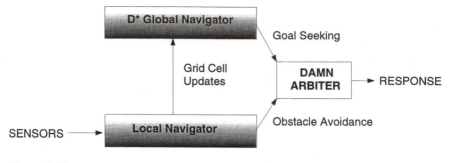

Figure 5.17
Navigational control system using D* as a behavior.

for the circumstances (figure 5.17). The system was tested at a slag heap near Pittsburgh, driving successfully in excess of 1.4 kilometers in a cluttered environment on its way to the goal. The authors claim it to be the first system that exhibits on a real robot both efficient goal acquisition and obstacle avoidance in an unstructured outdoor environment.

Another type of map, the *purposive map* (Zelinsky et al. 1995; Zelinsky and Kuniyoshi 1996), stores information regarding the utility of behaviors during navigation within the world (as opposed to spatial information regarding the world's structures). It is similar in spirit to Yamauchi's action memory described earlier. In Zelinsky's research, the behavioral controller consists of a subsumption-like arbiter, managing behaviors such as wander, collide, wall-follow, find-an-opening, move-to-goal, and the like. The purposive map monitors and coordinates behavioral state. The map itself lists features and associated scalar quantities that estimate the spatial relationships between features. Associated with each feature is an action to be used when it is encountered. The system designer enters the information in the map manually. Actually, this map is more of a plan than an environmental model since it ties task-specific actions with recognizable environmental conditions—an interesting twist on the use of representations, where the knowledge stored for later use is dependent not only on the state of the world but the robot's intentions as well.

5.3 PERCEPTUAL REPRESENTATIONS

The representations we have discussed thus far have been concerned with the *where* issues: where in the world the robot is located and where it is going. As chapter 2 discussed, there is strong neurophysiological evidence for dual cortical pathways: one concerned with spatial issues (where), the other with recognition (what) (Mishkin, Ungergleider, and Macko 1983). We briefly discuss in this section some representational issues as they relate to perception for behavior-based robotic systems. This discussion is a preview of a larger discourse in chapter 7, but it is important at this point to understand certain aspects of representational use for object recognition.

A very large body of work exists on model-based computer vision, which typically is concerned with object identification based on geometric models. Although this strategy is appropriate for certain classes of problems, traditional geometric models have less utility in the context of behavioral systems. Recall from chapter 3 that perception in the context of behavior-based robotic systems is best conducted on a need-to-know basis. Because perception is strongly related to the actions that the robot needs to undertake, we now briefly review some representational strategies that take into account the robot's ability to move within the world and that can reflect its intentional position. These representations are consistent with our notion of action-oriented perception and offer in some sense to try to capture the concept of affordance introduced in chapter 7.

The main class of representations we consider for sensory recognition are function based, addressing the problem of recognizing environmental objects that fit specific functions of value to the robotic agent at a particular time. These may include affordance-like functions such as sittable, throwable, provide-support, provide-storage-space, or what-have-you. A simple example involves assuming that you have a book in your hand and you need to place it down somewhere safely in a room in which you have never been before. Once you walk in, you might see many candidate surfaces (shelves, tables, beds, etc.) each of which to some degree will perform that function. How is the functional model represented for book stowability, and how can goodness of fit be measured with each candidate's environmental features? How can a decision be made as to the best place to put down the book? Functional models are concerned with these kinds of issues.

Stark and Bowyer (1991, 1994) developed one of the first examples of a functional representation. In this first attempt at a function-based model, no explicit geometry or structure is used. Instead a set of primitives (relative orientation, dimensions, stability, proximity, and clearance) defines functional properties. The flow of control for this system (figure 5.18) first takes as input a three-dimensional description of the object in terms of faces and vertices, then identifies potential functional elements (such as surfaces), attaches functional

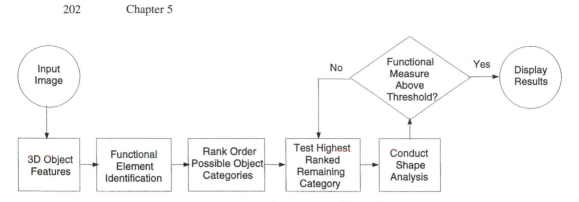

Figure 5.18
Control flow for functional interpretation.

labels to the individual features, and finally conducts a generate-and-test evaluation to determine if it indeed fits the functional criteria in question. The main example used for Stark and Bowyer's research has been identifying a chair as something that both "is sittable" and "provides stable support." An armchair would add the functions of "provides back support" and "provides arm support." In this strategy, objects with no express geometric models can be considered chairs if they meet the constraints the functional models for that object impose. Stark and Bowyer's work has yet to be integrated into a robotic system, but it appears to hold promise especially for behavior-based systems that involve affordance-like perceptual strategies.

More recently, Bogoni and Bajcsy (1994a) have studied functionality from an active-perception perspective. Functionality is related to observability and provides a basis for robotic sensors to investigate actively to determine the actual object's nature. Another study (Budenske and Gini 1994) provides a basis for recognizing doorways through a series of exploratory motions. Sonar data, which can be applied for this purpose, are notoriously misleading and error prone because of specular reflections, a wide sampling cone, and other artifacts of the sensing process (Everett 1995). In Budenske and Gini's work, initial sonar readings indicate a functional passageway that is potentially a door, but this is confirmed by other investigatory sensor-motor activities before the robot navigates through it. These activities include positioning the robot adjacent to the door opening, having the robot move back and forth in front of the opening to confirm its size and position, and centering the robot in the opening prior to passage. This information is then tied to a behavior-based robot, using behaviors referred to as logical sensors/actuators (LSAs), and the passage completed. The doorway per se is not directly represented; rather, the configuration of actions determines the doorway's function.

In research at the University of California at Berkeley, Stark developed the theory of scanpaths, another active representational strategy potentially suitable for use in behavior-based robotic systems (Noton and Stark 1971; Stark and Ellis 1981). In this theory of object recognition, models are created by the paths taken by the eye as its foveal region moves about the entire object. The connectivity of the focusing points and the order in which they occur constitute the *scanpath*. This ordering, which can be modeled on a computer by creating a network of visual features, can provide guidance as to where to focus perceptual processing to distinguish one object from another. Stark's work has yet to be tied to robotic systems but provides a clear alternative strategy to geometric model–based recognition for use in behavioral control systems.

There is much more to be said on the role of perceptual activity in the context of behavior-based robotics. We have touched on only some of the perceptual representation issues here. Chapter 7 investigates more thoroughly perceptual processing and control for this class of robots.

5.4   CHAPTER SUMMARY

■ The more predictable the world is, the more useful knowledge representations are.

■ Two important characteristics of knowledge include its predictive power and the need for the information stored to correlate with the environment in some meaningful way.

■ Knowledge can be characterized into three primary forms: explicit, implicit, and tacit.

■ Knowledge can be further characterized according to its temporal durability:

• transitory knowledge, which is derived from sensory data and corresponds to cognitive short-term memory.

• persistent cognitive maps, which may originate from either a priori knowledge or sensory data and corresponds to long-term memory.

■ Significant evidence exists from cognitive psychology that mental processing involves various forms of knowledge representation.

■ Using representational knowledge has several potential drawbacks within behavior-based systems:

• The stored information may be inaccurate or untimely.

• The robot must localize itself within the representational framework for the knowledge to be of value.

■ Representational knowledge's primary advantage lies in its ability to inject information beyond the robot's immediate sensory range into the robotic control system.

■ Examples of explicit representational knowledge use in behavior-based robots include short-term behavioral memory, sensor-derived cognitive maps, and a priori map-derived representations.

■ Short-term behavioral memory extends behavioral control beyond the robot's immediate sensing range and reduces the demand for frequent sensory sampling. This form of representation is tied directly to an individual behavior within the control system.

■ Grid-based representations are often used for short-term behavioral memory. The grids are typically either sector-based or regular and have resolutions that depend on the robot's environment and source of the grid data.

■ Grid representations of STM have been used to remember the robot's past positions, to buffer sensor readings for wall recognition, and to store observations of obstacles.

■ LTM maps are either metric or qualitative. Metric maps use numeric values to store the positions of observed events; qualitative maps use relational values.

■ The notion of distinctive places is central to the use of sensor-derived cognitive maps. Locations are remembered that incoming sensor data determine to be unique in some way.

■ Qualitative maps support general navigational capabilities and can provide behavioral support for moving to a goal, avoiding obstacles, invoking behavioral transitions, localization, and other related activities.

■ A priori map-derived representations offer the robot information regarding places where it has never been before. The data for the representations may come from preexisting maps, blueprints, floorplans, and the like.

■ Internalized plans inject a priori grid-based map knowledge directly into a behavior-based control system.

■ The D* method improves on the gradient map strategy used in internalized plans by permitting efficient sensor updates to the stored world knowledge.

■ STM and LTM cognitive maps address the "where" aspects of memory; function-based perceptual representations address the "what" aspects.

■ Function-based perceptual representations are most closely related to the affordance-based approach reactive robotics commonly uses.

■ Function-based methods are not based on standard geometric methods and require analysis of incoming sensor readings in terms of what the robotic agent needs to accomplish.

Chapter 6

Hybrid Deliberative/Reactive Architectures

In preparing for battle I have always found that plans are useless, but planning is indispensable.

—Dwight Eisenhower

It is a bad plan that admits of no modification.

—Publilius Syrus

Everybody's got plans . . . until they get hit.

—Mike Tyson

Few people think more than two or three times a year; I have made an international reputation for myself by thinking once or twice a week.

—George Bernard Shaw

Chapter Objectives

1. To understand the limitations of purely reactive and purely deliberative methods when each is considered in isolation.
2. To study biological models of hybrid reactive/deliberative systems.
3. To recognize the issues in establishing interfaces between reactive control and deliberative planners and to express several models for these interfaces.
4. To study several representative hybrid architectures, especially AuRA, Atlantis, Planner-Reactor, and PRS.

6.1   WHY HYBRIDIZE?

We have seen that reactive behavior-based robotic control can effectively produce robust performance in complex and dynamic domains. In some ways,
however, the strong assumptions that purely reactive systems make can serve
as a disadvantage at times. These assumptions include

1. The environment lacks temporal consistency and stability.
2. The robot's immediate sensing is adequate for the task at hand.
3. It is difficult to localize a robot relative to a world model.
4. Symbolic representational world knowledge is of little or no value.

In some environments, however, these assumptions may not be completely
valid. Purely reactive robotic systems are not appropriate for all robotic applications. In situations where the world can be accurately modeled, uncertainty is restricted, and some guarantee exists of virtually no change in the
world during execution (such as an engineered assembly work cell), deliberative methods are often preferred, since a complete plan can, most likely,
be effectively carried out to completion. In the real world in which biological
agents function, however, the conditions favoring purely deliberative planners
generally do not exist. If roboticists hope to have their machines performing
in the same environments that we, as humans, do, methods like behavior-based
reactive control are necessary. Many researchers feel, however, that hybrid systems capable of incorporating both deliberative reasoning and behavior-based
execution are needed to deliver the full potential of behavior-based robotic
systems.

   We saw in chapter 5 that introducing various forms of knowledge into a
robotic architecture can often make behavior-based navigation more flexible
and general. Deliberative systems permit representational knowledge to be
used for planning purposes in advance of execution. This potentially useful
knowledge may take several forms:

- Behavioral and perceptual strategies can be represented as modules and
configured to match various missions and environments, adding versatility.
- A priori world knowledge, when available and stable, can be used to configure or reconfigure these behaviors efficiently.
- Dynamically acquired world models can be used to prevent certain pitfalls
to which non-representational methods are subject.

   Hybrid deliberative/reactive robotic architectures have recently emerged
combining aspects of traditional AI symbolic methods and their use of ab-

stract representational knowledge, but maintaining the goal of providing the responsiveness, robustness, and flexibility of purely reactive systems. Hybrid architectures permit reconfiguration of reactive control systems based on available world knowledge through their ability to reason over the underlying behavioral components. Dynamic control system reconfiguration based on deliberation (reasoning over world models) is an important addition to the overall competence of general purpose robots.

Building such a hybrid system, however, requires compromise from both ends of the robotic systems spectrum (section 1.3). Furthermore, the nature of the boundary between deliberation and reactive execution is not well understood at this time, leading to somewhat arbitrary architectural decisions.

6.2   BIOLOGICAL EVIDENCE IN SUPPORT OF HYBRID SYSTEMS

Psychological and neuroscientific models of behavior provide an existence proof for the success of an integrative strategy involving elements of deliberative reasoning and behavior-based control. Flexibility in our use of the models scientists in other fields have developed is important, however, since we, as roboticists, are concerned primarily with creating functioning autonomous agents that may have some behavioral overlap with their biological counterparts, but not necessarily with reproducing their control and execution strategies verbatim.

Just as many psychologists moved from behaviorism (Watson 1925; Skinner 1974) to cognitive psychology (Neisser 1976) as an acceptable description of human information processing, research in the use of hybrid systems has expanded to include many concepts forwarded by this school of thought. The experimental evidence is compelling. Shiffrin and Schneider (1977) have indicated the existence of two distinct modes of behavior: willed and automatic. Norman and Shallice (1986) have modeled the coexistence of two distinct systems concerned with controlling human behavior. One system models "automatic" behavior and is closely aligned with reactive systems. This system handles automatic action execution without awareness, starts without attention, and consists of multiple independent parallel activity threads (schemas). The second system controls "willed" behavior and provides an interface between deliberate conscious control and the automatic system. Figure 6.1 illustrates this model.

This research characterized the tasks requiring willed control in humans involving deliberate attentional resources:

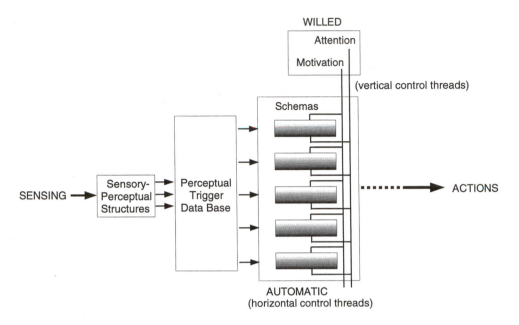

Figure 6.1
Model for integrated automatic and willed behavior (after Norman and Shallice 1986).

- planning or decision making
- troubleshooting
- novel or poorly learned actions
- dangerous or difficult actions
- overcoming habit or temptation

Other motor tasks are typically automatic and occur without the use of attention. Their modeling incorporates a contention scheduling mechanism for coordinating the multiple active motor schemas. Higher-level deliberative processes involving attention alter the threshold values for schemas (behaviors), dynamically changing the interplay between them. Psychological support for schema use in this strictly horizontal manner is well established (Schmidt 1975). The Norman-Shallice model incorporates aspects of both vertical and horizontal control threads. The horizontal control threads are used in a similar manner in the subsumption architecture (Brooks 1986). Deliberative influence is introduced when multiple horizontal behaviors are mediated by vertical threads that interconnect the various behaviors and allow for their dynamic modulation as a result of attentional resources, such as planning, troubleshooting, etc. Perceptual events trigger the schemas themselves but attentional processes modulate them. This provides a coherent psychological model for integrating multiple concurrent behaviors controlled by higher-level processing.

The Norman-Shallice model points out several connections between deliberate and automatic control:

- Automatic schemas are modulated by attention arising from deliberate control.
- Schemas (behavioral tasks) compete with each other.
- Schema selection is deliberate control's principal function. Vertical threads provide the selection mechanism.
- Neuropsychological experiments are consistent with this model.

The evidence supporting the existence of a distinct supervisory attentional system is considerable. The model lacks a mechanism by which the deliberative process is conducted; this is left for others to elucidate. Even if this theory ultimately fails to explain the basis for human psychological motor behavior and planning, the model may nonetheless prove useful in its own right as a basis for integrating deliberative and behavioral control systems in robots.

6.3 TRADITIONAL DELIBERATIVE PLANNERS

Deliberative planners are often aligned with the hierarchical control community within robotics. (Hierarchical control is also referred to as intelligent control; see section 1.3.1.) Hierarchical planning systems typically share a structured and clearly identifiable subdivision of functionality relegated to distinct program modules that communicate with each other in a predictable and predetermined manner. Numerous examples illustrate this deliberative/hierarchical planning strategy (e.g., Albus, McCain, and Lumia 1987; Saridis and Valvanis 1987; Meystel 1986; Keirsey et al. 1984; Ooka et al. 1985). A generalized model appears in figure 6.2.

A typical subdivision of functionality depends on both the spatial planning scope and temporal constraints. At a hierarchical planner's highest level, the most global and least specific plan is formulated. The time requirements for producing this plan are the least stringent. As one proceeds down the planning hierarchy, the scope becomes narrower, focusing on smaller regions of the world but requiring more rapid solutions. At the lowest levels, rapid real-time response is required, but the planner is concerned only with its immediate

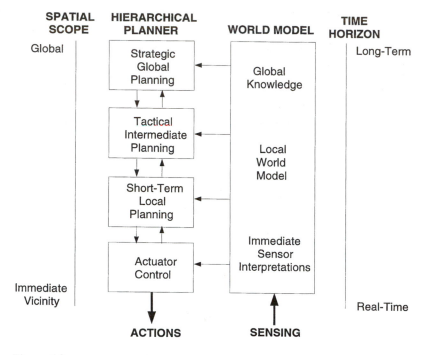

Figure 6.2
Deliberative/hierarchical planning.

surroundings and has lost sight of the "big picture." Meystel (1986) has developed a theory for hierarchical planning that emphasizes the significance of scope and invokes the concept of nested controllers.

Hierarchical planners rely heavily on world models, can readily integrate world knowledge, and have a broader perspective and scope. Behavior-based control systems, on the other hand, afford modular development, real-time robust performance within a changing world, and incremental growth, and are tightly coupled with arriving sensory data. Hybrid robotic architects believe that a union of the deliberative and behavior-based approaches can potentially yield the best of both worlds. If done poorly, however, it can yield the worst of both worlds. The central issue then becomes how to develop a unifying architectural methodology that will ensure a system capable of robust robotic plan execution yet take into account a high-level understanding of the nature of the world and a model of user intent.

6.4   DELIBERATION: TO PLAN OR NOT TO PLAN?

The integration of knowledge-based deliberation and reactive control requires the confrontation of many difficult problems. Each of these methods addresses different subsets of the complexities inherent in intelligent robotics. The hybrid system's architect contends that neither approach is entirely satisfactory in isolation but that both must be taken into account to produce an intelligent, robust, and flexible system.

The hierarchical approach is best suited for integrating world knowledge and user intent to arrive at a plan prior to its execution. Replanning with this method, however, at levels where sensory data is merged into world models is cumbersome at best. Deliberative planning without consideration for the difficult issues of plan execution can lead to restricted usage within very narrow problem domains (i.e., the ecological niche is extremely small and focused) and extremely brittle robotic systems. A robot must have the ability to respond rapidly and effectively to dynamic and unmodeled changes that occur within its world. If a purely deliberative system attempts to model and preplan for all eventualities, it risks becoming so bogged down that the planning process never terminates (the qualification problem) (see box 6.1). It is also unsafe for a robot to make gross assumptions about the world that do not reflect its dynamic nature.

Box 6.1

> The *qualification problem* is related to a never-ending "what if?" questioning stream. Qualifications to a plan's utility make it more and more restrictive and less general. There are just too many "what-ifs" (preconditions) to be able to enumerate them all in advance for any real-world domain. Thus since we cannot adequately qualify a plan's applicability, it may possibly fail when applied.

The reactive approach, on the other hand, is well situated to deal with the immediacy of sensory data but is less effective in integrating world knowledge. A clear-cut distinction can be seen in the hierarchical planner's heavy reliance on world models (either a priori or dynamically acquired) as compared to the avoidance in most reactive behavior-based systems of world representations entirely. When reactive behavior-based systems are considered in isolation, robustness is gained at the expense of some very important characteristics: flexibility and adaptability. The issues of action and perception are addressed, but cognition is ignored, often limiting these robots to mimicking low-level life forms. Hybrid system research assumes that representational knowledge *is* necessary to enhance and extend the behaviors of these machines into more meaningful problem domains. This includes the incorporation of memory and dynamic representations of the environment. Dynamic replanning must be affected not only in a reactive manner but also in the context of a more abstract plan, one representing the robot's goals and intents at a variety of planning levels. The research issues for these designers do not center on reactive versus preplanned deliberative control but rather on how to synthesize effectively a control regime that incorporates both methodologies.

The terms signifying each of the two major components of these hybrid architectures varies widely. Lyons (1992) uses planner and reactor. Malcolm and Smithers (1990) prefer cognitive and subcognitive systems, with the cognitive component performing high-level functions such as planning and the subcognitive portion controlling the robot's sensors and actuators. In this book we generally use deliberative and reactive to distinguish the two systems.

The central issue in differentiating the many approaches to hybrid architectures discussed in this chapter focuses on interface design: What is the appropriate boundary for the subdivision of functionality? How is coordination effectively carried out? This is one of the most interesting and pressing research areas in intelligent robotics today.

Lyons (1992) describes three different ways in which planning and reaction can be tied:

■ Hierarchical integration of planning and reaction: Deliberative planning and reactive execution are involved with different activities, time scales, and spatial scope. Hence a multilevel hierarchical system can be structured that integrates both activities (panel (A) in figure 6.3). Planning or reacting depends on the situation at hand. In many ways, this is closely aligned with the traditional deliberative approach with one fundamental distinction: the higher, deliberative level(s) are epistemologically distinct from the lower, reactive one(s), that is, the nature and type of knowledge and reasoning is distinct.

■ Planning to guide reaction: Another alternative model involves permitting planning to configure and set parameters for the reactive control system. Execution occurs solely under the reactive system's auspices, with planning occurring both prior to and concurrent with execution, in some cases projecting the outcome of continuously formulated plans and reconfiguring the reactive system as needed (panel (B) in figure 6.3).

■ Coupled planning-reacting: Planning and reacting are concurrent activities, each guiding the other (panel (C) in figure 6.3).

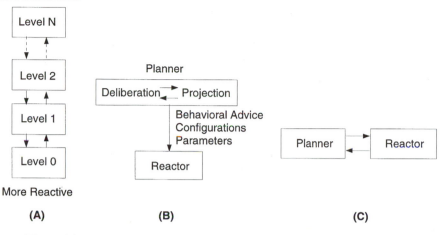

Figure 6.3
Typical deliberative/hierarchical planning strategies.

6.5 LAYERING

One outcome of a 1995 workshop on robot architectures (Hexmoor et al. 1995) was the observation that a multi-layered hybrid architecture comprising a top-layer planning system and a lower-level reactive system is emerging as the architectural design of choice (Hexmoor and Kortenkamp 1995). It was further observed that the interface or middle layer between the two components of such an architecture is the key function, linking rapid reaction and long-range planning.

Hybrid system designers look toward a synthetic, integrative approach that applies both of these paradigms (reaction and planning) to the issues of robot control, using each where most appropriate. After the decision has been made that both deliberative and reactive functionality are important for a particular application, the question arises as to how to effectively partition these functions. In general, two layers are needed at a minimum: one to represent deliberation and the other reactivity. Another common approach involves introducing an explicit third layer, concerned with coordinating the two components. Section 6.6 looks at specific instances of these hybridized architectures and gives examples of both. Indeed, in some cases, further resolution is added, producing even more layers. The bottom line, however, is that deliberation and reactivity need to be coordinated, and the architect decides where and how to implement this function.

6.6   REPRESENTATIVE HYBRID ARCHITECTURES

Four principal interface strategies are in evidence for the various hybrid architectural designs:

■ Selection: *Planning is viewed as configuration.* The planning component determines the behavioral composition and parameters used during execution. The planner may reconfigure them as necessary because of failures in the system.

■ Advising: *Planning is viewed as advice giving.* The planner suggests changes that the reactive control system may or may not use. This is consistent with the "plans as advice" view (Agre and Chapman 1990) in which plans offer courses of actions but the reactive agent determines whether each is advisable.

■ Adaptation: *Planning is viewed as adaptation.* The planner continuously alters the ongoing reactive component in light of changing conditions within the world and task requirements.

■ Postponing: *Planning is viewed as a least commitment process.* The planner defers making decisions on actions until as late as possible. This enables recent sensor data, by postponing reactive actions until absolutely necessary, to provide a more effective course of action than would be developed if an initial plan were generated at the beginning. Plans are elaborated only as necessary.

This section presents four major hybrid architectures, each of which typifies one of these strategies: AuRA for selection; Atlantis for advising; Planner-Reactor as adaptation; and PRS as postponement. A survey of several other hybrid architectures is then presented. Judging from the high level of activity, the hybrid approach is currently a particularly important research topic. Note especially the distinctions in how deliberation and reactivity are interfaced, as these are hallmark characteristics for each approach.

6.6.1   AuRA

Arkin (1986, 1987b) was among the first to advocate the use of hybrid deliberative (hierarchical) and reactive (schema-based) control systems within the Autonomous Robot Architecture (AuRA). Incorporating a conventional planner that could reason over a flexible and modular behavior-based control system, Arkin found that specific robotic configurations could be constructed that integrated behavioral, perceptual, and a priori environmental knowledge (1990b). Hybridization in this system arises from two distinct components: a deliberative hierarchical planner, based on traditional AI techniques, and a reactive controller, based on schema theory (Arbib 1992). Arkin's was the first robot navigational system to be presented in this integrative manner (1989d).

Figure 6.4 depicts the components of AuRA schematically. AuRA has two major planning and execution components: a hierarchical system consisting of a mission planner, spatial reasoner, and plan sequencer coupled with a reactive system, the schema controller. In the style of a traditional hierarchical planning system (Albus, McCain, and Lumia 1987; Meystel 1986; Saridis and Valvanis 1987), the highest level of AuRA is a mission planner concerned with establishing high-level goals for the robot and the constraints within which it must operate. In AuRA-based systems constructed to date, the mission planner has acted primarily as an interface to a human commander. The spatial reasoner, originally referred to as the navigator (Arkin 1987b), uses cartographic knowledge stored in long-term memory to construct a sequence of navigational path legs that the robot must execute to complete its mission. In the first implementation of AuRA, this was an A* planner operating over a meadow map (hybrid free space/vertex graph) representation (Arkin 1989c). The plan sequencer, referred to as the pilot in earlier work, translates each path leg the spatial reasoner generates into a set of motor behaviors for execution. In the original implementation, the plan sequencer was a rudimentary rule-based system. More recently it has been implemented as a finite state sequencer (Mackenzie, Cameron, and Arkin 1995). Finally, the collection of behaviors (schemas), specified and instantiated by the plan sequencer, is then sent to the robot for execution. At this point, deliberation ceases, and reactive execution begins.

The schema manager is responsible for controlling and monitoring the behavioral processes at run time. Each motor behavior (or schema) is associated with a perceptual schema capable of providing the stimulus required for that particular behavior. This action-oriented perception is the basis for this form of behavior-based navigation (Arkin 1990a). As described in section 4.4, each behavior generates a response vector in a manner analogous to the potential fields method. The schemas operate asynchronously, transmitting their results to a process (move-robot) that sums and normalizes these inputs and transmits them to the low-level control system for execution.

Within AuRA, a homeostatic control system (tested only in simulation to date) is interwoven with the motor and perceptual schemas (Arkin 1992c). Internal sensors, such as fuel level and temperature transducers, provide information over a broadcast network monitored by behaviors containing suitable receptors. These internal messages change the overall motor response's

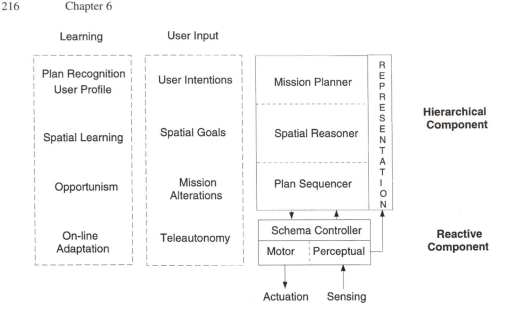

Figure 6.4
High-level AuRA schematic.

performance by altering the behaviors' and internal parameters' relative strengths in an effort to maintain balance and system equilibrium (homeostasis). Chapter 10 discusses homeostatic control further.

Once reactive execution begins, the deliberative component is not reactivated unless a failure is detected in the reactive execution of the mission. A typical failure is denoted by lack of progress, evidenced either by no motion or a time-out. At this point the hierarchical planner is reinvoked one stage at a time, from the bottom up, until the problem is resolved. First, the plan sequencer attempts to reroute the robot based on information obtained during navigation and stored in STM. Original implementations used sonar maps produced by the Elfes-Moravec algorithm for spatial world modeling (Elfes 1986). If for some reason this proves unsatisfactory (e.g., the route is completely blocked within this local context), the spatial reasoner is reinvoked and attempts to generate a new global route that bypasses the affected region entirely. If this still fails to be satisfactory, the mission planner is reinvoked, informing the operator of the difficulty and asking for reformulation or abandonment of the entire mission.

Modularity, flexibility, and generalizability as a result of hybridization constitute AuRA's principal strengths. The value of each aspect has been demonstrated both in simulation and on real robotic systems.

AuRA is highly modular by design. Components of the architecture can be replaced with others in a straightforward manner. This is particularly useful in research. Some examples include

- A specialized mission planner developed for an assembly task where boxes are pushed together into a specified arrangement. This planner was ported to a Denning mobile robot that competed in the 1993 American Association for Artificial Intelligence (AAAI) mobile robot competition. Stroulia (1994) further extended the planner to learn and reason over more general planning tasks.
- The original A* spatial reasoner has been replaced with Router (Goel et al. 1994), a multistrategy planner. Router models navigable routes as topological links between nodes instead of the metric meadow map representation used previously. The system was tested on a Denning mobile robot that successfully navigated from room to room and down corridors in an office and laboratory building.
- Perceptual schemas have been expanded to incorporate specialized action-oriented sensor fusion methods (Murphy and Arkin 1992) (section 7.5.7). Because of the recognition that in many cases multiple sensor sources are better than individual ones, specialized strategies were developed to fuse data within the context of action-oriented perception. Dempster-Shafer statistical methods provided the basis for evidential reasoning (Murphy 1991).
- The original rule-based plan sequencer has been replaced with a temporal sequencer (Arkin and MacKenzie 1994) based on FSAs (MacKenzie, Cameron, and Arkin 1995). The FSA is an expression of a plan, in which each state represents a specific combination of behaviors that accomplish one step of the task. Transitions are made from one state to another when significant perceptual events trigger them.

Another strength of AuRA is the flexibility it provides for introducing adaptation and learning methods. Chapter 8 will discuss these and other methods further. In early implementations of AuRA, learning arose only from STM of spatial information used for dynamic replanning. Since then, a variety of learning techniques have been introduced, including

- on-line adaptation of motor behaviors using a rule-based methodology (Clark, Arkin, and Ram 1992)
- case-based reasoning methods to provide discontinuous switching of behaviors based on the recognition of new situations (Ram et al. 1997)
- genetic algorithms that configure the initial control system parameters efficiently (Ram et al. 1994) and allow a robot to evolve toward its ecological niche in a given task environment

AuRA's generalizability to a wide range of problems is another strength. Various architectural components have been applied in a variety of domains, including

■ manufacturing environments (Arkin et al. 1989; Arkin and Murphy 1990).
■ three-dimensional navigation as found in aerial or undersea domains (Arkin 1992a).
■ indoor and outdoor navigation (Arkin 1987b).
■ robot competitions (Arkin et al. 1993; Balch et al. 1995).
■ vacuuming (MacKenzie and Balch 1993).
■ military scenarios (MacKenzie, Cameron, and Arkin 1995; Balch and Arkin 1995).
■ mobile manipulation (Cameron et al. 1993).
■ multirobot teams (Arkin 1992b; Balch and Arkin 1994).

AuRA's major strength results from the power of wedding two distinct AI paradigms: deliberation and reactivity. AuRA provides a framework for the conduct of a wide range of robotic research including deliberative planning, reactive control, homeostasis, action-oriented perception, and machine learning. It has been motivated but not constrained by biological studies, drawing insight wherever available as a guideline for system design.

AuRA's strengths lie in its modularity, which permits ready integration of new approaches to various architectural components; flexibility, as evidenced by the ease of introduction of various learning methodologies and novel behaviors; generalizability, demonstrated by its applicability to a wide range of domains, including robot competitions, among others; and most importantly, use of hybridization to exploit the strengths of both symbolic reasoning and reactive control.

6.6.2   Atlantis

At the Jet Propulsion Laboratory (JPL) Gat (1991a) developed a three-level hybrid system, Atlantis, that incorporates a deliberator that handles planning and world modeling, a sequencer that handles initiation and termination of low-level activities and addresses reative-system failures to complete the task, and a reactive controller charged with managing collections of primitive activities (figure 6.5). The architecture is both asynchronous and heterogeneous. None of the layers is in charge of the others, and activity is spread throughout the architecture.

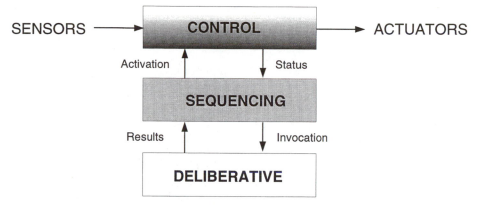

Figure 6.5
The Atlantis architecture.

Atlantis's control layer is implemented in ALFA (Gat 1991b), a LISP-based program language used to program reactive modules configured in networks connected via communication channels. ALFA is most closely related to Kaelbling's Rex (1987), a circuit-based language (section 3.2.4.2). This system was initially tested on Tooth (figure 6.6, panel (A)), a small precursor to the Mars microrovers used for NASA's Pathfinder program (Shirley and Matijevic 1995) (figure 6.6, panels (B) and (C)), and a Real World Interface (RWI) base for indoor navigational experiments.

The sequencing layer of Atlantis is modeled after Firby's RAPs (section 3.1.3). Conditional sequencing occurs upon the completion of various subtasks or the detection of failure. In particular, the notion of *cognizant failure* is introduced (Gat and Dorais 1994), refering to the robot's ability to recognize on its own when it has not or cannot complete its task. Monitor routines are added to the architecture to determine if things are not going as they should and then interrupt the system if cognizant failure occurs. Often these monitor routines are very task specific, such as checking alignment conditions when conducting wall following, but they can be more general, such as a time-out for the overall completion of a task.

Deliberation occurs at the sequencing layer's request (Gat 1992). The deliberator consists of traditional LISP-based AI planning algorithms specific to the task at hand. The planner's output is viewed only as advice to the sequencer layer: it is not necessarily followed or implemented verbatim.

(A)

(B)

Figure 6.6

(C)

Figure 6.6 *(continued)*
(A) Tooth, (B) Rocky 4, and (C) Sojourner.

Design in Atlantis proceeds from the bottom up: low-level activities capable of being executed within the reactive-controller level are first constructed. Suitable sequences of these primitive behaviors are then constructed for use within the sequencing level, followed by deliberative methods that assist in the decisions the sequencer makes.

Experiments have been performed on a large outdoor JPL Mars rover testbed called Robby (figure 6.7) (Gat 1992), which successfully undertook various complex navigational tasks in rough outdoor terrain. The primitive activities used in the reactive controller were based on Slack's NATs (section 3.3.2) and were guided by a strategic plan constructed by the deliberator. The sequencer was then able to abandon intermediate-level navigational goals if they became untenable as noted by advice from the deliberator.

Summarizing Atlantis's important features:

■ Atlantis is a three-layered architecture consisting of controller, sequencer, and deliberator.

■ Asynchronous, heterogeneous reactivity and deliberation are used.

Figure 6.7
Robby, a JPL Mars rover prototype.

■ The results of deliberation are viewed as advice, not decree.
■ Classical AI is merged effectively with behavior-based reactive control methods.
■ Cognizant failures provide an opportunity for plan restructuring.
■ The system has been exercised successfully on both indoor and outdoor robotic systems.

6.6.3 Planner-Reactor Architecture

Lyons and Hendriks (1992, 1995) forward the Planner-Reactor architecture as another means for integrating planning and reactivity. Their philosophy advocates the use of a planner as a mechanism to *continuously* modify an executing reactive control system. Figure 6.8 depicts this approach. The planner is in essence an execution monitor that adapts the underlying behavioral control system in light of the changing environment and the agent's underlying goals.

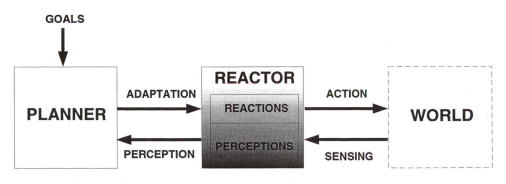

Figure 6.8
Planner-Reactor architecture.

The *RS* model, discussed in section 3.2.4.1, is used both to model and to implement the reactor component. It is assumed that a suboptimal reactor may be present at any time and that the planner's goal is to improve the performance of the reactor at all times. Loosely speaking, this is a form of *anytime planning,* where a significantly suboptimal solution may be initially chosen then improved on during execution.

Anytime planners provide approximate answers in a time-critical manner such that:

- At any point a plan is available for execution, and
- The quality of the available plan increases over time (cf. Dean and Wellman 1991).

Situations provide the framework for structuring sets of reactions. They can be hierarchically defined and often denote the state the robotic agent is currently in regarding a task. For the primary task studied in Lyons and Hendriks' (1993) work, parts assembly, a situational hierarchy can be structured as depicted in figure 6.9. Here, the situation where the robot needs to build kits consists of various constituent situations, each of which may in turn consist of further situational specifications. This hierarchy is not unlike the task/subtask hierarchies developed by traditional AI planning systems such as Noah (Sacerdoti 1975), but differs in that the situations specify behavioral structures for use in the reactor and not specific robotic commands.

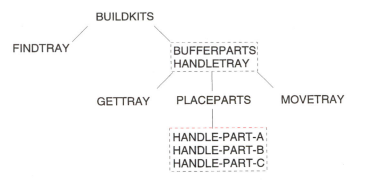

Figure 6.9
Partially expanded situations for kitting assembly tasks. (Dotted boxes denote concurrent situations.)

The situations themselves are also encoded using *RS* formalisms. Planning is viewed as a form of adaptation (Lyons and Hendriks 1994). A reactor executes under a set of operating assumptions. If any assumptions are violated regarding the utility of a particular reactor configuration, the planner modifies the reactor's control system to remove the assumption violation. If the violation occurs as a result of environmental changes, the strategy is referred to as *forced assumption relaxation*. Planner-directed relaxation of assumptions can also occur because of a change in high-level goals (e.g., from user input). The assumptions used within the Planner-Reactor architecture are generally highly domain specific (i.e., strong knowledge).

- *Strong Knowledge* involves information peculiar to a particular problem domain and has little or no general utility.
- *Weak Knowledge* is information that can be used across many domains and has broad utility.

For parts assembly by a robot in a manufacturing work cell, some of these assumptions within the Planner-Reactor architecture include

- Part quality: Each part meets the necessary criteria or specifications for use in the assembly.
- Non-substitutability of parts: Each part has only one type.
- No parts motion: Parts do not move once delivered into the work space.

- No downstream disturbance: Subsequent manufacturing processes are always ready to receive the assembled parts.
- Filled tray: All the parts are delivered to the work cell.
- Tray disturbance: The tray is not moved after arrival.
- Parts homogeneity: Parts arrival is evenly distributed.

Clearly, in the real world, violations of these assumptions are not only possible but likely. Each assumption has a monitor associated with it during run time to ensure its validity. If, for whatever reason, an assumption violation is detected, the planner relaxes the assumption and adapts the control system to deal with the new situation. These violations often occur because of environmental factors beyond the robot's control. The planner can reinstate assumptions later, once the original situation has been restored, along with a reactor reconfiguration and reinstantiation of a suitable assumption monitor. Figure 6.10 depicts the flow of control in this architecture. This process is recursive, as an adapted reactor can be further adapted by the planner.

A variation of the Planner-Reactor architecture has been developed for planning and controlling a multifingered robotic hand (Murphy, Lyons, and Hendriks 1993). The deliberative planner is referred to as the grasp advisor and has an associated grasp reactor. Grasp selection is based (ideally) on the task requirements, the feasibility of acquiring the part using the proposed grasp, and the stability afforded the part once grasped in that manner. The initial implementation, however, is concerned only with the stability criterion. Typical behavioral components for a reactive grasping system include find-objects, grasp-objects, and avoid-obstacles, which are all self-explanatory in function. The deliberative grasp advisor, using information obtained from environmental knowledge such as part information obtained through vision, communicates global constraints to the reactor, which then biases the actual grasp strategy used for initial contact with the part. This example task does not currently use assumptions within the grasp advisor in the same way that the kitting assembly system does but nonetheless exemplifies how deliberation and reactivity can be effectively integrated.

Summarizing, the key features of the Planner-Reactor methodology are as follows:

- Deliberation and reactivity are integrated through asynchronous interaction of a planner and a concurrent reactive control system.
- Planning is viewed as a form of reactor adaptation.
- Adaptation is an on-line process rather than an off-line deliberation.
- Planning is used to remove errors in performance when they occur.

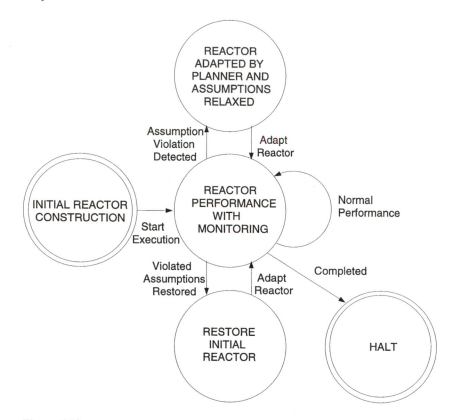

Figure 6.10
FSA representing flow of control for assumption-based planning.

■ The reactor undergoes situationally dependent on-line performance improvement.

■ The basic techniques, tested in both assembly work cell tasks and grasp planning for a robotic hand, are believed applicable to a broad range of applications, including mobile robot navigation and emergency response planning.

6.6.4   The Procedural Reasoning System

The Procedural Reasoning System, (PRS) (Georgeff and Lansky 1987), provides an alternative strategy for looking at the integration of reactivity and deliberation. Reactivity in this system refers to the postponement of the elaboration of plans until it is necessary, a type of least-commitment strategy.

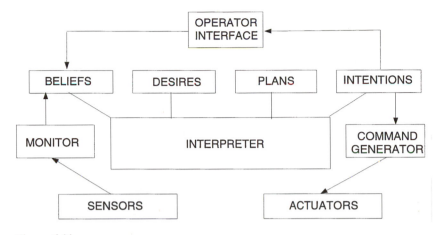

Figure 6.11
The Procedural reasoning system (PRS).

A *least-commitment strategy* defers making a decision until it is absolutely necessary to do so. The information necessary to make a correct decision is assumed to become available late in the process, thus reducing the need for backtracking.

In PRS, plans are the primary mode of expressing action, but these plans are continuously determined in reaction to the current situation. Previously formulated plans undergoing execution can be interrupted and abandoned at any time. Representations of the robot's beliefs, desires, and intentions are all used to formulate a plan. The plan, however, represents the robot's desired behaviors instead of the traditional AI planner's output of goal states to be achieved. Figure 6.11 depicts the overall PRS architecture. The interpreter drives system execution, carrying out whatever plan is currently deemed suitable. As new beliefs, desires, or intentions arise, the plan may change, with the interpreter handling the plan switching. A symbolic plan always drives the system, however, so it is not reactive in the normal sense of tight sensorimotor pair execution, but it is reactive in the sense that perceived changing environmental conditions permit the robotic agent to alter its plans on the fly.

The system was tested and developed on SRI's robot Flakey for use in office navigation tasks (figure 6.12). UM-PRS (Lee et al. 1994) is a later variation

Figure 6.12
Flakey. (Photograph courtesy of Kurt Konolige and SRI International.)

of this PRS system that has been applied to the Defense Advanced Research Project Agency Unmanned Ground Vehicle (DARPA UGV) Demo II project for outdoor off-road military scouting missions using HMMWVs. We revisit this system as a piece of the DARPA UGV Demo II program in chapter 9.

6.6.5   Other Hybrid Architectures

We now survey other efforts in the development of hybrid deliberative/reactive architectures. The solutions being explored are diverse, especially in regard to where deliberation should end and reactivity begin and whether planning should be viewed as selection, advising, adaptation, postponement, or something else.

■ SSS (Connell 1992): SSS, developed at the IBM T.J. Watson Research Center, is a hybrid architecture that descended directly from the subsumption architecture (section 4.3). The letters in SSS stand for each of its three layers: servo, subsumption, and symbolic. The interface between the servo layer and the symbolic is not particularly new: together they provide behavioral modularity and flexibility to the underlying servomotor controllers by providing parameters and set points for the servo loops in the same manner as subsumption. SSS's novelty lies in its use of world model representations, which are viewed as a convenience, but not a necessity, for certain tasks. The symbolic (deliberative) layer provides the ability to selectively turn behaviors on or off as well as provide parameters for those that require them. Once the behaviors are configured, they continue to execute without any intervention of the symbolic level. Restating, the symbolic level predetermines the behavioral configuration used during execution. The system was tested on a small mobile robot, TJ (figure 6.13), capable of moving at an average speed of a little under three feet per second in an indoor office environment. The symbolic level handles where-to-go-next decisions (strategic), whereas the subsumption level handles where-to-go-now choices (tactical). A coarse geometric map of the world is present at the strategic level, and route planning is conducted within this representation. Piecewise segmentation of the route in a manner similar to that of AuRA provides the behavioral configuration for each leg of the overall journey.

Also worth mentioning is an earlier system (Soldo 1990), considerably less developed, that advocates the use of behavioral experts coordinated by an AI planner using a world map. This system provides a framework for integrating deliberative planning and reactive control by allowing the planner to choose appropriate behaviors along the same lines as both SSS and AuRA.

Figure 6.13
TJ. (Photograph courtesy of Jon Connell.)

■ Multi-Valued Logic (Saffiotti et al. 1995): Researchers at SRI International, drawing heavily on many earlier ideas and synthesizing them formally, have developed a novel hybrid architecture that uses a multi-valued logic (MVL) representation for behaviors (motor schemas) as the reactive component coupled with gradient fields as goals in the manner of Payton's work (section 5.2.2). Multi-valued logic provides the ability to have a variable planner-controller interface that is strongly context dependent. In other words, the decision when to plan and when to react reflects the nature of the environment. Further, behavioral plans are included that draw inspiration from PRS-style deliberation. These provide a form of preplanned behavior that can be invoked and elaborated as necessary. This system has been successfully tested on the robot Flakey (figure 6.12) in various indoor office environments.

■ SOMASS Hybrid Assembly System (Malcolm and Smithers 1990): The SO-MASS system is an assembly system consisting of two parts: the cognitive (deliberative) and the subcognitive (reactive) components. The cognitive part consists of a symbolic planner designed to be as ignorant as possible—a virtue according to the system designers. The intent is to avoid clogging the reasoner with unnecessary knowledge. The planner itself is hierarchical in structure, concerned first with finding a suitable ordering of parts to produce the required assembly, then subsequently with determining gravitational stability consistent with the ordering, producing suitable grasps to acquire the part, insuring that assembly tolerances for handling errors are met, and translating the plan into executable robot code consisting of parameterized behavioral modules suitable for execution. The subcognitive component is concerned with the actual execution of the behaviors after the plan is downloaded to the robot. In this system, implemented on a working robotic arm, there is a clear-cut division between deliberation and planning but a limited ability to exchange information between them.

■ Agent Architecture (Hayes-Roth et al. 1993): Plans in this architecture are considered descriptions of intended courses of behavior. Two levels are specified within the agent architecture: the physical level, concerned with perception and action within the environment, and the cognitive level, for higher-level reasoning needs such as problem-solving and planning. According to the designers, finer resolution could yield more than two levels, but currently this number seems adequate. A plan is communicated from the cognitive level to the physical level, with feedback from the execution of the plan returned to the cognitive level. The designers claim that reactive and deliberative (planning) behaviors can coexist within each level, so the standard partitioning of reactivity and deliberation does not pertain. As examples, situation assessment can occur within the cognitive level, and limited path planning can occur within the physical level. The difference between levels is essentially epistemological and temporal, based on the following distinctions:

• Whether symbolic reasoning (cognitive) versus metric (physical) is employed.

• Time horizons for history and reaction are both significantly shorter for the physical level compared to the cognitive one.

• Greater abstraction is present at the cognitive level.

The system has been tested on mobile robots for both surveillance and delivery tasks.

■ Theo-Agent (Mitchell 1990): "Reacts when it can, plans when it must" is the motto for Theo-Agent. This hybrid system, developed at Carnegie-Mellon University, focuses predominantly on learning: in particular, learning how to become more reactive, more correct in its actions, and more perceptive about the world's features relevant to its performance. Stimulus-response (behavioral) rule selection and execution are the basis for reactive action, using an arbitration mechanism to choose the most appropriate rule. If no rules apply, then and only then is the planner invoked to determine a suitable course of action. As a result of the planning process, a new stimulus-response rule is added to the existing rule set. This new rule can be used again later should the same or similar situation arise, this time without the need for planning. Theo-Agent was tested on a Hero 2000 mobile robot given the task of locating garbage cans. A stimulus-response reaction took on the order of 10 milliseconds, whereas the planner required several minutes. Hence if the robot begins with few or no rules, its reaction time decreases from initially several minutes to under a second (about two orders of magnitude) as it experiences more and more of the world.

■ Generic Robot Architecture (Noreils and Chatila 1995): This hybrid architecture, developed in France, consists of three levels that bridge the spectrum of planning to reactivity:

• Planning level: Generates sequences of tasks to achieve the robot's high-level goals using a STRIPS-like planning system (Nilsson 1980).

• Control system level: Translates the plan into a set of tasks and configures the functional level prior to execution.

• Functional level: Corresponds to a set of functional modules (servo processes analogous to behaviors) concerned with reactive execution. Implemented behaviors include obstacle avoidance, wall following, and visual tracking.

This system is similar in structure to several of the selection style architectures already encountered in this chapter. A significant contribution of this work lies in the development of a task description language that provides a formal method for designing and interfacing these modules. Special attention has also been paid to diagnostic and error recovery procedures. The system has been tested on the Hilare series of robots, using vision for tracking tasks.

■ Dynamical Systems Approach (Schöner and Dose 1992): This approach has been significantly influenced by biological systems research as a basis for providing an integrative hybrid approach for reacting and planning. Suitable vector fields, designed using potential field methods (section 3.3.2), serve as the basis for planning and provide a clean bridge to behavior-based reactive execution. The deliberative planner operates within the reactive controller's representational space, dealing with the underlying controller's mathematics and dynamics rather than reasoning symbolically. Planning consists of selecting and providing parameters for each of the associated behavioral fields and determining their relative strength for summation purposes in light of the task's constraints. This work has been demonstrated in simulation only to date, but it provides an interesting way of rethinking the representational space in which high-level deliberative planning can operate.

■ Supervenience Architecture (Spector 1992): The supervenience architecture provides an environment for integrating reaction and deliberation based on abstraction, in particular the "distance from the world" (supervenience) that the abstracted concept represents. Although the ramifications of this work are often more concerned with philosophy than robotics, a multilevel implementation of the architecture referred to as the abstraction-partitioned evaluator (APE) has been implemented. It consists of multiple levels ranging from the perceptual/manual (lowest level), to spatial, temporal, causal, and finally conventional (highest level), connected in a strict hierarchy. To test these ideas, a simulated homebot capable of actions such as grab, move-object, move-right, rotate, and the like has been used. The main premise is that reactivity and deliberation are differentiated primarily by their levels of abstraction and how far they are removed from the real world. Supervenience provides an integrated formalism for describing these many levels of abstraction. As such, it somewhat blurs the distinctions that other hybrid architectures make and thus leans towards a more traditional hierarchical design (e.g., Albus 1991, Meystel 1986).

■ Teleoreactive Agent Architecture (Benson and Nilsson 1995): This hybrid deliberative/reactive architecture is based on the construction of a plan in the form of a set of teleoreactive (TR) operators (section 3.3.1) which an arbitrator then selects for reactive execution. The deliberative component involves hierarchical planning, yielding a tree-like structure that consists of TR programs. The TR formalism provides the unifying representation for both reasoning and reacting. The system has been tested in a simulated botworld environment.

■ Reactive Deliberation (Sahota 1993): The reactive deliberation architecture consists of two distinct layers: the deliberator and the reactive executor. The executor consists of action schemas operating at a level similar to that of RAPs (section 3.1.3). The deliberator enables a single action schema at a time and gives it parameters. Deliberation in this architecture refers not to higher-level abstract reasoning but rather to the selection of one of the many potential behaviors currently appropriate for execution in the given situation consistent with the agent's goals. In many respects this is merely an elaborated version of an action-selection mechanism, but it provides us with another way to think about the interface between planning and reactivity. This system has been tested using small robots for playing tabletop soccer. The behaviors for this domain consist of activities such as shoot, defend-red-line, clear, go-to-home-line, and so on.

■ Integrated Path Planning and Dynamic Steering Control (Krogh and Thorpe 1986): In early work demonstrated in simulation, a strategy for using path planning methods using relaxation over a grid-based world model was coupled with a potential fields–based steering controller. The path planner generated subgoals referred to as critical points for the steering controller. Potential fields methods (Krogh 1984), modified to provide real-time feedback similar to those used in AuRA, provided the local navigational capabilities for achieving the series of subgoals the path planner established. Though not really a behavior-based model, this early example provides a clear integration between path planning and reactive control.

■ UUVs: Hybrid architectures have been applied to undersea navigational tasks by several researchers. The rational behavioral model (Byrnes et al. 1996), a three-layer architecture consisting of execution, tactical, and strategic layers, reasons over behaviors at different levels. Although cast in a more hierarchical framework (cf. Saridis 1983), it uses primitive behaviors as the primary object for planning. Another system (Bonasso 1991) uses Gapps/Rex (section 3.2.4.2) as the underlying reactive control methodology and subsumption competences (behaviors) as the primary operators. This is an example more of hybridizing two different reactive strategies than of deliberation and reactivity. The target vehicle for both architectures is an undersea robot.

6.7   CHAPTER SUMMARY

■ Both deliberative planning systems and purely reactive control systems have limitations when each is considered in isolation.

■ Deliberative planning systems provide an entry point for the use of traditional AI methods and symbolic representational knowledge in a reactive robotic architecture.

■ The interface between deliberation and reactivity is poorly understood and serves as the focus of research in this area.

■ Strong evidence exists that hybrid deliberative and behavior-based systems are found in biology, implying that they are compatible, symbiotic, and potentially suitable for use in robotic control.

■ Hybrid models include hierarchical integration, planning to guide reaction, and coupled planning and reacting.

■ Another important design issue concerns the number of layers present within the overall architecture, with two or three currently being the most common.

■ AuRA is an early hybrid deliberative/reactive system using motor schemas and a traditional AI spatial planner. The planner configures the reactive control system prior to execution and reconfigures it in the event of task failure.

■ Atlantis is a three-layer hybrid architecture based on RAPs and NATs. It introduced the concept of cognizant failure in which a robot becomes aware of its inability to complete a task. Plans are viewed as advice rather than commands or instructions in this system.

■ The Planner-Reactor architecture consists of two major components. Planning is viewed as continuous adaptation of the reactive component. The *RS* model provides the underpinnings of all the architecture's components. Situations provide the context for sets of reactive actions.

■ PRS uses a least-commitment strategy to delay the elaboration of plans for execution until necessary. Although not strictly behavior based, it does react to changes in the environment detected via sensing and develops plans consistent with the robot's current observations, beliefs, desires, and intentions.

■ Selection (AuRA), advising (Atlantis), adaptation (Planner-Reactor), and postponing (PRS) are four major interface strategies frequently used in various hybrid architectures.

■ Many other hybrid architectures have also been developed along similar lines: SSS, MVL, agent architecture, Theo-Agent, Supervenience, and teleo-reactive agent architecture among others.

Chapter 7
Perceptual Basis for Behavior-Based Control

We don't see things as they are, we see them as we are.

—Anais Nin

It would be as useless to perceive how things "actually look" as it would be to watch the random dots on untuned television screens.

—Marvin Minsky

We have to remember that what we observe is not nature in itself but nature exposed to our method of questioning.

—Werner Karl Heisenberg

Chapter Objectives

1. To understand the intimate relationship between motor behavior and perception.
2. To appreciate how biology can inform the robotic designer regarding principles of perception.
3. To recognize the utility of modular perceptual strategies.
4. To explore the role of expectations, focus of attention, perceptual sequencing, and sensor fusion within behavior-based perception.
5. To see several representative examples of perceptual design for this class of robotic systems.

7.1   A BREAK FROM TRADITION

Without a doubt, a robot's ability to interpret information about its immediate surroundings is crucial to the successful achievement of its behavioral goals. To react to external events, it is necessary to perceive them. The real world is often quite hostile to robotic systems. Things move and change without warning, at best only partial knowledge of the world is available, and any a priori information available may be incorrect, inaccurate, or obsolete.

Machine perception research, and in particular computer vision, has a long and rich tradition, with a great part of it dissociated from the issues of real-time control of a robotic system. This work has focused on taking input sensor readings and producing a meaningful and coherent symbolic and/or geometric interpretation of the world. The top panel of figure 7.1 represents this viewpoint. Much of this research has ignored the fact that perceptual needs are predicated upon the consuming agent's motivational and behavioral requirements.

Certainly scapegoats can be found for the lack of progress in producing real-time robotic perception under this paradigm: Computer architectures were too primitive, or neuroscientists have not provided an adequate understanding of human vision. Perhaps, however, the means were not at fault, but rather the desired ends. The traditional approach has significant problems:

■ Perception considered in isolation: Is it wise to consider the perceiver as a disembodied process? This is perhaps similar to studying a living creature by chopping it up and handing out the pieces to different scientists. Perception is better considered as a holistic, synergistic process deeply intertwined with the complete agent's cognitive and locomotion systems.

■ Perception as king: There has been some elitism regarding much of the research in perceptual processing, computer vision in particular. Unquestionably, vision is a hard problem. Nonetheless perceptual activities need to be viewed as only one of the many requisite needs for a functioning intelligent agent. Vision researchers can benefit greatly by considering these other system components as partners, as opposed to servants.

■ The universal reconstruction: Much perceptual research has focused on creating three-dimensional world models. These models are often built without regard for the robot's needs. A deeper question is whether these reconstructive models are really needed at all.

Roboticists (Brooks 1991b) and psychologists (Neisser 1993) alike lament the pitfalls associated with the traditional approach to machine vision. Over-

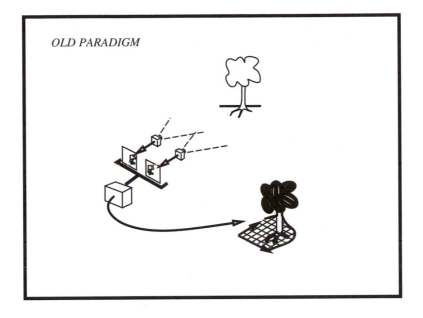

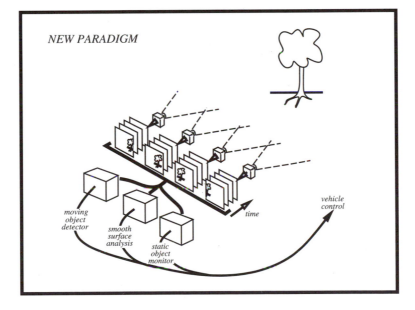

Figure 7.1
Approaches to perception. (Figure courtesy of Bob Bolles).

coming these difficulties requires a shift toward a new (or rather rediscovered) paradigm: viewing perception as a partner process with action. More accurately, a duality exists: The needs of motor control provide context for perceptual processing, whereas perceptual processing is simplified through the constraints of motor action. In either case, action and perception are inseparable.

Recently, in developments paralleling the advent of behavior-based robotic systems, new approaches have emerged that take this interplay into account. These methods are guided by the adage:

Perception without the context of action is meaningless.

The reflections of the new perceptual paradigm include:

- *Action-oriented perception:* An agent's perceptual processing is tuned to meet its motor activities' needs.
- *Expectation-based perception:* Knowledge of the world can constrain the interpretation of what is present in the world.
- *Focus-of-attention methods:* Knowledge can constrain where things may appear within the world.
- *Active perception:* The agent can use motor control to enhance perceptual processing by positioning sensors in more opportune vantage points.
- *Perceptual classes:* These partition the world into various categories of potential interaction.

The bottom panel of figure 7.1 captures some aspects of this new approach. Perception now produces motor control outputs, not representations. Multiple parallel processes that fit the robot's different behavioral needs are used. Highly specialized perceptual algorithms extract the necessary information and no more: Perception is thus conducted on a need-to-know basis.

To further advance this position, complexity analysis of the general task of visual search has provided illuminating results. Bottom-up visual search where matching is entirely data driven has been shown to be NP-complete and thus computationally intractable, whereas task-directed visual search has linear-time complexity (Tsotsos 1989). This tractability results from optimizing the available resources dedicated to perceptual processing (Tsotsos 1990). Attentional mechanisms that result from exploitation of the knowledge of the specific task provide just such constraints. The significance of these results for behavior-based robotic systems cannot be underestimated:

"Any behaviorist approach to vision or robotics must deal with the inherent computational complexity of the perception problem: otherwise the claim that those approaches scale up to human-like behavior is easily refuted." (Tsotsos 1992, p. 140)

The net outcome is that a primary purpose of perceptual algorithms is to support particular behavioral needs. In earlier chapters, we have seen that behaviors and their attendant perceptual processes can be executed in parallel. In reactive control, sensor information is not fused into a single global representation over which other planning processes then reason. This is in marked contrast to more traditional hierarchical views of robotic control which assume that perception's purpose is to construct a global world model (Barbera et al. 1984). The inherent parallelism and more targeted processing of behavior-based robotics permits much more efficient sensor processing.

To emphasize further the importance of perception itself, we revisit the symbol grounding problem in AI (chapter 1). Perception provides perhaps the only opportunity for us to provide physical grounding for the objects within an agent's world. The agent's interaction with these objects completes the grounding process by providing meaning through its resulting actions.

7.2   WHAT DOES BIOLOGY SAY?

A wide range of disciplines within the biological sciences have addressed the issues of perception as related to behavior. For roboticists, significant insights can be gleaned from these studies. This section provides an overview of a few important results from research in perception, neuroscience, psychology, and ethology of particular relevance to our study of behavior-based robotic systems.

7.2.1   The Nature of Perceptual Stimuli

To begin with, it is useful to distinguish between the different ways of categorizing perceptual stimuli. One such distinction can be based upon the origin of the received stimuli. *Proprioception* refers to perception associated with stimuli arising from within the agent. This includes information such as tendon or muscle tension, from which limb position or the number of times a particular action has been repeated (such as a leg movement) might be computed. *Exteroception* refers to perception associated with external stimuli. Here the environment transmits information to the agent via vision, audition, or some other sensor modality. The most common industrial robotic arms that compute their end effector positions through inverse kinematics rely on proprioceptive information. If, however, a vision system is coupled to the robot, exteroceptive data can provide environmental feedback as to where within the world the robot needs to move. Clearly, reactive robots tightly coupled to the environment through sensorimotor behaviors rely heavily on exteroceptive perception. Nonetheless, proprioceptive control has been widely observed by biologists in animals' generation of navigational trajectories. One of many such examples occurs in insects such as millipedes (Burger and Mittelstaedt 1972) and in desert spiders (Mittelstaedt 1985), where homing behavior is based upon proprioceptive sensations and is generated from the "sum of the momentary peripheral afferent inputs" (Burger and Mittelstaedt 1972). In other words, the distances traveled by the insects and spiders are believed to be stored in some manner, then used later by the organisms to return to their homesites. This process, referred to as *path integration,* relies entirely on proprioceptive inputs. The sensory data, generated by an accumulation of the animal's past movements and used to orient the animal within the world, is referred to as *ideothetic* information (Mittelstaedt 1983). In contrast, orientation information generated by landmarks, sun position, or other external cues is referred to as *allothetic* information. Allothetic information supports closed-loop control based on continuous feedback from an external source, whereas ideothetic information provides only open-loop control and is thus subject to greater error due to the inevitable noise during locomotion.

■ A *closed-loop control system* uses feedback from the results of its output actions to compute the deviation between what it was commanded to do and what it actually accomplished. This feedback is used as one of the inputs to the controller.
■ An *open-loop control system* has no means to evaluate the difference between the commanded action and the actual result, that is, no feedback is available.

In animal navigation, it is believed that both allothetic and ideothetic information are in use and integrative mechanisms are provided to reconcile the inevitable differences between them smoothly. We will study the issues concerning the combination of multiple, potentially conflicting data sources in section 7.5.7.

7.2.2   Neuroscientific Evidence

Now that we have categorized the types of stimuli that give rise to perception, we can briefly look at some of the neuroscientfic studies that address how this information is processed. Unfortunately, we do not know as much as we would like about the actual processing of perceptual information within the brain. Nonetheless, several relevant observations derived from neuroscience may be helpful in our understanding of perceptual processing's role in behavior.

Individual sensor modalities have spatially separated regions within the brain. Sight, hearing, and touch all have distinct processing regions. Even within a specific sensor type, spatial segregation is present: "Perhaps the most striking finding is that there is no single visual area in the brain. Different areas of the brain specialize in different aspects of vision such as the detection of pattern, color, movement, and intensity . . . " (McFarland 1981, p. 593). This observation holds not only for the human brain but that of lower animals as well. For example, a distinct neural region exists for looming detection in frogs associated with predator avoidance (Cervantes-Perez 1995). Neural structures associated with prey selection for these animals have also been observed (Fite 1976).

In the human and primate brain, visual processing is channeled into two distinct vision streams (Nelson 1995): the object vision stream, concerned with recognition of objects and foreground-background separation, and the spatial vision stream, which provides positional information useful for locomotion. The initial evidence for these "what" and "where" visual systems came from lesion studies conducted on primates (Mishkin, Ungergleider, and Macko 1983) indicating that the object stream is localized to the temporal area of the cortex, whereas the parietal regions are associated with spatial vision.

Further specialization occurs within the cortex itself. Orientation sensitivity to a particular stimulus occurs throughout layers of the visual cortex. A neuron at a particular level is sensitive to a stimulus at a preferred orientation, as has been observed in cats and macaque monkeys (Lund, Wu, and Levitt 1995).

Echolocation, analogous to sonar sensing in robots, also has specialized neural regions associated with it. In particular, the auditory cortex of the mustached bat is dedicated to this type of processing but has additional parcellation within itself (Suga and Kanwal 1995). The subdivisions are associated with varying ranges to targets, each of which likely has a differing behavioral response associated with it. Further analysis has revealed different specialized regions associated with target size and velocity.

One final observation that we mention is the space-preserving nature of the connections between the brain and the sensing system itself. These mappings are prevalent and are exemplified by the retinotopic maps projecting the eyes' output through the lateral geniculate nucleus onto the visual cortex; somatotopic maps projecting the peripheral inputs generated by touch onto its associated cortical regions; and tonotopic maps found preserving spatial relations produced by audition. Sensory information impinges upon the brain in a manner similar to its external source.

7.2.3   Psychological Insights

> The observer, when he seems to himself to be observing a stone, is really, if physics is to be believed, observing the effects of the stone upon himself.
> —Bertrand Russell

Finally, taking a psychological perspective, we can obtain additional insight. In particular we draw heavily upon the theories of J. J. Gibson and Ulric Neisser regarding perception's role in generating behavior.

7.2.3.1   Affordances

A relevant and important concept lies in the meaning of objects in relation to an organism's motor intents, a concept Gibson (1979) first introduced as *affordances*. As defined by Gardner (1985, p. 310), "Affordances are the potentialities for action inherent in an object or scene—the activities that can take place when an organism of a certain sort encounters an entity of a certain sort." The Gibsonian concept of affordances formulates perceptual entities not as semantic abstractions but rather by what opportunities the environment affords. The relationship between an agent and its environment afforded by a potential action is termed an affordance. All information needed for the agent to act resides within the environment, and mental representations are not used to codify perception. A chair can be perceived differently at different times, as something useful to sit in, as something blocking the way, or as something to throw if attacked. The way the environment is perceived depends on what we intend to do, not on some arbitrary semantic labeling (e.g., chair). A chair need not be explicitly recognized as a chair if it is serving only as a barrier to motion. Under those circumstances, it need be recognized only as an obstacle. If tired, it need be recognized only as a place to rest. From a robot designer's perspective this translates into designing algorithms that detect things that impede motion, afford rest or protection or other capabilities, but not in to designing algorithms that do semantic labeling and categorization.

The following steps characterize affordance research (Adolph, Gibson, and Eppler 1990):

1. Describe the fit between the agent and its environment.
2. Determine the agent-environment relationships regarding both the optimal performance of the action and the transitions between actions.
3. Analyze the correspondence between the actual and perceived agent-environment fit.
4. Determine the perceptual information required to specify the affordance.
5. Evaluate how to maintain and adapt action as necessary.

These guidelines, developed for psychologists, can also be of benefit in the design of perceptual algorithms to support behavior-based robotic systems. Many of the more radical camp that strictly maintain Gibson's views have lately fallen on hard times within the mainstream psychological community, but that in no way diminishes the potential value of his ecological stance on agent-environment interactions as a basis for robot perceptual algorithm generation (Pahlavan, Uhlin and Ekhlundh 1993; Blake 1993; Ballard and Brown 1993; Arkin 1990a). We, as roboticists, will use the term affordance to denote a perceptual strategy used to interact with the world, satisfying the need of some specific motor action.

7.2.3.2   A Modified Action-Perception Cycle

While I am not sure that access to movement-produced information and affordances would be sufficient to produce perceptual awareness in a machine, it is a necessary condition . . . (Neisser 1993, p. 29)

Neisser (1989) modifies the Gibsonian stance somewhat to permit Gibson's ecological perspective to account for the spatial vision stream (for locomotion) discussed earlier in this section, while forwarding a cognitive explanation for the object vision stream (for recognition). This approach acknowledges recent neurophysiological findings and presents a two-pronged explanation of vision reasonably consistent with the approaches used in some of the hybrid robotic architectures we encountered in chapter 6. Other robotics researchers have recognized these parallel pathways and used them to construct separate yet coordinated vision systems for determining what an object is apart from where it is located (Kelly and Levine 1995). If indeed there are multiple parallel perceptual systems in the brain as the evidence indicates, it is certainly possible that different methods exist as well of processing that information for action.

Neisser's perspective arises from the school of cognitive psychology (chapter 2) and leads us to the notion of *action-oriented perception*. This school

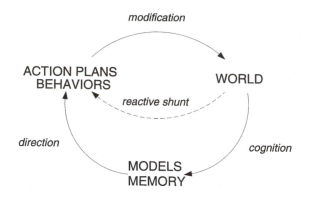

Figure 7.2
Modified action-perception cycle.

of thought acknowledges the fact that perception and action are intimately intertwined. Neisser (1976) elaborates the action-perception cycle as the basis by which humans interact with their environment (figure 7.2 presents a modified version). In this cycle, perceptions arising from interaction with the world modify the organism's internal expectations and behaviors, which in turn result in new exploratory activities that result in new perceptions. Anticipatory schemas play a crucial role in providing both the direction and context for interaction with the world. Neisser's initial version of this cycle does not include the reactive shunt, which, in my estimation, more directly ties perception and action together while still permitting the coexistence of plans for actions. The version presented here is believed to be more consistent with his later publications (Neisser 1989) which have evolved since the earlier exposition in Neisser 1976. In any case, this liberty was taken to provide a better reflection on how this cycle can be related to behavior-based robotic systems.

7.2.4   Perception as Communication—An Ethological Stance

Consider that the world is trying to tell us something, if only we knew how to listen. Sensing can thus be viewed as a form of communication—in which information flows from the environment to the attending agent. Obviously, if we don't know what to attend to we will have a hard, if not an impossible, time discerning the messages that the world is providing. The world is telling us something if only we would pay attention. Where and how our attentional and perceptual resources are directed depends strongly on our motivation or intentional state.

The ethological literature is replete with examples of sensed information providing cues for evoking behavior (e.g., Smith 1977; Tinbergen 1953). Indeed, evolution has provided biological agents with highly tuned apparatae to pick up efficiently the information necessary to carry out useful actions. The looming and prey detectors (Ewert 1980) mentioned earlier for guiding visual response in the frog are good examples.

In recognition behavior, we find that some agents are capable of discerning things others simply cannot (e.g., intraspecies kin recognition among birds (Colgan 1983)). Perceptual cues necessary for an organism's survival and routine functioning are extracted cheaply and efficiently from the environment whereas irrelevant information is not processed at all (i.e., it is not even discarded: pick up never occurs). In other words, these agents have evolved mechanisms that enable efficient communication with the world's salient features (salient, that is, in the context of that agent's needs). This implies that we need to have our robotic agents attend to what is necessary in the context of their (not our) needs. Depending on their internal conditions, motivational state or goals, and sensory limitations, we can develop algorithms that provide useful and focused information for these actors.

7.3   A BRIEF SURVEY OF ROBOTIC SENSORS

Sensor technology has advanced rapidly in the last decade, resulting in many low-cost sensor systems that can be readily deployed on behavior-based robots. Sensors can be categorized, in terms of their interaction with the environment, as either passive or active. Passive sensors use energy naturally present in the environment to obtain information. Computer vision is perhaps the most typical form of passive sensing. Passivity is particularly important in military applications, where detection of the robot should be avoided. Active sensors, on the other hand, involve the emission of energy by a sensor apparatus into the environment, which is then reflected back in some manner to the robot. Ultrasonic sensing and laser range finding are two common active sensor modalities used for behavior-based robots.

A very brief discussion of the operation of several representative sensor systems follows, including the use of shaft encoders for dead reckoning. Shaft encoders are not environmental sensors in the strictest sense, since they measure only the rotations of the robot's motors (i.e., they provide proprioceptive information). Nonetheless, they are widely used for positional estimation and warrant further discussion. The reader interested in more detailed information on a wide range of sensors useful for robots is referred to Everett 1995.

7.3.1 Dead Reckoning

Dead reckoning (derived originally from *ded*uced *reckoning*) provides information regarding how far a vehicle is thought to have traveled based on the rotation of its motors, wheels, or treads (odometry). It does not rely on environmental sensing. Two general methods for dead reckoning are available: shaft encoders and inertial navigational systems.

Shaft encoders are by far the most frequently used method of dead reckoning because of their low cost. These operate by maintaining a count of the number of rotations of the steering and drive motor shafts (or wheel axles) and converting these data into the distance traveled and the robot's orientation. Although shaft encoders can provide highly reliable positional information for robotic arms, which are fixed relative to the environment, through direct kinematics, in mobile systems they can be extremely misleading.

> *Direct kinematics* involves solving the necessary equations to determine where the robot's end effector is, given the joint coordinates (angles and length of links) of the robot arm.

If you have ever been stuck in mud or snow in an automobile, you can recognize that the information as to how many times the drive wheels have turned does not necessarily correlate well with the car's actual positional changes. Because shaft encoders are proprioceptive and only measure changes in the robot's internal state, they must be supplemented with environmental sensing to produce reliable results when determining the robot's actual location within the world.

An inertial navigational system (INS) does not measure the rotation of wheels or shafts but rather tracks the accelerations the robot has undergone, converting this information into positional displacements. This results in far more accurate dead reckoning systems, but with one major penalty: higher cost. INS is also prone to internal drift problems and must be periodically recalibrated to yield accurate information. The quality of the data makes it far more desirable than shaft encoders, but cost and power requirements frequently prevent its deployment.

Although not based on dead reckoning, global positioning systems (GPSs) can also provide geographic information as to the robot's whereabouts within the world. A battery of twenty-four Department of Defense earth-orbiting satellites relay positional data whereby the robot can deduce its position relative to a world coordinate system. Time of flight of the GPS signals and triangulation with three transmitting satellites enables the robot's altitude, longitude, and latitude to be computed. Global positioning systems are rapidly decreasing in cost but cannot be used inside buildings where the satellites' signals are blocked. Differential GPS (DGPS) can provide higher positional resolution than the standard nonmilitary GPS service, which is limited to approximately 100-meter accuracy (best case) (Everett 1995) because of an intentionally degraded public usage signal preventing unintended use by hostile military powers. DGPS requires a ground-based transmitter to supplement the satellites and can easily yield relative accuracies in submeter ranges.

7.3.2   Ultrasound

Sonar (ultrasonic sensing) is a form of active sensing. It operates on the same basic principle by which bats navigate through their environment. A high-frequency click of sound is emitted that reflects off a nearby surface and returns later at a measurable time. The delay time for receipt of the returning signal can be used to compute the distance to the surface that reflected the sound if the velocity of the sound wave is known. A typical ultrasonic sensor (Polaroid) emits a beam that receives echoes from a region approximately 30 degrees wide emanating from its source. These sensors can operate rapidly, returning ten or more depth data points per second. Accuracy for many working systems is typically on the order of 3 centimeters (0.1 foot) over a maximum range up to 10 meters. A wide range of sensors is commercially available covering a broad range of frequencies, each with variations in beam width and distance. Figure 7.3 shows a Nomadic Technologies sonar ring equipped with sixteen sensors.

Ultrasonic sensing has decided advantages: It is of low cost, provides coarse three-dimensional environmental information (distance to an object), and returns a tractable amount of data for interpretation. Its disadvantages are substantial as well: It has much poorer discriminatory ability than vision, is significantly susceptible to noise and distortion due to environmental conditions, frequently produces erroneous data because of reflections of the outgoing sound waves, and the sonar beam is prone to spread. Sonar has found its best use in obstacle detection and avoidance at short range. Its difficulty in discriminating different types of objects, for example, between an obstacle and a goal, limits

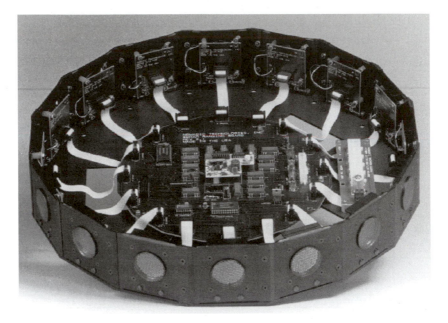

Figure 7.3
Ultrasonic sensors. (Photograph courtesy of Nomadic Technologies Inc., Mountain View, California.)

its applicability. Sonar cannot be used in outer space, as it requires a medium for the transmission of the sound wave. Progress has been made in the use of phased sonar arrays to provide greater information regarding the environment, but these currently are not in widespread use in robotic systems.

7.3.3 Computer Vision

Video technology has been available for at least half a century. Only recently, however, has charge-coupled device (CCD) camera technology advanced rapidly in terms of miniaturization and greatly lowered cost. Color imagery is now available at very affordable prices.

Although some digital cameras, are available, most robot vision systems consist of one or two black-and-white or color analog output CCD cameras, one or more digitizers, and an image processor. Because robots need real-time interpretation of incoming video data, they often require specialized architectures found in image processors for serious research and applications. Certain techniques provided through the use of behavior-based design, however, can provide very low-cost, complete vision systems for robots (Horswill and Yamamoto 1994). Figure 7.4 shows a high-end vision system used for real-time tracking of people in an autonomous helicopter. It consists of a low-light camera or conventional video mounted on a pan-tilt system with specialized image stabilization and real-time motion detection hardware (Cardoze and Arkin 1995). A behavior-based helicopter, designed by Montgomery, Fagg, and Bekey (1995) at the University of Southern California, won the 1994 International Aerial Robotics Competition. This vehicle integrated three sonar sensors for altitude measurements, a compass for heading control, three gyroscopes for controlling attitude, and a video camera for recognizing target objects.

The sheer volume of video information generated can be staggering. For a single camera, typical image resolution after digitization is on the order of 512 by 512 pixels (picture elements), with each pixel consisting of eight bits of information encoding 256 intensity levels. Multiply this value by three for color images (one image plane each for red, green, and blue) and then attempt to process at frame rate (30 times per second). We now have a receiving bandwidth of approximately 24 megabytes per second! Specialized and often costly image processing hardware can make this data flow tractable. We will see, however, that behavior-based robotic perception provides techniques, such as the use of expectations and focus-of-attention mechanisms, that constrain the amount of raw data that must be analyzed, significantly reducing the overall processing requirements. These behavior-based perceptual algorithms are generally designed to exploit task and behavioral knowledge wherever possible. Adaptive techniques that track features over multiple frames are also commonly used. Full-scale scene interpretation, the hallmark goal of mainstream image-understanding research, is generally not required.

7.3.4   Laser Scanners

Laser scanners are active sensors, emitting a low-powered laser beam that is scanned over a surface. Through techniques such as phase amplitude modulation, the distance to the individual points can be computed with the net result an array of image points, each of which has an associated depth. In effect, a three-dimensional image is obtained. Reflectance data is often also available, providing data regarding the nature of the surface as well. The product is an extremely rich three-dimensional data source. Figure 7.5 illustrates a representative commercially available system.

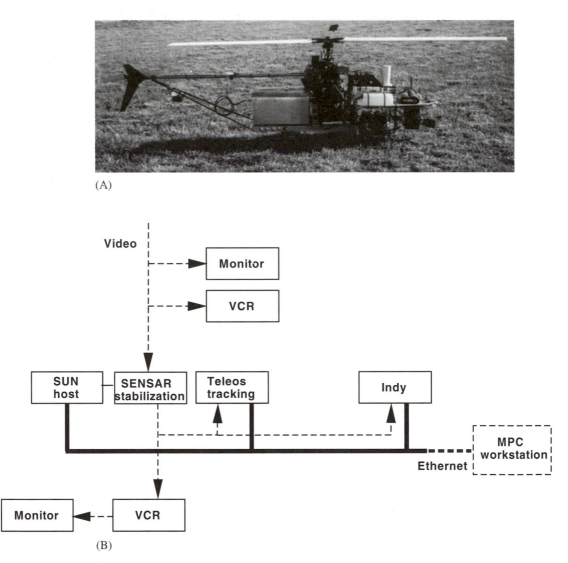

(A)

(B)

Figure 7.4
Vision system for an autonomous helicopter. The helicopter (A) has a color CCD video camera mounted on a pan-tilt mechanism on the nose. The video is transmitted to the ground station system (B), where the real-time tracking is conducted. (Photograph courtesy of Mark Gordon.)

Figure 7.5
LASAR™ Laser scanning system. (Photograph courtesy of Perceptron, Inc.)

Laser systems are not without their drawbacks. First and foremost is their cost, many orders of magnitude over ultrasonic ranging devices. Another problem arises from the mechanical instabilities associated with many current implementations of these devices (e.g., problems with nodding mirror designs used for mechanically scanning the laser beam). More subtle difficulties arise as a result of the sparse data sampling found at longer distances (a consequence of the imaging geometry), which can cause certain objects to go undetected, and problems with range periodicities when using phase modulated systems that force interpretation ambiguities on the incoming data regarding distance to the surface. Lower-cost linear array laser scanners are available, but they provide considerably less information. Nonetheless, as the underlying sensor technology improves in the next several years, these devices are expected to become more and more useful and commonplace. Their nature and use of low-powered lasers nonetheless poses some difficulties for various applications in terms of both safety and stealth.

7.4 MODULAR PERCEPTION

A child of five would understand this. Send someone to fetch a child of five.
—Groucho Marx

One of the essential characteristics of behavior-based robotics is the design of multiple parallel motor behaviors to provide overall control. This leaves two choices for tying in perception: generalized perception or modular perception.

Revising Marr's (1982) definition of general vision, generalized perception is a process that creates, given a set of input sensing, a complete and accurate representation of the scene and its properties. Thus stated, perception is conducted without regard for the agent's intentions or available repertoire of behaviors. But is there really a need for such a scene representation? The behavior-based roboticist, needs only to identify the necessary perceptual cues within the environment required to support the needed motor actions. Much of the difficulty inherent in the general perception problem vanishes, since there is no need to perform the complex and arduous task of full-fledged scene reconstruction.

As an alternative, modular perception advocates the design of perceptual specialists dedicated to extract the relevant information for each active behavior. This reprises the theme heard in Minsky's *Society of the Mind:* "Each mental agent by itself can only do some simple thing that needs no mind or thought at all. Yet we join these agents in societies—in certain very special ways—this leads to true intelligence" (Minsky 1986, p. 17). We have already studied the behavioral agents comprising our robotic designs, we now focus on the individual modules which, in toto, constitute perception.

Once committed to the paradigm of modular perception, we must determine what constitutes a module. Various definitions have been forwarded, which we now review.

7.4.1 Perceptual Schemas

Schema theory has a long and rich history, which we reviewed in chapter 2. We focus now on those aspects of schema theory that apply to perception and can be generalized to robotic systems. According to Arbib (1995a, p. 831),

"A perceptual schema embodies processes for recognizing a given domain of interaction, with various parameters representing properties such as size, location, and motion." Extracting several of the major features of schema theory relevant to modular perception (Arbib 1992):

- Schemas are a set of multiple concurrent active, not passive, processes focused on differing perceptual activities.
- Schemas contain both the control and knowledge required to complete a perceptual task.
- Schemas form an active network of processes functioning in a distributed manner specific for a particular situation and a set of agent intentions.
- Schema theory provides the basis for languages to define action-oriented perception (e.g., *RS* (Lyons and Arbib 1989) and the Abstract Schema Language (Weitzenfeld 1993)).
- The activation level associated with a schema can be related to the degree of belief in a particular perceptual event.

Perceptual schemas are somewhat related to Gibson's affordances, serving a similar purpose within an organism (Arbib 1981, Arkin 1990a). For the roboticist, the difficulty lies in how to operationalize this notion of affordance as a schema.

Each individual perceptual schema is created to produce only the information necessary for the particular task at hand. Remember that perceptual schemas are embedded within motor schemas, providing the information required for them to compute their reaction to the world (section 4.4). The question becomes one of saliency: How do we know what features of the environment are the correct ones to support a particular behavior? Even assuming that these can be clearly identified, we must then assess if it is feasible to extract this information in real time, as is necessary for robotic control, given the limitations of existing sensor and computational technology. Gibsonian affordances are preoccupied with the role of optic flow in navigational tasks. Although some progress has been made in using optic flow fields for behavior-based control (Duchon, Warren, and Kaelbling 1995), often other, more computationally feasible feature extraction algorithms are preferred for schema-based perception.

Let us examine some practical cases from our robot's world. If an avoid-static-obstacle schema is active, as is usually the case so the robot will not crash into things, some means for perceiving obstacles is necessary. An obstacle is defined as something that provides a barrier to the robot's motion, that is, it occupies space in the intended direction of motion. Objects within the environment are not considered obstacles until they get in the way. Further, they do not have to be semantically labeled as chairs, people, or whatever: they merely need to be recognized as an impediment to motion. The sensor or algorithmic source of the perception of the obstacles is of no concern to the motor schema, only the information regarding where the obstacles are located and, if available, a measure of the certainty of their perception. It is irrelevant to the motor schema if the obstacle information arises from vision, ultrasound, or some other form of sensing. From a design standpoint, it is necessary only to choose one or more of these sensor algorithms, embedding it within the motor schema itself. The obstacle-detection algorithm is unconcerned with other perceptual processing for other active motor schemas and thus can run asynchronously within the context of the avoid-static-obstacle schema. No world model of the environment is required, only reports as to where any obstacles are currently located relative to the robot. As this information is egocentric (centered on the robot's position), it eliminates the need for absolute coordinate frames of reference.

Another example involves road following when using a stay-on-path schema Arkin (1990a). The question of what perceptual features make a road or path recognizable to a robot has no single answer. Roads and paths vary widely in appearance, and weather and time of day further alter their visual presentation. For certain conditions, a possible solution involves tracking the paths' boundaries. One particular method uses a fast line-finding algorithm and is most successful when applied to well-defined roads, paths, or hallways (figure 7.6). An alternative perceptual schema, for use in different situations, exploits a fast region segmentation algorithm that is robust when the path boundaries are ill defined (figure 7.7). In some instances it may be preferable to have both of these perceptual processes active, arbitrarily choosing the most believable or fusing their results in some meaningful way (section 7.5.7). Many other more sophisticated ways exist to perform a road-following behavior, some of which are discussed in section 7.6.1.

7.4.2   Visual Routines

Visual routines, as developed by Ullman (1985), are another method for describing modular perception. In this approach, a collection of elemental perceptual operations can be assembled into a rich set of visual routines. These routines can be created to serve specific perceptual goals; they can share common elemental operations and can be applied at different spatial locations within the image. Control methods must be provided for sequencing the routine operations correctly and applying them at suitable locations within the image.

Visual routines embody both sequential processing through the choice of an ordered set of elemental operations as well as spatial, temporal and functional (i.e., specialization) parallelism.

Base representations are first created to which the visual routines are then applied. This approach has a more bottom-up processing flavor than perceptual schemas since a continually available substrate of low-level perceptual processing is assumed to be available. This strategy is consistent with Marr's (1982) primal and two-and-a-half–dimensional sketches. Box 7.1 describes these aspects of Marr's theory of vision.

Box 7.1

Marr's (1982) theory of vision uses three levels of representation:

- The *Primal Sketch* makes information regarding changes in intensity (brightness) explicit, such as edges, blobs, and textures.
- *The two-and-a-half–dimensional sketch* makes information about surfaces explicit at each point within the image (e.g., surface orientation).
- *The three-dimensional model* makes information regarding an object's shape within the world explicit (e.g., volume).

In Ullman's theory, a set of *universal routines* provides initial analysis of any image. These universal routines bootstrap the interpretation process, providing indices and thus guidance in the application of more specialized routines. There is inherently less reliance on expectations to provide effective choice in applying the set of perceptual modules. The application of visual routines is not purely bottom up, however, because routines are assembled on an as-needed basis from a finite set of elemental operations. Although a definitive set of elemental operations has not been created, several plausible operations include

- shifting the focus to different locations in the base representation
- bounded activation, restricting the applicability over the spatial extent of the base representations
- boundary tracing
- location marking
- indexing, based upon a location's sufficient distinctiveness from its surroundings

(A)

Figure 7.6
Fast line finding. (A) A Denning robot conducts sidewalk following using a fast line
finder. The algorithm uses expectations to anticipate the position of the sidewalk boundaries (both in terms of spatial and orientation constraints). (B) and (C) The results of
the grouping process and the computed centerline. These results are fed forward into
the next incoming frame as expectations as the robot proceeds down the sidewalk.

This theory, intended primarily as an explanation of biological perception, has led to the development of several approaches with applicability for
robotics. Chapman (1990) developed a perceptual architecture, SIVS, inspired
by Ullman's visual routine theory. Similar methods using visual routines were
also deployed in Chapman and Agre's earlier system, Pengi (Agre and Chapman 1987). Figure 7.8 depicts the SIVS architecture. Control inputs select from
among the primitive visual operators guiding the overall processing performed
on the substrates, referred to as early (retinotopic) maps in the figure. The
routines are selected in a task-specific, top-down manner based on the agent's
action requirements. The operators that have been defined in SIVS extend those
proposed by Ullman:

- Visual attention and search: where to look within the scene
- Tracking: following moving objects through the use of visual markers

(B)

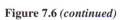

(C)

Figure 7.6 *(continued)*

(A)

Figure 7.7
Fast region Segmentation. This sequence shows the results of a fast region segmenter when used for path following. It is particularly useful when road edges are weak and the fast line finder is not suitable. Only the central portion of the path is extracted to obtain a more consistent segmentation. (A) shows the robot located on a gravel path whose edges are covered by grass. (B) shows the extracted region and (C) the computed path edges (least-squares fit) and the computed centerline.

- Spatial properties: the ability to compute distances, angles and directions to objects within the world, thus constructing concrete spatial relationships
- Activation: determining whether a selected region is bounded through spreading activation
- Others: including various housekeeping and marker manipulation operators.

This system was tested only in a video game environment and thus bypassed much of the difficulty of dealing with real perceptual algorithms. Nonetheless the overall control architecture is faithful to Ullman's approach and provides a solid step towards operationalizing it on a real robot.

Reece and Shafer (1991) implemented visual routines for potential use in robotic driving at Carnegie-Mellon University. Their system, called Ulysses, was inspired by Agre and Chapman's work (1987) and used fourteen routines

(B)

(C)

Figure 7.7 *(continued)*

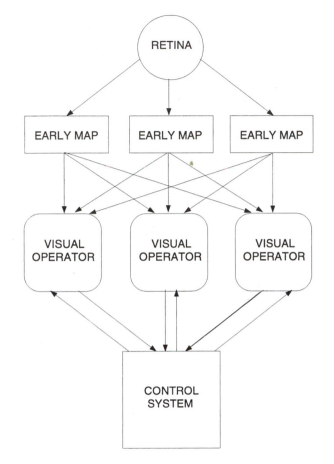

Figure 7.8
SIVS perceptual architecture.

(table 7.1) to provide the necessary control information for selecting steering and speed maneuvers for tactical driving. It was tested on a traffic simulator and showed that special purpose perceptual routines reduce the tactical driving task's computational complexity by several orders of magnitude.

7.4.3 Perceptual Classes

The notion of perceptual classes is particularly useful for describing perceptual requirements in behavior-based systems, because it permits defining perceptual tasks based on the agent's needs. The partitioning of perceptual events within the world into equivalence classes is based on the needs of a motor action:

Table 7.1
Perceptual Routines in Ulysses

Find-current-lane	Mark-adjacent-lane	Track-lane
Find-next-car-in-lane	Find-next-lane-marking	Profile-road
Find-next-sign	Find-back-facing-signs	Find-overhead-signs
Find-path-in-intersection	Find-next-car-in-intersection	Find-signal
Find-intersection-roads	Find-crossing-cars	

obstacle or nonobstacle; road or nonroad; landmark or anything else; moving object or stationary. The perceptual task directs the appropriate sensory processing mechanism to the consuming motor behavior. By channeling these perceptual tasks directly, the ability to execute them in parallel on separate processors is obtained, thus enhancing computational performance.

Donald and Jennings (1991a, 1991b) have contributed formalizations for this concept. They view the design of perception as the construction of recognizable sets: places or things the robot is capable of perceiving. Task-directed strategies for perception are a natural consequence, because the robot can be provided with expectations regarding what it should encounter (i.e., a definition of the characteristics of the perceptual class being sought) (Donald, Jennings, and Brown 1992). Sensing is considered a mapping of the robot's view of the world onto the set of possible interpretations, defined by the perceptual classes themselves. Careful construction of the perceptual classes can make this mapping easier than in an unconstrained interpretation. In defining the perceptual classes, what the robot is permitted to sense and understand is denoted. Correlating the resulting perceptual classes to the needs of the behaviors permits the extraction of information to be limited to only that required for a particular task. The notion of perceptual equivalence, whereby a large, disparate set of uncertain sensory readings is reduced to members of particular perceptual classes, renders computational tractability to the otherwise unduly complex interpretation problem. The notion of information invariants as the basis for equivalences has extended this work even further, pointing towards the eventual development of a calculus whereby robot sensor systems could be evaluated analytically (Donald 1993). This work involves the use of approaches employing computational theory permitting the reduction of one sensor into another.

The perceptual equivalence class method permits the minimization or elimination of map construction in a manner strongly supportive of purely reactive systems (Donald and Jennings 1991a). This research has focused primarily on spatial landmark recognition (where the robot is) rather than on which objects afford what actions. Nonetheless, the principles appear readily extensible to this broader problem.

7.4.4 Lightweight Vision

Horswill (1993a) has forwarded a considerably less theoretical, more pragmatic, but no less important approach to the design of perceptual algorithms. The overall approach, dubbed *lightweight vision*, focuses on specializing individual perceptual processes tailored to the behavioral tasks at hand. Horswill argues that although this specialization might lend the appearance of a collection of disjointed, ad hoc solutions, there are principled means by which these specialized modules can be analyzed to produce both generalization and potential reusability. This is accomplished in part by making explicit the assumptions that underlie the application of a perceptual algorithm for a given task environment.

Lightweight vision incorporates both task and environmental constraints. These explicit constraints provide the basis for design of the specialized perceptual module. The claim is made that for most real world task-environment pairs, a potentially large number of perceptual solutions exist. Each solution within that solution space is referred to as a "lightweight" system.

Lightweight vision is loosely related to Donald's methods in perceptual equivalence classes (section 7.4.3). An equivalence class is concerned with the theoretical equivalence of multiple perceptual systems in a task's context. Horswill acknowledges that many systems provide an equivalent solution for a given perceptual class (as defined by a task environment); it becomes the engineer's goal, however, to define a low-cost, highly efficient perceptual solution within that space of potential systems. Thus lightweight vision provides a design methodology for constructing specialized perceptual algorithms for use in behavior-based robotic systems (i.e., those that do not require reconstruction of the environment in some abstract representational form).

Design is accomplished through the explicit declaration of constraints imposed on the perceptual task. Habitat constraints refer to the set of environments within which the specialized system will operate. These constraints lead to the formulation of a computational problem that then lends itself to optimization. Polly (figure 7.9) is a robot whose purpose is to roam through the corridors of the MIT AI lab and provide tours for visitors as needed. A partial list of the percepts required for this task appears in table 7.2.

Table 7.2
Partial list of Percepts used within Polly.

open-left?	open-right?	blocked?
open-region?	blind?	vanishing-point?
light-floor?	dark-floor?	farthest-direction?
person-ahead?	person-direction?	wall-ahead?

Table 7.3 elaborates the habitat constraints that the environment provides for computation of depth recovery (needed for obstacle avoidance) and vanishing point (needed for heading information for navigation). These constraints pose tractable computational problems that in turn lend themselves to efficient, low-cost lightweight solutions for each of the perceptual modules required for the laboratory tour.

Polly's architecture consists of a coupled low- and high-level navigation system. The low-level architecture is composed of speed control, corridor follower, wall follower, and ballistic turn behaviors using a subsumption-style arbitration mechanism. The high-level navigation system provides directions as to where to go next in the tour and conducts place recognition to assist in verifying where the robot is, at various places within the tour script.

Polly is a very robust system, having given in excess of 50 tours in two different laboratories (MIT and Brown University). Perceptual specialization (also known as lightweight vision) has enabled a small, computationally weak robot to conduct a complex visual navigational task by permitting the design of algorithms that fit a specific task-environment pair. The vision modules may also be reused in similar tasks and environments. This system has clearly demonstrated the pragmatism of modular vision in behavior-based robotic design.

7.5   ACTION AND PERCEPTION

Perceptual modules and motor behaviors can be bundled together in different ways. To some extent, one may question whether perception is driving action or vice versa. Two different forms of behavioral perception have resulted:

■ *action-oriented perception*, in which behavioral needs determine the perceptual strategies used, and

■ *active perception*, in which perceptual requirements dictate the robot's actions.

Figure 7.9
Polly, a robotic tour guide. (Photograph courtesy of Rodney Brooks.)

Table 7.3
Two sets of exemplar habitat constraints and their use in Polly's task.

Perceptual Need	Constraint	Computational Problem	Optimization
Depth recovery for navigation	Ground plane assumption	use height in image (indoor level floor)	
	Background texture constant (carpet)	use texture algorithm	
Corridor vanishing point for heading	long corridor edges (office building)	line finding	use pixels as lines
	Strong corridor edges known camera tilt	edge detection clustering	low-cost detector 1D clustering

To some extent, this is a "chicken and egg" question, relating to the origin of perception in animals: Did perception result from the requirements of locomotion, or did the evolution of perception enable locomotory capabilities? We leave this question for others to answer and look instead at the impact of both of these approaches on the design of behavior-based robotic systems.

7.5.1   Action-Oriented Perception

Action-oriented perception requires that perception be conducted in a top-down manner on an as-needed basis, with perceptual control and resources determined by behavioral needs. As stated earlier, this is in contrast to more traditional computer vision research, which to a large extent takes the view that perception is an end in itself or that its sole purpose is to construct a model of the world without any understanding of the need for such a model. These non–action-oriented strategies burden a robotic system with unnecessary processing requirements that can result in sluggish performance.

Action-oriented perception is not a new concept. As we have seen, it has roots in both cybernetics (Arbib 1981) and cognitive psychology (Neisser 1976). The underlying principle is that perception is predicated on the needs of action: Only the information germane for a particular task need be extracted from the environment. The world is viewed in different ways based upon the agent's intentions.

Action-oriented perception has many aliases: selective perception (Simmons 1992), purposive vision (Aloimonos and Rosenfeld 1991), situated vision (Horswill and Brooks 1988), and task-oriented perception (Rimey 1992) are a few. The underlying thesis for this method is that the nature of perception is highly dependent on the task that is being undertaken. The task determines the perceptual strategy and processing required. This approach, developed in conjunction with reactive robotic systems, tailors perception to fit the needs of individual motor behaviors. Instead of trying to solve the so-called general vision problem by attempting to interpret almost everything an image contains, an advantage is gained by recognizing that perceptual needs depend on what an agent is required to do within the world. Avoiding the use of mediating global representations in the pathway between perception and action removes a time-constraining bottleneck from robotic systems.

In action-oriented perception, the motor behaviors provide the specifications for a perceptual process: what must be discerned from environmental sensing and constraints as to where it may be located. Focus-of-attention mechanisms play a role in directing the perceptual process as to where to look, and expectations provide clues (e.g., models) as to what the appearance of the event being sought is. How to perceive the desired event is captured in the perceptual module's computational process.

Behavior-based systems can organize perceptual information in three general ways: sensor fission (perceptual channeling), action-oriented sensor fusion, and perceptual sequencing (sensor fashion) (figure 7.10). Sensor fission is straightforward: a motor behavior requires a specific stimulus to produce a response, so a dedicated perceptual module is created that channels its output directly to the behavior. A simple sensorimotor circuit, numerous examples of which we have already encountered in chapter 3, results.

Action-oriented sensor fusion permits the construction of transitory representations (percepts) local to individual behaviors. Restricting the final percept to a particular behavior's requirements and context retains the benefits of reactive control while permitting more than one sensor to provide input, resulting in increased robustness. Section 7.5.7 explores these issues further.

Sometimes fixed-action patterns require varying stimuli to support them over time and space. As a behavioral response unfolds, different sensors or different views of the world may modulate it. Perceptual sequencing allows the coordination of multiple perceptual algorithms over time in support of a single behavioral activity. Perceptual algorithms are phased in and out based on the agent's needs and the environmental context in which it is situated. The phrase sensor *fashion* coarsely captures this notion of the significance of differing perceptual modules changing over time and space. Section 7.5.6 studies this aspect of coordinated perception in more detail.

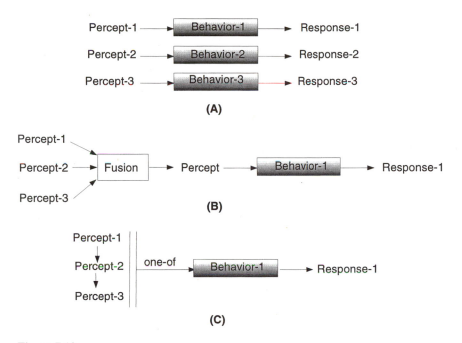

Figure 7.10
Dimensions of action-oriented perception: (A) Sensor fission—multiple independent motor behaviors, each with its own perceptual module; (B) Sensor fusion—multiple perceptual submodules supporting a single perceptual module within the context of a single motor behavior; and (C) Sensor fashion—multiple perceptual modules are sequenced within the context of a single motor behavior. The different dimensions can be composed together.

Crowley et al. (1994) have tried to formalize reactive visual processes. In their approach, a set of virtual sensors creates mappings onto an action space determined by actuators and their associated controllers. The behavior itself provides the mapping from perceptual space onto action space. Supervisory control permits the selection and control of the sequencing of individual perceptual processes in the style of hybrid architectures (chapter 6).

7.5.2   Active Perception

Active perception focuses primarily on the needs of perception, rather than the needs of action. The question changes from the action-oriented perspective of "How can perception provide information necessary for motor behavior?" to

"How can motor behaviors support perceptual activity?" These two viewpoints are not mutually exclusive; indeed, active perception and action-oriented perception are intimately related. What the agent needs to know to accomplish its tasks still dictates perceptual requirements, but active perception provides the perceptual processes with the ability to control the motor system to make its task easier as well. In contrast, Blake (1995) characterizes nonactive perceptual strategies that rely upon a single vantage point as the equivalent of a "seeing couch potato."

According to Pahlavan, Uhlin, and Eklundh's useful definition (1993, p. 22), "An active visual system is a system which is able to manipulate its visual parameters in a controlled manner in order to extract useful data about the scene in time and space." Bajcsy's (1988) seminal paper on active perception characterizes it as the application of intelligent control to perception using feedback from both low-level sensory processes and high-level complex features. Useful a priori knowledge of the world may be either numeric or symbolic and encodes sensor models and expectations. Active perception shares the view with action-oriented perception that sensory modules are a principal commodity, with perceptual goals embedded in these modules. Active perception is thus defined as an intelligent data acquisition process, intelligent in its use of sensors guided by feedback and a priori knowledge.

Work at the University of Toronto epitomizes this approach. Wilkes and Tsotsos (1994) define behaviors for controlling a video camera to extract the necessary information for object recognition. Three specific behaviors are defined for this purpose: *image-line-centering,* providing rotation to the camera to orient the object vertically within the image (rotational control); *image-line-following,* providing translations parallel to the image plane to track object features (tangential control); and *camera-distance-correction,* providing translation along the optical axis, in essence, zooming (radial control). Because these behaviors permit the camera to control its position in space, it can use active exploration strategies to confirm or annul hypotheses generated from the candidate object models available to the system. Figure 7.11 captures the system architecture. The camera actively pursues its goal, moving about at the end of a robotic arm to continually obtain more advantageous viewpoints until an identification is achieved. The system was tested successfully in complex scenes that suffered from high levels of occlusion. The ability to have multiple views guided by feedback from the recognition process reduces the computational complexity substantially over what may otherwise be an impossible task when data is from only a single or an arbitrary collection of prespecified cam-

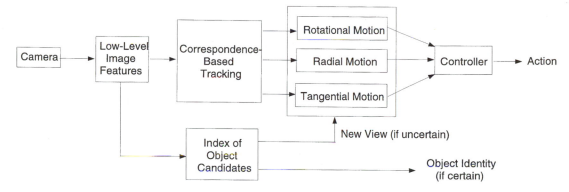

Figure 7.11
Exemplar active vision architecture.

era viewpoints. Similar research has also been conducted at the University of Wisconsin (Kutulakos, Lumelsky, and Dyer 1992).

Ballard (1989) has summarized the important characteristics of active vision (which he refers to as animate vision):

- An active vision system has control over its cameras: it can search, move in, change focus, and so forth.
- Active vision can move the camera in preprogrammed stereotypical ways, if needed.
- Image features can be isolated and extracted reliably without the use of models.
- Alternate coordinate systems become available for exploration instead of merely an egocentric frame of reference, as is often the case with purely reactive systems. Action and perception can be conducted with an object-centered frame of reference or with respect to some independent feature within the world.
- Fixation points provide the ability to servo within the visual frame of reference.
- Object-centered coordinate systems have inherent advantages due to their invariance with respect to observer motion.

Active vision has been treated in several other books (Aloimonos 1993; Christensen, Bowyer, and Bunke 1993) to which the interested reader is referred. Our discussion now returns to a more behavior-based action-oriented perspective in which an agent's intentions directly determine perceptual requirements.

7.5.3   What About Models?

A priori knowledge of the world can play a significant role during perceptual processing. Particular cases favor the appropriate use of this form of knowledge. These uses include providing expectations for perceptual processes: *what* to look for (section 7.5.4); providing focus-of-attention mechanisms: *where* to look for it (section 7.5.5); sequencing perceptual algorithms correctly: *when* to look for it (section 7.5.6); and initially configuring sensor fusion mechanisms: *how* to look for it (section 7.5.7). These uses, are entirely proper within the context of motor behavior. It is not so much in what form the representation appears but rather how it is used that distinguishes the action-oriented approach from other methods.

There is also the issue of percepts, events perceived within the environment, and how they should be encoded, if at all. The dictionary defines a percept as "an impression of an object obtained by use of the senses; sense-datum" (Webster 1984). A question arises as to whether it is at all necessary to create an abstract representation encoding such an event or impression. The pure reactivist would argue that the signal on a sensor circuit wire is the encoding of the sensor output and need not be made more persistent or abstract than that. Certainly stimulus-response pairs can be characterized in this manner, so why add any additional representation from a perceptual perspective? A recent response to this position (Agre and Chapman 1990), advocates the use of transient *deictic* representations which capture the agent's relationship with its environment at any particular point. As an example from their Pengi system (Agre and Chapman 1987), a video game environment including various animal agents such as penguins and bees, would include the-bee-I-am-chasing. The agent's intentions and the situation in which the agent finds itself define the particular bee in question. Pengi uses visual routines (section 7.4.2) to extract the relevant data for the situated task pair. These fleeting action-oriented representations are constructed as necessary in support of particular behavioral needs. The routines used in this system, however, were not physically tied to an operating sensor system.

Hayhoe, Ballard, and Pelz's (1994) work at Rochester embodied these ideas in a real system. Camera fixations provided the contextual bindings for the deictic representations. Perceptual information, instead of being stored as a history, is required immediately prior to its use. Descriptions created are relevant only to a particular task, avoiding the memory-consuming representations needed should traditional geometric models be stored. To some extent, the

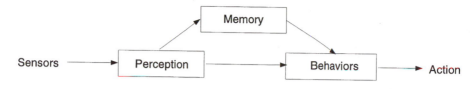

Figure 7.12
Control system using deictic spatial memory.

environment itself serves as the representational storehouse, requiring only suitable perceptual algorithms to extract the information as needed. The system was tested in a simple blocks world environment, with simple perceptual routines to GetColor and GetLocation to move the blocks from one location to another. Cognitive models of human performance motivated this study, which concluded that the visual representations humans use are "extremely scant" with "minimal information carried over between fixations." It can be argued that these conclusions serve as solid guidelines in the use of visual representations for behavior-based systems as well.

Brill's (1994) research at the University of Virginia argues for the extension of deictic representations to include local spatial memory. The impetus is to provide information that goes beyond the limits of reflex action, providing to the control system some history of events within the world that go beyond the sensory system's immediate range. Deictic representations again serve as the basis for the basic constructs, but added memory provides the robot with a broader perceptual layout. The system thus can both act from immediate sensory data, as in a typical reactive system, but can also react to spatial memory constructed in a task-oriented manner (figure 7.12), reminiscent of the structure seen in the modified action-perception cycle discussed earlier (section 7.5.1). It also resembles Payton's methods for internalizing plans (section 5.2.2.2) but is concerned with sensor-derived deictic models as opposed to incorporating a priori map knowledge. Brill's conceptual framework has been explored only in a preliminary manner thus far.

We now move on to investigating how information about the world, however it may be represented or derived, can help constrain the inherent complexity of perceptual interpretation as we examine the intertwined roles of expectations and focus-of-attention mechanisms.

7.5.4 Expectations

Expectations enable limited computational resources to perform effectively in real time. Psychological (e.g., Neisser 1976) and neuroscientific (e.g., Spinelli 1987) studies have consistently reaffirmed expectations' role in biological systems. Expectations can tell perceptual processes at least two things: where to look for a particular perceptual event and how that particular perceptual event will appear. Temporal continuity and consistency assumptions can enable a system to restrict the possible location of an object from one point in time to the next. Things generally do not disappear in one place and materialize in another. This fact, coupled with knowledge of the system's egomotion, allows significant constraints to be applied to sensory processing.

One way expectations can be exploited is by a recognition that much perceptual activity involves two major components: recognition and tracking. The recognition or discovery phase is often a model-driven approach based on the anticipation of what the object in question might look like. Its representation or characteristics can be retrieved from memory or may be hard-wired into a specific object recognition behavior. In some cases, as in the case of obstacles, a recollection of how specific obstacles actually appear need not be invoked but rather a recall of the affordances that make an obstacle an obstacle. Once recognition is achieved, this phase is abandoned in favor of the newly arrived percepts forming the basis for tracking the whereabouts of the object in question. This tracking phase is computationally far less demanding than discovery, because the expectations derived from perception are more immediate and hence more reliable and accurate than those long-term recall or a more abstract model provides.

Illustrating this process by example, suppose that an agent's instruction is to turn right just past the first oak tree. If the agent has previously traveled the route, some mental image may exist of what the particular tree in question looks like and where it might be located. This recollection may be imperfect, having been formed under different environmental conditions (night instead of day, fog versus sunshine, etc.). Additionally, the tree may have grown, been damaged, or been altered in some manner since last observed. Thus we must assume that our model can provide at best only limited knowledge of how the tree should appear.

It is also entirely possible that the agent may never have traveled the route before, and thus some generic model for an oak tree will need to be invoked. This forces greater computational demand for recognition, as fewer constraints can be placed upon the interpretation of incoming sensor data. Nonetheless some restrictions can be placed upon the scene interpretation regarding where oak trees are likely to occur in general and their typical characteristics (e.g., height, color, breadth, leaf shape, etc.).

Let us now assume that the recognition phase has successfully discerned the oak tree in question. The task remaining is simply to track the position of this tree until the next change in motor activity, which is the right turn, can occur. We no longer need to continually distinguish what type of tree it is, rather all that is needed is to track its position so that the turn can be made when the opportunity presents itself. The perceptual processing now concentrates on the tree's immediately extracted perceptual features and not on some vague or outdated representation. Color or shape may be adequate for tracking purposes in a setting where the tree is solitary. By exploiting the assumptions that the tree remains anchored in place and its reflectance is relatively constant, it can readily be tracked as the robot moves about. Although lighting variations and other environmental changes can and do occur, the expectations of the tree's tracked features are continuously updated largely independent of any a priori model. No independent sensor-based representation of the tree is maintained or needed at the reactive level. This form of adaptive tracking remains in effect until either the task is completed or the recognition occurs that some perceptual criteria has been violated, forcing a recall of the recognition phase.

Researchers at the University of Maryland (Waxman, Le Moigne, and Srinivasan 1985; Waxman et al. 1987) have looked at the recognition and following of roadways as part of the DARPA autonomous land vehicle project. Their process for road following is broken down into two distinct phases: bootstrap-image processing and feed-forward processing. The bootstrap system's purpose is to find the road's location without prior information regarding the vehicle's position. Once the road has been successfully identified and the vehicle is in motion, a feed-forward strategy is employed that relies heavily on the inertial guidance system for dead reckoning. Where the road should appear within the image is predicted based on its last appearance and the motions sensed by the INS. These predictions restrict the possible location of features so that processing can be limited to small subwindows centered on their expected positions, reducing the computation dramatically. The actual constraints based on error studies have been set at 0.25 meters and 1 degree of orientation—fine for inertial guidance but impractical for most lower-cost systems. To maintain these tolerances, an expensive pan-tilt mechanism is required as well. Line extraction, combining evidence from multiple image subwindows to yield the long parallel lines of the roadsides, is the principal feature used for road identification.

7.5.5   Focus of Attention

Focus of attention, closely related to expectations, provides information regarding where an agent should expend its perceptual resources, guiding where to look within the image or determining where to point the sensors. This in essence is a search reduction strategy. The problem can be phrased as how to prune the search space within which the desired perceptual event appears. Several techniques use hardware strategies such as foveated cameras or focus control; others exploit knowledge of the world to constrain where to look. We first examine the strong evidence supporting attentional mechanisms in human visual processing. The advantages from a computational perspective are presented, followed by examples of both hardware and software systems these issues have influenced.

7.5.5.1   The Role of Attention in Human Visual Processing

Vision in natural environments confronts the observer with a large number of potential stimuli within the field of view. Biederman (1990) claims that there are at least three reasons attentional mechanisms must select one entity for observation from the many potentially available:

- The eye itself is foveated; the retina contains only a small region (the fovea) capable of resolving fine detail. This is manifested in the *spotlight metaphor,* in which information is filtered so that attention is paid only at the center of attraction (Olshausen and Koch 1995).
- Shifting attention from one region to another does not necessarily require eye movements and thus can be done at very high speeds.
- Serial shifting of attention provides the ability to integrate and use different features, such as color and shape. This serialization has computational advantages as a consequence of the highly constrained manner in which a scene is explored.

Culhane and Tsotsos (1992) at the University of Toronto developed a strategy to reduce the computational complexity of visual search in machine vision. An attentional "beam," a localized region within an image, is used within a multilevel abstraction hierarchy that selectively inhibits irrelevant image regions (figure 7.13). The hierarchy represents various levels of visual processing, with the attentional beam applied to the most abstract level. This in turn controls low-level processing, thus reducing dramatically the amount of image processing required.

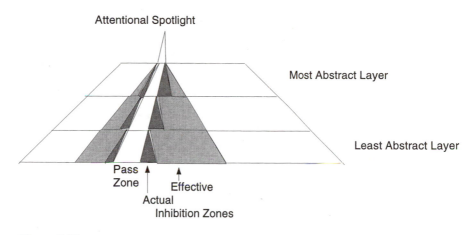

Figure 7.13
Attentional beam (after Culhane and Tsotsos 1992).

Culhane and Tsotsos characterize their method as a "continuous and reactive mechanism." This system focuses primarily on early vision and seems most appropriate for tasks such as target tracking. After the initial target location is determined, attention constrains processing at lower regions in the hierarchy by inhibiting computation in regions outside of where the target would be expected to appear within the next incoming image. This model can also handle object recognition via scan path methods (Stark and Ellis 1981) (section 5.3). A prioritized search for different features at different spatial locations within an image can be conducted easily by serially pointing the attentional beam at different image regions.

7.5.5.2   Hardware Methods for Focus of Attention

Hardware solutions for providing attention have also been studied. One strategy is to embed the spotlight notion directly into the hardware, using a foveated camera, similar in principle to the eye, from the onset. Kuniyoshi et al. (1995) reviews several such methods, where

- multiple images are acquired using a zoom lens, sequentially focusing in on the object being attended to.
- multiple cameras use differing fields of view (e.g., wide-angle and telephoto lens) while coordinating the cameras.

- a CCD chip is designed as an artificial retina with a dense foveated region.
- a specially designed lens is used with a conventional CCD array to produce a foveated space-varying image.

Although progress has been made in developing specialized hardware consistent with the eye and potentially capable of exploiting comparable focus-of-attention mechanisms, little work to date has incorporated them into complete robotic systems.

7.5.5.3 Knowledge-Based Focus-of-Attention Methods

Knowledge about the world can also guide the application of attentional processing. In research conducted at the University of Chicago, Fu, Hammond, and Swain (1994) have developed methods to link regularities present in the everyday world with perceptual activity. In their GroceryWorld example, in which an agent is shopping for food at a supermarket, domain-specific knowledge is exploited to guide perceptual processing. For example, foods are typically grouped together by types (soups, cereals, meats); within types, brands tend to be colocated; big items are stored low on the shelves, perishable items in freezers, and so forth. This heuristic knowledge generates expectations as to where in a store to find certain items. Perceptual activities are then structured in a manner that yields the desired outcome: finding the food item on the shelf. Visual routines in this system include a type-recognizer and an item-recognizer built from three simple and fast vision algorithms. These routines are highly specific to the task-environment in which the shopper operates (an image database of a grocery store). By exploiting the regularities within this domain, very simple perceptual algorithms can accomplish what would otherwise be a very difficult task.

Another approach is to introduce deep, causal knowledge about the world to focus attention. In a blocks world example using the BUSTER system developed at Northwestern University, Birnbaum, Brand, and Cooper (1993) applied causal analysis to explain why a complex configuration of blocks is capable of remaining standing. Expectations regarding the causes of physical support drive the investigation, allowing attention to be applied to regions of the image most likely to provide evidence for an explanation. Attention is first directed to lower parts of the image, where physical support begins. After establishing support at these lower regions, image processing proceeds upward, providing explanations as to why or how a particular blocks world configuration can indeed remain standing. This yields a visual attentional trace through the image not unlike the scanpaths discussed in section 5.3. Here, explanation drives visual attention: The agent's goal is to determine why something is the way it is. Causal semantics eventually will be embedded in a complete robotic system, and the resulting progress will certainly be of interest.

7.5.6   Perceptual Sequencing

It is entirely possible, and in many instances highly desirable, to have more than one perceptual algorithm associated with a single motor behavior at different stages during its activation. Sensor fission is concerned with multiple parallel independent concurrent algorithms, and sensor fusion is concerned with combining multiple related concurrent perceptual algorithms. Sensor fashion (perceptual sequencing), on the other hand, is concerned with the sequencing of multiple related perceptual algorithms.

Sensor fashion, an aspect of action-oriented perception, recognizes that the perceptual requirements for even a single motor behavior often change over time and space. For example, different perception is required to recognize an object when it is far away than when it is close. Often, entirely different perceptual cues may be used over the course of a single behavior.

Assume, for example, that a mobile robot's task is to dock with a workstation in a factory (Arkin and MacKenzie 1994). One of the behaviors necessary for this task is *Docking,* which provides the response regarding how to move relative to the perceived workstation stimulus. Because this operation is carried out over a wide range of distances (from as much as 100 feet away to immediately in front of the workstation), no single perceptual algorithm is adequate for the task. Instead, four distinct perceptual algorithms are coordinated sequentially. When the robot is far away from the workstation, the limitations of the video lens make it impossible to discern the dock's structure. The first perceptual algorithm cues either from lighting conditions at the workstation or from motion, to generate a hypothesis about the workstation's location. The docking behavior influences the robot and it starts moving toward the hypothesized target. As the robot approaches the workstation, it must positively identify it. A more computationally expensive algorithm, exploiting a spatially constrained version of the Hough transform (a model-based object recognition algorithm), is used to make a positive identification, confirming that the perceptual event in question is truly the workstation. As soon as the workstation is positively identified, an adaptive tracking methodology is used, based on region segmentation. At the final stages of docking, ultrasound positions the robot.

The primary issues in perceptual sequencing are when to use each of these algorithms and how to determine the best time to switch perceptual strategies. In our example, while the robot is far from the dock, we use the long-range detection algorithm, heading directly towards the dock; when within an expected recognition range, the model-based strategy is used with the resulting cue triggering the approach of the docking behavior. As the range closes, a transition from vision to ultrasound occurs as the camera's field of view becomes useless at close range.

Related to this is the notion of a *perceptual trigger,* a perceptual process that invokes a change in either the behavioral or perceptual state of the robot. The behavior-based robot's control system is reconfigured when a perceptual trigger fires, changing either the set of active behaviors, the set of active perceptual processes, or both. These triggers can be quite simple, such as proximity information or detection of a color or motion (e.g., a cloak waved in front of a bull), or they can be more complex, like the dock recognition algorithm mentioned above. We have seen, in section 4.4.4, how perception can be used to trigger different behaviors for a foraging task.

An experimental run for our example shows the robot using four different perceptual schemas in the course of traversing a distance from thirty feet to one-half foot. A finite state acceptor (FSA) (figure 7.14) is used to express the relationships among the individual perceptual strategies in the context of the docking behavior. Allowing failure transitions to be present within the FSA ensures robustness. Figures 7.15 and 7.16 illustrate the example docking run.

At the University of Pennsylvania, Kosecka, Bajcsy, and Mintz (1993) have developed a similar approach based on discrete event systems (DES). This method uses supervisory control to enable and disable various perceptual and motor events: Abrupt sensory events trigger different strategies. Bogoni and Bajcsy's (1994b) extension of the DES approach to the investigation of functionality uses a supervisory overseer for controlling, arbitrating, and fusing evidence from multiple sensory vantage points. In their work, developed for the manipulation domain, an overseer uses FSAs to control multiple sensors (figure 7.17). The overseer's state is reflected to the two subordinate sensors (in the example shown, tactile and vision). Tactile sensing provides only contact information whereas vision can be informative for all states.

Figure 7.18 shows a considerably more complex mapping for a piercing task (detecting when a screwdriver has pierced a styrofoam box).

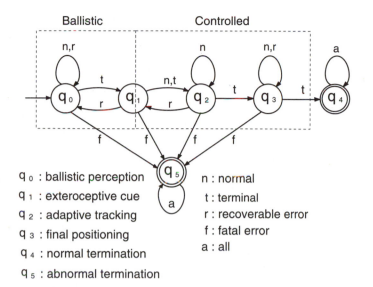

q₀ : ballistic perception
q₁ : exteroceptive cue
q₂ : adaptive tracking
q₃ : final positioning
q₄ : normal termination
q₅ : abnormal termination

n : normal
t : terminal
r : recoverable error
f : fatal error
a : all

Figure 7.14
FSA encoding temporal sequencing used for docking behavior.

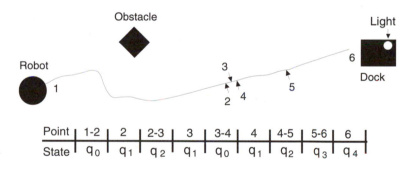

Figure 7.15
Trace of docking run with an obstacle present. Active behaviors include docking, noise, and avoid-static-obstacles.

(A)

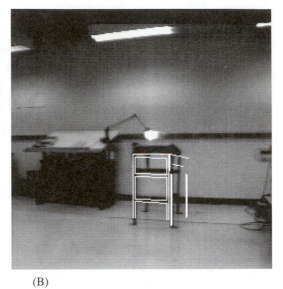

(B)

(C)

(D)

Figure 7.16

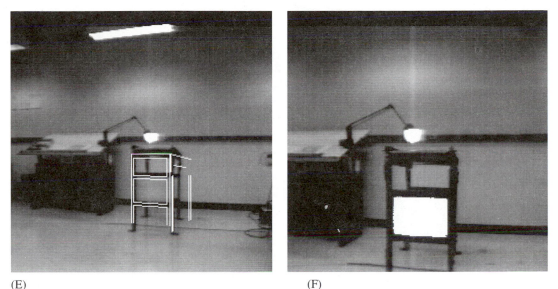

(E)   (F)

Figure 7.16 *(continued)*
Perceptual Sequencing for Docking: (A) Phototropic long-range dock detection; (B) Successful model-based dock recognition; (C) Adaptive tracking using region segmentation; (D) Loss of region due to obscuration; (E) Rerecognition using model-based technique; and (F) Final adaptive tracking image followed by final positioning using ultrasound.

7.5.7   Sensor Fusion for Behavior-Based Systems

A man with a watch knows what time it is; a man with two watches isn't so sure.
—Anonymous

Sensor fusion's traditional role has been to take multiple sources of information, fuse them into a single global representation, and then reason over that representation for action, an approach at odds with the basic view of representation's role in behavior-based robotics. This does not mean, however, that sensor fusion no longer has any place within behavior-based robots, for multiple sources of information can significantly enhance the way an agent acts within the world.

Action-oriented sensor fusion advocates that sensor reports be fused only within the context of motor action and not into some abstract, all-purpose global representation. Fusion is based on behavioral need and is localized within the perceptual processes that support a particular behavior.

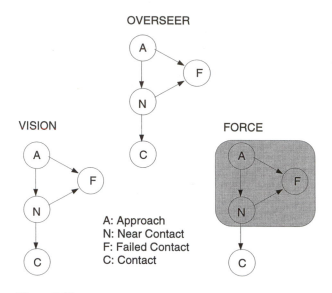

Figure 7.17
In this simple example of the DES approach, the overseer's states are mapped into two sensors, vision and force, each contributing when it can. The shaded area indicates no useful information is available for that particular set of states.

Sensor fusion, in any case, is not as simple as it sounds; incoming evidence may be complementary (i.e., in support of other observations) or competitive (i.e., in contradiction). Further, the incoming evidence may be arriving at different times (asynchronously), as some sensors take longer to process than others. Often there are qualitative distinctions in the nature of the information provided: Vision may yield color information regarding the presence of a soda can, a laser striper may yield shape data, and a tactile sensor the can's surface texture. The information may also be coming from widely separated viewpoints. Deciding what to believe is a complex task, and the behavior-based roboticist's goal is to provide a single coherent percept consistent with the incoming evidence.

Pau (1991) considered the role of behavior in sensor fusion, recognizing that a behavior-based system would appear as a collection of subsystems in support of a particular behavioral actor. His cognitively inspired approach strives to provide fusion support in the context of each individual agent's requirements, in contrast to the traditional method of constructing task-independent representations. Formalisms have been provided for specifying fusion processes relative to actors, but they have not been tested within the confines of a robotic system.

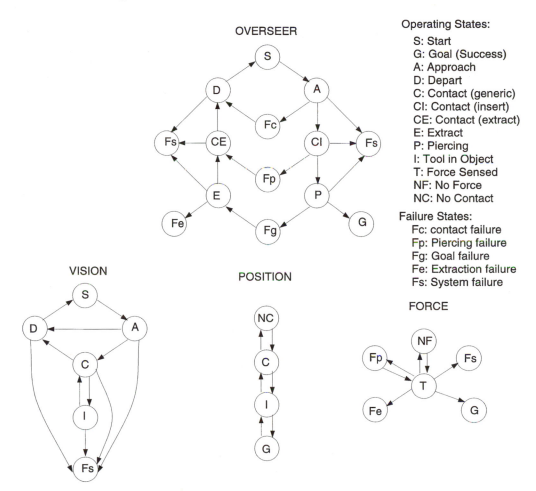

OVERSEER

VISION

POSITION

FORCE

Operating States:
S: Start
G: Goal (Success)
A: Approach
D: Depart
C: Contact (generic)
CI: Contact (insert)
CE: Contact (extract)
E: Extract
P: Piercing
I: Tool in Object
T: Force Sensed
NF: No Force
NC: No Contact

Failure States:
Fc: contact failure
Fp: Piercing failure
Fg: Goal failure
Fe: Extraction failure
Fs: System failure

Figure 7.18
The more complex piercing task requires the coordination of three sensors: vision, position and force. The figure shows the mappings from the overseer onto the individual sensors. When the overseer changes state, the sensor states change as well.

Kluge and Thorpe's (1989) work at Carnegie-Mellon University took a more practical approach to coordinating multiple sources of information. The FERMI system, used for road following, employs a collection of road trackers, each tracking different features about the road, with all providing their information to the robot controller for road following. Five different road trackers have been developed: two edge-based methods oriented to a particular feature, another that extracts linear features such as road stripes, a boundary detector using color information, and a feature-matching algorithm. All of the trackers provide information regarding the road's location. Trackers are fused using a Hough-based method in which each tracker votes for a particular location of a road spine (centerline). This voting process determines the winning candidate road position.

Arbib, Iberall, and Lyons (1985) were among the first to introduce the notion of a task-dependent representation in the context of robotics. Their work advocated the coordinated use of a set of perceptual schemas to provide the necessary information for a motor task. Murphy (1992) has furthered this notion of coordinated perceptual schemas as the basis for action-oriented sensor fusion. Her model draws heavily on psychological theories of sensor fusion (Bower 1974; Lee 1978) and uses a state-based mechanism to control important sensor interactions such as cooperation, competition, recalibration, and suppression. Contributing perceptual subschemas dedicated to individual sensors and funneled into a controlling parent perceptual schema provide the means for expressing this model. Murphy's work coalesced in the development of the SFX architecture (Murphy and Arkin 1992).

SFX's analog of the underlying psychological model has three states:

State 1. *Complete Sensor Fusion:* All sensors cooperate with each other in determining a valid percept.
State 2. *Fusion with the possibility of discordance and resultant recalibration of dependent perceptual sources:* Recalibration of suspect sensors occurs rather than the forced integration of their potentially spurious readings into the derived percept.
State 3. *Fusion with the possibility of discordance and a resultant suppression of discordant perceptual sources:* Spurious readings are entirely ignored by suppressing the output stream of the sensor(s) in question.

The task-specific perceptual schemas used for fusion yield percepts directly related to the needs of a motor behavior. Perceptual subschemas feed their parent schema, which in turn support higher-level schemas. Ties to the actual sensor data emanating from each source eventually ground this recursive for-

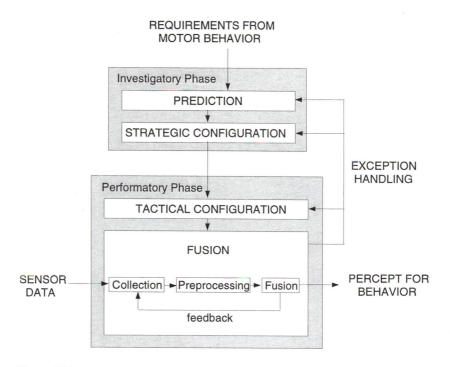

Figure 7.19
The SFX architecture.

mulation. A parent perceptual schema combines the incoming subschema information using statistical uncertainty management techniques (Murphy 1991) to produce a percept and a measure of its belief to be used within the motor schema itself.

Figure 7.19 depicts the overall control flow within the SFX architecture. The perceptual schema and subschema arrays are configured prior to execution during the fusion process's investigatory phase based on the active motor behaviors' needs. This investigatory phase is analogous to the preexecution configuration of behaviors found in many hybrid architectures (chapter 6). The performatory phase of sensor fusion similarly matches the execution aspects of reactive control and proceeds without hierarchical supervision. An observation directed acyclic graph (oDAG) incorporates the sensing activity (algorithms and sensors) to generate the necessary behavioral percept (figure 7.20). This unique control scheme (Murphy 1992) has been developed to provide error recovery capabilities in light of potential sensor failures or uncertain readings.

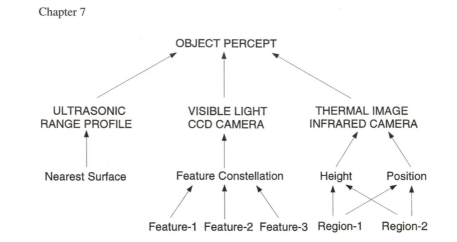

Figure 7.20
This oDAG represents the generation of a percept associated with an object using evidence gathered from three different sensors: ultrasound, video, and thermal imagery. Features and their associated belief values are propagated upward to generate the belief in the overall percept.

7.6 REPRESENTATIVE EXAMPLES OF BEHAVIOR-BASED PERCEPTION

Perceptual processing for mobile systems is notoriously difficult. Working in a partially known and uncertain environment with sensors that are in motion and subjected to bouncing, the perceptual system must provide information to a robot that is both useful and accurate. In this section we investigate three representative tasks: road following, visual tracking, and robotic head control.

7.6.1 Road Following

Driving is a spectacular form of amnesia. Everything is to be discovered, everything to be obliterated.
—Jean Baudrillard

Many research centers have expended and continue to expend a significant effort on providing perceptual support for road following. We will survey only two of the most successful efforts, one in Europe and the other in the United States.

Dickmanns and Zapp (1985) have developed a high-speed road following system at the Military University of Munich. This system operates using a windowing technique to enforce focus-of-attention mechanisms to meet real-time processing constraints. High-speed vehicle dynamics have been considered in their initial test bed, a panel truck called VaMoRS (panel (A) of figure 7.21).

Autonomous road following has been achieved at speeds up to the vehicle's limit (100 km/hour). A dedicated microprocessor assigned to each feature tracks it in its own window. Anticipatory control is utilized via a "preview" window, based on the vehicle's modeled dynamics. Figure 7.22 illustrates the overall control architecture. Limited obstacle recognition has also been provided (Graefe 1990). An even faster vehicle, vaMP (panel (B) of figure 7.21), further pushes the envelope of high-speed, autonomous road following. Additional research has extended this method to autonomous landing of an airplane (Dickmanns 1992).

In the United States, Carnegie-Mellon University has a long track record in road-following autonomous robots. Figure 7.23 shows one of their earliest systems, Terregator (TERREstrial naviGATOR), that was used, among other things, for following sidewalks on campus (Wallace et al. 1985). Initially, the only environmental sensor used was a single black-and-white video camera but it was later upgraded to color (Wallace et al. 1986).

Wallace's (1987) subsequent work at Carnegie-Mellon on the Navlab (figure 7.24) demonstrated the ability to follow roads streaked with shadows and poorly registered in the color spectrum. A pattern classification scheme based on pixel values on a color surface distinguishes sunny and shaded road from nonroad regions. The image pixels associated with the road are grouped into a single region that is then used to steer the vehicle. This approach evolved into the SCARF system described below.

We have already discussed two other recent road-following methods developed at Carmegie-Mellon: Ulysses, in section 7.4.2, and FERMI, in section 7.5.7. We will now review several others.

The SCARF system was initially developed at CMU by Crisman (1991). This road-following system relies on color imagery to detect roads with which feature-based algorithms had serious difficulties: for example, roads with degraded edges and surfaces, and those with significant shadowing. No three-dimensional road model is constructed (consistent with the behavior-based approach) while SCARF robustly provides control feedback regarding road position. In its most recent implementation (Zeng and Crisman 1995), color categories are provided within the RGB (red-green-blue) space of the imagery. Pixels are mapped onto these categories as received, reducing the 24-bit RGB color image to a 6-bit format. Statistics are respectively gathered on those pixels that correspond to road and nonroad areas, and in some cases these are further partitioned into shaded and nonshaded areas. A Gaussian road model,

(A)

(B)

Figure 7.21

(C)

Figure 7.21 *(continued)*
High-speed road-following autonomous robots: (A) VaMoRS, (B) vaMP, and (C) vaMP
vision system. (Photographs courtesy of Ernst Dickmanns.)

generated from the statistics of previous imagery, is then used to classify the 6-
bit format into road and nonroad regions, providing the necessary information
on road location for steering purposes.

Also at Carnegie-Mellon, Pomerleau (1993) developed another classification system, based on neural nets, called ALVINN (Autonomous Land Vehicle
in Neural Nets). An image array or retina of 30 × 32 pixels served as the input layer. This was connected to four hidden units that in turn projected onto
the output layer, quantizing the steering into thirty discrete units ranging from
sharp-right to straight-ahead to sharp-left (figure 7.25). The system was tested
on the Navlab system (panel (A) of figure 7.24) and later ported for use for
road-following tasks for the UGV Demo II project (chapter 9).

For training purposes, a human driver first takes the vehicle over the road.
During driving, the back-propagation method trains the network (section 8.4).
After training, the system is capable of following the road types and conditions
it encountered. ALVINN has had successful runs up to 90 miles without human

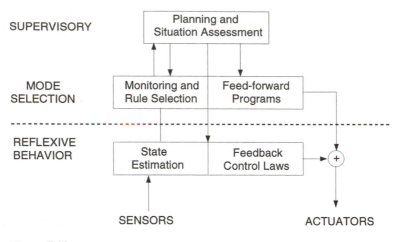

Figure 7.22
Architecture used in VaMoRS project. Note the partitioning along the lines of hybrid systems discussed in chapter 6.

Figure 7.23
Terregator. (Photographs courtesy of The Robotics Institute, Carnegie-Mellon University.)

intervention on highways and has also been successfully used on single- and multilane dirt and paved roads of various types.

The No Hands Across America Navlab 5 USA tour is one of the most ambitious exhibitions of autonomous driving to date (panel (B) of figure 7.24). The vehicle, a modified 1990 Pontiac TransSport, drove almost 3,000 miles autonomously, from Pittsburgh, Pennsylvania, to San Diego, California. Autonomous visual steering was used for 98.2 percent of the trip at speeds averaging 57 miles per hour. The vision system used for this project, developed at Carnegie-Mellon, and called RALPH (Pomerleau 1995), has a simple control process:

1. An image is acquired.
2. Irrelevant portions of the image are discarded (i.e., a focus-of-attention trapezoid is used to constrain the processed data).
3. The remaining image is subsampled to yield a 30×32 image array that includes important road features.
4. The road curvature is then computed using a generate-and-test strategy, shifting the rows' low-resolution imagery by a predicted curvature until it becomes "straightened." The curvature hypothesis with the straightest features wins.
5. The vehicle's lateral offset relative to the road's centerline is then computed using template matching (from a template created when the vehicle is centered in the lane) on a one-dimensional scan line across the road.
6. A steering command is then issued, and the process begins again from step 1.

Only the template in Step 5 needs to be modified when RALPH encounters new road types. This template can be created as needed during driving without human intervention, using look-ahead and rapid adaptation, and swapped in automatically as needed. The highest speed RALPH has achieved on the Navlab 5 is 91 miles per hour on a test track.

7.6.2   Visual Tracking

Even if you're on the right track, you'll get run over if you just sit there.
—Will Rogers

Visual tracking has been a heavily researched area for several decades. Instead of attempting a comprehensive survey, we present just three examples of recent work that have been fielded on actual robotic hardware and that exploit, at some level, the notion of task directedness.

(A)

Figure 7.24

(B)

Figure 7.24 *(continued)*
(A) Navlab 1 and (B) Navlab 5. (Photographs courtesy of The Robotics Institute, Carnegie-Mellon University.)

Woodfill and Zabih's research at Stanford University (1991) produced a motion-based tracking algorithm for keeping a moving person in view of a mobile robot by panning the robot's camera as necessary. Correlational matching was performed on a pixel by pixel basis to compute an initial disparity map that was subsequently smoothed by comparing each pixel's values to its neighbors' and assigning it the most popular one for the neighborhood. This algorithm ran on a 16,000-node connection machine (a very powerful computer) processing 15 pairs of images per second. Segmentation of the moving object from the motion field was then performed using histogramming techniques. The tracking process also projected the object's location to constrain the interpretation of the motion field. This system worked for both indoor and outdoor scenes sufficiently textured to produce a rich motion field.

Prokopowicz, Swain, and Kahn's work at the University of Chicago (1994) takes advantage of the wide range of well-developed tracking algorithms available, including a simplified version of the Woodfill and Zabih algorithm described above, a correlation-based tracker, and a color histogram tracker that takes advantage of the target's color properties. Additional trackers based on

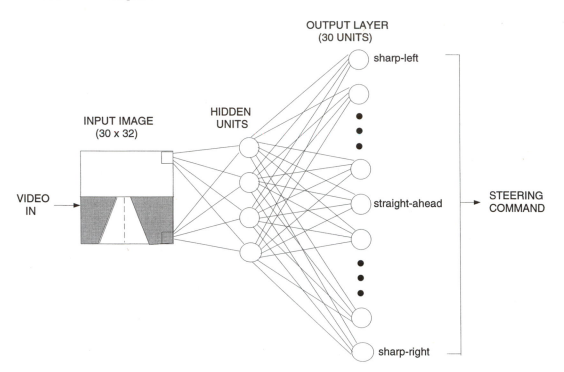

OUTPUT LAYER
(30 UNITS)

sharp-left

INPUT IMAGE
(30 x 32)

HIDDEN
UNITS

VIDEO
IN

straight-ahead

STEERING
COMMAND

sharp-right

Figure 7.25
ALVINN's neural network architecture.

binocular vision are being developed. This approach focuses on understanding the relationship between the algorithms, the target, and the environment within which the agent operates. Three behavioral tracking tasks are defined:

- *Watch*: where the robot is stationary and the target is moving.
- *Approach*: where the robot is moving and the target is stationary.
- *Pursue*: where both the robot and target are moving.

By defining the target class properties (speed, locale, appearance changes, etc.) for a wide range of objects, a set of environmental background characteristics (background motion, uneven lighting, visual busyness, and so forth) and the conditions under which the various tracking algorithms succeed or fail, selection of the algorithms at run time based on agent intention, target properties, and environmental conditions becomes feasible. This approach explicitly acknowledges these interdependencies, and by doing so, significantly enhances the system's overall robustness.

Figure 7.26
Rochester balloon-juggling robot. (Photograph courtesy of Brian Yamauchi.)

Another interesting tracking system developed at the University of Rochester (Yamauchi and Nelson 1991), was used to control a robotic manipulator for the task of juggling a balloon (figure 7.26). Three concurrent parallel behavioral agents were implemented:

- Rotational tracker: keeps the robot facing in the balloon's direction.
- Extensional tracker: keeps the arm extended so that it remains beneath the balloon's position.
- Hitter: provides the upward force to the balloon when the balloon is immediately above the paddle held by the arm.

The balloons were partially inflated with helium to slow them during fall. An average of 20 experimental runs yielded 7.0 bounces with a 39.4-second duration with a maximum run of 20 bounces with a 104-second duration. Other work in juggling systems with conventional balls abounds (e.g., Aboaf, Drucker, and Atkeson 1989; Buhler, Koditschek, and Kindlmann 1989) but it often employs the reasonably predictable physics of the situation. Balloon juggling is inherently more complex and unpredictable, making it more suitable for behavior-based solutions.

7.6.3   Robotic Heads

All I ask of my body is that it carry around my head.
—Thomas Alva Edison

To many, the pinnacle of visual sensing occurs in the design and development of a robotic head. A typical head consists of two video cameras, each of which has several controllable degrees of freedom (DOFs). To coordinate such a complex system, several behavioral control subsystems may be used (Brown 1991):

- Saccade: the open-loop rapid slewing of the camera in a given direction, often used to reposition a camera when a target moves out of the field of view.
- Smooth pursuit: continuous tracking of a moving target.
- Vergence: measuring the disparity between the two cameras focused on a target and then moving one of the cameras to reduce or eliminate it.
- Vestibulo-ocular reflex: open-loop control used to stabilize the head cameras relative to body movement, eliminating apparent motion due to translation or rotation of the robot base.
- Platform compensation: used to prevent the camera positioning systems from reaching their limits. When a limit is approached for any particular DOF, open-loop motion repositions the joints of the robotic platform without moving the cameras themselves.

Robotic heads can range widely in complexity and cost. At the low end of the price scale, we can find a robotic head that costs less than $1000 (Horswill and Yamamoto 1994). It includes two low-resolution CCD cameras and a four-DOF active head. It has been used for experiments in vergence and saccadic motion.

Ferrier and Clark (1993) at Harvard have developed a more complex head capable of saccades, pursuit, and vergence (panel (A) of figure 7.27). An even more complicated system (panel (B) of figure 7.27) with thirteen DOF has been developed in Sweden (Pahlavan and Eklundh 1993). Primary reflexes developed for this KTH (Kungl Tekniska Högskolan) head include smooth pursuit, vergence, and involuntary saccades. A large number of robotic heads have been developed. The interested reader is referred to Christensen, Bowyer, and Bunke 1993 for more information.

Perhaps, the most ambitious robotic head (and torso as well) project to date is Cog, a robot constructed by Brooks and Stein (1994) at the MIT AI Laboratory (figure 7.28). This robot is equipped with auditory as well as visual sensors (with pan-tilt, vergence, and saccade capabilities) and has in its initial configuration two six-DOF arms and a torso with a three-DOF hip and a three-DOF neck. Conductive rubber sensors will be used later to impart touch sensing to the robot. Cog is intended ultimately to encompass most of the aspects of behavior-based visual perception we have discussed throughout this section: saccades, smooth pursuit, vergence, vestibulo-ocular reflex, visual routines, and head-body-eye coordination. This project confronts head on the issues of scalability in subsumption-based behavioral methods.

7.7   CHAPTER SUMMARY

- Traditional perception has been concerned with constructing an intention-free model of the world. Newer approaches, generated for behavior-based systems, take the system's motor requirements into account in their design.
- These behavior-based algorithms are highly modular, providing targeted capabilities for specific motor needs and environments.
- Biological studies have provided significant insight into the design of these systems:
• Affordances provide a new way of thinking about how to perceive based on what environmental opportunities are afforded the robotic agent.
• The dual systems of what and where can be associated with hybrid architectural design.
- Common robotic sensors include shaft encoders for dead reckoning, inertial navigation systems, global positioning systems, ultrasound, video, and laser scanners.
- Schema theory, visual routines, perceptual classes, and lightweight vision provide differing methods for describing perceptual modules.
- Action-oriented perception provides three means by which perceptual modules can be coordinated:
• Sensor fission: Individual modules are dedicated to each behavior.
• Action-oriented sensor fusion: Recursively defined modules combine multiple sources of information into a single percept.
• Sensor fashion (perceptual sequencing): Various perceptual modules are activated and coordinated at differing points in time and space as needed.
- Active perception enables the perceptual process to control supporting motor behaviors.
- Expectations and focus of attention can be used to constrain the perceptual process's inherent complexity.

(A)

Figure 7.27

■ Significant results have been achieved in the areas of high-speed robotic road following, visual tracking, and the design of complex robotic heads.

■ The following list summarizes the design principles for perceptual algorithms in support of reactive robotic systems:

• Don't design one algorithm that does everything: rather, tailor perception modularly to meet motor requirements.

• Closely couple perception and motor control.

• Action-oriented perception is central to achieving rapid response.

• Exploit expectation knowledge when available (from previous images, object models, etc.).

• Use focus-of-attention mechanisms to constrain search; use computational power where it is most likely to yield results.

• Organize perceptual strategies using sensor fission, fusion, or fashion as needed.

(B)

Figure 7.27 *(continued)*
(A) Harvard head. (Photograph courtesy of Nicola Ferrier.) (B) KTH head. (Photograph courtesy of Jan-Olof Eklundh.)

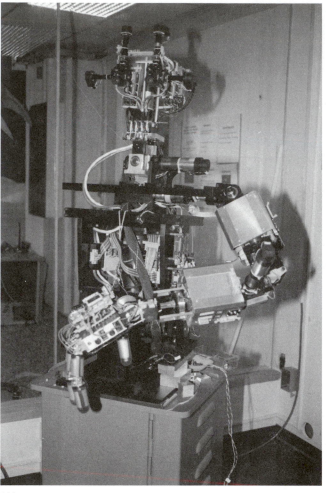

(A)

Figure 7.28

(B)

Figure 7.28 *(continued)*
Cog: (A) full view; (B) head. (Photographs courtesy of Rodney Brooks.)

Chapter 8
Adaptive Behavior

It is impossible to begin to learn that which one thinks one already knows.

—Epictetus

A mind once stretched by a new idea never regains its original dimension.

—Oliver Wendell Holmes

The reasonable man adapts himself to the world; the unreasonable man persists in trying to adapt the world to himself. Therefore, all progress depends on the unreasonable man.

—George Bernard Shaw

Chapter Objectives

1. To understand why robots need to have learning capabilities.
2. To recognize the opportunities for learning within behavior-based systems.
3. To understand the major types of learning algorithms used for behavior-based systems, including reinforcement learning, neural networks, genetic algorithms, and learning in fuzzy behavioral control.

8.1   WHY SHOULD ROBOTS LEARN?

Learning is often viewed as an essential part of an intelligent system. Indeed some argue that without this ability, there cannot be intelligence present at all: "Learning is, after all, the quintessential AI issue . . . . I will now give a definition of AI that most of our programs will fail. AI is the science of endowing programs with the ability to change themselves for the better as a result of their own experiences" (Schank 1987, pp. 63–64).

But what do we mean by learning or adaptation? As with many other terms we have encountered, there is no universal definition:

- "Modification of a behavioral tendency by experience" (Webster 1984).
- "A learning machine, broadly defined, is any device whose actions are influenced by past experiences" (Nilsson 1965).
- "Any change in a system that allows it to perform better the second time on repetition of the same task or on another task drawn from the same population" (Simon 1983).
- "An improvement in information processing ability that results from information processing activity" (Tanimoto 1990).

Our operational definition will be:

Learning produces changes within an agent that over time enable it to perform more effectively within its environment.

Although this definition will not satisfy all, it provides us with a means for measuring learning by defining performance metrics against which an agent can be measured before, during, and after learning has occurred.

How then can we relate learning and adaptation? Adaptation refers to an agent's learning by making adjustments in order to be more attuned to its environment. Phenotypic adaptation occurs within an individual agent, whereas genotypic is genetically based and evolutionary. Adaptation can also be differentiated on the basis of time scale: acclimatization is a slow process, but homeostasis is a rapid, equilibrium-maintaining process. We differentiate four types of adaptation (adapted from McFarland 1981):

- Behavioral adaptation: An agent's individual behaviors are adjusted relative to one another.
- Evolutionary adaptation: Descendents change over long time scales based on the success or failure of their ancestors in the environment.
- Sensor adaptation: An agent's perceptual system becomes more attuned to its environment.
- Learning as adaptation: Essentially anything else that results in a more ecologically fit agent.

Adaptation may produce habituation, an eventual decrease in or cessation of a behavioral response when a stimulus is presented numerous times. This process is useful for eliminating spurious or unnecessary responses. Sensitization is the opposite, an increase in the probability of a behavioral response when a stimulus is repeated frequently. Habituation is generally associated

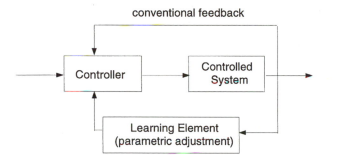

Figure 8.1
Adaptive control system.

with relatively insignificant stimuli such as loud noise, whereas sensitization occurs with more dire stimuli like electric shocks.

From a controls perspective, we can more easily differentiate adaptation and learning. Adaptive control, an early 1950s example of a system's changing to better fit its environment, uses feedback to adjust the controller's internal parameters (Aström 1995). Figure 8.1 illustrates an adaptive system that uses feedback in both the traditional sense and for internal modification of the controller itself.

Learning, on the other hand, can improve performance in additional ways, by

- introducing new knowledge (facts, behaviors, rules) into the system.
- generalizing concepts from multiple examples.
- specializing concepts for particular instances that are in some way different from the mainstream.
- reorganizing the information within the system to be more efficient.
- creating or discovering new concepts.
- creating explanations of how things function.
- reusing past experiences.

Artificial intelligence research has devoted considerable effort to determining the mechanisms by which a robotic system can learn some of these things, leading to a wide range of learning systems, including

- **Reinforcement learning:** Rewards and/or punishments are used to alter numeric values in a controller.
- **Neural networks:** This form of reinforcement learning uses specialized architectures in which learning occurs as the result of alterations in synaptic weights.

- **Evolutionary learning:** Genetic operators such as crossover and mutation, are used over populations of controllers, leading to more efficient control strategies.

- **Learning from experience**

• **Memory-based learning:** Myriad individual records of past experiences are used to derive function approximators for control laws.

• **Case-based learning:** Specific experiences are organized and stored as a case structure, then retrieved and adapted as needed based on the current situational context.

- **Inductive learning:** Specific training examples are used, each in turn, to generalize and/or specialize concepts or controllers.

- **Explanation-based learning:** Specific domain knowledge is used to guide the learning process.

- **Multistrategy learning:** Multiple learning methods compete and cooperate with each other, each specializing in what it does best.

Many of the above learning methods have been explored to varying degrees in behavior-based robotic systems. In this chapter we look at how learning methods can be effectively exploited in behavior-based robots and study a wide range of constructed systems that provide these agents with the ability to improve their performance within their environments.

8.2   OPPORTUNITIES FOR LEARNING IN BEHAVIOR-BASED ROBOTICS

Learning is not compulsory. Neither is survival.

—W. Edwards Deming

Where can learning occur within a behavior-based robotic control system? To answer this effectively, we need to revisit some of the notation we developed in chapter 3. Recall that a functional mapping β_i defines an individual behavior that acts upon a given stimulus $\mathbf{s}_i$ to produce a specific response $\mathbf{r}_i$. A gain value g_i is used to modify the response's overall strength as a multiplicative constant.

$$\mathbf{r}_i = g_i * \beta_i(\mathbf{s}_i)$$

Within the context of the individual behavior, what can be learned?

1. What is a suitable stimulus for a particular response? That is, given a desired $\mathbf{r}_i$, what $\mathbf{s}_i$ is appropriate?

2. What is a suitable response for a given stimulus? That is, given a particular s_i, what is r_i? This identifies a point behavioral response for a single stimulus but does not specify β_i in its entirety.

3. What is a suitable behavioral mapping between an existing stimulus domain and range of responses? That is, what is the form of β_i?

4. What is the magnitude of the response? That is, what is the value of g_i?

5. What constitutes a whole new behavior for the robot (i.e., new stimuli and/or responses)?

Recall further (section 3.4.2) that behaviors are grouped into assemblages that specify the global response ρ of the robot for a set of behaviors **B** with associated gains **G** and a given set of stimuli **S** when subjected to a coordination function **C**:

$$\rho = \mathbf{C}(\mathbf{G} * \mathbf{B}(\mathbf{S})).$$

C is generally either competitive (arbitration) or cooperative (fusion) or some combination of the two.

Within the context of a behavioral assemblage, what can be learned?

1. What set of behaviors β_i constitutes the behavioral component of an assemblage **B**?

2. What are the relative strengths of each behavior's response within the assemblage? That is, what is **G**?

3. What is a suitable coordination function **C**?

Problems often accompany opportunities, and learning is not different in this respect.

▪ Credit assignment problem: How is credit or blame assigned to a particular piece or pieces of knowledge in a large knowledge base or to the component(s) of a complex system responsible for either the success or failure of an attempt to accomplish a task?

▪ Saliency problem: What features in the available input stream are relevant to the learning task?

▪ New term problem: When does a new representational construct (concept) need to be created to capture some useful feature effectively?

▪ Indexing problem: How can a memory be efficiently organized to provide effective and timely recall to support learning and improved performance?

▪ Utility problem: How does a learning system determine that the information it contains is still relevant and useful? When is it acceptable to forget things?

Robots can potentially learn how to behave by either modifying existing behaviors (adaptation) or by learning new ones. This type of learning can be related to Piaget's theory of cognitive development (Piaget 1971), in which *assimilation* refers to the modification or reorganization of the existing set of available behaviors (schemas) and *accommodation* is the process involved with the acquisition of new behaviors. Robots can also learn how to sense correctly by either learning where to look or determining what to look for.

A robot can also learn about the world's spatial structure. We discussed this in chapter 5 in the context of short-term behavioral memory and long-term memory maps. We do not discuss spatial memory and learning further in this chapter and focus instead on learning and adaptation within the behavioral control system.

As we have seen, robots learn by widely varied methods that can be classified along several dimensions (Tan 1991):

■ Numeric or symbolic: Symbolic learning associates representations with the numbers inherently generated within control systems. These can result in symbolic structures such as logical assertions, production rules, and semantic networks. Numeric methods of learning manipulate numeric quantities. Neural networks and statistical methods are prime examples of numeric approaches.
■ Inductive or deductive: Generalizing as a result of learning from examples or experiments is typical of inductive learning. Deductive learning produces a more efficient concept from an initial one originally provided to the robot.
■ Continuous or batch: Learning can occur either during the robot's interaction with the world (continuous and on-line) or instead through its acquisition of a large body of experience prior to making any changes within the behaviors (batch).

Most of the methods applied to behavior-based robotic control systems to date are both numeric and inductive. Some of these methods are on-line and continuous and others are more batch oriented. The remainder of this chapter reveals more about various types of learning paradigms successfully applied to different aspects of behavioral control systems.

8.3   REINFORCEMENT LEARNING

The man who sets out to carry a cat by its tail learns something that will always be useful and which will never grow dim or doubtful.
—Mark Twain

Reinforcement learning is one of the most widely used methods to adapt a robotic control system. It is numeric, inductive, and continuous. It is motivated by an old psychological concept, the Law of Effect, which states: "Applying a

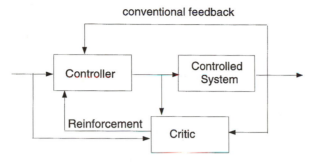

Figure 8.2
Reinforcement learning system.

reward immediately after the occurrence of a response increases its probability of reoccurring, while providing punishment after the response will decrease the probability" (Thorndike 1911). This notion of reward and punishment reinforces the causative behavior. Modern psychology largely disputes the Law of Effect as the major basis for animal learning, but the law still provides a useful model for robotic behavioral modification.

To send the necessary reinforcement signal to the control system, we need a component capable of evaluating the response, which we will refer to as the *critic*. The critic applies reinforcement to the control system in light of its evaluation (figure 8.2).

This form of *unsupervised learning* includes no notion of a particular target goal state that the system is trying to achieve, in contrast to *supervised learning*, in which there is an explicit notion of correctness in terms of an optimal behavior established a priori. In reinforcement learning, the feedback to the control provides information regarding the quality of the behavioral response. It may be as simple as a binary pass/fail or a more complex numeric evaluation. There is no specification as to what the correct response is, only how well the particular response worked.

One of the major problems associated with reinforcement learning is credit assignment. Suppose, for example, we have a collection of N active behaviors $\beta_i(\mathbf{s}_i)$ generating a global response ρ. The critic evaluates the results from executing ρ and determines that a reward or punishment needs to be applied, perhaps by changing the components of $\mathbf{G}$, the relative strengths of each behavioral component. How can the critic either increase or decrease its strength in accordance with the Law of Effect? It is hard to determine directly which of the individual components is largely responsible for the success or failure of a response. We will see how each of the actual learning systems presented addresses this particular problem. Neural network architectures, a special case of reinforcement learning, are discussed separately in the following section.

A common means for expressing reinforcement learning involves a decision policy. A robotic agent may have many possible actions it can take in response to a stimulus, and the policy determines which of the available actions the robot should undertake. Reinforcement is then applied based on the results of that decision, and the policy is altered in a manner consistent with the outcome (reward or punishment). The ultimate goal is to learn an optimal policy that chooses the best action for every set of possible inputs.

The issues in the design of robotic reinforcement learning systems can be summarized as follows (Krose 1995):

■ Which reinforcement learning algorithm should we choose? Two types predominate:

• Adaptive Heuristic Critic (AHC) learning: The process of learning the decision policy for action is separate from learning the utility function the critic uses for state evaluation (panel (A) in figure 8.3). Section 8.4.2 discusses connectionist variations of this algorithm, typically used for behavior-based robotics.

• Q-learning: A single utility Q-function is learned to evaluate both actions and states (panel (B) in figure 8.3) (Watkins and Dayan 1992). Lin's (1992) study comparing Q- and AHC-based reinforcement learning methods for enhancing an agent's survivability in a simulated dynamic world provides evidence that Q-learning is the superior method for reactive robotic applications. Indeed, Q-learning currently dominates behavior-based robotic reinforcement learning approaches.

■ How do we approximate the control function most effectively? Should we use lookup tables or discrete or continuous approximations, and what aspects of the control states do we need to represent?

■ How fast do we need to learn? This is strongly dependent on the problem domain in which the robot is operating. Learning that is too slow may not be worth the extra computational overhead, particularly if the environment in which the agent is operating is also subject to change.

Although a large body of literature exists on robotic learning, much research to date has been carried out only in simulation. Because there is often a large leap from implementing studies successfully in simulation to constructing actual robotic hardware, we restrict our discussion primarily to learning systems that have actually been fielded on robots. The remainder of this sec-

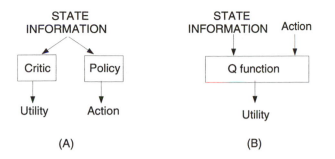

Figure 8.3
Learning architectures: (A) Adaptive Heuristic Critic; (B) Q-learning.

tion offers a representative sampling of a range of tasks that benefit from reinforcement learning strategies. Many additional simulation studies of behavioral learning systems have been conducted within the artificial life community. Because this book is concerned with robotics, we focus on real world systems.

8.3.1   Learning to Walk

We studied earlier (section 2.5.3) the problem of coordinating multiple leg controllers in a legged robotic system. Obtaining efficient gaits is a nontrivial problem. We have seen also in section 2.5.3 that a neural controller can generate gaits that correspond to those of biological systems such as the cockroach. Numeric reinforcement learning methods can also be applied in learning legged locomotion in a behavior-based control system.

Maes and Brooks (1990) studied learning using Genghis, a robot hexapod (figure 3.6). They used a rule-based subsumption architecture for the controller, which consists of thirteen high-level behaviors using two sensor modalities for feedback: two touch sensors located on the bottom of the robot (fore and aft) to determine when the body of the robot hits the floor and a trailing wheel to measure forward progress (figure 8.4). Genghis's task was to learn to move forward. Negative feedback results when either of its touch sensors makes contact with the ground and positive feedback when its measurement wheel indicates that the robot is moving forward. These feedback results are binary (i.e., the sensors are either on or off). High-level behaviors include six swing forward behaviors, six swing backward behaviors, and a horizontal balance behavior that corrects all of the legs to produce a stable horizontal position.

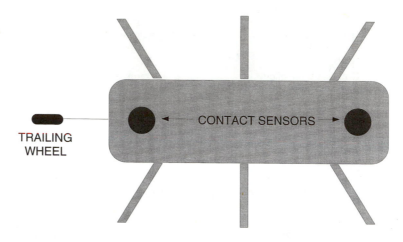

Figure 8.4
Sensors used in Genghis for reinforcement learning. Underbelly touch sensors to detect ground contact provide negative feedback and the trailing wheel provides positive feedback when the robot moves forward.

8.3.1.1   The Learning Algorithm

Reinforcement is used to alter the precondition list of the subsumption behaviors on the criteria of their being: *relevant*, that is, positive feedback is received more frequently when the behavior is more active than when it is not, and negative feedback is not received at all when the behavior is active or is received less frequently when the behavior is more active than not; or *reliable*, that is, the feedback results (either positive or negative) are consistent when the behavior is active (i.e., the probability of the behavior's occurrence approaches either 0 or 1).

Each behavior is modified independently beginning with a minimally restrictive precondition list. Each maintains its own performance record—a matrix consisting of the number of times that feedback (both positive and negative) is on or off and whether or not the behavior is active or not during that time. The results are decayed over time so that only a recent history is maintained. The correlation for positive feedback for a behavior B is computed by

$$\text{corr}(P, B) = \frac{(j * m) - (l * k)}{\sqrt{(m + l) * (m + k) * (j + k) * (j + l)}}, \tag{8.1}$$

where

j = number of times the behavior is active when positive feedback is present;

k = number of times the behavior is not active when positive feedback is present;

l = number of times the behavior is active when no positive feedback is present; and

m = number of times the behavior is not active when no positive feedback is present.

The same equation is used for correlating negative feedback simply by substituting negative feedback for positive feedback in equation 8.1. A value near -1 for the correlation indicates that feedback is not likely when the behavior is active and $+1$ indicates that it is quite likely.

The behavior's relevance is determined by computing the difference between the correlations between positive and negative feedback:

$$\text{corr}(P, B) - \text{corr}(N, B). \tag{8.2}$$

If this value approaches $+2$, the behavior is highly likely to be active and is considered relevant, that is, positive feedback is received when the behavior is active.

The behavior's reliability is then computed by

$$\min(\max(\frac{j_p}{j_p + l_p}, \frac{l_p}{j_p + l_p}), \max(\frac{j_n}{j_n + l_n}, \frac{l_n}{j_n + l_n})), \tag{8.3}$$

where j and l have the meaning as before and the subscripts p and n denote positive and negative feedback respectively. If this value is close to 1, the behavior is considered highly reliable, but very unreliable if it is near 0.

If the behavior proves relevant but not reliable, a different perceptual condition is monitored to see if it is responsible for the lack of reliability. If it is, the behavioral rule's precondition list will be altered. New performance statistics are gathered correlating the robot's performance when the new perceptual condition is either present or absent. A correlation with feedback is then computed, as in equation 8.1, by substituting the new perceptual condition's being either on or off for the behavior's being either active or inactive. If the resultant correlation value is near $+1$, the precondition list of the behavior is modified to require the new perceptual condition to be on; if the correlation value is near -1, the requirement that the new perceptual condition be off is added. If no strong correlation either way is apparent, a new perceptual condition is monitored. These conditions are continually reevaluated until a sufficiently high reliability is achieved.

During execution, the behaviors are grouped based on common actuator control. A probabilistic selection is made based on their relevance, reliability, and newness regarding its appearance in each group. The behaviors are then activated and feedback obtained. These probabilistic aspects insure experimentation to avoid premature convergence to a suboptimal solution.

> *Convergence* in a learning system refers to the point at which additional training does not result in any additional improvement in performance.

8.3.1.2   Robotic Results

The following results were produced using this learning algorithm:

■ Using solely negative feedback with the balance and six swing forward behaviors, Genghis learned to adopt a stable tripod stance, keeping three legs on the ground at all times (the middle leg from one side and the front and rear from the other).

■ A second experiment, using both positive and negative feedback, resulted in Genghis's walking using the tripod gait, in which it alternately swings two sets of three legs forward as the robot moves.

8.3.2   Learning to Push

At IBM, Mahadevan and Connell (1991) used Q-learning to teach a behavior-based robot how to push a box. The robot, Obelix, was built on an RWI 12-inch-diameter base. There are eight ultrasonic sensors, four of which look forward, two each to the left and right. Sonar output is quantized into two ranges: NEAR (from 9–18 inches) and FAR (18–30 inches). A forward-looking infrared detector has a binary response of four inches used to indicate when the robot is in a BUMP state. The current to the drive motors is also monitored to determine if the robot has become physically STUCK (the input current exceeds a threshold). Only 18 bits of sensor information are available: 16 bits from the ultrasonic sensors (NEAR or FAR) and two for BUMP and STUCK.

Motor control outputs are limited to five choices: moving forward, turning left or right 22 degrees, or turning more sharply left or right at 45 degrees. The robot's learning problem involves deciding, for any of the approximately

Reward/Punishment

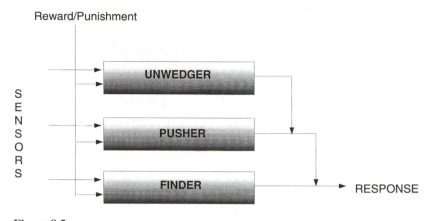

Figure 8.5
Obelix's behavioral controller (colony architecture).

250,000 perceptual states, which of the five possible actions will enable it to find and push boxes around a room efficiently without getting stuck.

The behavioral controller, based on Connell's colony architecture (section 4.5.3), consists of three behaviors (figure 8.5):

■ *Finder* behavior, which is intended to move the robot toward possible boxes. This behavior is rewarded whenever the input vector contains NEAR bits. If the robot moves forward and the forward looking NEAR bits are turned on, a +3 reward is given. If any NEAR bits that were already on are turned off, a −1 punishment is applied. Finder is active only when neither of the other behaviors is active.

■ *Pusher* behavior occurs after BUMP results from a box find and continues at least until the box is wedged against an immovable object, such as a wall. The robot's reward is +1 if it continues to move forward and remains in BUMP, and its punishment is −3 if it stops being in the BUMP state (loses the box). The pusher behavior remains active for a short time after BUMP contact is lost so that it may recover from possible small errors in pushing. Boxes tend to rotate when pushed by the circular robot if not pushed directly through the center of drag, making this task considerably more difficult than it might first appear.

■ *Unwedger* behavior removes the robot when the box becomes no longer pushable. The robot's reward is +1 if the STUCK state goes to 0, or its punishment is −3 if it persists in the STUCK state. This behavior is active whenever the STUCK bit is on and persists for a short time after it goes off to ensure safe extrication.

8.3.2.1   The Learning Algorithm

Q-learning provides the ability to learn, by determining which behavioral actions are most appropriate for a given situation, the correct global robotic response ρ for a given set of stimuli $\mathbf{S}$ presented by the world. An update rule is used for the utility function $Q(x, a)$, where x represents the states and a the resulting actions:

$$Q(x, a) \leftarrow Q(x, a) + \beta(r + \lambda E(y) - Q(x, a)),   \tag{8.4}$$

where

β is a learning rate parameter;
r is the payoff (reward or punishment);
λ is a parameter, called the discount factor, ranging between 0 and 1;
$E(y)$ is the utility of the state y that results from the action and is computed by $E(y) = max(Q(y, a))$ for all actions a.

Reward actions are also propagated across states so that rewards from similar states can facilitate their learning as well. The issue here is what constitutes a similar state. One approach uses the weighted Hamming distance as the basis for the similarity metric. The 18-bit state representation is compacted to 9 bits, then the difference between the number of set bits between different states is computed. Some state characteristics are considered more important than others in preserving distinctiveness. In particular, BUMP and STUCK each have a weight of five, NEAR sonar has a weight of two, and all other bits have a unit weight. Arbitrarily, two states are considered similar if their weighted Hamming distance is less than three.

The utility function is used to modify the robot's behavioral responses as follows:

```
Initialize all Q(x,a) to 0.
Do Forever
    Determine current world state s via sensing
    90% of the time choose action a that maximizes Q(x,a)
        else pick random action
    Execute a
    Determine reward r
    Update Q(x,a) as above
    Update Q(x',a) for all states x' similar to x
End Do
```

Another variant of Q-learning that uses statistical clustering for the similarity metric instead of weighted Hamming distances has also been investigated.

8.3.2.2   Robotic Results

The methods described were tested on the robot Obelix. It was observed that using Q-learning over a random agent substantially improved box pushing. The robot's performance using Q-learning was also compared to its performance when controlled by a hand-coded, hand-tuned behavioral controller. Mahadevan and Connell (1991) state that the robot was "fairly successful at learning to find and push boxes and unwedge from stalled states" (p. 772). The ultimate performance after learning was said to be "close to or better than the hand-coded agent" (ibid.). This work's importance lies in its empirical demonstration of Q-learning's feasibility as a useful approach to behavior-based robotic learning.

8.3.3   Learning to Shoot

Researchers at Osaka University (Asada et al. 1995) have applied vision-based reinforcement learning to the task of shooting a ball into a goal, using Q-learning as their system's underlying methodology. In this instance the set of states for the utility function $Q(x, a)$ is defined in terms of the input visual image obtained from a camera mounted on the robot. The ball's location within the image is quantized in terms of position (left, center, or right) and distance (large/near, middle, or small/far). The goal's location is quantized in terms of the same two qualities plus relative angle (left-, right-, or front-oriented). The set of states defined by all allowable combinations of these substates totals 319. Two additional states each exist for when the ball or goal is lost either to the right or left. These states assist in guiding the robot to move in the correct direction, as opposed to moving randomly, should the stimulus not be directly present within the image.

The robot's action set consists of the inputs for each of the two independent motors that power each wheel. Each wheels action subset consists of three commands: forward, stop, and back. This yields a total set of nine possible actions for the robot. The robot continues in a selected action until its current state changes.

The reward value is set to 1 if the ball reaches the goal and 0 otherwise. The discount factor, λ, is set to 0.8. Because of the difficulty in associating a particular state action in the past with the reward generated, convergence is very hard to achieve if the robot is started in a random state. This difficulty, referred to as the delayed reinforcement problem, is related to the credit assignment problem discussed earlier in the chapter. The problem is addressed here by having a good teacher who provides an intelligent design for learning experiences.

The trainer devises easy situations (such as head-on approaches that are near) to allow the system initially to improve its performance in this constrained situation. As this level of competency is mastered, more difficult and challenging states are progressively introduced. This procedure improves learning performance convergence dramatically. Suitable training instance selection is used to facilitate many types of learning. An early example is Winston's (1975) ARCH program, which illustrated the power of using proper training sequences for achieving convergence in inductive concept formation tasks.

8.3.3.1   Robotic Results

The system was implemented on a tracked robot equipped with a radio/video link to an offboard real-time image processing system and Sun control computer. The ball was painted red and the goal box blue to make feature extraction simpler. The experiments were run on the laboratory floor. The actual success rate was about 50 percent as compared to 70 percent predicted by simulation studies. Such a difference in actual and predicted success rates is not uncommon because of the significant inaccuracies in simulation models and noise in the input sensors. Looking at the final action-state data, approximately 60 percent of the stimulus-response mappings were correctly created. Considering that the robot had no ability whatsoever to get the ball into the goal initially, these results are encouraging and support earlier claims that Q-learning is a feasible method for behavior-based robotic learning.

8.4   LEARNING IN NEURAL NETWORKS

Although learning in neural networks can be viewed as a form of reinforcement learning, neural networks are sufficiently distinct to warrant a discussion on their own. In chapter 2 we presented the rudiments of neural network systems. In this section, we discuss methods for encoding behavior-based robotic control using neural networks and the adaptation methods that can be used to modify the synaptic weights that encode the means by which the robot can respond.

Hebb (1949) developed one of the earliest training algorithms for neural networks. Hebbian learning increases synaptic strength along the neural pathways associated with a stimulus and a correct response, strengthening frequently used paths. Specifically,

$$w_{ij}(t+1) = w_{ij}(t) + \eta * o_i o_j, \tag{8.5}$$

where:

$w_{ij}(t)$ and $w_{ij}(t+1)$ are the synaptic weights connecting neurons i and j before and after updating, respectively;
η is the learning-rate coefficient; and
o_i and o_j are the outputs of neurons i and j, respectively.

Perceptrons, introduced in section 2.2.3.2, have also been used for robotic learning. Perceptron learning uses a method different from Hebbian learning for synaptic adjustment. The overall training procedure is as follows:

```
Repeat
   1. Present an example from a set of positive and negative
      learning experiences.
   2. Verify the output of the network as to whether it is
      correct or incorrect.
   3. If it is incorrect, supply the correct output at the
      output unit.
   4. Adjust the synaptic weights of the perceptrons in a
      manner that reduces the error between the observed
      output and correct output.
Until satisfactory performance as manifested by convergence
achieved (i.e., the network has reached its limit of performance)
      or some other stopping condition is met.
```

Various methods are used for updating the synaptic weights in step 4. One such method, the delta rule, is used for perceptrons without hidden layers. It modifies synaptic weights according to the formula

$$\Delta(w_{ij}) = \eta * w_{ij} * (t_j - o_j), \tag{8.6}$$

where:

$\Delta(w_{ij})$ is the synaptic adjustment applied to the connection between neurons i and j;
η is the learning-rate coefficient; and
t_j and o_j are the correct and incorrect outputs, respectively.

The delta rule strives to minimize the error term $(t_j - o_j)$ using a gradient descent approach.

Gradient descent refers to learning methods that seek to minimize an objective function by which system performance is measured. At each point in time, the policy is to choose the next step that yields the minimal objective function value. This in essence states that one should continue to improve one's state condition as fast as one can for as long as one can. The learning rate parameters, commonly found in these algorithms, refer to the step size taken at each point in time. Each step during the descent is computed only on the basis of local information (a local optimization procedure), which is extremely efficient, but introduces a myopia that can result in traps at local minima. *Hill climbing* is the analogous process whereby the objective function is maximized.

Back-propagation is probably the most commonly used method for updating synaptic weights. (See Werbos 1995 for a review.) It employs a generalized version of the delta rule for use in multilayer perceptron networks (a common form of neural networks used in robotic control and vision). Usually the synaptic weights' initial values are set randomly, then adjusted by the following update rule as training instances are provided:

$$w_{ij}(t + 1) = w_{ij}(t) + \eta \delta_j o_i, \tag{8.7}$$

where

$\delta_j = o_j(1 - o_j)(t_j - o_j)$ for an output node; and

$\delta_j = o_j(1 - o_j)\Sigma_k \delta_k w_{jk}$ for a hidden layer node.

The errors are propagated backward from the output layer.

8.4.1   Classical Conditioning

Classical conditioning, initially studied by Pavlov (1927), assumes that unconditioned stimuli (US) automatically generate an unconditioned response (UR). The US-UR pair is defined genetically and is appropriate to ensure survival in the agent's environment. In Pavlov's studies, the sight of food (US) would result in a dog's salivation (UR). Pavlov observed that associations could be developed between a conditioned stimulus (CS), which has no intrinsic survival value, and the UR. In the dog's case, when a bell was rung repeatedly

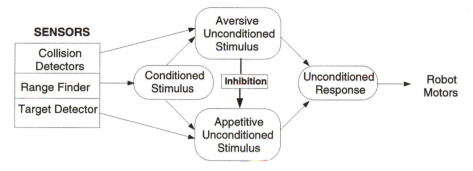

Figure 8.6
Learning architecture supporting classical conditioning.

with the sight of food, over time an association was made so that the ringing of the bell alone was sufficient to induce salivation. Hebbian learning can produce classical conditioning.

An international research group (Vershure, Krose, and Pfeifer 1992; Vershure et al. 1995) has looked at classical conditioning methods as a basis for the self-organization of a behavior-based robotic system. Instead of hard-wiring the relationships between stimuli and responses, the learning architecture (figure 8.6) permits these associations to develop over time.

In their early simulation studies (1992), Vershure, Krose, and Pfeifer divide the positive US fields into four discrete areas in which the attractive (appetitive) target may appear: ahead, behind, left, and right. A significant turning response is required when the target is considerably to the left or right, a lesser one (if any) if it is to the front or rear. The UR set consists of six possible commands: advance, reverse, turn right 9 degrees, turn right 1 degree, turn left 9 degrees, and turn left 1 degree. Two additional collision sensors serve as negative US, producing a response consisting of a reverse and turning 9 degrees away from the direction of the collision. The negative (aversive) US can inhibit the positive US, ensuring that managing collisions takes precedence over target acquisition.

The CSs use a range sensor capable of producing a distance profile of 180 degrees in the direction in which the robot is heading. The readings are divided into varying discrete levels of resolution based on the robot's heading: for the forward area, ranging from −30 to +30, there are twenty units covering 3 degrees each; for the area to the right, ranging from +30 to +60, there are five units covering 6 degrees each; and for the area to the far right, ranging from $+60$ to $+90$, there are three units covering 10 degrees each. Areas to the left and far left have resolutions similar to those of the right and far right, respectively, making a grand total of 36 units of range data.

For the neural network implementation, perceptron-like linear threshold units with binary activation values are used. The synaptic weights are updated by the following rule:

$$\Delta w_{ij} = \frac{1}{N} \left(\eta o_i o_j - \epsilon \bar{o} w_{ij} \right),$$ (8.8)

where

η is the learning rate;
ϵ the decay rate;
N is the number of units in the CS field;
o_i, o_j is the binary output value of units i and j respectively; and
$\bar{o}$ is the average activity of the US field.

The robot's task is to learn useful behaviors by associating perceptual stimuli with environmental feedback. The behaviors include avoidance, in which the robot learns not to bump into things, and avoidance, combined with approach to a desired target. Note that the robot has no a priori understanding of how to use the range data to prevent collisions from occurring in the US set: This must be learned from the CS.

The simulation studies indicate that successful emergent behavior does occur in a manner consistent with the agent's goals. The authors likened these results to the development of an adaptive field by the construction of a sensor-driven control schema. These learned behaviors are consistent with specialized variants of schema-based navigation, discussed in section 4.4, in which the agent constructs the required responses through environmental interactions.

More recently, this work has been extended to vision-based navigation for an actual mobile robot, NOMAD (Vershure et al. 1995). The robot's learning task involves sorting colored blocks that conduct electricity, either strongly or weakly, based on feedback from an aversive or appetitive response. Because the robot can obtain the US only when it is in actual contact with the block, its goal is to learn the correct response to the color characteristics associated with each block type. In this case the UR arises from a conductivity sensor, and the CR uses color vision.

The synaptic update rule used is

$$w_{ij}(t + 1) = w_{ij}(t) + v(t)a_i(t)(\eta a_j(t) - \epsilon w_{ij}(t)),\qquad(8.9)$$

where

$v(t)$ is the average activation of the value units, where the value units provide constraints on the system;

a_i is the neuron's firing rate;

a_j is the firing rate of the presynaptic neuron j; and

η and ϵ are the learning rate parameters for potentiation and depression of synaptic strength, respectively.

Three different variations were used in the study:

1. A value system is present. (Equation 8.9 is used as is.) This value system exerts an influence on alterations in synaptic strength based on relevant sensory inputs independent of whether they are aversive or appetitive.
2. The value system is turned off by setting $v(t) = 1$ in equation 8.9.
3. A model is used that corresponds to Hebbian learning, with no value units and a dropping of the dependency of synaptic depression on a_j (i.e., the last term in equation 8.9 becomes $\eta a_i t a_j(t) - \epsilon w_{ij}(t)$).

In the study, the robot successfully learned to accomplish the task. The learning performance varied depending on the method chosen, with method 2 resulting in the best performance and fastest development of conditioned responses.

Others have used classical conditioning methods: Scutt (1994), for example, taught a Braitenberg-like robot (section 1.2.1) consisting of a neural net of only five neurons to seek light. In another example, Gaussier and Zrehen (1994) used a variation of Hebbian learning to teach a small mobile robot, using a neural network, to develop a topological map, learning suitable responses at different locations within its world. These researchers showed that learned encodings similar to potential fields could be developed using classical conditioning methods capable of representing learned landmark positions (Gaussier and Zrehen 1995).

8.4.2   Adaptive Heuristic Critic Learning

With adaptive heuristic critic (AHC) reinforcement learning methods, a critic learns the utility or value of particular states through reinforcement. These learned values are then used locally to reinforce the selection of particular actions for a given state (panel (A) in figure 8.3). A research group in Spain (Gachet et al. 1994) has studied the use of connectionist AHC reinforcement as a basis for learning the relative strengths (i.e., **G**) of each behavior's response within an active assemblage. The study's specific goals were to learn how to coordinate effectively a robot equipped with the following behaviors: goal attraction, two perimeter-following behaviors (left and right), free-space attraction, avoiding objects, and following a path. The output for each of these behaviors is a vector that the robot sums before execution, in a manner very similar to that of the schema-based methods discussed earlier (section 4.4).

The AHC network (figure 8.7) starts with a classification system that maps the incoming sonar data onto a set of situations, either thirty-two or sixty-four depending upon the task, that reflect the sensed environment. An output layer containing a weight matrix W, called the associative search element (ASE), computes the individual behavioral gains g_i for each behavior. Each element W_{ki} of the weight matrix is updated as follows:

$$W_{ki}(t+1) = W_{ki}(t) + \alpha b_i(t)e_{ki}(t), \tag{8.10}$$

where α is the learning rate and $e_{ki}(t)$ is the eligibility of the weight W_{ki} for reinforcement (maintained and updated as a separate matrix).

A separate adaptive critic element (ACE) determines the reinforcement signal $b_i(t)$ to be applied to the ASE. Its weights V are updated independently as follows:

$$V_{ki}(t+1) = V_{ki}(t) + \beta b_i(t)X_k(t), \tag{8.11}$$

where β is a positive constant and X_k is the eligibility for the ACE. This partitioning of the reinforcement updating rules from the action element updating is a characteristic of AHC methods in general.

The task for the non-holonomic robot (named Robuter) is to learn the set of gain multipliers **G** for a particular task-environment. Three different missions are defined for the robot. The first mission involves learning to explore the environment safely. The second involves learning how to move back and forth between alternating goal points safely, and the third is to follow a predetermined path, also without collisions.

In the exploration mission, initially the robot moves randomly within the world. When a collision occurs, negative reinforcement is applied and the robot is moved back to a position it occupied N steps earlier ($N = 30$ for the simulations, 10 for the actual robot because of tight quarters). For the other goal-oriented missions, negative reinforcement occurs under two conditions: when a collision is imminent, and when the robot is pointing away from the goal (or next path point) and no obstacles nearby are blocking its way to the goal. Tests on Robuter in a relatively confined laboratory environment showed

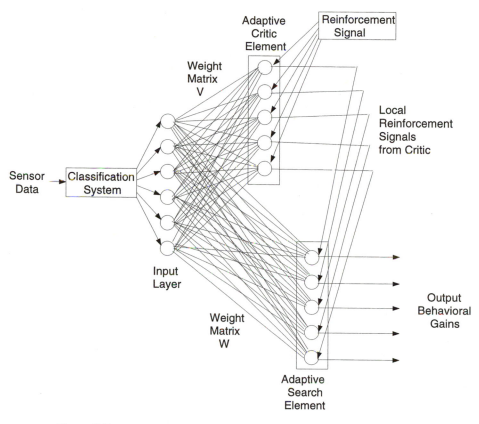

Figure 8.7
Connectionist AHC learning system (after Gachet et al. 1994).

successful learning for the first and second missions. Successful simulation results were reported for the third mission as well.

Millan (1994) also used AHC learning methods for navigation tasks. A Nomadics robot named Teseo used temporal differencing methods (Sutton 1988) as a specific instance of AHC learning. In this work, the robot learns behavioral patterns efficient for a particular task, such as moving from one location to another. The robot learns to avoid unfruitful paths (e.g., dead ends) on the way to achieving its navigational goals. Basic reactive reflexes are used as primitive behaviors. Similarly, researchers at the University of Southern California (Fagg et al. 1994) have used temporal differencing as a form of connectionist AHC learning to permit a robot to learn collision avoidance, wall following, and environmental exploration.

A research team at the University of Karlsruhe (Ilg and Berns 1995) applied AHC learning methods to teach leg coordination and control to a hexapod robot name LAURON (figure 8.8). Here also a critic element generates a reward for the current state and a separate action element generates the choice of how to act next. Individual leg actions were learned (return and power strokes) as well as coordinated control between the legs.

8.4.3   Learning New Behaviors Using an Associative Memory

A research group at the University of Edinburgh (Nehmzow, Smithers, and Mc-Gonigle 1993; Nehmzow and McGonigle 1994) has studied ways to increase a robot's behavioral repertoire (i.e., learn new β_i) through a connectionist associative memory. Two of their robots, named Alder and Cairngorm, were equipped with two whisker sensors, one each on the vehicle's left and right front, used to signal collisions. The robot was also able to sense when it is moving forward. In later work a more sophisticated robot, the Edinburgh R2, used five bump sensors, eight infrared sensors for proximity detection, and six light-dependent resistors to detect the presence of light.

Instinct rules, the first approach taken, were established for the agent, which resulted in various forms of locomotion. The motor responses that became associated with these rules correspond closely to behaviors in a priority-based system such as the subsumption architecture. Example behaviors learned by Alder and Cairngorm include (Nehmzow, Smithers, and McGonigle 1993):

- Rule 1—Keep forward motion sensor on: The robot learns to move forward.
- Add Rule 2—Keep whiskers straight: The robot learns to avoid bumping into obstacles.
- Add Rule 3—Make whiskers respond after four seconds: The robot learns wall-following behavior.
- Add Rule 4—Make alternate whiskers respond: The robot learns corridor-following behavior.

Figure 8.9 depicts the learning architecture for the Edinburgh R2 (Nehmzow and McGonigle 1994). As is the case for their other robots, the two-layer perceptron-based neural network's goal is to associate novel sensor information with recently undertaken actions. A novelty detector determines when conditions have changed sufficiently to warrant a change in action, which occurs when either the robot's heading has changed significantly or there is a significant net difference in the proximity sensor data. The associative memory acts on a sensor vector containing the proximity data (quantized into a range

(A)

(B)

Figure 8.8
(A) Hexapod robot LAURON and (B) its successor LAURON II. (Photographs courtesy of Karsten Berns.)

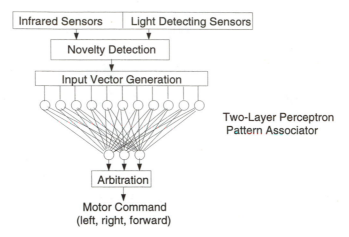

Figure 8.9
Two-layer perceptron learning architecture.

between 0 and 3) and light-detector data (digitized into a normalized range between 0 and 255). The output of this associative memory passes into an arbiter that selects the most appropriate action. Only three actions are defined: swift left turn, swift right turn, and move forward.

This two-layer perceptron (eleven input, three output nodes), in contrast to the multilayer neural networks already discussed, has the advantage of rapid learning, often with only one positive example. These perceptron networks, however, can learn only linearly separable functions (Minsky and Papert 1969), although this has not yet proven to be a problem for this type of application. Scalability issues are as yet unresolved.

The synaptic weight update rule used appears in equation 8.6. For the R2, teaching is supervised by a human, in contrast to the instinct rules used earlier. The experimenter provides critical feedback on its performance directly to the robot by covering or uncovering a light sensor on its top. The robot considers itself to be behaving correctly while the sensor is dark (positive feedback). When the sensor is uncovered (negative feedback) the robot tries different actions until it finds a suitable one, at which point the sensor is covered again. Clearly a good teacher is essential for proper learning in this instance. This process of applying external feedback is likened to "shaping," a process of behavior modification used for training animals.

This robot has learned four basic behaviors: obstacle avoidance, box pushing, wall following, and light seeking. Combinations of these behaviors are also teachable, permitting the robot to learn how to navigate through a maze, for example, by using avoidance, light seeking, and wall following in a learned order.

8.5   GENETIC ALGORITHMS

Biologically the species is the accumulation of the experiments of all its successful individuals since the beginning.
—H. G. Wells

The genetics of behavior has been well studied in the context of biological systems. Breeds of animals are created to possess certain useful behavioral properties such as disposition (e.g., viciousness or friendliness in dogs). It is also possible to use computational analogies of behavioral genetics to configure robotic characteristics. In this section, we first review how certain classes of genetic algorithms operate, then look at specifically how they can be used within robotic systems. We also examine how their strengths can be combined with the strengths of neural networks to yield hybrid adaptive robotic control systems.

8.5.1   What Are Genetic Algorithms?

Genetic algorithms (GAs) form a class of gradient descent methods in which a high-quality solution is found by applying a set of biologically inspired operators to individual points within a search space, yielding better generations of solutions over an evolutionary timescale (Goldberg 1989). The fitness of each member of the population (the set of points in the search space) is computed using an evaluation function, called the fitness function, that measures how well each individual performs with respect to the task. The population's best members are rewarded according to their fitness, and poorly performing individuals are punished or deleted from the population entirely. Over generations, the population improves the quality of its set of solutions. Although GAs, and gradient descent methods in general, are not guaranteed to yield an optimal global solution, they generally produce high-quality solutions within reasonable amounts of time for certain problem spaces. As we will see, this includes the learning of control strategies for behavior-based robots.

Genetic algorithms usually require specialized knowledge representations (encodings) to facilitate their operators' operation. The encodings typically take the form of position-dependent bit strings in which each bit represents a gene in the string *chromosome*. An initial population (a representative set of bit strings) is established by some means, often by randomization. Genetic

Reproduce

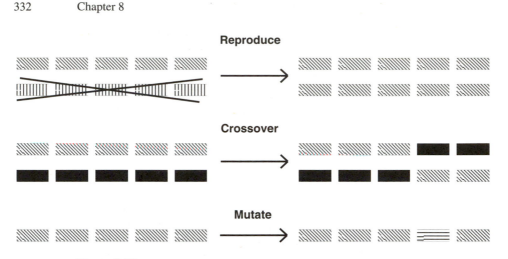

Crossover

Mutate

Figure 8.10
The genetic operators reproduction, crossover, and mutation.

operators are then applied to the bit string encoding of the population members. The three most frequently used operators are *reproduction, crossover*, and *mutation.* (figure 8.10).

Prior to the operator's application, each individual's fitness is computed using the fitness function. For a behavior-based system, this may involve running a robot through a series of experiments, using the encoding of the behavioral controller represented by the particular individual bit string encoding being evaluated. The fitness function returns a value capturing the robot's overall performance for the set of conditions being tested.

Using the reproduction operator, the fittest individuals are copied exactly and replace less-fit individuals. This is done probabilistically, usually using weighted roulette-wheel selection, increasing the likelihood of but not guaranteeing the fittest individuals' reproduction. This operator's net effect is an increase in the ratio of highly fit individuals relative to the number of poor performers, loosely following the Darwinian principle of survival of the fittest.

Crossover involves two individual encodings, exchanging information through the transfer of some part of their representation to another individual. This process creates new individuals that may or may not perform better than the parent individuals. Which individuals to cross over and what bit string parts to exchange are usually chosen randomly. The net effect is an increase in the overall population.

Mutation, a simple probabilistic flipping of bit values in the encoding, affects an individual only and does not increase the overall population size. This random effect provides the ability to escape local minima, a common problem associated with gradient descent methods. Just as in biological mutations, most mutations will lead to inferior individuals, but occasionally a more fit one will emerge. Because the probability of mutation is generally very low and copies of the most fit individuals result from reproduction, this randomness permits high-quality solutions to emerge that would otherwise be unattainable.

The use of these genetic operators results in a varying population over time. Some individuals created have a lower fitness than their parents, but on average the entire population's overall fitness as well as that of the best individuals improves with successive generations. If properly designed, the learning system eventually settles on a set of highly fit, near-optimal individuals with similar bit strings. The final solution's quality and length of time to obtain it depend heavily on the nature of the problem and the values for the many parameters that control the GA. Fortunately, control problems, and in particular behavior-based control methods, are highly compatible with these methods, as they generally have a reasonable parameter set size.

8.5.2   Genetic Algorithms for Learning Behavioral Control

GAs, although a powerful technique for developing control systems, require some restrictions on implementation compared to the individual learning methods we have already investigated. Since these methods typically require a significant population of robots for fitness testing, and the robots must be further tested over many, many generations, much of the learning in genetic algorithms is of necessity conducted in simulation off line. As an evolutionary timescale is needed, it is generally infeasible to conduct real-time learning. Simulated learning, fortunately, can generally be conducted at speeds orders of magnitude faster than real-world testing. Assuming that a simulation has a reasonable degree of fidelity to the real robot and environment, the control parameters from the fittest simulated individual developed over many generations can then be transferred to the actual robot for use.

An example from such a simulation appears in figure 8.11 (Ram et al. 1994). In this particular system, GA-Robot, a schema-based behavioral controller is evolved using genetic algorithms. An encoding is created that represents the individual gains of the component behaviors (goal attraction, obstacle avoidance, and noise) and additional parameters internal to certain behaviors (obstacle sphere of influence, noise persistence). In this work, instead of using a more slowly converging bit string, an encoding using floating-point values for the gains and parameters is used.

```
begin
    Obstacles.Create;              /* Make a new environment */
    Population.Build;              /* Make a new population */
    for 1 to NUMBER_GENERATIONS do
      begin
        for 1 to RUNS_PER_GENERATION do
          begin                      /* Let Robots try to reach goal */
            for 1 to MAX_NUMBER_STEPS do
              begin
                Robots.Move;
              end
            Obstacles.Recreate; /* Update environment */
          end
            /* Prepare next generation */
        Robots.Reproduce;
        Robots.Crossover;
        Robots.Mutate;
      end
end
```

Figure 8.11
GA-Robot's main evolutionary algorithm.

Fitness for an individual is defined as a function of weighted penalties:

```
raw_fitness = collision_weight * number_of_collisions
            + time_weight * number_of_steps
            + distance_weight * distance_traveled
```

By altering the penalty weights for each component of the fitness functions, three different classes of robots are evolved, each specialized for a particular ecological niche (figure 8.12):

- Safe: optimized to avoid hitting obstacles while still attaining the goal.
- Fast: optimized to take the least amount of time to attain the goal.
- Direct: optimized to take the shortest path (which may be slower because of reduced speeds in cluttered areas).

The different behavior of a single class of evolved robots across differing environments is also in evidence in figure 8.13. Although these robots are optimized to avoid collisions, they can still find relatively direct paths in low clutter environments. As the clutter increases, however, the paths begin to diverge, until the robots find many indirect and slow but safe routes through the obstacle field. Using GAs in this way permits an environment-specific control

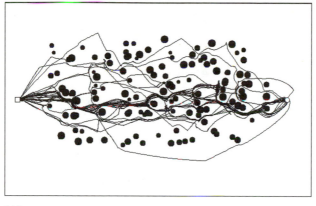

(A)

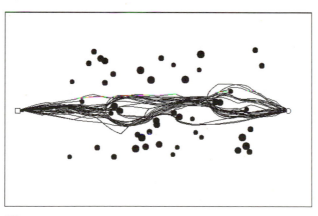

(B)

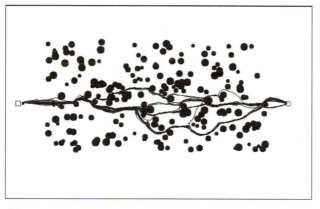

(C)

Figure 8.12
Final paths through 25% cluttered general worlds of (A) safe, (B) fast, and (C) direct
robots.

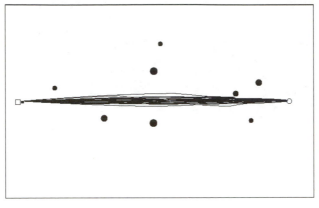

(A)

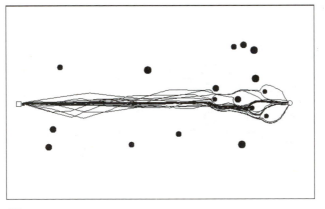

(B)

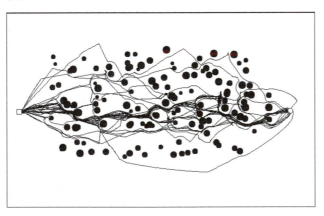

(C)

Figure 8.13
Final paths of safe robots through (A) 1%, (B) 10%, and (C) 25% cluttered general
worlds.

system to be evolved if desired, filling targeted ecological niches (e.g., fast robots in highly cluttered worlds).

8.5.3 Classifier Systems

Other variations on representational encodings are also used. One common alternative strategy is the use of a *classifier system* (Booker, Goldberg, and Holland 1989). Here, genetic operators act upon a set of rules encoded by bit strings. The performance element of a classifier system works in the manner of a production system: Preconditions for a set of rules are checked to determine their applicability given the current situational context. The preconditions have fixed-length bit encodings with values 0, 1, or # (don't care). The action side of the rule is also a fixed-length encoding with values of 0, 1. Conflict resolution methods are used to select which one from a set of potential rules will be used. The performance element then executes the selected rule. Credit assignment is performed by a separate critic module that evaluates the results of the chosen actions (i.e., the fitness) and is used, as always, to guide learning. A learning element creates new rules using genetic operators.

We saw earlier (section 3.3.1) that rule-based systems are a useful encoding method for behavior-based robotic systems. GA-based classification systems are a natural fit. One international research group centered in Milan has used these methods to evolve behavioral control in a system called ALECSYS (figure 8.14). Testing on a series of small robots (AutonoMouse), the researcher's have demonstrated phototaxis: learning to approach both stationary and moving light sources (Colombetti and Dorigo 1992). In simulation, they have further demonstrated the coordination of three different primitive behaviors—approaching, chasing, and escaping—using several different potential coordination operators (e.g., combination, suppression, and sequencing). The chase behavior operates along the following lines: A sensor encodes in a four-bit string the location of the object to be chased. This particular encoding can serve as the precondition for a rule that has an action encoding consisting of five bits, the first three encoding the direction to move, one bit for whether or not to move, and a one-bit flag to notify the behavior coordinator that an action is recommended by the rule. These bit strings representing rules evolve using the genetic operators described earlier, creating new rules as necessary and deleting useless ones according to the results of the critic's fitness assessment. ALECSYS has also been applied to manipulator control, learning to coordinate vision (exteroceptive) and encoder (proprioceptive) sensors to

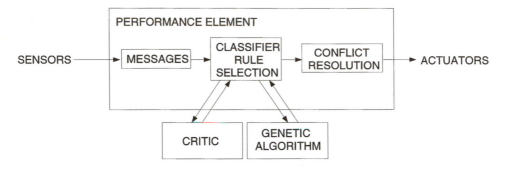

Figure 8.14
ALECSYS learning architecture.

produce gross motion guiding the manipulator to a target object (Patel et al. 1995).

Another important approach combining the power of production rules and genetic algorithms is SAMUEL, a system developed at the Naval Research Laboratories and tested on a Nomad robot (Grefenstette and Schultz 1994). The task for this system is to learn how to avoid obstacles and to safely navigate to a goal in a cluttered environment using sonar and infrared sensors. At each time step an action is produced consisting of moving at a linear speed between −1 and 5 inches per second and a turning speed of −40 to +40 degrees per second. The standard set of genetic operators of selection, crossover and mutation are employed. Performance for the top five individuals improved significantly (from approximately 72 percent to 93 percent success) for a set of fifty individual rule sets evaluated over twenty trials each and evolved over fifty generations. The initial rule set was obtained from a set of human-created rules and machine-generated variations. Significant simulation results were also generated for behavioral scenarios involving evasion, dogfighting, minefield navigation, and prey tracking (Schultz and Grefenstette 1992).

8.5.4   On-Line Evolution

Though most GAs evolve different individuals over time, it is also possible to permit the continuous evolution of the control system during execution using genetic algorithms. Steels (1994) accomplishes on-line adaptation by treating the behavioral controller as a population of concurrent active behavioral processes. The goal for the robotic agent (in this case a small machine constructed from LegoTechnics) is to survive; this means finding adequate energy sources (which are depletable) and not getting stuck in obstacle traps while seeking them out. An initial population of behavioral processes is generated that compete for actuator control, producing changes in speed or turning. Fitness is evaluated over some history window, typically looking about one second into the past, according to how well the system responds to satisfying its survival needs. During this time interval each process's contribution to (impact on) the robot's control is logged. The fitness and impact a process had during its last history window guides reproduction. New process creation involving GA operators is used to keep the total number of active processes in the system constant. Significant performance enhancements over initial behavioral configurations have been achieved using this approach.

In this system, an individual agent has the ability to respond to continual changes in its environment. Most GA methods assume that the behavioral controller is fixed during a particular agent's lifetime. This method permits continuous adaptation, which can potentially provide greater flexibility in adapting to evolving ecological niches and it explicitly recognizes an agent's need to change in response to ongoing environmental change.

8.5.5   Evolving Form Concurrently with Control

Sims (1994) has developed an interesting approach to evolving entire robotic creatures using GAs. Given the question being studied, Sim's work has of necessity been tested only in simulation. Sims allows for the evolution of not only the agent's controller, but also its morphology (form). Genotypes encoded as directed graphs are used to produce phenotypic structures that constitute the corresponding three-dimensional kinematic systems. Rigid, revolute, twist, spherical and other joint types are permitted. The genotype encoding determines points of attachment. Sensors attached to the independently evolved control system include contact, joint angle, and photosensors. A neural controller maps sensor inputs onto effector outputs.

To evaluate fitness, a high-fidelity physical simulation is created. Various objective functions are established: for swimming and walking, the distance traveled by the agent's center of mass per unit time; for jumping, the maximum clearance achieved by the lowest part of the agent; and for following, the average speed of approach to a light source. Figure 8.15 shows several successfully evolved creatures for swimming and walking.

Reproductive selection is based upon fitness, as is normally the case. Crossover operations on genotypic encodings involve combining components of the

(A)

Figure 8.15

directed graph rather than bit string manipulation. Mutation is also conducted by adding random nodes to the genotype graph.

    The results of these simulation studies are impressive. It is hard to envision, given the current state of the art, how these kinds of kinematic variations could be conducted autonomously. Nonetheless, it is certainly important to recognize that behavioral robotics is limited if one considers only a fixed spectrum of physical robotic structures to control. Nature provides this flexibility to its creatures. Roboticists would also do well to consider these aspects of morphological adaptation, at the very least within the design process.

8.5.6   Hybrid Genetic/Neural Learning and Control

Several systems have combined the power of neural controllers and genetic algorithms. Researchers at the Center for Neural Engineering at the University of Southern California (Lewis, Fagg, and Bekey 1994) have used GA methods

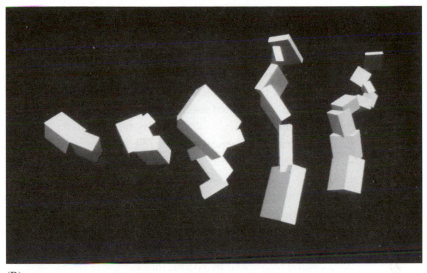

(B)

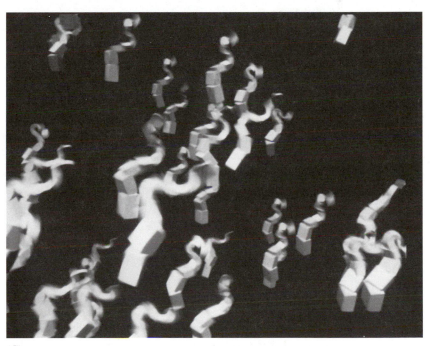

(C)

Figure 8.15 *(continued)*
Evolved creatures, (A) Walking creatures, (B) Evolutionary ancestors of the water snake, and (C) Swimming water snakes. (Photographs courtesy of Karl Sims.)

to evolve the weights for a neural controller for a robotic hexapod, named Rodney, rather than using traditional neural learning (e.g., back-propagation). Fitness functions were defined for first learning oscillatory control for each of the legs and then coordinating the oscillations to produce effective gaits. The tripod gait manifested itself, but surprisingly the robot preferred to walk backward rather than forward: Evidently this was more efficient for this particular mechanical structure. Similar results for a hybrid genetic/neural system were obtained at Case Western Reserve University (Gallagher and Beer 1992).

In other work, a Braitenberg-style neural controller was implemented on a small commercially available Khepera robot equipped with three ambient light sensors pointed to the floor and eight infrared proximity sensors (Mondada and Floreano 1995; Floreano and Mondada 1996) (figure 8.16). Fitness functions were defined for various behaviors, including

- Navigation and obstacle avoidance: Fitness maximizes motion and distance from obstacles.
- Homing: Fitness ensures that the power is kept at adequate levels by adding a light-seeking behavior to guide it to its black recharging area when power becomes low.
- Grasping of balls using an added gripper: Fitness maximizes the number of objects (balls) gripped in an obstacle-free environment.

Genetic algorithms are used to evolve the synaptic weights for the neural controller. In all three cases, the targeted behavior is learned to varying degrees. Here also backward locomotion is a preferred method for the evolved mobile gripper controller. The most successful individual backed up until it encountered something, then turned around and attempted to grip it.

8.6 FUZZY BEHAVIORAL CONTROL

Any fool can make a rule
And every fool will mind it.
—Henry D. Thoreau

In this section, we belatedly introduce fuzzy behavioral control, a variant of discrete rule-based encodings (section 3.3.1). We review first the basic principles of fuzzy logic and then its applications specific to robotic systems. Some aspects of learning of fuzzy control are then presented for reactive robots.

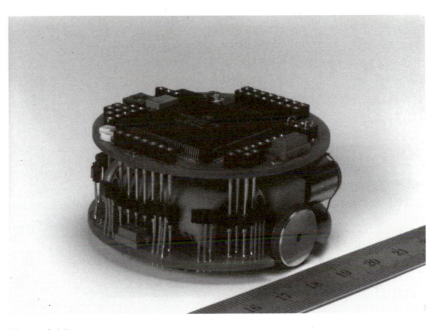

Figure 8.16
Khepera robot. (Photograph courtesy of E. Franzi, F. Mondada, and A. Guignard. Photographed by Alain Herzog.)

8.6.1   What Is Fuzzy Control?

Fuzzy control systems produce actions using a set of fuzzy rules based on fuzzy logic, which is different from conventional predicate logic. In conventional logic, assertions about the world are either true or false: there is nothing in between. Values such as true and false are referred to as *crisp*, that is, they have one exact meaning. Fuzzy logic gives us a different perspective, allowing variables to take on values determined by how much they belong to a particular fuzzy set (defined by a membership function). In fuzzy logic these variables are referred to as linguistic variables, which have noncrisp meanings (e.g., fast, slow, far, near, etc.). Membership functions measure numerically the degree of similarity an instance of a variable has in its associated fuzzy set.

A fuzzy logic control system (figure 8.17) consists of the following:

■ Fuzzifier: which maps a set of crisp sensor readings onto a collection of fuzzy input sets.
■ Fuzzy rule base: which contains a collection of IF-THEN rules.

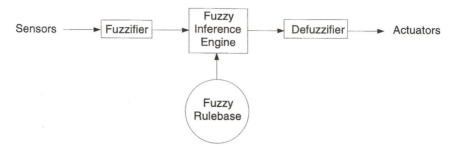

Figure 8.17
Fuzzy logic control system architecture.

- Fuzzy inference engine: which maps fuzzy sets onto other fuzzy sets according to the rulebase and membership functions.
- Defuzzifier: which maps a set of fuzzy output sets onto a set of crisp actuator commands.

Consider an example of linguistic variables that may be useful for behavior-based robotics: steering control. It might be useful to instruct the robot to turn in some direction, but we may not want the behavior to specify the value of a turn too crisply (e.g., turn right 16.3 degrees). Instead it may be desirable to have a fuzzy output, such as turn-hard-right, or slightly-right, or don't turn (and similarly for the left). Membership functions encoding this information might appear somewhat as shown along the horizontal axis in figure 8.18. Note the overlap in membership between linguistic classes. Suppose similarly we have obstacle detection sensors that provide linguistic information such as clear-ahead, obstacle-near-right, obstacle-far-right, and similarly for the left. (Example membership functions are also shown on the vertical axis in figure 8.18). Simple fuzzy rules can then be created, such as

- IF clear-ahead THEN don't turn.
- IF obstacle-near-right THEN turn-hard-right.
- IF obstacle-far-right THEN turn-slightly-right.

A fuzzy control system of this sort would start with crisp sensor readings (e.g., numeric values from ultrasound); translate them into linguistic classes in the fuzzifier; fire the appropriate rules in the fuzzy inference engine, generating a fuzzy output value; then translate these into a crisp turning angle in the defuzzifier, as ultimately the motor must be commanded to turn at a particular discrete angle.

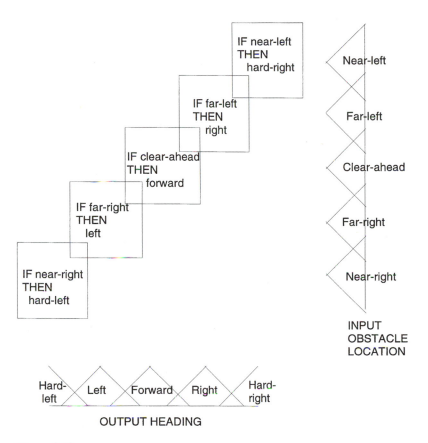

Figure 8.18
Fuzzy logic for steering control, showing input and output membership functions and fuzzy rules relating them.

Fuzzy systems have more flexibility than conventional rule-based methods and permit more robust integration of sensorimotor commands than conventional production systems. Fuzzy control systems are now pervasive in consumer products: washing machines, camcorders, and VCRs, to name a few. Additional introductory information on fuzzy logic can be found in Kosko and Isaka 1993.

8.6.2   Fuzzy Behavior–Based Robotic Systems

Successfully fielded systems show the advantages of behavioral fusion or blending using fuzzy logic. We review two of these efforts.

8.6.2.1   Flakey

At SRI, Saffiotti, Ruspini, and Konolige (1993b) have designed a reactive fuzzy controller for the robot Flakey (figure 6.12). Specific behaviors are encoded as collections of fuzzy rules. One such example rule for obstacle avoidance is:

■ IF obstacle-close-in-front AND NOT obstacle-close-on-left THEN turn sharp-left.

Fuzzy rules can also invoke whole behavioral rule sets, providing context for interpreting sensor data. These meta rules describe the applicability of a behavior for a given situation: IF $context_i$ THEN $apply(B_i)$. For example, the rules below specify which behaviors should be active depending on whether a collision is imminent.

■ IF collision-danger THEN apply(keep-off)
■ IF NOT(collision-danger) THEN apply(follow)

Remember that the applied behaviors themselves are fuzzy, so depending on the membership function structure, each may be active to varying degrees, thus blending their responses smoothly. The behaviors are implemented as schemas, each consisting of three components:

■ Context determines a particular behavior's relevancy to a given situation.
■ A desirability function is implemented as a set of rules specifying the control regime.
■ A descriptor set defines the objects that must be perceived or acted upon during execution (e.g., places and things in the world).

Using fuzzy control, Flakey can pursue multiple goals, blending behaviors using rules without requiring strict arbitration. Fuzzy control also permits integration of a deliberative planner to yield a hybrid architecture (Saffiotti, Ruspini, and Konologe 1993a). Using this controller, Flakey, deployed primarily in an office environment, successfully competed at the first AAAI mobile robot competition in San Jose, winning second place in a competition emphasizing the ability to navigate in an obstacle-strewn environment.

8.6.2.2   MARGE

Another robot using fuzzy logic, MARGE (figure 8.19), developed at North Carolina State University (Goodridge and Luo 1994), was a winner in the following year's AAAI robot competition. MARGE used fuzzy logic differently

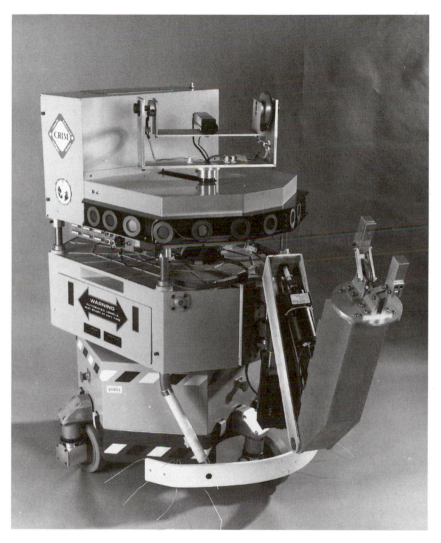

Figure 8.19
MARGE. (Reprinted with permission from Janet et al. 1996 © 1996 IEEE.)

however. Instead of allowing context to enable and disable behavioral rule sets, MARGE's controller uses a networked collection of distributed fuzzy agents, all independent and concurrent. Implemented fuzzy behavioral agents include goal seeking, obstacle avoidance, wall following, and docking. Fuzzy behavioral fusion is conducted, using additional fuzzy controllers as multiplexers to adjust the gains (g_i) for each behavior. Weighted vector summation is the method for producing the final defuzzified command signal. A finite state machine sequences between fuzzy controllers suitable for the competition's tasks, such as office rearrangement, which required moving boxes from one location to another in a cluttered world. MARGE won first place in this event.

8.6.3   Learning Fuzzy Rules

Learning in fuzzy control systems for behavior-based robots has predominantly focused on learning the fuzzy rules themselves. In work conducted at the Oak Ridge National Laboratories, Pin and Watanabe (1995) provide one example for automatically generating a fuzzy rule base from a user-provided qualitative description of behavior. Learning is viewed differently in this system, which is given the ability to reflect the user's intentions more effectively. A traditional rule-based learning system, TEIRESIAS (Davis 1982), that was layered on top of production expert systems served a similar purpose: to facilitate the transfer of knowledge into a usable form and assist in the development of a rule base.

In this fuzzy approach, the rule base is generated automatically by the following process:

1. The user enters the rule strategy for reacting to a given stimuli (the base behavior) in a qualitative form using a template.
2. The user defines the input membership functions for the stimulus specifically for each behavior.
3. The system creates a skeleton rule base for this information and verifies its completeness regarding coverage of the stimulus-and-response space. Output membership functions are initially set to a standard value.
4. Specialized metarules are then generated to suppress or inhibit behaviors (in the subsumption sense). The membership functions of the rules are automatically adjusted to reflect the desired dominance relationships.

Successful results have been achieved using automatically generated fuzzy rule bases for both indoor and outdoor robotic systems.

In a system more closely related to the other types of learning discussed earlier in this chapter, work at the Laboratoire d'Informatique Fondamentale et d'Intelligence Artificielle (LIFIA) in France (Reignier 1995) has used supervised incremental methods for learning fuzzy rules. The task here is to find a collection of fuzzy rules that captures the robot's existing supervised behavior. Temporal difference learning methods (discussed in section 8.4.2) are used. In particular, the system is capable of rule creation, adaptation (parameter modification of THEN part of rule), and generalization (modification of IF part). Positive reinforcement results when the robot reaches the goal, negative reinforcement when it bumps into something. Learning occurs while the robot moves through the world on the way to the goal. At this writing only preliminary simulation results were available, but nonetheless this work shows more traditional reinforcement learning methods' extensibility to more unusual behavioral control regimes such as fuzzy logic.

8.7 OTHER TYPES OF LEARNING

Several other methods for learning have been applied to or have potential for application in behavior-based systems. A brief survey follows.

8.7.1 Case-Based Learning

Case-based learning methods use the results of past experiences to guide future action (Kolodner 1994). Experiences are stored as structured cases. The basic algorithm for case-based learning and acting is as follows:

1. Classify the current problem.
2. Use the resulting problem description to retrieve similar case(s) from case memory.
3. Adapt the old case's solution to the new situation's specifics.
4. Apply the new solution and evaluate the results.
5. Learn by storing the new case and its results.

At Georgia Tech, Ram et al. (1997) have applied these methods in simulation only to a schema-based behavioral controller called ACBARR. Cases comprise three components: a set of gains **G** and several internal parameters used for wandering and obstacle avoidance that represent a particular behavioral assemblage; environmental information indicating when this configuration was in use; and some local bookkeeping information. The goal becomes learning which situations should be associated with which case's behavioral configurations. Figure 8.20 shows the overall system architecture. The system begins with a particular configuration determined by the parameters of the behaviors. When performance inadequacies are determined by such criteria as not making progress toward the goal or not moving sufficiently, a new case more appropriate for the task is selected. On-line adaptation of the case occurs by a method referred to as *learning momentum* (Clark, Arkin, and Ram 1992). This method, succinctly summarized, states that if the system is doing well, do the same thing a little more strongly; if doing poorly, alter the behavioral composition to improve its performance. For example, if the system moves from a relatively obstacle-free area to a more cluttered one, obstacle avoidance begins to increase and goal attraction to decrease until satisfactory performance is achieved.

Whenever ACBARR encounters a sufficiently novel environment or significantly modifies the original case retrieved, that information is stored for future reference, i.e., it learns to use those behaviors the next time it encounters a similar situation. The system is capable of escaping box canyons and navigating complex mazes using these methods, which a purely reactive system would not normally be able to do (figure 8.21).

8.7.2   Memory-based Learning

Memory-based learning can perhaps be viewed as case-based learning taken to the extreme, in which explicit numerical details of every experience are remembered and stored. Although it has not yet been applied in behavioral controllers, it has been proven an effective technique in robots for learning functional control law approximators for tasks such as pole balancing, juggling, and billiards (Atkeson, Moore, and Schaal 1997; Moore, Atkeson, and Schaal 1995). Simply speaking, in memory-based learning, complex control functions are approximated by the interpolation of locally related past successful experiences. These *lazy learning* methods are well-suited for complex domains with large amounts of data.

8.7.3   Explanation-Based Learning

Explanation-based learning (EBL) methods use models (typically symbolic) of the domain to guide the generalization and specialization of a concept by induction. Learning occurs on an instance-by-instance basis, with refinement of the underlying model occurring at all steps in the process, guided by an underlying model or theory (explanation of the world). Domain-specific knowledge is crucial for this process to operate effectively, contrary to the numeric methods of reinforcement and neural learning we discussed earlier. The robot generates a plan of action based on its goal, current perceptions, and underlying

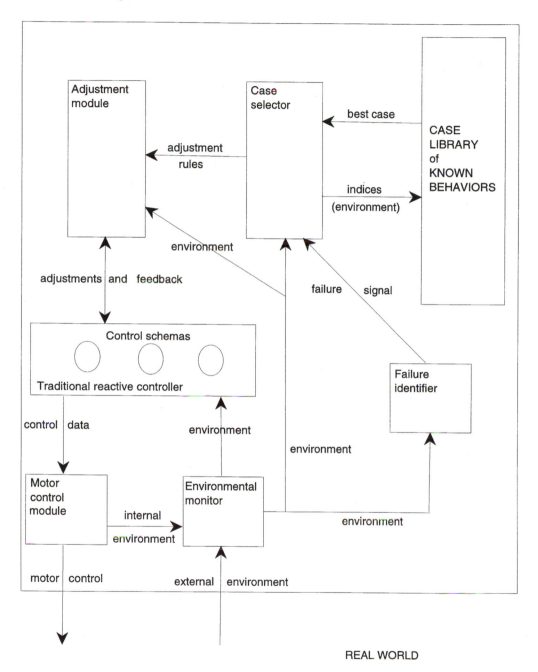

Figure 8.20
ACBARR system architecture.

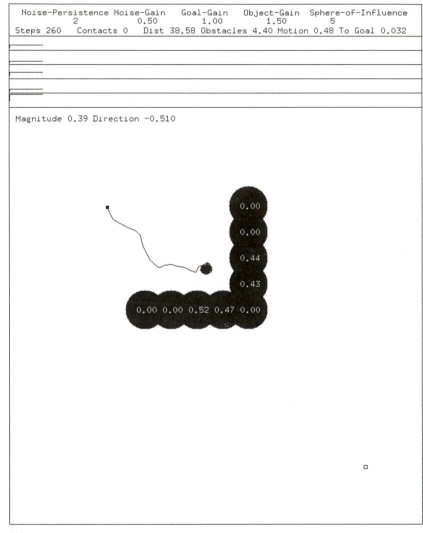

(A)

Figure 8.21
Effects of Adaptation on Box Canyon Performance: (A) Purely reactive, no learning or
adaptation; (B) No cases used, only on-line adaptation; (C) Case-based reasoning and
on-line adaptation (ACBARR).

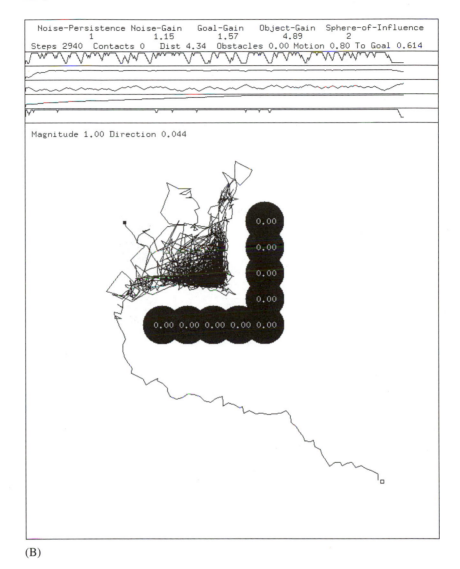

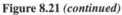

(B)

Figure 8.21 *(continued)*

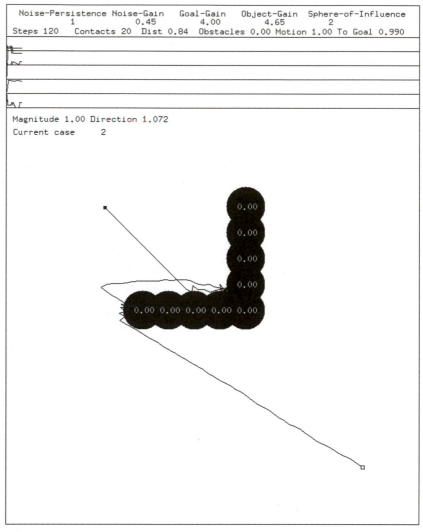

(C)

Figure 8.21 *(continued)*

theory of the world it inhabits. Based on the plan's success or failure, future plans are chosen as guided by the theory.

Learning sequences of operations in manipulation tasks seems to be the domain of choice for EBL scientists studying robotics (Segre and Dejong 1985). Other research in the manipulation domain has demonstrated that the underlying theory required in EBL can also be learned (Christiansen, Mason, and Mitchell 1991). Here, not only is the plan selection process affected, but the underlying theoretical explanation of action is learned as well.

Thrun (1995) has demonstrated hybrid EBL, Q-learning, and neural learning for the navigation of the mobile robot XAVIER (figure 5.15), whose particular task here is to recognize and then move to a specific target (green soda can) using sonar, vision, and laser stripe range data. Navigation consists of a sequence of specified actions, rather than being controlled by a set of active behaviors. Seven actions are permissible, including sharp turns, moving forward, and a specialized, hard-coded obstacle avoidance routine should something get in the way. A learning episode consists of the robot starting at some point within the lab and terminating when either the robot is directly in front of the target soda can (rewarded) or the target leaves the field of view (penalized). Q-learning is used to determine the action policies. The domain theory, instead of being symbolically represented by rules, which is usually the case in EBL, is captured in a neural network in advance using back-propagation training. The training set for Thrun's experiments includes 3,000 instances from 700 navigation episodes. These neural networks are used to predict (explain) the reinforcement that would result from the application of a particular action. The learning process proceeds first by an ex post facto explanation using the domain theory of the current training example's result. Generalization then occurs based on the explanation of the training instance in accordance with the existing weight space derived from previous examples. Finally, refinement occurs by minimizing the error between the training example and the synaptic weights in the networks. The net effect in Thrun's trials was successful and relatively rapid on-line learning (less than ten minutes) and navigation for this particular task. EBL has yet to be extended to behavior-based systems, but there appears to be significant potential for its use, based upon these other results.

8.8   CHAPTER SUMMARY

- Robots need to learn in order to adapt effectively to a changing and dynamic environment.
- Behavior-based robots can learn in a variety of ways:

- They can learn entire new behaviors.
- They can learn more effective responses.
- They can learn to associate more appropriate or broader stimuli with a particular response.
- They can learn new combinations of behaviors (assemblages).
- They can learn more effective coordination of existing behaviors.

■ Learning can either be continuous and on-line or be conducted at the end of an episode or many episodes.

■ Reinforcement learning is a battery of numerical techniques that can be effectively used in adaptive behavior-based robots:

- Using statistical correlation to associate rewards with actions.
- Adaptive heuristic critic methods, in which the decision policy is learned independently from the utility cost function for state evaluation. These AHC methods often are implemented in neural network systems.
- Q-learning in which actions and states are evaluated together.

■ Neural networks, a form of reinforcement learning, use specialized, multi-node architectures. Learning occurs through the adjustment of synaptic weights by an error minimization procedure such as Hebb's rule or back-propagation.

■ Classical conditioning in which a conditioned stimulus is eventually, over time with suitable training, associated with an unconditioned response, can be manifested in robotic systems as well.

■ Simple associative memories implemented as two-layer perceptrons can produce rapid learning for simple tasks.

■ Genetic algorithms operate over sets of individuals over multiple generations using operators such as selection, crossover and mutation.

■ Effective fitness functions must be defined for the particular task and environment for successful evolutionary learning. By suitable selection, particular ecological niches can be defined for various behavioral classes of robots (e.g., safe, fast, etc.)

■ A classifier system uses fixed-length bit string rule-based representations for discrete behavioral encodings for use with genetic operators.

■ Evolutionary strategies have been used for on-line adaptation and changes in physical structure in addition to the more common application to off-line learning of control system parameters.

■ Fuzzy control uses rule-based methods that involve taking crisp sensor inputs, fuzzifying them, conducting fuzzy inference, and then producing a crisp response.

■ Membership functions map the inputs onto the degree of membership for a particular linguistic variable.

■ Learning can be accomplished in fuzzy behavior–based robot systems by capturing designer intentions through the automatic generation and refinement of suitable fuzzy rules for an application or by adapting the rules directly using reinforcement learning methods.

■ Many other powerful learning methods have just begun to be explored in the context of robotics, including memory-based, case-based, and explanation-based learning.

■ Behavioral learning systems have enabled robots to learn to walk, to push boxes, to shoot a ball into a goal, and to navigate safely toward a goal, among other things.

Chapter 9
Social Behavior

The mob has many heads but no brains.
—English proverb

A team effort is a lot of people doing what I say.
—Michael Winner

Chapter Objectives

1. To understand the benefits and complexities of multiagent robotic systems.
2. To be able to characterize the different dimensions along which teams of robots can be organized.
3. To recognize the differences in communication, perception, learning and adaptation associated with social behavior when compared to solitary robotic agents.

9.1 ARE TWO (OR *N*) ROBOTS BETTER THAN ONE?

When is it better to go it alone, and when to have teammates? This question applies not only to human endeavors but robotics as well. As expected, teaming robots together has both an upside and a downside. The positive aspects:

- Improved system performance: Where tasks are naturally decomposable, the "divide and conquer" strategy is wholly appropriate. By exploiting the parallelism inherent in teaming, tasks can be completed considerably more efficiently overall for a wide range of tasks and environments using groups of robots working together.
- Task enablement: The ability to do certain tasks that would be impossible for a single robot.

- Distributed sensing: Information sharing beyond the range of an existing sensor suite on an individual robot.
- Distributed action at a distance: A robot team can simultaneously carry out actions at many different locations.
- Fault tolerance: Agent redundancy and reduced individual complexity can increase overall system reliability.

The negative aspects:

- Interference: The old adage "Too many cooks spoil the broth" pretty much sums it up. The fact that actual robots have physical size provides the opportunity for blockage or robot-robot collisions. The volume of the agents themselves results in an overall reduction of navigational free space when more than one robot is used. This is especially significant in tight quarters.
- Communication cost and robustness: Communication is not free. It generally requires additional hardware, computational processing, and energy. Communication can also suffer because of noisy channels, electronic countermeasures, and deceit by other agents, complicating reliability.
- Uncertainty concerning other robots' intentions: Coordination generally requires knowing what the other agent is doing, at least to some extent. When this is unclear because of lack of knowledge or poor communication, robots may compete rather than cooperate.
- Overall system cost: In some cases, two robots may cost more than one. If the team can be designed using simpler, less complex, robots than would be required individually, this is not necessarily the case.

In light of the potentially significant advantages afforded by multirobot teams despite the potential drawbacks, researchers are investigating cooperative societies, bringing a wide range of perspectives to bear on social behavior:

- Ethological: Studying how animals cooperate and communicate (Arkin and Hobbs 1992).
- Organizational: Looking at how human organizations are structured (Carley 1995).
- Computational models: Drawing from computer science in the areas of multiprocessing and parallel system design (Wang 1995).
- Distributed artificial intelligence: Dealing with the problems of agency and cooperation using negotiation, deception, and methods for communication (Lesser 1995).
- Motion planning: Addressing the geometric and kinematic problems of multiple objects moving about in space (Latombe 1991).

■ Artificial life: Studying the relationships the multiagent teams form with their environments, typically including aspects of competition as well as co-operation (Langton 1995).

Independent of the perspective taken, many potentially useful jobs for robotic societies have been identified. Some of the most commonly studied tasks for multiagent robotic systems include

■ Foraging, where randomly placed items are distributed throughout the environment, and the team's task is to carry them back to a central location.

■ Consuming, which requires the robots to perform work on the desired objects in place, rather than carrying them back to a home base. This may involve assembly or disassembly operations, such as in a land mine field.

■ Grazing, which requires a robot team to cover an environmental area adequately. The potential applications of this social behavior include lawn mowing, surveillance operations for search and rescue, and cleaning operations such as vacuuming.

■ Formations or flocking, which require the team of robots to assume a geometric pattern (approximate in the case of flocking, specific in the case of formations) and maintain it while moving about the world. Early work in this area has been concerned with theoretical and simulated results (e.g., Sugihara and Suzuki 1990; Parker 1992; Chen and Luh 1994). Behavior-based methods for coordinating multiple graphical agents have also had a significant impact within the computer animation community (Reynolds 1987; Hodgins and Brogan 1994). Real robots have demonstrated both formation (Balch and Arkin 1995) and flocking (Mataric 1993a) behaviors.

■ Object transport, which probably can be viewed as a subtask of certain types of foraging, typically requires the distribution of several robots around the desired object with the goal being to move it to a particular location. Particular examples include box pushing (Kube and Zhang 1992) and coordinated pallet lifting and transport (Johnson and Bay 1995).

Scientists and engineers in Japan were among the first to study coordinated mobile multirobot systems. An early cellular robotic (CEBOT) system (Fukuda et al. 1989), involving the docking of several small robot units to produce a larger robot, illustrated communication mechanisms that can be used to support coordinated behavior. Interrobot communication devices included infrared photodiodes used for messaging that provided positional information regarding dock location. The CEBOT program research has continued over the years, resulting in an architecture (Cai et al. 1995), depicted in figure 9.1, that consists

**INPUT
DEVICES**

**OUTPUT
DEVICES**

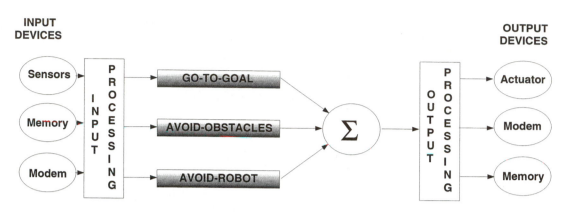

Figure 9.1
CEBOT Mark V control system.

of multiple parallel behaviors using vector summation as the basis for behavioral integration (section 3.4.3.2). Small teams of mobile robots (figure 9.2) were successfully tested for multirobot goal-oriented navigation among obstacles. These agents use a behavioral suite consisting of go-to-goal, avoid-obstacles (using infrared and ultrasonic sensors), and an avoid-robot-collision behavior that produces a right turn whenever another robot is within a certain distance.

At the University of Tsukuba, Premvuti and Yuta (1995) experimented with a multiagent robotic system using Yamabico robots equipped with ultrasound, dead reckoning for position estimation, and a communication network capable of transmitting position information. This work focused on cooperation between robots to avoid collisions as they moved about corridors and through intersections.

9.2   ETHOLOGICAL CONSIDERATIONS

As has been our practice throughout this book, we look toward biological systems, whenever feasible, to provide insights regarding the design of behavior-based robotic systems. Ethological studies show clearly that multiagent societies offer significant advantages in the achievement of community tasks. A wide range of animal social structures exists to support agent-agent interactions. For example, uni-level organizations are found in schooling fish, hierarchical systems are found in baboon societies, and caste systems are typified by many insect colonies (e.g., bees). The relationships between these agents often

Figure 9.2
CEBOT Mark V robot team. (Reprinted with permission from Cai et al. 1995. © 1995 IEEE.)

determine the nature and type of communication essential for the social system to succeed. The converse also holds in that the communication abilities somewhat determine the most effective social organizations for a particular class of agents.

Tinbergen's (1953) influential work on animal behavior describes a broad range of social activity:

- Simple social behaviors
- Sympathetic induction, or doing the same things as others (e.g., the yawn-yawn response)
- Reciprocal behavior, such as coital activity or feeding young through induced regurgitation
- Antagonistic behavior or simple conflict
- Mating behaviors
- Persuasion and appeasement
- Orientation or approach
- Family and group life behaviors
- Flocking and herding defense-related behaviors, such as communal attack (mobs), warning (the flock is as alert as the most observant individual), and crowding (reducing vulnerability by confusing predators)
- Congregation, using smell or vision

- Infectious behaviors that spread throughout the society, such as alarm, sleep, and eating
- Fighting behaviors
- Reproductive fighting: Preventing rivals from being at same location
- Mutual hostility: Spreading the society over a region
- Peck order: Establishing a dominance hierarchy and ultimately reducing fighting

One of the most commonly studied social biological systems is that of ants. Excellent references on their social organization and communication methods include Holldobler and Wilson 1990 and Goetsch 1957. Ants typically use chemical communication to convey information to one another. We have seen earlier (section 2.5.1) an example of a robotic system capable of a primitive form of chemotaxis inspired by ants' communication methods. Foraging mechanisms are considerably more sophisticated in ant colonies, however, than in any robotic system thus far developed. Foraging ants lay down chemical trails, dramatically increasing the efficiency of foraging while avoiding the need for explicit memory in the organism. Decision making is a collective effort rather than a master-slave decision (Deneubourg and Goss 1989). This pattern is consistent with the goal of avoiding hierarchical decisions in a behavior-based robotic society. Different foraging patterns for different ant species have been simulated, exploiting their tendencies of collecting different-sized food particles, among other characteristics (Goss et al. 1990). One study (Franks 1986) has looked in particular at the behavior of army ants in the context of group retrieval of prey, evaluating the relationship of the mass of retrieved objects and the velocity of their return.

A sampling of other interesting social ethological studies includes:

- the impact of environmental factors such as food supply, hunger, danger, and competition on the foraging behavior of fish (Croy and Hughes 1991).
- mob behavior and communication in the whip-tail wallaby, illustrating the emergent organization of multiple agents and the nature of communication that supports this group behavior (Kaufmann 1974).
- primate studies regarding the organization of colonies (Altmann 1974) relative to their environment.
- the role of display behavior for parsimonious communication mechanisms (e.g., Moynihan 1970).

(See also section 2.4 for additional discussion of ethological studies' influence on behavior-based robotics.)

9.3 CHARACTERIZATION OF SOCIAL BEHAVIOR

Designing a society of robots involves many different considerations. A team of agents (either animal or robotic) can be characterized along a number of dimensions, including reliability, organization, communication, spatial distribution, and congregation.

9.3.1 Reliability

System reliability is defined as the probability that the system can act correctly in a given situation over time. Parallelism, in general, increases reliability, eliminating the potential for single-point failures that would be found in serially structured systems. Holldobler and Wilson (1990), based on their studies of ants, argue that redundancy within an organization should occur at low levels rather than high levels. Redundancy at the agent level itself, as opposed to redundant teams of agents, is considered more important. The agents must be predisposed in some manner to work together as well. This may be something as simple as not interfering with each other by staying out of each other's way or as complex as the development of a complex vocabulary for exchanging messages.

9.3.2 Social Organization

Animal societies are very diverse. Wilson (1975) established ten "qualities of sociality": group size, demographic distribution, cohesiveness, amount and pattern of connectedness, permeability, compartmentalization, differentiation of roles, integration of behavior, information flow, and fraction of time devoted to social behavior. Deegener defined over forty categories of animal societies (Allee 1978). A few distinct examples of social organization include multilevel hierarchical structures (e.g., ant caste systems), flat single-level structures (e.g., schooling fish), dynamic, loosely structured mobs (e.g., whip-tail wallabies), and dominance systems or peck orders (e.g., roosting place competition for fowl). The number and types of constituent agents ultimately determine the society's performance. Specialization (heterogeneity) should be based upon societal need. One heuristic states that if an event occurs regularly within the society's lifetime, a particular class of agents should be present to handle it (Wilson 1975), implying, for robotics, that heterogeneous societies should be developed if there is a demand for specialized skills. For example, it might be better to create robots that are experts at gathering material and then delivering

Table 9.1
Modes of Animal Communication

Mode	Directionality	Distance	Relevant Uses
Audition	Low-Medium	Far	Alarm, individuality
Luminescense	High	Medium	Location
Chemical	Low	Low	Mass communication
Reflected light	Medium	Medium	Social distance (Box 1973)
Tactile	High	Low	Contact
Electric	Low	Low	Aggression

it to robots that are experts at assembling structures than to try to make all of them competent for both tasks. The cliche "jack of all trades and master of none" may apply to robot societies as well.

9.3.3   Communication

Communication has two major aspects:

■ Information Content: Most animal communication mechanisms operate at a very low bandwidth. Even when vision is used, the signals between agents generally have a low information content. Messages in animal societies are often very limited: For ants, there are typically ten to twenty different chemical signals (Holldobler and Wilson 1990); and mammals, birds, and fish have been estimated to have approximately fifteen to thirty-five distinct major display behaviors (Moynihan 1970). Note that these may be graded by intensity.
■ Mode: Different animal societies use a surprisingly wide range of communication mechanisms, including chemical, bioluminescence, reflected-light, tactile, acoustic, echolocation, infrared, and electric communication (table 9.1).

9.3.4   Spatial Distribution

Spatial distribution is particularly important for activities such as foraging for food. Spatial considerations include small versus large groups or overlapping versus non-overlapping foraging ranges. Resource density, an environmental factor, often has a direct bearing on overall society size (the more resources, the larger the group) and also influences the foraging patterns, so that the more restricted the resource, the greater the overlap of foraging ranges (Altmann 1974; Carr and MacDonald 1986). A generalization resulting from this relationship is Horn's Principle of Group Foraging, which states that if a resource is evenly distributed, it is better for the agents (in this case, birds) to form individual, non-overlapping foraging ranges instead of roosting and foraging together (Wilson 1975). Various models for ant foraging have also been developed relating foraging ranges and strategies to resource density and distribution (Deneubourg and Goss 1989; Goss et al. 1990). Similar considerations of resource-task allocation should also affect robot societies' social behavior.

9.3.5   Congregation

Coordinating activity is important for a society. How can the society remain together over time? Simple tasks such as finding other agents can be difficult in a large group or broad area. Animals use various strategies to accomplish this task:

- By defining a colony location as a predefined meeting point recognized by other agents, agents can converge at this location. Colonies have the advantages of having common storage of resources and good defense capabilities.
- *Lekking* is a group behavior that involves the generation of a loud noise by a number of similar agents (e.g., animals of the same sex), simultaneously increasing the likelihood of other agents' hearing and then joining and strengthening the group's lekking.
- Distinctive calls can be used to help find lost agents or to indicate that an agent is lost.
- Specific assembly calls by a single agent can also muster a group of agents that is widely dispersed.

9.3.6   Performance

To effectively evaluate societal system performance, specific metrics must be introduced. One useful metric is *speedup* ($S[i, j]$), a measure of the performance of a team of N robots relative to N times the performance of a single robot. Formally, the speedup for a team of i robots carrying out j task actions is

$$S[i, j] = \frac{P[1, j]i}{P[i, j]},\tag{9.1}$$

where $P[i, j]$ is a performance measure. $P[i, j]$ can be measured in many different ways, depending on what is important to the task. It could be the total time taken to complete a task, the total length of travel for the robots, the energy used during task achievement, or various combinations of these or other metrics (Balch and Arkin 1994). Speedup results can be categorized into sublinear performance ($S[i, j] < 1$), where multiples of a single agent perform better than a team; superlinear performance ($S[i, j] > 1$), where a team performs better; and linear performance ($S[i, j] = 1$), a break-even point where the overall performance is comparable (Mataric 1992c).

9.4   WHAT MAKES A ROBOTIC TEAM?

The issue of what makes a robotic team influences how designers of robotic systems and societies make intelligent decisions regarding what organization, communication, behavioral strategies, and the like are appropriate for a particular task environment. We now examine some ways in which robot teams can be structured and in so doing help define the design space for these societies.

Early researchers in Tsukuba, Japan (Premvuti and Yuta 1990; Yuta 1993), categorized several important aspects regarding the organization of multirobot teams, delineating each society according to

- Active or non-active cooperation: Robots either share or do not share a common goal.
- Level of independence: Control is either distributed or centralized (the robots' decisions are made either locally or by some external global agent) or some combination of both.
- Types of communication: Communication is either
- explicit (where a signal is intentionally shared between two or more robots) or
- implicit (where information is shared by observation of other agents' actions).

These first steps towards a taxonomy as well as a proliferation of multiagent robotics research led a Canadian research group (Dudek et al. 1993) to propose a more complete taxonomy capable of categorizing the variety of multiagent robotic systems being created by laboratories around the world. It characterizes teaming along these lines:

- **Team size**: Refers to the number of robots and consists of the following subclasses: alone (one robot), pair (two robots), limited group (a relatively small number of robots given the magnitude of the task), or infinite group (for all practical purposes an infinite number of robots).
- **Communication range**: Refers to each robot's ability to communicate directly with other team members and consists of the following subclasses: none (no direct communication), near (only robots within a short distance can be communicated with directly), and infinite (no limit to the robots' direct communication capabilities).
- **Communication topology**: Refers to the pathways by which communication can occur. The subclasses are broadcast (all information is sent and received by all robots within range), addressed (direct messaging is allowed on a named basis), tree (only hierarchical communication is permitted), and graph (arbitrary communication pathways can be established).
- **Communication bandwidth**: Refers to the amount of communication available. The subclasses are high (communication is for all practical purposes free), motion-related (motion and communication costs are approximately the same), low (communication costs are very high), and zero (no communication is available).
- **Team reconfigurability**: Refers to the flexibility regarding the structure and organization of the team, with subclasses static (no changes are permitted), communication coordinated (robots in communication with each other can reorganize), and dynamic (arbitrary reorganization is permitted).
- **Team unit processing ability**: Refers to the underlying computational model used. Subclasses include non-linear summation units, finite state automata, push down automata, and Turing machine equivalent.
- **Team composition**: Refers to the composition of the agents themselves. The subclasses are homogeneous (all the same), and heterogeneous (more than one type).

Cao et al. (1995) at UCLA's Commotion Lab made another attempt at capturing the design space of multirobot systems. It describes four principal research axes:

- Architecture: Whether the system's control is centralized or decentralized.
- Differentiation of agents: Whether the constituent agents' structure and control systems are identical (homogeneous) or different (heterogeneous).
- Communication structures:
- Via environment: for example, a trail left by the robot
- Via sensing: by observing other robots' actions

• Via communication: by intentional signaling

■ Models of other agents' intentions, capabilities, states, or beliefs: This aspect incorporates ideas from the distributed AI community.

It is probably premature to assume that any one of these categorizations or taxonomies can adequately express the wide range of robotic team possibilities. In the remainder of this chapter, we will focus instead on social organization and structure, interrobot communication, distributed perception, and societal learning, concluding with a case study of a successful application. As in previous chapters, despite the large body of simulation studies, we concentrate on those systems tested on actual robotic hardware.

9.5 SOCIAL ORGANIZATION AND STRUCTURE

The behavioral architecture for a robotic society's constituent agents is only one of many commitments made during team design. The permissible communication protocols between team members and the societal structure (homogeneous or heterogeneous agents) are also extremely important. We now look at a range of architectural strategies for robotic societies. Often the issues discussed within these particular systems transcend the individual agents' behavioral architecture. The systems described are only representative of the field and do not constitute a complete survey by any means.

9.5.1 The Nerd Herd

An intellectual descendent of Brooks, Mataric has expanded subsumption-style architectures for applications of robotic teams (Mataric 1994a). We encountered this multiagent approach in the context of a subsumption-based foraging system in section 4.3.4. A broad range of basic social behaviors has been specified, including

■ Homing: Each agent strives to move to a common home base.
■ Aggregation: Agents try to gather while maintaining a specified separation.
■ Dispersion: Agents cover a large area, establishing and maintaining a minimum separation between robots.
■ Following: Robots follow one after the other.
■ Safe wandering: Robots move around while avoiding collisions with obstacles and each other.

As is standard for subsumption, a rule-based encoding is used. For example:

Figure 9.3
The Nerd Herd. (Photograph courtesy of M. Mataric.)

```
Aggregate:
 If an agent is outside the aggregation distance
     turn toward the aggregation centroid and go.
 Else
     stop.
```

Similar simple rules are constructed for the other behaviors.

Two different coordination mechanisms are used: direct combination, which is a vector summation process, and temporal combination, which sequences through a series of behavioral states. Perceptual information is encoded as a series of predicates (e.g., at-home? have-puck? crowded? behind-kin? sense-puck?) used to encode the sensory data needed to activate the relevant behaviors.

The system has been evaluated both in simulation and on a set of up to twenty small mobile robots, the so-called Nerd Herd (figure 9.3). The basic behaviors, described earlier, can be combined to yield more complex social interactions, including

- flocking, consisting of safe wandering, aggregation, and dispersion.

- surrounding, consisting of safe wandering, following, and aggregation.
- herding, consisting of safe wandering, surrounding, and flocking.
- foraging, consisting of safe wandering, dispersion, following, homing, and flocking.

Note that in herding, for example, composite behaviors such as surrounding are also used as building blocks.

The contributions of this work lie not in architectural advances but rather in the study of new rule-based behaviors for multiple physically embodied agents capable of interacting with each other. This social interaction can lead to physical interference with each others' goals, complicating overall societal task completion.

9.5.2   Alliance Architecture

Another offshoot of the subsumption approach is the Alliance architecture, which includes special consideration for heterogeneous teams of robots (Parker 1994, 1995). Alliance varies significantly from subsumption in its addition of behavior sets and a motivational system. Behavior sets enable different groups of low-level behaviors to be active together or to hibernate, permitting a reconfigurability atypical of subsumption-style architectures. Motivational behaviors enable or disable these behavior sets. They operate by accepting, in addition to the normal inputs from sensors and inhibition from other behaviors commonplace in subsumption architectures, information from interrobot communication and the existing agent's internal motivational state. Internal motivation allows the robot to respond effectively when trapped by permitting it to become impatient or by allowing it to acquiesce (give up) on a task if it is overly difficult or unachievable. To some extent Alliance can be viewed as adding a layer above the subsumption architecture that embodies these new capabilities (figure 9.4).

The direct input of communication signals from other robots into an agent's active behaviors facilitates cooperation between agents. Explicit models of interrobot communication provide predicates supporting information transfer between two robots regarding a specific task over a given time period.

Impatience relates to a robot's waiting for the completion of a task by another robot that is a prerequisite for the impatient robot's next action. In Alliance, it is implemented using an impatience rate function and a binary impatience_reset function. These functions control the motivational variable representing impatience within the robot. Acquiescence is similar but deter-

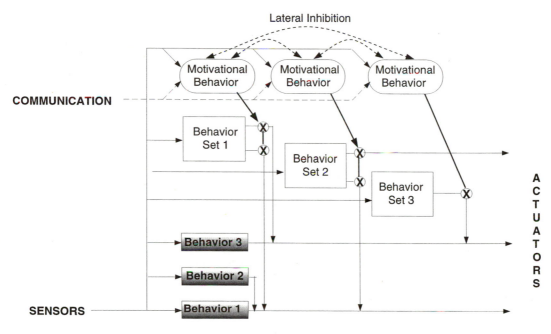

Figure 9.4
The Alliance architecture.

mines when to change behavior in deference to another robot. Each robot's (r_i) overall motivation for a behavioral set a_{ij} is computed by the following equations:

$$m_{ij}(0) = 0, \text{ and}$$

$$m_{ij}(t) = [m_{ij}(t-1) + impatience_{ij}(t)] * sensory\_feedback_{ij}(t) *$$

$$activity\_suppression_{ij}(t) * impatience\_reset_{ij}(t) * acquiescence_{ij}(t),$$

where $impatience_{ij}(t)$ is the impatience rate function that determines how quickly the robot becomes impatient; $sensory\_feedback_{ij}(t)$ is a binary predicate that indicates whether the preconditions for the behavioral set are satisfied or not; $activity\_suppression_{ij}(t)$ is a binary predicate indicating whether or not another behavioral set a_{ik}, $j \neq k$ is active at time t; $impatience\_reset_{ij}(t)$ is a binary predicate that is 0 when another robot is making progress on the task that the robot is waiting on, and otherwise 1; and $acquiescence_{ij}(t)$ is a binary predicate that determines whether to give up on a task or not. Thus the motivation for a behavioral set will continue to grow unless sensor data indicates that it is

Table 9.2
Example tasks for Alliance

Task	Robots	Behavioral sets
Box pushing	Genghis R-2	push, go-home push-left, push-right
Hazardous waste cleanup	3 R-2	find-locations-methodically, find-locations-wander, move-spill, report-progress
Janitorial service	Simulation	empty-garbage, dust-furniture, clean-floor
Bounding overwatch	Simulation	join-group, emerge-leader, follow-leader, lead-to-waypoint, overwatch

not needed, another competing behavior is active, another robot has taken over the task, or the robot gives up on the task. When the motivation value crosses an arbitrarily predefined threshold, then behavioral set a_{ij} becomes active in robot r_i. The robot then concurrently and periodically broadcasts to all other robots the fact that a_{ij} is active.

Alliance has been used for a wide range of mission scenarios, as table 9.2 shows. Figure 9.5 shows two snapshots of the hazardous waste cleanup mission being conducted by three R-2 robots.

9.5.3   Stagnation Behaviors

Kube and Zhang (1994) of the University of Alberta have studied a common problem in multirobot tasks: avoiding stagnation during task completion. Stagnation occurs when team members are not cooperating effectively with each other. Alliance addresses this problem through motivational variables such as acquiescence and impatience, relying to a large degree on interrobot broadcast communication. An alternative approach adds a new stagnation behavior to the overall architecture consisting of one or more specific strategies used to overcome the particular difficulty confronting the team. In box pushing, for example, stagnation may result from individual agents' pushing in opposite directions, effectively canceling each other's forces.

Figure 9.6 depicts a three-behavior arbitration-based architecture for a box-pushing task. Stagnation is defined in this context as when a robot is in contact with the box, but the box is not moving. To handle this potential event, each agent's stagnation behavior is composed of several strategic behaviors including realignment, which changes the direction in which the robot is pushing, and

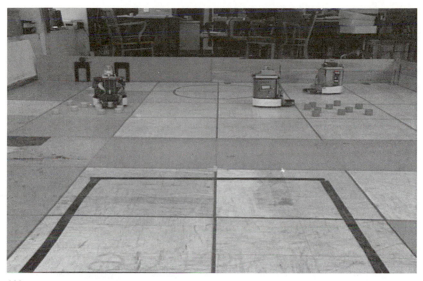

(A)

(B)

Figure 9.5
In a mock-up mission, a team of robots (A) retrieve and (B) deliver spill objects (the dark pucks) to the disposal area (the square region in the foreground). (Photographs courtesy of Lynne Parker.)

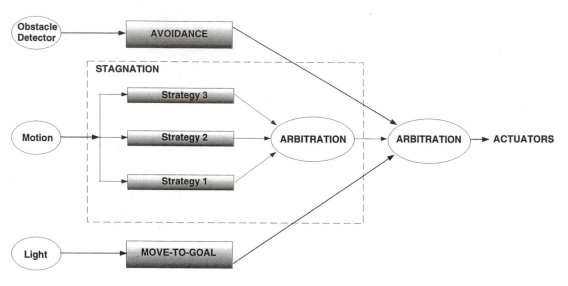

Figure 9.6
Behavioral architecture, incorporating stagnation behavior.

repositioning, which moves the robot to a different random location along the box's perimeter. These stagnation strategies can be assigned priorities according to the length of time the stagnation condition has persisted. (In this case, realignment is attempted before repositioning.)

In contrast to Alliance, no explicit communication is required between robots, nor knowledge of the other agent's intentions, to eliminate the stagnation condition. The behavioral control architecture has been successfully verified in experiments with teams of small robots (figure 9.7).

9.5.4   Societal Agents

Multiagent schema-based robotic architectures have also been developed and fielded. In the Societal Agent Theory (MacKenzie 1996), a single representational syntax is used to express not only primitive sensorimotor behaviors and assemblages but also teams of physical agents. This approach, inspired by Minsky's Society of Minds (Minsky 1986), makes no distinction between the methods used to deploy intra- and interagent behaviors. A society consists of a collection of behaving agents that may or may not be spatially distributed (i.e., may or may not have multiple physical embodiments). A team of robots can thus be viewed as an assemblage itself.

Figure 9.7
A team of small robots pushing a box.

Earlier work at Georgia Tech (Arkin 1992b) provided conceptual proof that robotic team cooperation was feasible in the absence of any explicit robot-to-robot communication. This was shown first for foraging tasks, then extended to consuming and grazing scenarios (Balch and Arkin 1994). A straightforward extension of schema-based reactive control (section 4.4) was used, but there was no direct modeling of the robot society as an entity itself.

The subsequent Societal Agent Theory provides a new means for expressing both homogeneous and heterogeneous teams. This in turn facilitates the design of robot teams and has been incorporated into a multiagent design and specification system called *MissionLab* (section 9.9.2) (MacKenzie, Cameron, and Arkin 1995).

Multiagent behaviors such as formation control, which allows cooperative motion of robots relative to each other (Balch and Arkin 1995), and team teleautonomy, where a single human operator can effectively influence the

(A) Robots in line formation.

Figure 9.8
Two Denning Robots moving across the laboratory, initially starting in line formation (side by side), then transitioning to column formation (one following the other)—note change in orientation relative to stripes on floor.

behavior of an entire team of robots (Arkin and Ali 1994), have been developed within this framework (sections 9.9.1 through 9.9.3). These behaviors have been tested in simulation, on Denning mobile robots (figure 9.8), and on military vehicles as part of the Defense Advanced Research Project Agency's (DARPA's) Unmanned Ground Vehicle (UGV) Demo II Program (section 9.9).

9.5.5 Army Ant Project

At Virginia Tech, Johnson and Bay (1995) have focused on cooperation by teams of robots in payload transportation. A controller (figure 9.9) consisting of four behaviors using a vector summation coordination mechanism has been developed for each of the agents to direct a transport task that involves lifting a pallet containing material and moving it to a goal location. The orientation behavior strives to keep the pallet level, independent of its height. A force

(B) Robots in column formation.

Figure 9.8 *(continued)*

behavior coordinates the forces exerted by the individual robot with those of other members of its team using interagent broadcast communication to distribute the load as evenly as possible. The pallet-contact behavior ensures that the robot maintains contact with the pallet as it moves, while the height behavior determines the level at which the pallet should be held. Although tested only in simulation to date, this research provides compelling results for cooperation in lifting, transporting, and lowering payloads over rough terrain.

9.6   INTERROBOT COMMUNICATION

Communication between robots is an extremely important consideration in the design of a multirobot society. In this section we will consider the following issues:

- Whether communication is needed at all
- Over what range communication should be permitted
- What the information content should be
- What guarantees can be made regarding communication and performance

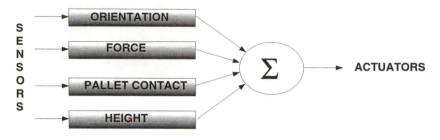

Figure 9.9
Behavioral controller for payload transport.

9.6.1   The Need for Communication

A fundamental issue in effecting cooperative behavior in a team of robots is the level of appropriate interagent communication. Communication is not free and can be undependable. It can occur explicitly, through direct channels, or indirectly, through the observation of behavioral displays or changes left in the environment (e.g., trail marking). In hostile environments, electronic countermeasures may be in effect, jamming information flow between agents or introducing deceit into the information stream.

So what should a robot listen to and believe if it is to work together with other robots? How should a designer of a multiagent robot system incorporate communication into the system? Identifying the major roles of communication in robot teams should help in the design process. They include (Fukuda and Sekiyama 1994):

- *The synchronization of action:* Certain tasks require certain actions to be performed in a particular sequence or simultaneously. Communication between agents provides the ability to coordinate these activities.
- *Information exchange:* Different agents have varying perspectives on the world based on their spatial position or knowledge of past events. It is often useful to share this information.
- *Negotiations:* Decisions may need to be made regarding who should do what. This avoids the duplication of effort yielding a more efficient society. The communication and sharing of goals and intentions can lead to productive changes in behavior based on other agents' projected actions.

Is communication important for cooperation? Werner and Dyer (1990) have studied the evolution of communication in synthetic agents. They demonstrated that directional mating signals can evolve in these systems given the presence of societal necessity. MacLennan (1991) has also studied this problem and has similarly concluded that communication can evolve in a society of simple robotic agents. In his studies, the societies in which communication evolved were 84 percent fitter than those in which communication was suppressed. In simulation research conducted at the Environmental Research Institute of Michigan, Franklin and Harmon (1987) used a rule-based cooperative multi-agent system to study the role of communication, cooperation, and inference and how these relationships lead to specialized categories of cooperative systems. Regarding communication, they recognized that information need not be explicitly requested by a receiver to be potentially useful to a multiagent system as a whole. All of these studies argue for the utility of some level of communication in robotic teams. Nonetheless, Arkin (1992b) has established that for certain classes of tasks, explicit communication is not a prerequisite for cooperation.

9.6.2   Communication Range

A tacit assumption is often made that louder is better; that is, that the wider a robot's communication range, the better its performance will be. This is not necessarily the case. Agah and Bekey (1995a) studied calls for help in the context of a multirobot object-carrying task at the University of Southern California. In their tropism system cognitive architecture, a set of attractive and aversive actions is selected based on an agent's current sensory input. From this set, a single action is chosen based on a weighted roulette wheel strategy that incorporates a degree of nondeterminism into the robot's response. In one example, two small robots have been constructed to carry out the task of pipe transport (figure 9.10). In a simulated cooperative foraging task using homogeneous robots, it was demonstrated that societal performance can decrease substantially with increases in a robot's communication radius. The trade-off is that too weak a call for help prevents an agent from being heard, but too strong a call brings the entire colony together and prevents effective exploration of the environment. Loudest is indeed not best for all tasks.

A probabilistic approach to determining the optimal communication range for multirobot teams under different conditions appears in Yoshida et al. 1995. This range is determined by minimizing the communication delay time between robots, assuming they are moving randomly. If more robots send information than the receiving agent can handle, resulting in complete blockage of communication flow, the optimal range $\chi_{optimal}$ (represented as the

Figure 9.10
Two small robots cooperatively carrying a pipe. (Photograph courtesy of A. Agah and G. Bekey.)

average number of robots within the output range) is computed as follows:

$$\chi_{optimal} = \frac{\sqrt[c]{c!}}{p}, \tag{9.2}$$

where c is the information acquisition capacity, an integer representing the upper limit on the number of robots that can be received at any one time without loss of information, and p is the probability of information output for each robot.

9.6.3   Communication Content

But what should be said between robots? Yanco and Stein (1993), at MIT, studied communication specifically in the context of robotic systems. In their research, a task is defined that requires communication to coordinate two robots, Ernie (the follower) and Bert (the leader) (figure 9.11). The robots have an extremely limited vocabulary (two words) that self-organizes over time, improving the performance. The target task involves the follower robot's mimicking the leader's behavior by either spinning or moving forward. Both

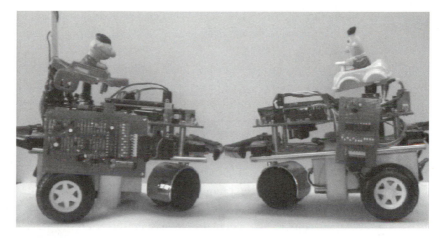

Figure 9.11
Ernie and Bert. (Photograph courtesy of Holly Yanco.)

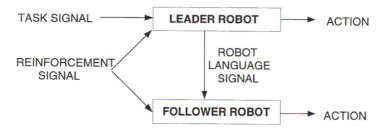

Figure 9.12
Learning coordination via communication.

robots receive reinforcement from a human instructor. Figure 9.12 depicts the
relationships between the robots and instructor-provided reinforcement.

At Georgia Tech, researchers studied communication's impact on the performance of multiagent robotic teams. Initial studies (Arkin 1992b) indicated
that robots could cooperate in foraging tasks even in the absence of explicit
communication. Cooperation in this context is evidenced as the phenomena of
recruitment, the shared effort of many robots to perform a task. Holldobler and
Wilson (1990, p. 265) have defined recruitment as "communication that brings
nestmates to some point in space where work is required." Although communication mechanisms can enhance the speed at which multiple agents converge
at a common work location, recruitment-like behavior in the absence of direct

communication between the agents has also been demonstrated. This result argues that although communication may be useful, it is not necessary for certain types of tasks.

For example, in a foraging task, each of the agents, operating independently, can discover a common attractor. As discovery occurs, more agents acquire the same object and work together to transport it to a common goal. As they converge on the attracting object, the speed at which it is retrieved increases because of the larger number of actors transporting it, yielding a cooperative effect. In most cases, objects too large for movement by a single agent can still be recovered successfully after multiple agents have arrived at the work site.

But what is gained if communication ability is added? Embarking from the minimalist approach (i.e., what can be accomplished in the absence of any communication), additional studies were performed to quantify performance improvements based on adding explicit communication to foraging, consuming, and grazing tasks (section 9.1). Two new classes of communication between agents were introduced (Balch and Arkin 1994):

■ State communication: A single bit of information is transmitted, indicating which state(s) the transmitting agent is in. Figure 9.13 shows a partitioning of the foraging FSA, where transmission of a 0 indicates that the robot is wandering, and transmission of a 1 indicates that it is goal-directed: either acquiring the detected attractor or returning it to the home base. Instead of heading directly toward the attractor object, the robot moves toward the transmitting agent, following it until within detection range of the object itself. This type of communication is analogous to display behavior in animals.

■ Goal communication: Going one step further, the location of the detected attractor is transmitted to the attending agent. Here the robot can move directly to the goal object without following the other agent.

Some examples from simulation studies qualitatively show the variation in performance with these methods: figure 9.14 for foraging behavior shows in a Rorschach-like display the reduction of effort in accomplishing the society's task as more communication is introduced; figure 9.15, showing the consuming task, depicts a marked reduction for state communication but no noticeable difference when state communication is replaced by goal. These results were ported to Denning mobile robots for further experimentation (figures 9.16 and 9.17).

Quantitative analysis of extensive simulation studies yielded the following conclusions regarding communication content (Balch and Arkin 1994):

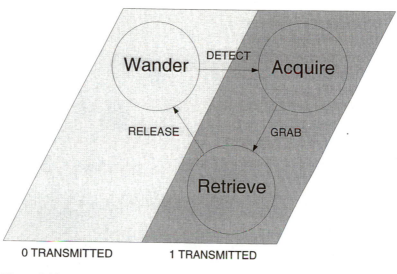

Figure 9.13
State communication during foraging task.

■ Communication improves performance significantly in tasks involving little implicit communication (foraging and consuming). In the grazing task, robots leave evidence of their passage, since the places they visit are modified. This fact is observable by the other robots. These types of communication are referred to as *implicit,* since they require no deliberate act of transmission.

■ Communication is not essential in tasks that include implicit communication.

■ More complex communication strategies (goal) offer little benefit over basic (state) communication for these tasks, confirming that display behavior is indeed a rich communication method.

9.6.4   Guaranteeing Communication

Formal theoretical methods have been applied in a limited way to ensure the quality of communication in multiagent robotic systems. At the University of California at Riverside, Wang (1995) has looked at distributed mutual exclusion techniques for coordinating multirobot systems. In Wang's research, no centralized clock or shared memory is used between agents. Only limited communication in immediate neighborhoods is required to provide deadlock

No Communication

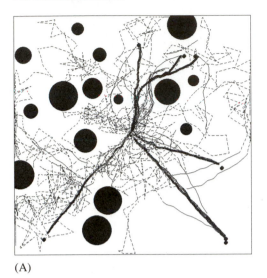

(A)

State Communication

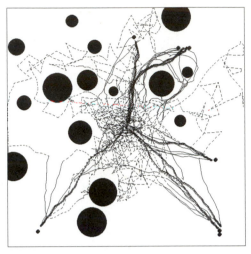

(B)

Goal Communication

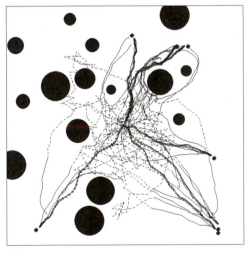

(C)

Figure 9.14
Typical run for foraging task with (A) no, (B) state, and (C) goal communication. The figures show the paths two robots took in retrieving seven attractors. Note that moving from (A) through (C) the society becomes progressively more goal directed. The simulations required 5,145, 4,470 and 3,495 steps, respectively, to complete. Additional communication consistently improves performance.

No Communication

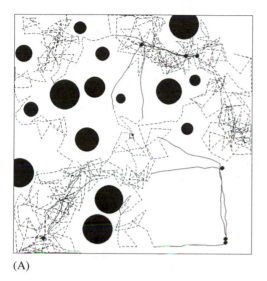

(A)

State Communication

(B)

Goal Communication

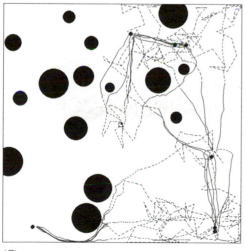

(C)

Figure 9.15
The consuming task with (A) no, (B) state, and (C) goal communication. The simulations required 9,200, 8,340 and 8,355 steps, respectively, to complete. Note that state and goal communication performance are approximately equal in this task.

(A)

(B)

Figure 9.16
(A) Two Denning robots, Ren and Stimpy, demonstrate the foraging task, in this case without explicit communication. (B) Ren tags an attractor.

(C)

(D)

Figure 9.16 *(continued)*
(C) Stimpy "tags" an attractor. (D) Ren and Stimpy deliver the attractors to home base.

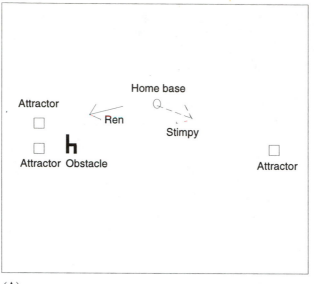

(A)

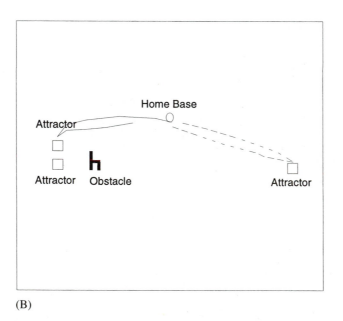

(B)

Figure 9.17

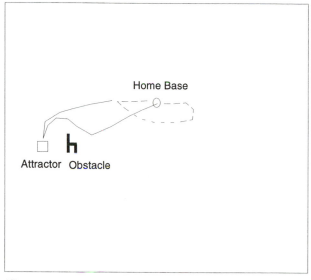

(C)

Figure 9.17 *(continued)*
A reconstruction of the path taken (from previous figure) in the foraging demonstration. Note the cooperation in retrieving the last object in figure (C).

detection (a stagnation condition) or to coordinate multiple agents competing for a single resource (e.g., passing through a narrow corridor or crossing at an intersection). Robots use "signboard" communication (Wang 1994), a specific low-bandwidth message protocol displayed by a device on each robot and perceivable only by nearby robots. Although the results have yet to be fielded on actual robots, they can be proven correct within their formal framework.

Lin and Hsu (1995) at the National Taiwan University developed a deadlock-free cooperation protocol for a multiagent object-sorting task. The protocol uses broadcast communication to sort agent priorities after a deadlock condition has been detected. Specialized behavioral strategies have been developed for helping other robotic agents, for performing load-balancing among the robots, and for selecting partners for the task of moving a set of randomly placed objects to specific goal locations. An object, O_i, requires i robots to move it to its goal location. Deadlock can easily occur when the robots do not help each other. This is a variation on the foraging task and can be represented as an FSA, as in figure 9.18.

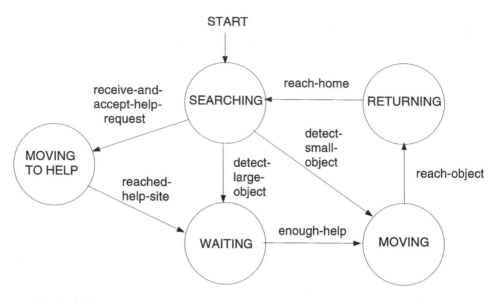

Figure 9.18
Simplified FSA for object sorting. A help request is emitted when the robot enters the
wait state after detecting an object too large to move by itself.

The robots are capable of broadcasting requests for help and sending out
point-to-point offers to help in response to particular requests. In one strategy, deadlock is prevented by establishing priorities for the objects to be
moved and helping to move the one with the highest priority first. Priorities
are based on the object's distance to its final destination. If there is still a
conflict, x-coordinates are compared, and if still needed, y-coordinates are
used for tie breaking. Since no two objects can possess the same x- and y-
coordinates, deadlock cannot occur as long as sufficient agents are available to
help move the largest possible object. More complex strategies involve detecting deadlock conditions after they occur and then remedying the situation or
generating a feasible sequence of actions that prevents deadlock from occurring at all while simultaneously balancing the workload among the available
robots.

9.7   DISTRIBUTED PERCEPTION

Our discussions of communication have focused on how information can be
shared among robotic agents. Further issues involve how perceptual activity

can be coordinated among a team of robots, what sensory or perceptual information is worth sharing, and how a team of robots, as distinct from an individual robot, should view the world.

One important perceptual task, relating to the notion of perceptual classes (section 7.4.3), is that of distinguishing team members from other environmental features. Kin recognition is the term used to refer to this particular perceptual ability (Mataric 1993b). In biology, specialized neural circuitry often accomplishes this task. Prosopagnosia, the inability to recognize faces, occurs in humans when there are lesions, typically due to strokes, on the underside of the occipital lobes, providing strong evidence that "some neural network within this region is specialized for the rapid and reliable recognition of human faces" (Geschwind 1979, p. 112).

In multiagent robotic systems, kin recognition may or may not be useful, depending on the circumstances. A robotic team that does not have this ability often has only two distinct perceptual classes: obstacles and target objects. Team member robots are indistinguishable from obstacles. Kin recognition, however, when implemented, provides information regarding other robots' position and, if needed, their identity. Thus behaviors can be developed that allow the robots to interact more effectively and minimize interference with each other (Mataric 1992c). This information can be provided in various ways: for example, by transmitting the positional information directly (Mataric 1992c) or instead using specific perceptual cues, such as making the robots a unique color relative to their environment (e.g., green in the case of the 1993 AAAI mobile robot competition (Balch et al. 1995).

The information shared by perception between agents can go far beyond simply recognizing each other; an agent's intentions can also be discerned. Cooperation by observation refers to this sharing of perceived information in the absence of explicit communication. More specifically, cooperation by observation involves observing another agent's action, then choosing appropriate actions based on the observed action and the current task situation (adapted from Kuniyoshi et al. 1994). This is closely related to the notion of plan recognition in the distributed AI community, in which an agent's intentions are inferred by observing its actions (Huber and Durfee 1995). In work at Japan's Electrotechnical Laboratory, Kuniyoshi (1995), using a team of small robots equipped with stereo vision, has defined several perceptual functions to accomplish the task of figuring out what another robot is doing:

- Find: Directs the observing agent's attention to a new target.
- Track: Follows the target agent as it moves through the world.
- Anticipate: Recognizes potential collisions or other hazardous situations and prevents them.
- Event Detection: Recognizes certain preconditions to synchronous action with other robots. This may involve spatial coordination or a team member's release of an object.

The event detection algorithms must be designed in a task-specific manner to provide the information necessary for the job at hand (section 7.5.1).

A number of kinds of applications require multiagent perception including

- Convoying: A common task for teams of robots traveling from one location to another is follow-the-leader or convoying. This task has use in both intelligent vehicle highway systems and military logistical operations. In some cases, a mixed human-robot system may be deployed, with the human driver leading the convoy and the other robots following safely behind. One representative perceptual system, developed at the University of Tennessee for two heterogeneous robots, uses a 10 DOF robotic head performing correlation-based visual tracking tied to a fuzzy logic controller (Marapane, Holder, and Trivedi 1994). Numerous other examples include work at Georgia Tech (Balch and Arkin 1995) that uses GPS sensor data for maintaining column formation in a team of unmanned ground vehicles (section 9.9.1).
- Landmine detection: This task involves coordinated spatial exploration and probing of a geographically bounded region. A wide range of sensors is available for this task including magnetic, X-ray, acoustic subsoil sensors, and ground-penetrating radar systems. A team of UCLA and U.S. Army researchers (Franklin, Kahng, and Lewis 1995) have proposed a prototype heterogeneous society consisting of ten R-3 robots and a small X-Cell 60 aerial robot. Clearly, for this mission, it is crucially important that agents share information to prevent their traversing an already-detected mine and also to increase the efficiency and coverage of an area by avoiding redundant search.
- Reconnaissance and surveillance: Teams of robots concerned with monitoring an area for incursion by an intruder must have the ability to coordinate their spatial and perceptual activities. It is not advantageous for robots to spend time looking at the same location while ignoring others. Gage (1992) has defined a variety of coverage methods prescribing the location of robots for surveillance, including

- blanket coverage, in which each robot takes up a station and remains there to watch for intruders.
- barrier coverage, in which a static line of robots is created to prevent crossing of the barrier without detection.
- sweep coverage, in which a team of robots moves through an area attempting to ensure that no enemy or intruder activity is present.

Sensor pointing must be controlled in a manner consistent with the other robots' positions and sensor deployments. Section 9.9.1 describes decision-theoretic methods for accomplishing this.

■ Map making: Expanding upon the notion of cooperation by observation, behavior-based navigation using shared maps by a team of robots has been developed in a joint U.S.-Japan effort (Barth and Ishiguro 1994). In contrast to the use of panoramic vision for global localization discussed in section 5.2.2.1, these robots can cooperate by providing to one another information regarding the relative whereabouts of team members. A schema-based control approach is used, with behaviors including avoid-obstacle, avoid-other-robot, group-moment-attraction (drawing the robots toward the center of mass of the other perceived robots to help keep the group together), and object-range-uncertainty-attraction (guiding the robot toward regions of uncertainty to gather more information). Small mobile robots with panoramic vision systems (figure 9.19) are being developed to provide exploration and formation capabilities that realize the results of Barth and Ishiguro's simulations.

9.8 SOCIAL LEARNING

Teams of robots offer new opportunities for learning, particularly how to self-organize and become more cooperative over time. Mataric (1994b) defines the basic forms of social learning as imitation or mimicry, in which one agent acquires the ability to repeat or mimic another's behavior, and social facilitation, in which existing behaviors are expressed more effectively as a direct consequence of social interactions. An inherent tension exists between individual and group needs. Agents may be strongly self-interested and have no concern for the society's overall well-being. What ecological pressures can be brought to bear that encourage nongreedy strategies that benefit the society and yet may be detrimental to the individual and how can social rules be developed that transcend an individual agent's goals?

(A)

Figure 9.19
Robot equipped with panoramic vision (A) and a panoramic view of a laboratory (B).
(Reprinted with permission from Barth and Ishiguro 1994. © 1994 IEEE.)

9.8.1   Reinforcement Learning

Reinforcement learning (section 8.3), a common strategy used for individual robotic learning, has been applied in multirobot contexts as well. Optimization functions in social robotics typically center on minimizing interference between agents and maximizing the society's reward. Reinforcement can result from an agent's actions directly, from observation of another agent's actions, or from observation of the reinforcement another agent receives (vicarious reinforcement).

Mataric (1994a) conducted experiments in social learning within a foraging context. A team of four robots was equipped with adaptive behaviors for safe wandering, dispersion, resting and homing. Perception was encoded as a set of predicates: have-puck? at-home? near-intruder? night-time? The robots learned over time to associate the correct perceptual preconditions with the appropriate behavior in this societal context. Both delayed-reinforcement Q-learning (section 8.3) and a progress estimator reinforcement summation algorithm were

(B)

Figure 9.19 (*continued*)

tested. The progress estimator approach yielded better results, presumably due to the task's non-Markovian nature (a consequence of the inherent noise in perception and actuation). Subsequent work compared learning using two additional social rules: *yielding*, in which a robot yields the right-of-way when on one side of an oncoming teammate and continues when on the other, and *sharing*, in which a robot broadcasts information to other robots. Reinforcement learning using these social rules always improved performance over those methods that used solely greedy strategies.

9.8.2   L-Alliance

Parker (1994) has extended the Alliance architecture described in section 9.5.2 to include learning mechanisms. Learning in L-Alliance involves parametric adjustment and improves team and mission performance, eliminating the need for a human operator to tune behavioral parameter settings. Each team member within L-Alliance maintains statistical data regarding its own past performance as well as that of each of its teammates. The time history is relatively small, typically five previous trials. This small history window permits rapid responsiveness yet allows reasonable predictions to be made regarding future performance requirements.

One learning problem unique to multirobot systems concerns optimizing task distribution over the available robotic agents, which is not unlike load balancing in multiprocessor systems. Indeed, different task allocation strategies based on results from the parallel processor community were tested. Techniques such as trying to accomplish the longest task first (based on descending first fit [Garey and Johnson 1979]) were found to result in terrible performance, however, because multirobot tasks had a high rate of failure during execution. Other allocation strategies using shortest task first or random selection produced better results. The learned parametric values include influence and motivation parameters that affect task selection and impatience and acquiescence values that affect task completion. The metrics used to measure performance were time and energy consumption.

During the initial active learning phase, the robots initially are maximally patient and minimally acquiescent. In the subsequent adaptive learning phase, the robots start with the parametric values learned during the active learning phase. Ad hoc update equations specific for each of the adjusted parameters have been used to achieve results within 20 percent of optimal for one particular simulated control strategy.

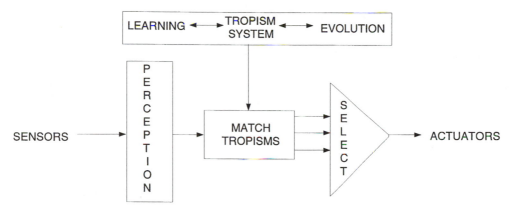

Figure 9.20
Tropism-based cognitive architecture (after Agah and Bekey 1997).

9.8.3   Tropism System Cognitive Architecture

Figure 9.20 depicts the tropism system cognitive architecture, developed at the University of Southern California and introduced in section 9.6.2. A weighted roulette wheel action-selection mechanism based on each action's strength (its tropism value) arbitrates between whatever tropisms are matched with current sensory inputs. Recall that tropisms represent the robot's "likes and dislikes." This architecture introduces three types of learning (Agah and Bekey 1995b):

- In *perceptual learning*, a new tropism is created, and the oldest one is removed from the tropism set. The new tropism consists of the four-tuple $(\sigma, \rho, \alpha_{random}, \tau_{initial})$ where σ is the novel sensed entity, ρ is the state, α_{random} is a random action, and $\tau_{initial}$ is an initial tropism value used by the action-selection mechanism.
- *Learning from success* resembles Q-learning (section 8.3), gradually increasing the tropism value τ by a fixed increment up to a maximum value, making it more likely to occur the next time the system finds itself in the same situation.
- *Learning from failure* changes α_{random} in the four-tuple to a new action when the last randomly generated one has proven unfruitful.

In contrast to L-Alliance, in which each robot maintains statistical data on other robots' performance through communication, here each robot learns independently of the others. Performance improvement was demonstrated in simulation studies using three different metrics: total number of tasks performed, total energy consumption of the colony, and energy consumed per task completed.

Genetic algorithms (section 8.5) have also been applied within this architecture. These methods strongly resemble classifier systems in their approach, with the tropisms encoded similarly to production rules. Fitness evaluation is based on the number of tasks completed and energy consumption. The major difference between these and other GA approaches lies in the performance's being measured at the societal level, rather than at the individual. In addition to simulation studies, a small set of robots in an actual implementation learned to gather objects and cooperate in carrying them (Agah and Bekey 1997).

9.8.4   Learning by Imitation

Imitation involves first *observing* another agent's actions (either human or robot), then *encoding* that action in some internal representation, and finally *reproducing* the initial action. According to Bakker and Kuniyoshi (1996), observation of an action involves

- being motivated to find a teacher.
- finding a good teacher.
- identifying what needs to be learned from the teacher.
- perceiving the teacher's actions correctly.

Representation of an action involves

- selecting a suitable encoding that matches the observation to the action.
- capturing a particular observation in the chosen representational format.

Reproduction of an action involves

- being motivated to act in response to an observation.
- selecting an action for the current context.
- adapting the action to the current environment.

We have already seen an example of action-imitation in Yanco's work (section 9.6.3), when Ernie the robot learns to coordinate itself with Bert's motor activities. Another example of learning by imitation involves a robot imitating a robotic teacher moving within a maze (Hayes and Demiris 1994). During training, the learning agent observes whether the leader either turns 90 degrees or continues moving forward at a given point within the maze. It then encodes a rule associating the environment with that particular action. Later the agent is able to determine, via sensing, which action rule is appropriate for its current position within the maze.

9.9   CASE STUDY: UGV DEMO II

DARPA conducted a research program in the mid-1990s focused on providing support for battlefield scouting operations. Behavior-based robotic systems clearly can play a role in this highly uncertain and dynamic domain. The UGV Demo II program employed a team of unmanned ground vehicles as scouts, capable of conducting reconnaissance, surveillance, and target acquisition operations in a coordinated manner. In conventional military operations, motorized scouts typically move in advance of the main force to report on enemy positions and capabilities.

Incorporated on each individual vehicle (HMMWV—High Mobility Multipurpose Wheeled Vehicle; see figure 9.21) is an architecture consisting of a suite of behaviors (figure 9.22). These include

- Stripe: A teleoperation behavior used by the operator to establish intermediate way points for the vehicle, then automatically create a path that the vehicle strives to follow.
- Cross country: A path-following behavior that uses GPS data for localization.
- Ranger: A navigational behavior using geometric data derived from both sensor and map data.
- Ganesha: An obstacle avoidance behavior that uses a local map derived from laser range finder data (Langer, Rosenblatt, and Hebert 1994).
- Safety: Obstacle detection and avoidance using stereo vision (Chun et al. 1995).
- Alvinn: A neural network road-following behavior (section 7.6.1).
- Formation: Formation control for multiple vehicles (section 9.9.1).

The DAMN arbiter (section 4.5.5) is used to coordinate these behaviors.

At Demo A, the first of a series of demonstrations, in 1993, a single vehicle showed the capability of road following using Alvinn and Stripe teleoperation (Chun and Jochem 1994). Off-road navigational capabilities were added at Demo B in 1994 using stereo vision for obstacle avoidance (Chun et al. 1995). Since this chapter discusses multiagent systems, we focus on the capabilities developed for Demo C's multivehicle demonstrations, conducted in 1995, including multiagent formation control, mission specification and planning, and team teleautonomy.

(A)

(B)

Figure 9.21
Unmanned ground vehicles from the DARPA UGV Demo II program: (A) Single
HMMWV scout; (B) Entire Demo II HMMWV UGV team. (Photographs courtesy of
Lockheed-Martin, Denver, Colorado.)

BEHAVIORS

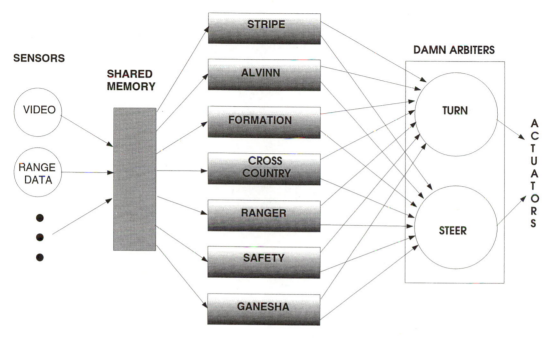

Figure 9.22
UGV Demo II software architecture (behavioral components).

9.9.1   Formation Behaviors

Formation control has significant utility for a wide range of potential applications in the unmanned vehicle community. In UGVs, formation control can be used for military scouting missions and logistical support in convoying. Scout teams employ specific formations for particular tasks. Column formation is usually associated with road-following activities, whereas line formations are used to cross large expanses of open terrain. Robotic behaviors were implemented to accomplish the four primary formations for scout vehicles listed by U.S. Army manuals (1986): *diamond, wedge, line,* and *column* (figure 9.23).

These formation control behaviors were successfully tested first in simulation studies, then on Denning mobile robots in the Georgia Tech Mobile Robot Laboratory and on two HMMWVs at Demo C of the UGV Demo II program in July 1995 in Denver. Figure 9.24 depicts a sequence of images from the demonstration in which the vehicles started initially in a column formation,

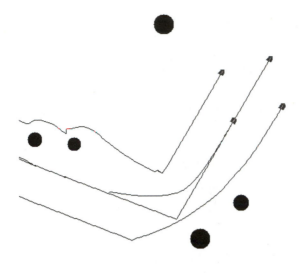

(A)

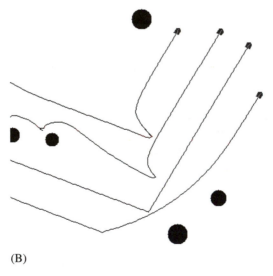

(B)

Figure 9.23

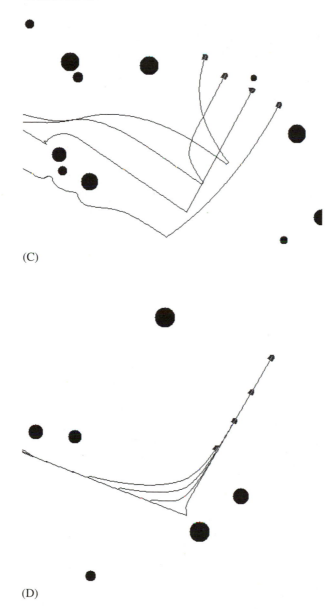

(C)

(D)

Figure 9.23 *(continued)*
Four simulated robots in leader-referenced (A) diamond, (B) wedge, (C) line, and
(D) column formations executing a 90-degree turn in an obstacle field.

(A)

(B)

Figure 9.24

(C)

Figure 9.24 *(continued)*
Demo C Formation tech demo: Two UGVs traveling in (A) column, (B) wedge, then (C) line formation.

then transited to wedge formation, then moved to line formation, and finally reverted to column formation with the vehicles' initial position reversed. Waypoint navigation and formation maintenance were concurrently active, and the vehicles switched among formations smoothly and autonomously at set GPS-designated points. Differential GPS provided the vehicles' position relative to each other.

The formation behavior itself is comprised of two main components: a perceptual schema detect-formation-position and a motor schema maintain-formation. The perceptual schema determines the robot's desired location for the formation type in use, its relative position in the overall formation, and the other robots' locations. Maintain-formation computes a vector toward this position whose magnitude is based on how far out of position the robot is. Three zones are defined (figure 9.25):

■ **Ballistic zone**: The robot is far from the desired position, so the output vector's magnitude is set at its maximum, which equates to the schema's gain value, with its directional component pointing toward the center of the computed dead zone.

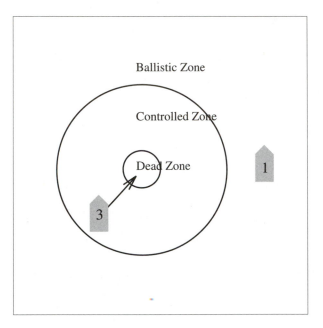

Figure 9.25
Zones for the computation of maintain-formation magnitude.

- **Controlled zone**: The robot is midway to slightly out of position, with the vector's magnitude decreasing linearly from a maximum at the zone's farthest edge to zero at the inner edge. The directional component points toward the dead zone's center.
- **Dead zone**: The robot is within acceptable positional tolerance. Within the dead zone, the vector's magnitude is always zero.

In figure 9.25, Robot 3 attempts to maintain a position to the left of and abeam Robot 1. Robot 3 is in the controlled zone, so the behavior generates a moderate force toward the desired position (forward and right).

Each robot must compute its own position in the formation continuously. Three techniques for this computation have been identified:

- **Unit-center-referenced**: A unit-center is computed by averaging the x- and y-coordinates of all robots involved in the formation. Each robot determines its own formation position relative to that center.
- **Leader-referenced**: Each robot determines its formation position in relation to a designated lead robot. The leader does not attempt to maintain formation;

the other robots are responsible for maintaining suitable offsets relative to the leader.

■ **Neighbor-referenced**: Each robot maintains its position relative to an adjacent robot.

Some interesting observations from this research (Balch and Arkin 1995) provide guidance in the use of formations. For example, the unit-center approach requires a transmitter and receiver for each robot and a protocol for exchanging position information. On the other hand, the leader-referenced approach requires only one transmitter for the leader and one receiver for each following robot, reducing communications bandwidth requirements significantly and making it a preferable approach in communications-restricted applications. Also, regarding the use of kin recognition instead of explicit communication: unit-center–referenced formations place a heavy demand on any passive sensor systems (e.g., vision) used. In a four-robot visual formation, for instance, each robot would have to track three other robots that may be spread across an extremely wide field of view. Leader- and neighbor-referenced formations, on the other hand, require tracking only one other robot.

A related question is how the available sensor resources can be used effectively to perform efficient scout reconnaissance for a given formation. Research at the University of Texas at Arlington considers how to coordinate perception over multiple vehicles (Cook, Gmytrasiewicz, and Holder 1996). Figure 9.26 shows a simulation of sensor-pointing algorithms fielded on a team of two robotic vehicles as part of DARPA's UGV Demo II program.

Using decision-theoretic methods, utility values for individual fields-of-regard are assigned to each member of a formation, allocating specific time in each relative position (figure 9.27). The utility value for scanning an area A using sensor S from position P is determined by the following equation:

$$U_{scan}(A, S, P) = \int_A \sum_k P1_c(x, y) P2_k(x, y) V I_k dx dy, \qquad (9.3)$$

where $P1_c(x, y)$ is the conditional probability that a target at location (x, y) will be identified correctly from position P using sensor S; $P2_k(x, y)$ is the prior probability that a target of type k exists at location (x, y); and $V I_k$ is the value of information regarding a target of type k. These utility values are continuously recomputed taking into account dynamic factors such as terrain, security, and focus of attention and are used to update the field-of-regard selection weights. Weighted roulette wheel methods are used for the selection

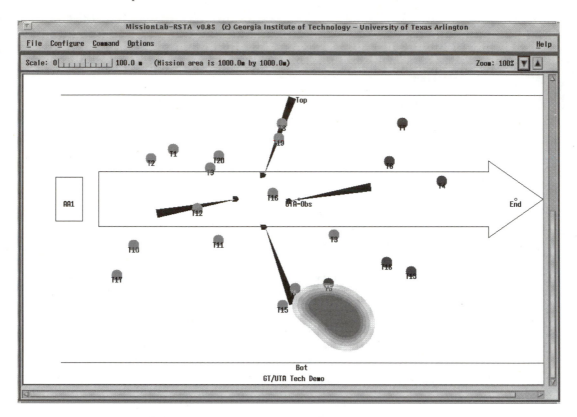

Figure 9.26
A simulation of sensor pointing as a team of four robots travels left to right in a diamond formation conducting reconnaissance operations. Triangles looking outward from each robot represent the video sensors' fields of view. All targets (represented as circles) are successfully detected during the mission. (Figure courtesy of Diane Cook.)

of new fields-of-regard values, introducing nondeterminism into the observational strategy that increases the likelihood of hostile target detection while reducing the effectiveness of countermeasures.

9.9.2   Multiagent Mission Specification

To effectively design a mission for a team of robots, suitable tools must be available. Several different approaches were developed for use within the Demo II program addressing different aspects of this problem. This section focuses on the *MissionLab* tool set. At the University of Michigan, Lee et al.

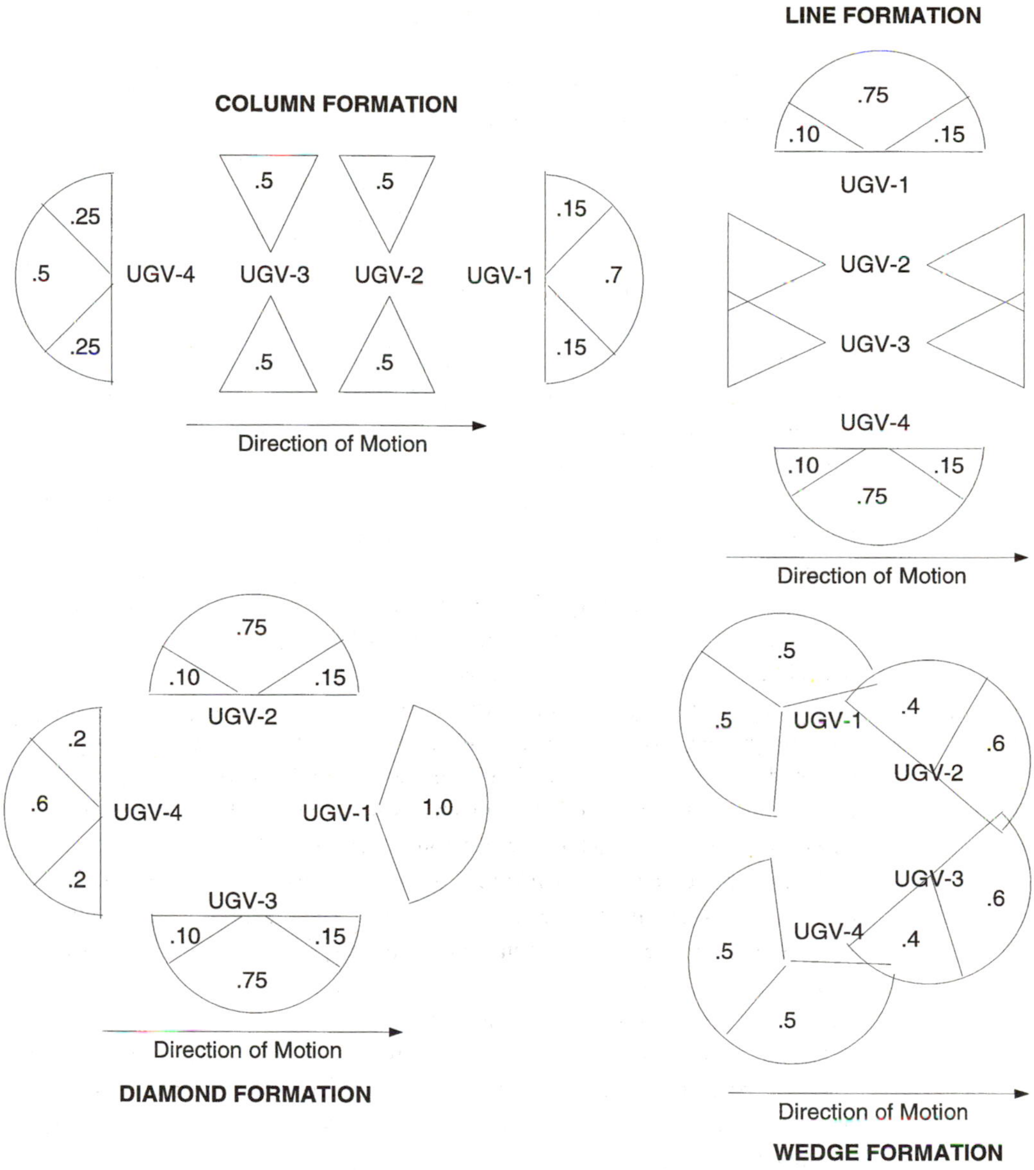

Figure 9.27
Example fields of regard for various formations. The number in each sector represents the percentage of time spent on reconnaissance activity within that area.

(1994) developed another system, UM-PRS, based on the Procedural Reasoning System (section 6.6.4). It elaborates plans for the current environmental context consistent with long-term goals. Although successfully fielded on a robot named MAVERIC (Kenny et al. 1994), only limited results have been reported to date for its use in multivehicle missions.

MissionLab,[1] a multiagent mission specification system developed at Georgia Tech, uses an agent-oriented philosophy as the underlying methodology, permitting the recursive formulation of societies of robots. It includes a graphical configuration editor, a multiagent simulation system, and two different architectural code generators. This software system embodies the Societal Agent Theory described in section 9.5.4. A society is viewed as an agent that consists of a collection of either homogeneous or heterogeneous robots. Each individual robotic agent consists of assemblages of behaviors, coordinated in various ways. Temporal sequencing (Arkin and MacKenzie 1994) affords transitions between various behavioral states naturally represented as a finite state acceptor. Coordination of parallel behaviors can be accomplished via fusion (vector summation), action-selection, priority (e.g., subsumption) or other coordination operators as necessary. These individual behavioral assemblages consist of groups of primitive perceptual and motor behaviors ultimately grounded to the robot's physical sensors and actuators.

Creating a multiagent robot configuration involves three steps: determining an appropriate set of skills for each of the vehicles; translating those mission-oriented skills into sets of suitable behaviors (assemblages); and constructing or selecting suitable coordination mechanisms to ensure that the correct skill assemblages are deployed for the mission's duration.

An important feature of *MissionLab* is its ability to delay binding to a particular behavioral architecture (e.g., schema based, UGV Demo II, subsumption) until after the desired mission behavior has been specified. Binding to a particular physical robot occurs after specification as well, permitting the design to be both architecture- and robot-independent.

Figure 9.28 shows the *MissionLab* system, which has separate software libraries for abstract behaviors, specific architectures, and various robots. The user interacts through a design interface tool (the configuration editor) that permits him to visualize a specification as it is created.

Specifications are represented graphically as icons, which can be created as needed or reused from an existing repertoire available in the behavioral library.

---

1. *MissionLab* is available via the world wide-web at:
http://www.cc.gatech.edu/ai/robot-lab/research/MissionLab.html.

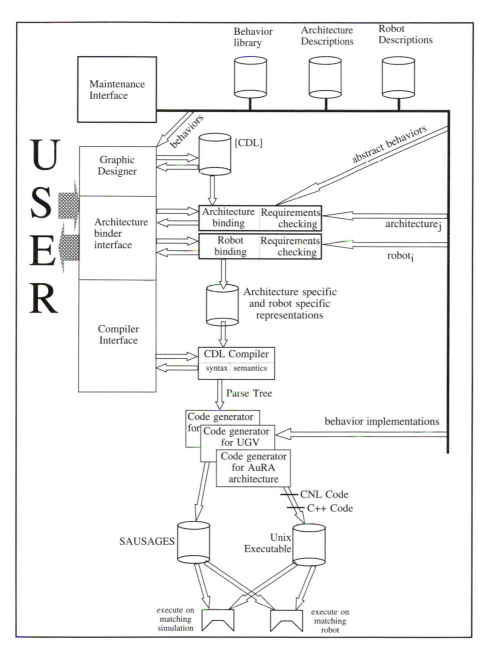

Figure 9.28
MissionLab system architecture.

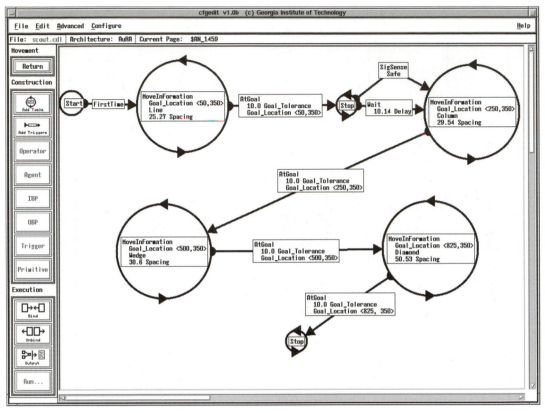

(A)

Figure 9.29

Multiple levels of abstraction, which can be targeted to the designer's abilities, range from entire robot mission configurations down to the low-level language for a particular behavior. After the behavioral configuration is specified, the architecture and robot types are selected. Then compilation occurs, generating the robot executables, which can be run within a simulation environment provided by *MissionLab* or, through a software switch, downloaded to the actual robots for execution.

Panel (A) of figure 9.29 depicts a finite state diagram specifying a simple military scouting mission. In this case, explicit GPS coordinates are used as destinations. The remaining panels show four robots during execution of the scout mission in the *MissionLab* simulator. Notice that the robots begin moving in line formation from the bottom left corner. They then switch to column

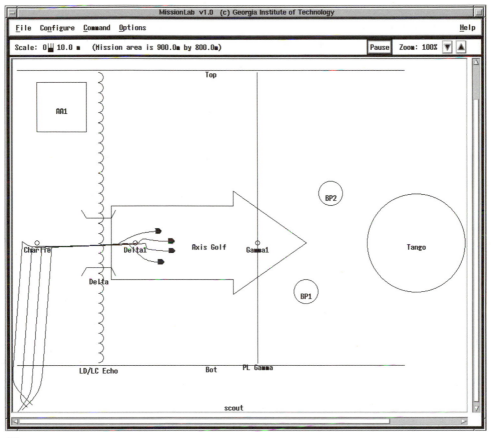

(B)

Figure 9.29 *(continued)*

formation to traverse the gap in the forward lines (passage point). The robots travel along the axis of advance in wedge formation and finally occupy the objective in a diamond formation.

9.9.3   Team Teleautonomy

Another important aspect of multiagent control involves introducing an operator's intentions into an autonomous robotic team's ongoing performance. Software developed as part of the UGV Demo II program provides this capability in two ways (Arkin and Ali 1994):

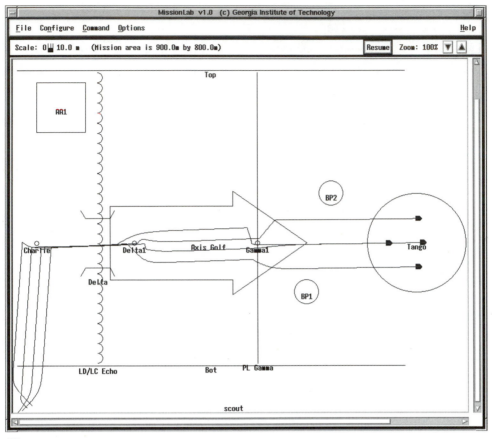

(C)

Figure 9.29 *(continued)*

A finite state configuration, constructed within *MissionLab* and corresponding to a scouting mission, appears in (A). The mission, consisting of a sequence of coordinated actions in differing formations, is shown at various stages of execution in (B) and (C) (moving initially upward in line formation, then to the right in a column, then changing to wedge, and finally occupying the objective in a diamond formation).

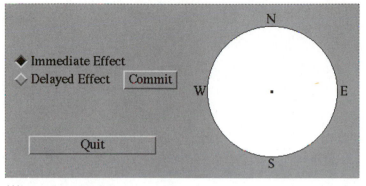

(A)

(B)

Figure 9.30
(A) On-screen joystick for teleautonomous directional control; (B) Personality slider bars for team behavioral modification.

- **The operator as a behavior**: In this approach, a separate behavior is created that permits the operator to introduce a heading for the robot team using an on-screen joystick (panel (A) of figure 9.30). This biases the ongoing autonomous behavioral control for all of the robots in a particular direction. Indeed, all other behaviors are still active, typically including obstacle avoidance and formation maintenance. The output of this behavior is a vector representing the operator's directional intentions and command strength. All of the robotic team members generate the same teleautonomous behavioral response to the operator's intentions. The entire team acts in concert without any knowledge of one another's behavioral state.

- **The operator as a supervisor**: Using this method, the operator is permitted to conduct behavioral modifications during run-time. This can occur at two levels:

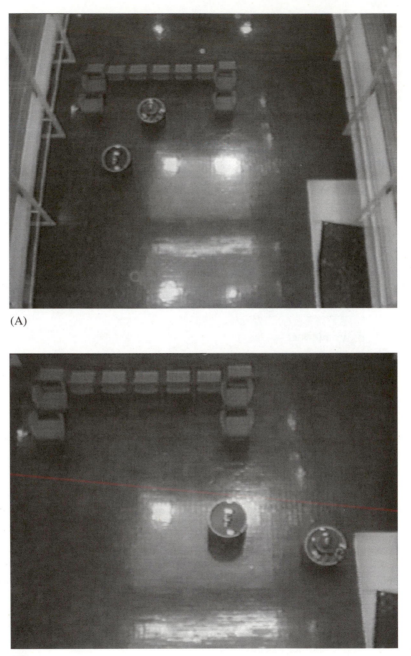

(A)

(B)

Figure 9.31

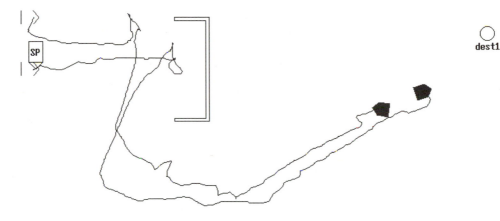

Team of Denning MRV2 Robots

(C)

Figure 9.31 *(continued)*
Teleautonomous extrication from a box canyon of a team of 2 Denning mobile robots (viewed from above). (A) shows robots trapped in box canyon, and (B) after teleautonomous removal. (C) provides the execution trace of the robotic run (rotated 90 degrees clockwise relative to the photographs).

• The knowledgeable operator can adjust the low-level gains and parameters of the active behavioral set for the entire team directly if desired, varying the relative strengths and behavioral composition as the mission progresses.

• For the normal operator, team behavioral traits ("personality characteristics") are abstracted and presented on screen for adjustment (panel (B) of figure 9.30). These include characteristics such as aggressiveness (inversely adjusting the relative strength of goal attraction and obstacle avoidance) and wanderlust (inversely varying the strength of noise relative to goal attraction and/or formation maintenance). These abstract qualities are more natural for an operator unskilled in behavioral programming. This approach permits the concurrent behavioral modification of all of the robots in a team according to the operator's wishes.

An example illustrating the utility of the directional control approach involves the extrication of teams from potential traps. Panels (A) and (B) of figure 9.31, show (from above) a run using two Denning mobile robots. The active behaviors include avoid-static-obstacle, move-to-goal, and column-formation. The robots wander into the box canyon and become stuck trying to make their way to the goal point specified just behind the box canyon. The operator intervenes, using the joystick to direct the robots to the right. While moving, they continue to avoid obstacles and maintain formation. Once clear of the trap, the operator ceases directing the robots and they proceed autonomously to their earlier prescribed goal. The overall execution trace is depicted in panel (C) of the figure.

9.10   CHAPTER SUMMARY

- Teams of robots afford significant advantages over individual robots in terms of performance, sensing capabilities, and fault tolerance. Problems involving interference, communication costs, and uncertainty in the actions of others can prevent full realization of the benefits of teaming.
- Typical generic tasks for societies of robots include foraging, flocking, consuming, moving material, and grazing.
- Ethological studies provide insights into social behaviors and interagent communication.
- Multiagent robotic systems can be characterized along the lines of reliability, social organization, communication content and mode, spatial distribution, congregation, and performance.
- Useful taxonomies exist for defining the relationships in robotic teams.
- Behavior-based architectures have been expanded to include social behavior.
- The Nerd Herd and Alliance are variants of the subsumption architecture.
- The Societal Agent Theory extends schema theory to multiagent robotics.
- Communication plays a central role in coordinating teams of robots.
- Communication is not necessary for cooperation but is often desirable.
- Range, content, and guarantees for communication are important factors in the design of social behavior.
- Distributed perception over multiple robots involves sharing discerned information between them.
- Various forms of machine learning have been applied to robotic teams, including reinforcement learning and imitation.
- The UGV Demo II program provides an example of teams of robots in action, including aspects of mission specification, formation maintenance, and team teleautonomy.

Chapter 10
Fringe Robotics: Beyond Behavior

"They're made out of meat."

"Meat?"

"Meat. They're made out of meat."

"Meat?"

"There's no doubt about it. We picked up several from different parts of the planet, took them aboard our recon vessels, and probed them all the way through. They're completely meat."

"That's impossible. What about the radio signals? The messages to the stars?"

"They use the radio waves to talk, but the signals don't come from them. The signals come from machines."

"So who made the machines? That's who we want to contact."

"They made the machines. That's what I'm trying to tell you. Meat made the machines."

"That's ridiculous. How can meat make a machine? You're asking me to believe in sentient meat."

"I'm not asking you, I'm telling you. These creatures are the only sentient race in that sector and they're made out of meat."

"Maybe they're like the orfolei. You know, a carbon-based intelligence that goes through a meat stage."

"Nope. They're born meat and they die meat. We studied them for several of their life spans, which didn't take long. Do you have any idea what's the life span of meat?"

"Spare me. Okay, maybe they're only part meat. You know, like the weddilei. A meat head with an electron plasma brain inside."

"Nope. We thought of that, since they do have meat heads, like the weddilei. But I told you, we probed them. They're meat all the way through."

"No brain?"

"Oh, there's a brain all right. It's just that the brain is made out of meat! That's what I've been trying to tell you."

"So . . . what does the thinking?"

"You're not understanding, are you? You're refusing to deal with what I'm telling you. The brain does the thinking. The meat."

"Thinking meat! You're asking me to believe in thinking meat!"

"Yes, thinking meat! Conscious meat! Loving meat. Dreaming meat. The meat is the whole deal! Are you beginning to get the picture or do I have to start all over?"

—Terry Bisson, Nebula Award Nominee, from "They're Made out of Meat" (OMNI Magazine, April 1991). (Reprinted with the permission of Mr. Bisson.)

Chapter Objectives

1. To explore the concept and ramifications of a robotic mind with particular regard to thought, consciousness, emotion, and imagination.
2. To consider unusual aspects of robotic control, including homeostasis, immune systems, and nanotechnology.
3. To entertain the notion of human-robot equivalence.

In this chapter, we move relatively far from mainstream robotics and probe its fringe areas. Quite often, practicing roboticists become enmeshed in pragmatic issues and ignore their work's philosophical, ethical, and even metaphysical ramifications. We now explore some of the deeper questions regarding the potential for robotic intelligence and in so doing discover a wide range of views on the subjects of robot mind and body. Certainly interesting subjects, often controversial, with nothing broadly agreed upon: Intelligence may or may not be achievable by computation; robots may or may not be able to attain consciousness; the roles, if any, that emotions and imagination play in artificial systems; what other biological models, such as hormonal and immune control systems, have to offer; what of incredibly small nanorobots; and in what sense, if any, a robot can be viewed as equivalent to or a successor to human beings.

10.1   ISSUES OF THE ROBOT MIND

The idea of artificial minds has been a central philosophical question in AI research since its inception. Attributing a mind to a robot is viewed by many as a substantial leap of faith for a scientist. The very concept may be disturbing to many of us, for it can raise fears regarding robots as potential competitors at all levels of human endeavor. Can robots think? Can robots be conscious or self-aware? Can they feel or dream as we do? It is certainly easy, at this point, to dismiss these questions. It is useful, however, to examine a broad perspective of these issues, often less scientific and more philosophical than what we have become accustomed to, but nonetheless worthy of exploration with an open mind.

10.1.1   On Computational Thought

We begin with a caveat: This section is not intended as a discourse on philosophy but rather a brief review of several notable opinions on this and other questions regarding mind as it pertains to machines in general and robots in particular.

Should a machine be said to think if it can fool a human who is merely observing it into believing it is capable of thought? This performance-based approach is the basis for the classic Turing Test of machine intelligence, in which the definition of thought is based not on machine consciousness but rather on human fallibility (Turing 1950; Epstein 1992). This definition by deception carries enough weight to prompt the annual sponsoring of the Loebner Competition, which offers a $100,000 prize to a machine that can successfully pass the Turing Test.

> One popular version of the Turing Test involves a person sitting in front of two terminals. This intelligence tester is free to ask any questions to the respondents on the other end of the terminals, one of which is a computer and the other a human being. If the questioner cannot discriminate between the computer and the human subject, the computer is said to have passed the Turing Test.

Those for whom the proof of possession of thought is based solely upon observed action have little reason to read further. For those who believe that a thinking agent must possess more than merely the ability to exhibit plausible actions for a wide range of situations in order to be considered able to think, we proceed.

Bellman (1978) states that since no one knows what "think" really means anyway, we cannot fairly answer the question of whether a machine can truly think. He argues from a mathematical perspective that computers can perform processes representative of human thought (i.e., decision making and learning), but since no one can precisely define what constitutes thinking, the question cannot be rigorously answered.

A different stance expressed by Weizenbaum and echoed by Albus (1981, p. 297) states: "For robots to truly understand humans they would have to be indistinguishable from humans in bodily appearance as well as physical and mental development and remain so throughout a life cycle identical of humans." This leads to the strong conclusion that robots will never be able to comprehend humans' values, and thus never be able to think as humans do. Brooks (1991, p. 22), on the other hand, argues that these aspects of intelligence are a naturally occurring by-product of a behavior-based effort: "Thought and consciousness will not need to be programmed in. They will emerge."

Roger Penrose can easily be characterized as AI's most ardent opponent. He denies the possibility that computational processes can ever lead to thought and presents four alternate perspectives on the issues of thinking and awareness (Penrose 1994):

1. All thinking is computation, thus computers are capable of thought. (This position is often referred to as *Strong AI*).
2. Thought is a result of the brain's physical actions. Computers can simulate this action, but a simulation is *never* the same as the thing simulated, and thus computers cannot think.
3. The brain's actions cannot even be simulated computationally.
4. Awareness cannot be explained by any scientific approach and thus is unattainable computationally.

In *The Emperor's New Mind* (1989), Penrose presents strong arguments against computational intelligence based on pillars of mathematics and computational theory, Göedel's Incompleteness Theorem and the Church-Turing Thesis, among others. The reader is referred to Penrose's books for the full development of his dismissal of AI as a means for producing thought, consciousness, and self-aware machines.

Obviously Penrose's point of view has met stiff resistance within the AI community. Most (e.g., Brooks and Stein 1994) point out that his arguments are fundamentally flawed and have been contradicted by earlier mathematical investigations (Arbib 1964). Caustically, Brooks states:

" . . . Penrose . . . not only makes the same Turing-Göedel error, but then in a desperate attempt to find the essence of mind and applying the standard methodology of physics, namely to find a simplifying underlying principle, resorts to an almost mystical reliance on quantum mechanics" (Brooks and Stein 1994, p. 23).

Nonetheless, Penrose steadfastly devotes a major portion of his second book, *Shadows of the Mind* (1994), to disputing the plethora of arguments against his position, dismissing some far more easily than others. He states that intelligence requires understanding, and understanding requires awareness, an aspect of consciousness. Most puzzling is his optimism in holding out for the possibility of a type of noncomputational intelligence based on a new science of quantum physics. He contends that intelligence is a consequence of this sort of activity naturally manifested within the microtubules located within the brain's neurons. Much of this argument is speculative, but nonetheless intriguing, especially given the recent advances in the theory of quantum computation (Lloyd 1996; Hogg 1996).

> Quantum computers are currently hypothetical devices that operate on the scale of atoms. They exploit quantum parallelism (the probabilistic wavelike nature of particulate state), existing in superpositions of a set of discrete states. This ability endows them with the capacity to do everything classical computers can do and more using quantum logic. Factoring (Shor 1994) and the simulation of quantum computers (Lloyd 1996) are two examples of problems proven to have inherently more efficient solutions on this class of machines.

Despite the raging debate on the very possibility of thinking machines, there is demonstrable value in pursuing their development. The successes achieved in behavior-based robotic systems generally do not lay claim to human-level intelligence, nor do they argue that the systems created are aware. To most robotics researchers this is an irrelevant question, their goal being to build useful and, at the very least, debatably intelligent machines. The commonly held belief that engineers and scientists have successfully proven that a bumblebee is incapable of flight may also have implications for the issues surrounding philosophers and thinking robots.

10.1.2 On Consciousness

Chalmers (1995, p. 81) characterizes the most mysterious aspect of consciousness as "how physical processes in the brain give rise to subjective experience," i.e., the experiences of color, pain, emotion, and feelings in general. Some philosophers boldly argue that they have unshrouded this mystery. In *Consciousness Explained*, Dennett (1991, p. 433) argues, using reductionism, that "all that complicated slew of activity in the brain amounts to conscious experience." His conclusions assume that the brain can be viewed as an information-processing system, a computer if you will, from which he further concludes that software-based computer systems can give rise to consciousness.

Perhaps the single most disputed thought experiment used to deflate the potential of machine consciousness is Searle's Chinese Room (1980):

An English speaker (the CPU), who can speak no other language, is locked in a room with a writing device (output), blank paper (mass storage), and a rule book (the program) that says what to do when presented with specific undecipherable Chinese characters. A slip of paper containing Chinese characters (the input) is presented through a small opening in the door. The human uses the rule book to perform transformations in Chinese, first by matching the characters from the input slip to corresponding entries in the rule book and then by carrying out the instructions specified in the book, creating new Chinese characters. This process generates correct answers in Chinese to the incoming Chinese questions. These are then passed in written form (output) to the outside through another small opening. The system can be envisioned as successfully passing the Turing Test, if a computer takes the place of the human. Searle contends that clearly the translator has no understanding of what the slips of paper contain and thus does not understand Chinese. Merely coming up with the right answer by any means possible does not constitute understanding.

Searle ultimately asserts that no robot could ever be conscious (Boden 1995). Just as Penrose's arguments met with widespread disclaim, so did the Chinese Room refutation of strong AI. Dennett counters that these types of "thought experiments 'work' precisely because they dissuade the reader from trying to imagine, in detail, how software could accomplish this" (Dennett 1991, p. 435).

The believers in computational consciousness persist. McCarthy (1995) believes consciousness is not only possible for robots, but necessary. This consciousness is intended to be different from a human's and, according to McCarthy, should not have humanlike emotions, in order to make robots more servile. A robot consciousness requires the ability to observe many things, including its own physical body, the extent of its knowledge (what it does or does not know), its goals and intentions, the history or basis for its beliefs, and what it is capable of achieving.

Bellman (1978, p. 94) attempts to draw mathematics into the fray with the observation that although "the general area of consciousness cannot be made precise" . . . "many aspects of consciousness can be treated by mathematical means, which means that we can have a computer be conscious in certain ways." The result is a characterization of consciousness as a control process.

Moravec (forthcoming) states that a robot's consciousness will eventually exceed that of people: "Some configurations will make a robot more thoroughly conscious than the average human. . . . " This view is consistent with his long-time articulated expectation that robots are humans' natural successors. These machines constitute the next logical step in evolution, our "mind children," ultimately capable of transcending human biological frailty (Moravec 1988).

Consciousness may be overrated anyway. Minsky (1986, p. 29) argues "In general, we're least aware of what our minds do best" and that consciousness arises when our automatic systems begin to fail. Moravec (1988, p. 44), despite his own tendencies to the contrary, observes that "robotics research is too practical to seriously set itself the explicit goal of producing machines with such nebulous and controversial characteristics as emotion and consciousness." Most roboticists are more than happy to leave these debates on consciousness to those with more philosophical leanings.

10.1.3   On Emotions

Several roboticists, however, recently have paid attention to emotional state and its impact on behavior. We can intuitively understand that emotions indeed influence behavior. When someone is angry, they generally behave differently than when they are happy. The effect may be anywhere from subtle to quite strong, depending upon the individual and the strength of the emotion. But what is this emotional stuff, and why would it be of possible importance or use to a robot?

We have already seen examples of the attribution of emotion to behavior-based systems. Braitenberg, in particular, unabashedly describes his vehicles as possessing fear, love, and aggression (as discussed in section 1.2.1). Albus (1981, p. 208) states: "Emotions play a crucial role in the selection of behavior." Though lower life forms exhibit simple emotions (pleasure or pain), humans apparently have a much broader range (hate, love, anger, fear, happiness, disgust, among others). Neurologically, it is generally acknowledged that human emotion originates within the brain's limbic system.

Modifying Associate U.S. Supreme Court Justice John Paul Stevens' famous quotation, we can't define emotion, but we know it when we see it. And perhaps that is the crux of the argument that robots can indeed possess emotions. Moravec (1988) contends that a robot is actually experiencing fear when, upon encountering a stairwell, it backs away from the danger because of a detect-cliff sensing system coupled with a deal-with-cliff action system. Is emotion then in the eye of the observer? For each of us, speaking of ourselves, we would clearly answer that it certainly is not. We know when we are angry, happy, or whatever, independent of external observation. But we ascribe this emotional capacity to others primarily through observation. So how do we know whether a robot is or is not experiencing emotion?

Minsky (1986, p. 163) states: "The question is not whether intelligent machines can have any emotions, but whether machines can be intelligent without any emotions." Emotional capacity may better adapt robots to deal with the world: Love can provide social behavior useful when cooperating with other agents (human or robotic); anger can be useful when competing with other agents; and pain or pleasure can be used for reinforcement learning and self-protection. As Moravec (forthcoming) observes: "In general, robots will exhibit some of the emotions found in animals and humans because those emotions are an effective way to deal with the contingencies of life in the wide, wild world."

To date, Japanese scientists have conducted most of the pragmatic research on giving robots emotions. Frustration, an emotion not uncommon to robotics researchers, often serves as the basis for emotional control. Research at Nagoya University (Mochida et al. 1995) has looked at robots that can experience two states: pleasantness and unpleasantness. A variable representing frustration represents the states: low frustration is pleasant, but high frustration is to the contrary. Simulations have been conducted using a Braitenberg-style architecture supplemented with a neural emotional model that alters the system's behavior as it becomes more or less frustrated. This enables it to escape traps, such as box canyons, which it cannot accomplish without this emotional behavioral switching.

Research at MITI in Japan (Shibata, Ohkawa, and Tanie 1996) extends the use of frustration to multirobot systems. In the context of empty-can collection tasks, frustration arises not only from the agent's own behavior but also from other team members' performance. The frustration level alters the action-selection process, appearing to result in greater cooperation than would occur otherwise. Section 10.2.1 describes an actual vacuum cleaning robot, Sozzy, that also uses emotions as a basis for action-selection.

Of course, the debate will continue as to whether these robots really experience emotion. An important point to take from this discussion, however, is that biological emotional control systems may have some utility in the context of behavior-based robotics, even if they serve merely to inspire models that are quite limited or rather far afield.

10.1.4 On Imagination

What of imagination? "Imagination gives us the ability to think about what we are going to do before committing ourselves to action" (Albus 1981). This capacity for simulation (imaging future actions) provides potentially useful

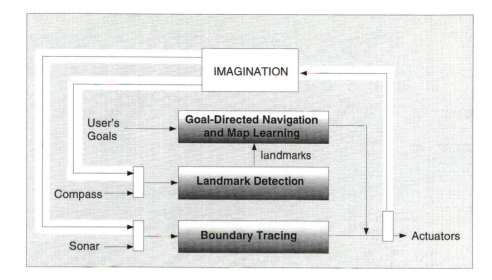

Figure 10.1
MetaToto's architecture. Highlighted components are those added above and beyond Toto's core capabilities.

feedback as to the utility and relevance of any plans under consideration. The quality of feedback is directly related to the quality of the simulation itself and the accuracy of its underlying assumptions about the world.

At MIT, imagination, in at least one sense, has been integrated into the subsumption architecture (Stein 1994). Cognition, viewed here as high-level deliberative reasoning or planning, is treated as imagined interaction with the world. This cognitive system is not disjoint from the robot control architecture, as is the case in many hybrid architectures (chapter 6), but rather uses the underlying behavioral architecture as the simulator itself.

This novel approach was embodied in MetaToto, extending the earlier navigational work using representation within the subsumption architecture of Toto (section 5.2.2.1). Figure 10.1 depicts the robot's controller, which reuses Toto's architecture in its entirety, wrapping the imagining simulator around it. Sensing is imagined using very simple sonar models and a straightforward scan-line algorithm. Acting is imagined by the updating of three positional variables: x-position, y-position, and heading. In essence, this is a rudimentary simulator.

MetaToto, however, is capable of exploring floor plan drawings and imagining how it would move in these previously unexplored environments, whereas Toto could not. The actual sonar and compass readings in the robot architecture have been replaced with imagined ones. Although simulators that use the same control code as actual robots are not new (e.g., *MissionLab*, section 9.9.2), the cognitive framework in which this work is couched is interesting. Whether this is truly an example of robot imagination is subject to debate, just as were the notions of robotic thought, consciousness, and emotion discussed in the preceding sections.

10.2   ISSUES OF THE ROBOT BODY

We now examine some fringe areas not directly related to the debate regarding the robot mind. Nonneural control systems have the potential for contributing to intelligent robotic systems. In animals, the endocrine system uses chemical messages for autoregulatory purposes whereas the immune system responds to external events in a defensive manner. This section explores the implications of these alternate control paradigms for robotics, then examines the issue of scale: What if robots could be made to operate at a molecular level? This draws us into the field of nanotechnology, currently little more than a dream but of potentially great importance.

10.2.1   Hormones and Homeostasis

The endocrine system in mammals, using hormones as chemical messengers, serves as a means for both information processing and control. This homeostatic control system is concerned with maintaining a safe and stable internal operating environment, whether for animal or machine. Homeostasis is a term typically applied to biological systems for the process by which that safe and stable state is achieved and maintained.

Gerald (1981) describes the endocrine system's basic role as follows: "[The endocrine system] may be compared to an orchestra, in which, when one instrument is out of tune, a perfect ensemble is impossible. . . . It is constantly monitoring the internal environment, and it is ideally situated to function in response to psychic stimuli." (Boyd 1971, p. 421).

A basic biological function of the endocrine system is to maintain the organism's internal self-consistency (homeostasis). This is accomplished by the endocrine (ductless) glands' directly secreting their chemical messengers (hormones) into the bloodstream. The circulatory system then carries these messengers (in essence, broadcasts) to all the organism's cells. Different cells have differing responses to endocrine secretions, some reacting markedly to certain hormones, others not at all. Selective tissues, called *target tissues*, are selectively aroused by a specific hormone. An example is a hormone secreted by the thyroid gland that targets bone tissue specifically. Some hormones are nonspecific, such as insulin, which acts on almost all cells (with the notable exception of most brain cells), affecting their energy (glucose) uptake.

Negative feedback mechanisms are fundamental to endocrine system control. One typical example (Boyd 1971) illustrates how the hypothalamus monitors the release of several different hormones and coordinates their effects based on central nervous system inputs. By applying this negative feedback control regime, the system, when stressed, can be restored to a steady state, an ability crucial to the process of homeostasis.

The biological endocrine system is concerned with three different areas: growth and development, nervous system function, and metabolism regulation, with the latter perhaps paying the highest dividends in robotics. Lehninger (1975, p. 363) defines metabolism as "a highly coordinated purposeful activity in which many sets of interrelated . . . systems participate, exchanging both matter and energy between the cell and its environment." This is resource management at a very low level. The question is what resources we should be concerned with in the robotics domain.

Energy management is one choice. Just as glucose fuels most of the body's cells, some form of energy must be made available for the robot. In mammals, two typical modes of glucose metabolism are found, "feast or famine." Cellular processes are always drawing energy from their environment. When glucose is abundant in the blood, insulin is released, signaling to the cells that their energy uptake can be increased. If the glucose level drops off, the hormone level also drops, signifying a fasting state. This hormonal release also affects biological organ tissues markedly, in addition to single cells, by bringing entire subsystems into either high or low states of activity depending on the organism's current state. This aspect of energy management is highly suitable for incorporation into a robotic homeostatic control subsystem.

Another potential application is that of thermoregulation. Warm-blooded animals must maintain constant temperatures throughout their lifetimes. Robots do not live within such rigid constraints, but nonetheless suitable operating ranges must be adhered to if we expect reliable performance. Robots are expected to perform in more hostile environments than people (e.g., space) and must have the ability to regulate internal temperature. It is not proposed that the cooling and heating mechanisms for robots be analogous to those of mammals; that would be absurd. Whatever temperature management system is used, however, two types of stresses can be anticipated:

■ Global stress: Heat must be exchanged between the robot and its surroundings to restore acceptable conditions (e.g., a robot on the sunny side of Mercury).

■ Local stress: Heat must be redistributed within the robot to maintain reliable operation of a particular subsystem. The failure of a single subsystem could have the domino effect, ultimately resulting in the robot's complete failure. An example of local stress would be the overheating of a robot's arm while servicing a furnace.

In either case, temperature must be regulated by a control system. Since this regulation occurs unconsciously in mammals (global stress through sweating or panting, local stress by dilation or constriction of blood vessels), homeostatic control can effectively manage this function.

Emergency notification and resultant behavioral parameter alterations can also be carried out quickly and efficiently using a broadcast communication mechanism. This loosely parallels the secretion of epinephrine (adrenaline) that markedly and rapidly increases the rate of a creature's processes in response to an unanticipated event. The fact that dormancy can be induced rapidly, over the same channels, should not be overlooked. Indeed much of the "fight or flight" response can be embedded in this manner.

10.2.1.1   The Homeostat

Ashby (1952) was among the first to develop the notion of homeostasis in a cybernetic context, extending the principles of biology to machines. In particular, he argued that adaptation is essential and that it is achieved by maintaining certain essential state variables within acceptable physiological limits, citing blood glucose level maintenance and thermoregulation as two examples, among others. Because he saw maintaining stability as essential to a system's survival, he created an unusual device called a homeostat that embodies these principles. It consists of four interacting units each containing an electromagnet and a water-based potentiometer (figure 10.2). The units are fully interconnected: each receives inputs from and each sends outputs to the others. In tests of the system, certain settings produced stable behavior (with the magnets moving to a central position and resisting displacement) whereas other settings yielded runaway instability (with the magnets' velocities increasing uncontrollably). Although a seemingly uninteresting device given the complexity of today's robots, the homeostat provided a test bed for the notions of homeostatic stability in machines in the 1950s.

(A)

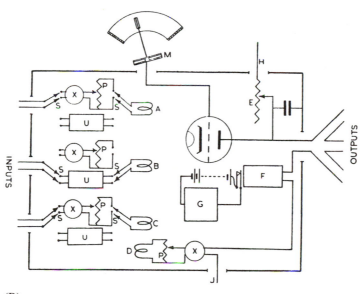

(B)

Figure 10.2
Ashby's homeostat: (A) the actual device; (B) the circuit for a single unit.

10.2.1.2   Schema-Based Homeostatic Control

The addition of a new class of behavioral control units called signal schemas
(Arkin 1988) provides a means for a robot to sense and transmit to motor
behaviors information regarding its own internal state. These signal schemas
are of two types: transmitter schemas, associated with specific internal sensors, and receptor schemas, embedded within motor schemas. The hormonal
concept of targetability is achieved by allowing the transmitter schemas to
broadcast their information to all active behaviors. Only those motor schemas
whose activity is dependent on a particular type of information contain receptor
schemas sensitive to those specific broadcast messages.

Transmitter schemas send information pertaining to one particular aspect
of the robot's internal state. Their role is to provide the feedback required to
achieve homeostatic control. For example, a sensor can measure a robot's available fuel reserves. In the case of battery-powered vehicles, this might involve
an ammeter; for petroleum-powered vehicles, a fuel tank measuring device
could be used. The rate of consumption can also be monitored, providing additional information for negative feedback analysis.

Receptor schemas, embedded within the motor schemas, provide the mechanism for modulating the motor behavior itself. In response to the information the transmitter schema broadcasts, the receptor schema alters parameters
within its motor schema, changing its output. If fuel reserves are running low,
motor rates are tuned to run at more efficient levels. Internal changes can produce shorter, albeit more risky, paths when fuel depletion warrants the risks.
The unit has one receptor schema for each transmitter to which it is sensitive,
implementing the concept of targetability by specifying which, if any, of the
transmitted signals the behavioral controller should be aware of. Figure 10.3
depicts these relationships.

In the case of energy management, a transmitter message emanates from an
internal sensor reporting available fuel reserves. Since this message is transmitted globally, it affects all targeted motor behaviors uniformly. In the case
of energy reduction, this produces smooth, more efficient (albeit slower) motion. In thermoregulation, decreasing the rate of motion reduces the amount
of heat produced per unit of time, allowing the motors to dissipate heat more
effectively and use power more efficiently.

As an example, figure 10.4 shows the effects on navigation as the robot's
initial fuel reserves range from full to almost empty. As the energy supplies
dwindle, the robot comes closer and closer to the obstacles, moving at a slower
and more efficient speed. Eventually, the course of the path taken actually

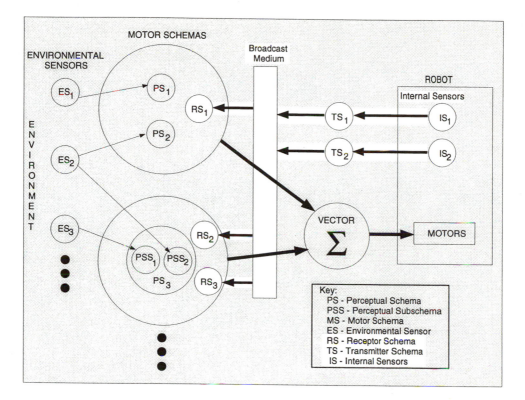

Figure 10.3
Homeostatic schema-based control architecture. The highlighted components pertain to homeostatic control.

switches, producing a much shorter path (in terms of distance but not time) in reaction to low fuel conditions. This set of paths clearly indicates the impact of available fuel reserves on the schema-based navigation process. Additional results, including those concerning thermoregulation, appear in Arkin 1992c.

10.2.1.3   Subsumption-Based Hormonal Control

Another application of the notion of hormonal control involves the development of a hormone-driven autonomous vacuum cleaner named "Sozzy" (figure 10.5) (Yamamoto 1993). This system is really a mixed metaphor in which hormonal analogies are used to modify the robot's "emotions," specifically fatigue, sadness, desperation, and joy. Figure 10.6 shows the means by which an emotion-suppressing behavior is added to an underlying subsumption-style

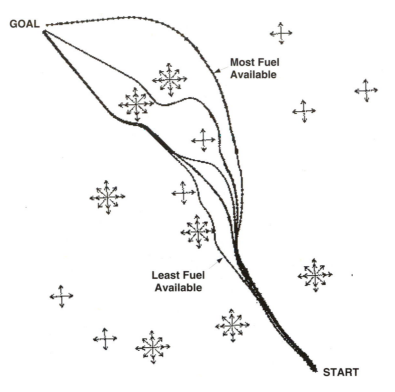

Figure 10.4
Collection of paths reflecting different fuel reserves. Note as the fuel reserves become depleted, the paths get closer and closer to the obstacles, finally resulting in a complete change in the path's general quality as it eventually changes from detouring to the upper regions to moving more closely around the obstacles at slower speeds.

control system that modifies the underlying active behavioral constituency. Hormonal state variables that reflect the various emotional states are maintained within the emotion-suppressing behavior. A function that receives both internal (e.g., battery level, time expired) and external stimuli (e.g., loss of beacon) regulates these states. The net result is behavioral switching as opposed to behavioral modification as seen in the schema-based hormonal controller. A robot implementing the system was tested in a laboratory setting where the hormone levels corresponding to the various emotional states rose and fell over time. This changed the robot's overall behavior, giving it the subjective appearance of being "more friendly and more lively" (Yamamoto 1993, p. 221) than when the hormonal system was inactive.

Figure 10.5
Sozzy: A hormone-driven robot. (Photograph courtesy of Masaki Yamamoto.)

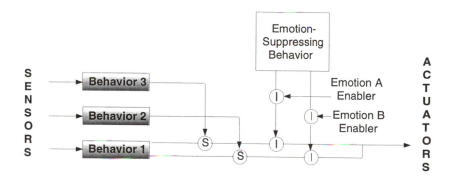

Figure 10.6
Hormonal behavioral switching. Inhibition from the emotion-suppressing behavior keeps the robot inactive until an emotion is enabled, which in turn inhibits the inhibition, effectively selecting a suitable behavioral set.

10.2.2   Immune Systems

Another biological control system parallel explored in the context of robotics involves the immune response. Immune networks detect and attack antigens (alien nonself materials such as bacteria) by producing antibodies. The bone marrow and thymus gland create lymphocytes of various types that regulate the production of antibodies and circulate throughout the lymphatic system in mammals. Specific antibodies attack specific antigens by recognizing particular antigenic determinants, forming a complex control system capable of recognizing and eliminating both previously encountered and new antigens.

In Japan, researchers have applied principles inspired by immune networks to robotic control problems. Using immune system models initially derived for fault tolerance (Mizessyn and Ishida 1993), the simulated learning of gait acquisition for a six-legged robot has been achieved (Ishiguro, Ichikawa, and Uchikawa 1994). Immune system models have been extended to include multiagent robotic systems (Mitsumoto et al. 1996). Here parallels are drawn at several levels: The robot and its environment are modeled as a stimulating antibody-antigen relationship, and robot-robot interactions can be both stimulating and suppressing (analogous to antibody-antibody relations). Each robot decides its next action based on these relationships with other robots and the world, organizing itself to effectively conduct the task. The system has been tested in simulation only on a foraging task, with an eye toward moving it onto a six-agent microrobot colony.

Both of these examples are based loosely on the idiotype network model (Jerne 1973), in which novel, randomly created antibodies are initially treated as antigens, resulting in systemwide stimulation or suppression of other antibodies, eventually resulting in steady-state conditions. The presence of other antigenic material can disrupt this equilibrium and, as in homeostasis, the system then responds in a manner to restore or achieve a new steady-state condition. Others (e.g., Bersini 1992) have used immune response models as an inspiration for reinforcement learning methods similar to Q-learning (section 8.3), but this has as yet not been applied to actual robot control systems.

10.2.3   Nanotechnology

What if we could build *really small* robots, robots so small that they could operate at the molecular level? As fantastic sounding as it is, this is the domain of nanotechnology, where machines operate on atomic scales. It is not as absurd as it first sounds. One could argue that nanomachines already exist operating within cells. These however result from natural sources. Protein enzymes routinely are involved in the assembly and disassembly of the stuff of which we are made. Is it really so implausible that engineered machines could be devised to serve similar purposes?

Drexler's vision of nanotechnology has served as the foundation of the field. In *Engines of Creation* (1986) Drexler describes a future in which molecular machines are commonplace. Cell repair machines, for example, have the ability to cure disease, reverse aging, or serve as active shields against infection. He also raises the spectre of their being used for evil ends or destructive purposes. Drexler's subsequent book *Nanosystems* (1992) provides more of a scientific basis for his earlier vision, describing the techniques by which molecular manufacturing could potentially be achieved. Molecular manufacturing has more in common with biochemistry than with engineering in terms of precision, control, defect rate, product size, and cycle time.

Moravec (1988) envisions nanotechnology as the means by which robots could truly become self-assembling. For example, a robot bush (figure 10.7) could self-construct and would have a structure unlike anything we've seen thus far. Robotic cilia would propel the bush about, and its shape could change dynamically. Local reflexes might handle much of the control.

Nothing close to an actual nanorobot has yet been produced, but many researchers are still working on a very small scale. This is the domain of microrobots, very small robotic systems that can do fundamentally different tasks in different ways than the more conventional systems we have already studied. On these scales, friction becomes the dominant force rather than gravity. Gnat robots have been proposed (Flynn 1987) and built (Flynn et al. 1989) that can fit on a single electronic chip. These systems have numerous potential uses: bugs for the CIA, multiagent swarms for space exploration, autonomous billboards, eye microsurgery, and patching holes in or removing barnacles from a ship's hull (Flynn, Brooks, and Tavrow 1989.)

MIT's AI Lab has developed several microrobot systems:

- Squirt: a low-cost prototype microrobot built for robotics education (Flynn et al. 1989).
- The Ants: a colony of microrobots being developed for explosive ordnance disposal applications (figure 10.8).
- The Rockettes: a colony of microrobots on the order of 10 grams each being developed for planetary exploration.

Perhaps the most unusual microrobot encountered thus far is the hybrid insect robot Takeuchi (1996) has developed at the University of Tokyo. This system is part robot and part cockroach: two severed cockroach legs serve

Figure 10.7
A self-assembling robot bush. (Figure courtesy of Hans Moravec.)

as the actuators for a single chip microcontroller. It is able to walk when an artificial body is attached to the legs. This roboroach is reportedly capable of functioning for approximately one hour and uses four electrodes inserted into the cockroach legs.

10.3   ON EQUIVALENCE (OR BETTER)

We now briefly examine some issues surrounding the ultimate relationship between robots and humans. Will robots inherit the earth? Will humans ultimately reside in robotic form? This section discusses the positions of those who believe either (or both) of those things will happen. Although it may be easy to disregard these points of view, let us open-mindedly explore these positions.

Figure 10.8
Ant microrobots. (Photograph courtesy of Rodney Brooks.)

Minsky (1994, p. 109) responds to the question, "Will robots inherit the earth?": "Yes, as we engineer replacement bodies and brains using nanotechnology. We will then live longer, possess greater wisdom and enjoy capabilities as yet unimagined." Minsky's answer also touches on the issue of humans as robots. According to this view, the transcendence from biology to technology is a cause for celebration rather than fear. We will ultimately be freed from our biological limitations. Even the option of immortality is posed. Humans become machines and vice versa—ultimately there is no distinction. This somewhat radical viewpoint flies in the face of the counterarguments against machine intelligence, thought, and consciousness we encountered earlier in this chapter but we continue our exploration nonetheless.

Moravec (1988) argues that this is our destiny, that, as stated earlier, these future robots are our mind children. But how do we become our robotic equivalent? This process of a person's becoming a machine is referred to as transmigration, which might occur in several ways (according to Moravec):

1. One approach might involve a high-fidelity surgical neuron-by-neuron replacement of your brain with an electronic neuron counterpart. As this would be a step-by-step process conducted with verifying simulations at every replacement step, at what point do you stop being a human and become a robot?

2. Another strategy would involve a high-resolution brain scan that, in a single operation, would create a new you "while you wait."

3. Perhaps a computer that you would wear throughout your lifetime would record all of your life experiences. Once it learned what it was like to be you and could act equivalently to you, the record could be transferred to a machine substrate.

4. Another approach would be to sever the corpus callosum, which connects the brain's two hemispheres, and attach each end to a computer that at first passes the messages through while also recording them. Eventually your biological brain would die, but during your lifetime this computer would have learned how to be you and could continue in that capacity indefinitely.

The net result, according to this view, is that the sum total of you is a program independent of where the program resides: in carbon-based life forms, in silicon, or perhaps in something else. You could run (think?) at speeds millions of times faster than the limitations biology imposes on you. It matters not if your frail biological life form dies—you still exist: "If the machine you inhabit is fatally clobbered, the [backup] tape can be read into a blank computer, resulting in another you, minus the experiences since the copy. With enough copies, permanent death would be very unlikely" (Moravec 1985, p. 145).

Fringe robotics indeed. For this point of view Moravec has been labeled a "DNA traitor" by many who either fear or dismiss the consequences of these thoughts.

10.4 OPPORTUNITIES

In concluding this book, it might be wise to provide some guidance to those who follow by describing what problems remain to be solved to advance the science of robotics. Many open questions warrant further investigation. Just a few are mentioned below:

■ Identifying ecological niches where robots can successfully compete and survive, making them sufficiently adaptable to changes in the world they inhabit.

■ Increasing accessibility: bringing robotics to the masses through suitable interface, specification, and programming systems.

■ Representing and controlling sensing by viewing it as a form of dynamic agent-environment communication.

- Improving perception: new sensors, selective attention mechanisms, gaze control and stabilization, improved eye-hand coordination, foveal vision, and specialized hardware, among others.
- Further exploitation of expectations, attention, and intention in extracting information about the world.
- Understanding more deeply the relationship between deliberation and reaction, leading to more effective and adaptive interfaces for hybrid architectures.
- Evaluating, benchmarking, and developing metrics: In order to be more accurately characterized as a science, robotics needs more effective means for evaluating its experiments. Although progress is beginning to be made in this area (Gat 1995) much more remains to be done.
- Satisfying the need for far more advanced learning and adaptation capabilities than are currently available.
- Creating large societies of multiagent robots capable of conducting complex tasks in dynamic environments.
- Using robots as instruments to advance the understanding of animal and human intelligence by embedding biological models of ever-increasing complexity in actual robotic hardware.

Certainly, the roboticist's plate is full of a myriad of important and exciting problems to explore.

10.5   CHAPTER SUMMARY

- The issue of whether or not robots are capable of intelligent thought or consciousness is quite controversial, with a broad spectrum of opinion ranging from "absolutely not" to "most assuredly so."
- Robotic emotions may play a useful role in the control of behavior-based systems, although their role is just beginning to be explored.
- Homeostatic control, concerned with managing a robot's internal environment, can also be useful for modulating ongoing behavior to assist in survival.
- Immune systems are also beginning to be explored as a means for controlling both individual and group robot behavior.
- Nanorobots and microrobots can revolutionize the way in which we think about robotic applications.
- One school of thought in robotics asserts that these machines are mankind's natural successors.
- As in any important endeavor, there are a wide range of questions waiting to be answered as well as opportunities to be explored.

References

Aboaf, E., Drucker, S., and Atkeson, C. 1989. "Task-Level Robot Learning: Juggling a Tennis Ball More Accurately," *Proceedings of the International Conference on Robotics and Automation*, Scottsdale, AZ, pp. 1290–95.

Adolph, K., Gibson, E. J., and Eppler, M.A. 1990. "Perceiving Affordances of Slopes: The Ups and Downs of Toddlers' Locomotion," *Emory Cognition Project Report #16*, Department of Psychology, Emory University.

Agah, A., and Bekey, G. 1995a. "In a Team of Robots The Loudest Is Not Necessarily the Best," *Proceedings of the International Conference on Systems, Man, and Cybernetics*, Vancouver, B.C.

Agah, A., and Bekey, G. 1995b. "Learning from Perception, Success, and Failure in a Team of Autonomous Mobile Robots," *Proceedings of the Seventh Portuguese Conference on Artificial Intelligence (EPIA 1995)*, Madeira Island, Portugal.

Agah, A., and Bekey, G. 1997. "Phylogenetic and Ontogenetic Learning in a Colony of Interacting Robots," *Autonomous Robots*, Vol. 1, No. 4, January, pp. 85–100.

Agre, P. E., and Chapman, D. 1987. "Pengi: An Implementation of a Theory of Activity," *Proceedings of the American Association of Artificial Intelligence Conference (AAAI-87)*, pp. 268–71.

Agre, P. E. and Chapman, D. 1990. "What Are Plans For?" *Robotics and Autonomous Systems*, Vol. 6, pp. 17–34.

Albus, J. 1981. *Brains, Behavior, and Robotics*, BYTE Books, Peterborough, NH.

Albus, J. 1991. "Outline for a Theory of Intelligence," *IEEE Transactions on Systems, Man and Cybernetics*, Vol. 21, No. 3, May-June, pp. 473–509.

Albus, J., McCain, H. and Lumia, R. 1987. "NASA/NBS Standard Reference Model for Telerobot Control System Architecture (NASREM)," NBS Technical Note 1235, Robot Systems Division, National Bureau of Standards.

Allee, W., 1978. *Animal Aggregations*, Univ. of Chicago Press, Chicago, IL.

Aloimonos, Y. (ed.) 1993. *Active Perception*, Lawrence Erlbaum Assocciates, Hillsdale, NJ.

Aloimonos, Y., and Rosenfeld, A. 1991. "Computer Vision," *Science*, Vol. 253, pp. 1249–53, September.

Altmann, S. A. 1974. "Baboons, Space, Time, and Energy," *American Zoologist*, Vol. 14, pp. 221–48.

Anderson, J. A. 1995. "Associative Networks," in *The Handbook of Brain Theory and Neural Networks*, ed. M. Arbib, MIT Press, Cambridge, MA, pp. 102–7.

Anderson, T., and Donath, M. 1991. "Animal Behavior as a Paradigm for Developing Robot Autonomy," in *Designing Autonomous Agents*, ed. P. Maes, MIT Press, Cambridge, MA, pp. 145–68.

Andresen, F., Davis, L., Eastman, R., and Kambhampati, S. 1985. "Visual Algorithms for Autonomous Navigation," *Proceedings of the IEEE International Conference on Robotics and Automation*, St. Louis, MO, pp. 856–61.

Arbib, M.A. 1964. *Brains, Machines, and Mathematics*, McGraw-Hill, New York.

Arbib, M. A. 1981. "Perceptual Structures and Distributed Motor Control," in *Handbook of Physiology—The Nervous System II: Motor Control*, ed. V. B. Brooks, American Physiological Society, Bethesda, MD, pp. 1449–80.

Arbib, M. A. 1992. "Schema Theory," in *The Encyclopedia of Artificial Intelligence*, 2nd ed., ed. S. Shapiro, Wiley-Interscience, New York, N.Y., pp. 1427–43.

Arbib, M. A. 1995a. "Schema Theory," in *The Handbook of Brain Theory and Neural Networks*, ed. M. Arbib, MIT Press, Cambridge, MA, pp. 830–34.

Arbib, M. A. 1995b. *The Handbook of Brain Theory and Neural Networks*, ed. M. Arbib, MIT Press, Cambridge, MA.

Arbib, M., and House, D. 1987. "Depth and Detours: An Essay on Visually Guided Behavior," in *Vision, Brain, and Cooperative Computation*, ed. M. Arbib and A. Hanson, MIT Press, Cambridge, MA, pp. 129–63.

Arbib, M., Iberall, T., and Lyons, D. 1985. "Coordinated Control Programs for Movements of the Hand," in *Hand Function and the Neocortex*, eds. A. Goodman and I. Darian-Smith, Springer-Verlag, New York, pp. 135–70.

Arbib, M. A., Kfoury, A. J., and Moll, R. N. 1981. *A Basis for Theoretical Computer Science*, Springer-Verlag, New York.

Arkin, R. C. 1986. "Path Planning for a Vision-Based Autonomous Robot," *Proceedings of the SPIE Conference on Mobile Robots*, Cambridge, MA, pp. 240–49.

Arkin, R. C. 1987a. "Motor Schema Based Navigation for a Mobile Robot: An Approach to Programming by Behavior," *Proceedings of the IEEE Conference on Robotics and Automation*, Raleigh, NC, pp. 264–71.

Arkin, R. C. 1987b. "Towards Cosmopolitan Robots: Intelligent Navigation in Extended Man-Made Environments," Ph.D. Dissertation, COINS Technical Report 87-80, University of Massachusetts, Department of Computer and Information Science.

Arkin, R. C. 1988. "Homeostatic Control for a Mobile Robot: Dynamic Replanning in Hazardous Environments," *Proceedings of the SPIE Conference on Mobile Robots III*, Cambridge, MA, pp. 407–13.

Arkin, R. C. 1989a. "Neuroscience in Motion: The Application of Schema Theory to Mobile Robotics," in *Visuomotor Coordination: Amphibians, Comparisons, Models, and Robots*, eds. J.-P. Ewert and M. Arbib, New York: Plenum Press, pp. 649–72.

Arkin, R. C. 1989b. "Motor Schema-Based Mobile Robot Navigation," *International Journal of Robotics Research*, Vol. 8, No. 4, pp. 92–112.

Arkin, R. C. 1989c. "Navigational Path Planning for a Vision-based Mobile Robot," *Robotica*, Vol. 7, pp. 49–63.

Arkin, R. C. 1989d. "Towards the Unification of Navigational Planning and Reactive Control," working notes, *AAAI Spring Symposium on Robot Navigation*, Stanford University, CA, March.

Arkin, R. C. 1990a. "The Impact of Cybernetics on the Design of a Mobile Robot System: A Case Study," *IEEE Transactions on Systems, Man, and Cybernetics*, Vol. 20, No. 6, November/December, pp. 1245–57.

Arkin, R. C. 1990b. "Integrating Behavioral, Perceptual, and World Knowledge in Reactive Navigation," *Robotics and Autonomous Systems*, Vol. 6, pp. 105–22.

Arkin, R. C. 1991. "Reactive Control as a Substrate for Telerobotic Systems," *IEEE Aerospace and Electronics Systems Magazine*, Vol. 6, No. 6, June, pp. 24–31.

Arkin, R. C. 1992a. "Behavior-Based Robot Navigation for Extended Domains," *Adaptive Behavior*, Vol. 1, No. 2, pp. 201–225.

Arkin, R. C. 1992b. "Cooperation without Communication: Multi-agent Schema Based Robot Navigation," *Journal of Robotic Systems*, Vol. 9, No. 3, April, pp. 351–64.

Arkin, R. C. 1992c. "Homeostatic Control for a Mobile Robot: Dynamic Replanning in Hazardous Environments," *Journal of Robotic Systems*, Vol. 9, No. 2, March, pp. 197–214.

Arkin, R. C. 1993. "Modeling Neural Function at the Schema Level: Implications and Results for Robotic Control," in *Biological Neural Networks in Invertebrate Neuroethology and Robotics*, eds. T. McKenna, R. Ritzmann and R. Beer, San Diego, CA, pp. 383–410.

Arkin, R. C., and Ali, K. 1994. "Integration of Reactive and Telerobotic Control in Multi-Agent Robotic Systems," *Proceedings of the Third International Conference on Simulation of Adaptive Behavior (SAB94) [From Animals to Animats]*, Brighton, UK, August, pp. 473–78.

Arkin, R. C., Balch, T., Collins, T., Henshaw, A., MacKenzie, D., Nitz, E., Rodriguez, R., and Ward, K. 1993. "Buzz: An Instantiation of a Schema-Based Reactive Robotic System," *Proceedings of the International Conference on Intelligent Autonomous Systems (IAS-3)*, Pittsburgh, PA, February, pp. 418–27.

Arkin, R. C., and Hobbs, J. D. 1992. "Dimensions of Communication and Social Organization in Multi-Agent Robotic Systems," *From Animals to Animats 2: Proceedings of the Second International Conference on Simulation of Adaptive Behavior*, Honolulu, HI, December, MIT Press, Cambridge MA, pp. 486–93.

Arkin, R. C., and Lawton, D. 1990. "Reactive Behavioral Support for Qualitative Visual Navigation," *Proceedings of the IEEE International Symposium on Intelligent Motion Control*, Istanbul, Turkey, 1990, pp. IP21–28.

Arkin, R. C., and MacKenzie, D. 1994. "Temporal Coordination of Perceptual Algorithms for Mobile Robot Navigation," *IEEE Transactions on Robotics and Automation*, Vol. 10, No. 3, June, pp. 276–86.

Arkin, R. C., and Murphy, R. R. 1990. "Autonomous Navigation in a Manufacturing Environment," *IEEE Transactions on Robotics and Automation*, Vol. 6, No. 4, August, pp. 445–54.

Arkin, R. C., Murphy, R., Pearson, M., and Vaughn, D. 1989. "Mobile Robot Docking Operations in a Manufacturing Environment: Progress in Visual Perceptual Strategies," *Proceedings of the IEEE International Workshop on Intelligent Robots and Systems*, Tsukuba, Japan, pp. 147–54.

Aron, S., Deneubourg, J., Goss, S., and Pasteels, J. 1990. "Functional Self-Organization Illustrated by Inter-Nest Traffic in Ants: The Case of the Argentine Ant," in *Biological Motion*, eds. W. Alt and G. Hoffmann, Springer-Verlag, Berlin, pp. 533–47.

Asada, M., Noda, S., Tawaratsumida, S., and Hosoda, K. 1995. "Vision-Based Reinforcement Learning for Purposive Behavior Acquisition," *Proceedings of the IEEE International Conference on Robotics and Automation*, May, pp. 146–53.

Ashby, W. R. 1952. *Design for a Brain: The Origin of Adaptive Behavior*, J. Wiley, New York, 1952 (Second edition 1960).

Aström, K. 1995. "Adaptive Control: General Methodology," in *The Handbook of Brain Theory and Neural Networks*, ed. M. Arbib, MIT Press, Cambridge, MA, pp. 66–69.

Atkeson, C., Moore, A., and Schaal, S. 1997. "Locally Weighted Learning for Control," *Artificial Intelligence Review*, February, Vol. 11. No. 1–5, pp. 11–73.

Badal, S., Ravela, S., Draper, B., and Hanson, A. 1994. "A Practical Obstacle Detection and Avoidance System," *Proceedings of the Second IEEE Workshop on Applications of Computer Vision*, Sarasota, FL, December, pp. 97–104.

Badler, N., and Webber, B. 1991. "Animation from Instructions," in *Making the Move: Mechanics, Control and Animation of Articulated Figures*, eds. Badler, Barsky, and Zeltzer, Morgan Kaufmann, San Mateo, CA, pp. 51–93.

Bajcsy, R. 1988. "Active Perception," *Proceedings of the IEEE*, Vol. 76, No. 8, August, pp. 996–1005.

Bakker, P., and Kuniyoshi, Y. 1996. "Robot See, Robot Do: An Overview of Robot Imitation," *AISB Workshop on Learning in Robots and Animals*, Brighton, UK, April.

Balch, T., and Arkin, R. C. 1993. "Avoiding the Past: A Simple but Effective Strategy for Reactive Navigation," *Proceedings of the IEEE International Conference on Robotics and Automation*, Atlanta, GA, May, Vol. 1, pp. 678–85.

Balch, T., and Arkin, R. C. 1994. "Communication in Reactive Multiagent Robotic Systems," *Autonomous Robots*, Vol. 1, No. 1, pp. 27–52.

Balch, T., and Arkin, R. C. 1995. "Motor Schema-Based Formation Control for Multiagent Robot Teams," *Proceedings 1995 International Conference on Multiagent Systems*, San Francisco, CA, pp. 10–16.

Balch, T., Boone, G., Collins, T., Forbes, H., MacKenzie, D., and Santamaría, J. 1995. "Io, Ganymede, and Callisto—A Multiagent Robot Trash-Collecting Team," *AI Magazine*, Vol. 16, No. 2, Summer, pp. 39–51.

Ballard, D. 1989. "Reference Frames for Animate Vision," *Proceedings of the Eleventh International Joint Conference on Artificial Intelligence (IJCAI-89)*, Detroit, MI, pp. 1635–41.

Ballard, D., and Brown, C. 1993. "Principles of Active Perception," in *Active Perception*, ed. Y. Aloimonos, Lawrence Erlbaum Associates, Hillsdale, NJ, pp. 245–82.

Barbera, A., Fitzgerald, M., Albus, J., and Haynes, L. 1984. "RCS: The NBS Real-time Control System," *Proceedings of the Robots 8 Conference*, Detroit, MI, June, pp. 19.1–19.38.

Barth, M., and Ishiguro, H. 1994. "Distributed Panoramic Sensing in Multiagent Robotics," *Proceedings of the IEEE International Conference on Multisensor Fusion and Integration for Intelligent Systems*, Las Vegas, NV, October, pp. 739–46.

Bartlett, F. C. 1932. *Remembering: A Study in Experimental and Social Psychology*, London, Cambridge University Press.

Basye, K. 1992. "An Automata-Based Approach to Robotic Map Learning," working notes, *AAAI Fall Symposium on Applications of AI to Real-World Autonomous Mobile Robots*.

Beer, R. 1990. *Intelligence as Adaptive Behavior: An Experiment in Computational Neuroethology*, Academic Press, New York, NY.

Beer, R., Chiel, H., and Sterling, L. 1990. "A Biological Perspective on Autonomous Agent Design," *Robotics and Autonomous Systems*, Vol. 6, pp. 169–86.

Bekey, G., and Tomovic, R. 1986. "Robot Control by Reflex Actions," *IEEE International Conference on Robotics and Automation*, San Francisco, CA, April, pp. 240–47.

Bekey, G., and Tomovic, R. 1990. "Biologically Based Robot Control," *Proceedings of the Annual International Conference of the IEEE Engineering in Medicine and Biology Society*, Vol. 12, No. 5, pp. 1938–39.

Bellman, R. 1978. *Artificial Intelligence: Can Computers Think?* Boyd and Frasier Publishing Co., Boston, MA.

Benson, S., and Nilsson, N. 1995. "Reacting, Planning, and Learning in an Autonomous Agent," in *Machine Intelligence 14*, eds. K. Furukawa, D. Michie, and S. Muggleton, Clarendon Press, Oxford, UK.

Bersini, H. 1992. "Immune Network and Adaptive Control," *Proceedings of the First European Conference on Artificial Life*, Paris, France, pp. 217–26.

Biederman, I. 1990. "Higher-Level Vision," in *Visual Cognition and Action*, Vol. 2, ed. N. Osherson, S. Kosslyn, and J. Hollerbach, MIT Press, Cambridge, MA.

Birnbaum, L., Brand, M., and Cooper, P. 1993. "Looking for Trouble: Using Causal Semantics to Direct Focus of Attention," *Proceedings of the Fourth International Conference on Computer Vision (ICCV-93)*, Berlin, Germany, May, pp. 49–56.

Bizzi, E., Mussa-Ivaldi, F., and Giszter, S. 1991. "Computations Underlying the Execution of Movement: A Biological Perspective," *Science*, Vol. 253, July, pp. 287–91.

Blake, A. 1993. "Computational Modelling of Hand-Eye Coordination," in *Active Perception*, ed. Y. Aloimonos, Lawrence Erlbaum Assocociates, Hillsdale, NJ, pp. 227–44.

Blake, A. 1995. "Active Vision," in *The Handbook of Brain Theory and Neural Networks*, ed. M. Arbib, MIT Press, Cambridge, MA, pp. 61–63.

Boden, M. 1995. "AI's Half-Century," *AI Magazine*, Vol. 16, No. 2, Winter, pp. 96–99.

Bogoni, L., and Bajcsy, R. 1994a. "Active Investigation of Functionality," *Proceedings of the Workshop on the Role of Functionality in Object Recognition*, 1994 Conf. on Computer Vision and Pattern Recognition, Seattle, WA, June.

Bogoni, L., and Bajcsy, R. 1994b. "Functionality Investigation Using a Discrete Event System Approach," *Robotics and Autonomous Systems*, Vol. 13, No. 3, October, pp. 173–96.

Bohm, C., and Jacopini, G. 1966. "Flow Diagrams, Turing Machines, and Languages with Only Two Formation Rules," *Communications of the ACM*, May. Vol. 9, No. 5, pp. 366–71.

Bonasso, P. 1991. "Underwater Experiments Using a Reactive System for Autonomous Vehicles," *Proceedings of the AAAI*, pp. 794–800.

Bonasso, P. 1992. "Reactive Control of Underwater Vehicles," *Applied Intelligence*, Vol. 2, No. 3, September, pp. 201–04.

Booker, L., Goldberg, D., and Holland, J. 1989. "Classifier Systems and Genetic Algorithms," *Artificial Intelligence*, Vol. 40, No. 1-3, pp. 235–82.

Borenstein, J., and Koren, Y. 1989. "Real-Time Obstacle Avoidance for Fast Mobile Robots," *IEEE Transactions on Systems, Man, and Cybernetics*, Vol. 19, No. 5, September, pp. 1179–87.

Borenstein, J., and Koren, Y. 1991. "The Vector Field Histogram—Fast Obstacle Avoidance for Mobile Robots," *IEEE Transactions on Robotics and Automation*, Vol. 7, No. 3, June, pp. 278–88.

Bower, T. 1974. "The Evolution of Sensory Systems," in *Perception: Essays in Honor of James J. Gibson*, eds. R. MacLeod and H. Pick, Cornell University Press, Ithaca, NY, p. 141.

Box, H. 1973. *Organisation in Animal Communities: Experimental and Naturalistic Studies of the Social Behavior of Animals*, Butterworths, London.

Boyd, W. 1971. *An Introduction to the Study of Disease*. Lea & Febiger, Philadelphia, PA.

Brady, M. 1985. "Artificial Intelligence and Robotics," *Artificial Intelligence and Robotics*, Vol. 26, pp. 79–121.

Braitenberg, V. 1984. *Vehicles: Experiments in Synthetic Psychology*, MIT Press, Cambridge, MA.

Brill, F. 1994. "Perception and Action in a Dynamic Three-Dimensional World," *Proceedings of the IEEE Workshop on Visual Behaviors*, Seattle, WA, June, pp. 60–67.

Brooks, R. 1986. "A Robust Layered Control System for a Mobile Robot," *IEEE Journal of Robotics and Automation*, Vol. RA-2, No. 1, pp. 14–23.

Brooks, R. 1987a. "Planning is Just a Way of Avoiding Figuring Out What to Do Next," *Working Paper 303*, MIT AI Laboratory, September.

Brooks, R. 1987b. "A Hardware Retargetable Distributed Layered Architecture for Mobile Robot Control," *Proceedings of the IEEE International Conference on Robotics and Automation*, Raleigh, NC, May, pp. 106–10.

Brooks, R. 1989a. "A Robot That Walks: Emergent Behaviors from a Carefully Evolved Network," *Proceedings of the IEEE International Conference on Robotics and Automation*, May, pp. 692–94.

Brooks, R. 1989b. "The Whole Iguana," in *Robotics Science*, ed. M. Brady, MIT Press, Cambridge, MA, pp. 432–56.

Brooks, R. 1990a. "The Behavior Language," *A.I. Memo No. 1227*, MIT AI Laboratory, April.

Brooks, R. 1990b. "Elephants Don't Play Chess," in *Designing Autonomous Agents*, ed. P. Maes, MIT Press, Cambridge, MA, pp. 3–15.

Brooks, R. 1991a. "Intelligence Without Reason," *A.I. Memo No. 1293*, MIT AI Laboratory, April.

Brooks, R. 1991b. "New Approaches to Robotics," *Science*, Vol. 253, September, pp. 1227–32.

Brooks, R., and Flynn, A. 1989. "Robot Beings," *Proceedings of the IEEE/RSJ International Conference on Intelligent Robotics and Systems (IROS-89)*, Tsukuba, Japan, pp. 2–10.

Brooks, R. A., and Stein, L. 1994. "Building Brains for Bodies," *Autonomous Robots*, Vol. 1, No. 1, pp. 7–25.

Brown, C. 1991. "Gaze Behaviors for Robots," in *Active Perception and Robot Vision*, eds. A. Sood and H. Wechsler, Springer-Verlag, Berlin, pp. 115–39.

Budenske, J., and Gini, M. 1994. "Why Is It So Difficult for a Robot to Pass through a Doorway Using Ultrasonic Sensors?" *Proceedings of the IEEE International Conference on Robotics and Automation*, pp. 3124–29.

Buhler, M., Koditschek, D., and Kindlmann, P. 1989. "A Family of Robot Control Strategies for Intermittent Dynamical Environments," *Proceedings of the International Conference on Robotics and Automation*, Scottsdale, AZ, pp. 1296–1301.

Burger, M., and Mittelstaedt, H. 1972. "Course Control by Stored Proprioceptive Information in Millipedes," *Biocybernetics*, Vol. IV, ed. H. Drischel and P. Dettmar, Fischer-Verlag, Berlin, June 1972.

Byrnes, R., Healey, A., McGhee, R., Nelson, R., Kwak, S., and Brutzman, D. 1996. "The Rational Behavior Software Architecture for Intelligent Ships," *Naval Engineers Journal*, Vol. 108, No. 2, March, pp. 43–55.

Cai, A., Fukuda, T., Arai, F., Ueyama, T., and Sakai, A. 1995. "Hierarchical Control Architecture for Cellular Robotic System—Simulations and Experiments," *Proceedings of the IEEE International Conference on Robotics and Automation*, June, pp. 1191–96.

Cameron, J., MacKenzie, D., Ward, K., Arkin, R., and Book, W. 1993. "Reactive Control for Mobile Manipulation," *Processing of the International Conference on Robotics and Automation*, Atlanta, GA, pp. 228–35.

Cao, Y., Fukunaga, A., Kahng, A., and Meng, F. 1995. "Cooperative Mobile Robotics: Antecedents and Directions," *Proceedings of the IEEE/RSJ International Conference on Intelligent Robotics and Systems (IROS '95)*, Pittsburgh, PA, pp. 226–34.

Cardoze, D., and Arkin, R. C. 1995. "Development of Visual Tracking Algorithms for an Autonomous Helicopter," *Proceedings of the Mobile Robots X*, Philadelphia, PA, pp. 145–56.

Carley, K. 1995. "Computational and Mathematical Organization Theory: Perspective and Directions," *Computation and Mathematical Organization Theory*, Vol. 1, No. 1, pp. 39–56.

Carr, G. M., and MacDonald, D. 1986. "The Sociality of Solitary Foragers: A Model Based on Resource Dispersion," *Animal Behavior*, Vol. 34, pp. 1540–49.

Cervantes-Perez, F. 1995. "Visuomotor Coordination in Frogs and Toads," in *The Handbook of Brain Theory and Neural Networks*, ed. M. Arbib, MIT Press, Cambridge, MA, pp. 1036–42.

Chalmers, D. 1995. "The Puzzle of Conscious Experience," *Scientific American*, Vol. 273, No. 6, pp. 80–86, December.

Chapman, D. 1990. "Intermediate Vision: Architecture, Implementation, and Use," Technical Report TR-90-06, Teleos Research, Palo Alto, CA, October.

Chen, L., and Luh, J. 1994. "Coordination and Control of a Group of Small Robots," *Proceedings of the International Conference on Robotics and Automation*, May, pp. 2315–20.

Christensen, H., Bowyer, K., and Bunke, H., eds. 1993. *Active Robot Vision: Camera Heads, Model-Based Navigation and Reactive Control*, World Scientific, Singapore.

Christiansen, A., Mason, M., and Mitchell, T. 1991. "Learning Reliable Manipulation Strategies without Initial Physical Models," *Robotics and Autonomous Systems*, Vol. 8, No. 1, pp. 7–18.

Chun, W., and Jochem, T. 1994. "Unmanned Ground Vehicle Demo II: Demonstration A," *Unmanned Systems*, Winter, pp. 14–20.

Chun, W., Lynch, R., Shoemaker, C., and Munkeby, S. 1995. "UGV—Demonstration B," *Unmanned Systems*, Summer, pp. 20–25.

Clark, R. J., Arkin, R. C., and Ram, A. 1992. "Learning Momentum: On-Line Performance Enhancement for Reactive Systems," *Proceedings of the IEEE International Conference on Robotics and Automation*, Nice, France, May, pp. 111–16.

Colgan, P. 1983. *Comparative Social Recognition*, J. Wiley, New York.

Collins, T. R., Arkin, R. C., and Henshaw, A. M. 1993. "Integration of Reactive Navigation with a Flexible Parallel Hardware Architecture," *Proceedings of the IEEE International Conference on Robotics and Automation*, Atlanta, GA, May, Vol. 1, pp. 271–76.

Colombetti, M., and Dorigo, M. 1992. "Learning to Control an Autonomous Robot by Distributed Genetic Algorithms," *From Animals to Animats 2: Proceedings of the Second International Conference on Simulation of Adaptive Behavior*, Honolulu, HI, December, MIT Press, Cambridge MA, pp. 305–12.

Connell, J. 1987. "Creature Building with the Subsumption Architecture," *Proceedings of the International Joint Conference on Artificial Intelligence (IJCAI-87)*, Milan, Italy, pp. 1124–26.

Connell, J. 1989a. "A Behavior-Based Arm Controller," *IEEE Transactions on Robotics and Automation*, Vol. 5, No. 6, December, pp. 784–91.

Connell, J. 1989b. "A Colony Architecture for an Artificial Creature," *Technical Report No. 1151*, MIT AI Laboratory, August.

Connell, J. 1992. "SSS: A Hybrid Architecture Applied to Robot Navigation," *Proceedings of the IEEE International Conference on Robotics and Automation*, Nice, France, pp. 2719–24.

Connell, J., and Viola P. 1990. "Cooperative Control of a Semi-Autonomous Mobile Robot," *Proceedings of the IEEE International Conference on Robotics and Automation*, pp. 1118–21.

Connolly, C., and Grupen, R. 1993. "On the Applications of Harmonic Functions to Robotics," *Journal of Robotic Systems*, Vol. 10, No. 7, pp. 931–46.

Cook, D., Gmytrasiewicz, P., and Holder, L. 1996. "Decision-Theoretic Cooperative Sensor Planning," *IEEE Transactions on Pattern Analysis and Machine Intelligence*, Vol. 18, No. 10, October, pp. 1013–23.

Craig, J. 1989. *Introduction to Robotics: Mechanics and Control*, 2nd Ed., Addison-Wesley, Reading, MA.

Crisman, J. 1991. "Color Region Tracking for Vehicle Guidance," *Active Vision*, MIT Press, Cambridge, MA, pp. 107–20.

Crowley, J., Bedrune, J., Bekker, M., and Schneider, M. 1994. "Integration and Control of Visual Processes," *Proceedings of the IEEE Workshop on Visual Behaviors*, Seattle, WA, June, pp. 45–52.

Croy, M., and Hughes, R. 1991. "Effects of Food Supply, Hunger, Danger, and Competition on Choice of Foraging Location by the Fifteen-spined Stickleback," *Animal Behavior*, Vol. 42, pp. 131–39.

Culhane, S., and Tsotsos, J. 1992. "An Attentional Prototype for Early Vision," *Proceedings of the Second European Conference on Computer Vision*, ed. G. Sandini, LNCS-Series Vol. 588, Springer-Verlag, Berlin, May, pp. 551–60.

Davis, R. 1982. "Applications of Meta-Level Knowledge to the Construction, Maintenance, and Use of Large Knowledge Bases," in *Knowledge-Based Systems in Artificial Intelligence*, eds. R. Davis and D. Lenat, McGraw-Hill, New York, pp. 229–490.

Dean, T., Angluin, D., Basye, K., Engelson, S., Kaelbling, L., Kokkevis, E., and Maron, O. 1995. "Inferring Finite Automata with Stochastic Output Functions and an Application to Map Learning," *Machine Learning*, Vol. 18, No. 1, pp. 81–108, Jan.

Dean, T., and Wellman, M. 1991. *Planning and Control*, Morgan-Kaufmann, San Mateo, CA.

Deneubourg, J., and Goss, S. 1984. "Collective Patterns and Decision-Making," *Ethology, Ecology, and Evolution*, Vol. 1, pp. 295–311.

Dennett, D. 1982. "Styles of Mental Representation," *Proceedings of the Aristotelian Society*, Vol. LXXXIII, pp. 213–16.

Dennett, D. 1991. *Consciousness Explained*, Little, Brown, and Co., Boston, MA.

Dickmanns, E. 1992. "A General Dynamic Vision Architecture for UGV and UAV," *Applied Intelligence*, Vol. 2, No. 3, September, pp. 251–70.

Dickmanns, E., and Zapp, A. 1985. "Guiding Land Vehicles along Roadways by Computer Vision," *AFCET Conference*, Toulouse, France.

Donald, B. 1993. "Information Invariants in Robotics: Part II—Sensors and Computation," *Proceedings of the International Conference on Robotics and Automation*, Vol. 3, pp. 284–90.

Donald, B., and Jennings, J. 1991a. "Sensor Interpretation and Task-Directed Planning Using Perceptual Equivalence Classes," *Proceedings of the International Conference on Robotics and Automation*, Anaheim, CA, pp. 190–97.

Donald, B., and Jennings, J. 1991b. "Perceptual Limits, Perceptual Equivalence Classes, and a Robot's Sensori-Computational Capabilities," *Proceedings of the IEEE/RSJ International Conference on Intelligent Robotics and Systems (IROS '91)*, pp. 1397–1405.

Donald, B., Jennings, J., and Brown, R. 1992. "Constructive Recognizability for Task-Directed Robot Programming," *Robotics and Autonomous Systems*, Vol. 9, No. 1–2, pp. 41–74.

Drexler, E. 1986. *Engines of Creation: The Coming Era of Nanotechnology*, Anchor Press/Doubleday, New York.

Drexler, E. 1992. *Nanosystems: Molecular Machinery, Manufacturing and Computation*, Wiley-Interscience, New York.

Duchon A., Warren W., and Kaelbling, L. 1995. "Ecological Robotics: Controlling Behavior with Optic Flow," *Proceedings of the Seventeenth Annual Conference of the Cognitive Science Society*, pp. 164–69.

Dudek, G., Jenkin, M., Milios, E., and Wilkes, D. 1993. "A Taxonomy for Swarm Robots," *Proceedings of the IEEE/RSJ International Conference on Intelligent Robots and Systems (IROS '93)*, Yokohama, Japan, pp. 441–47.

Elfes, A. 1986. "A Sonar-Based Mapping and Navigation System," *Proceedings of the IEEE International Conference on Robotics and Automation*, San Francisco, CA, pp. 1151–56.

Epstein, R. 1992. "Can Machines Think?" *AI Magazine*, Vol. 13, No. 2, Summer, pp. 80–95.

Erman, L., Hayes-Roth, F., Lesser, V., and Reddy, D. 1980. "The Hearsay II Speech Understanding System: Integrating Knowledge to Resolve Uncertainty," *Computing Surveys*, Vol. 12, No. 2, pp. 213–53.

Espenscheid, K., Quinn, R., Chiel, H., and Beer, R. 1994. "Biologically-Inspired Hexapod Robot Control," *Proceedings of the Fifth International Conference on Robotics and Manufacturing (ISRAM '94)*, August, Maui, HI, pp. 89–102.

Everett, B. 1995. *Sensors for Mobile Robots*, A.K. Peters, Wellesley, MA.

Ewert, J-P. 1980. *Neuroethology: An Introduction to the Neurophysiological Fundamentals of Behavior*, Springer-Verlag, Berlin.

Eysenck, M. 1993. *Principles of Cognitive Psychology*, Lawrence Erlbaum Associates, Hove, UK.

Fagg, A., Lotspeich, D., and Bekey, G. 1994. "A Reinforcement-Learning Approach to Reactive Control Policy Design for Autonomous Robots," *Proceedings of the IEEE International Conference on Robotics and Automation*, pp. 39–44.

Ferrell, C. 1994. "Robust Agent Control of an Autonomous Robot with Many Sensors and Actuators," M.S. Thesis, MIT AI Laboratory, Cambridge, MA.

Ferrier, N., and Clark, J. 1993. "The Harvard Binocular Head," in *Active Robot Vision: Camera Heads, Model-Based Navigation and Reactive Control*, eds. H. Christensen, K. Bowyer, and H. Bunke, World Scientific, Singapore, pp. 9–31.

Fikes, R., and Nilsson, N. 1971. "STRIPS: A New Approach to the Application of Theorem Proving to Problem Solving," *Artificial Intelligence*, Vol. 2, pp. 189–208.

Firby, R. J. 1989. "Adaptive Execution in Complex Dynamic Worlds," Ph.D. Dissertation, Technical Report YALEU/CSD/RR #672, Yale University, New Haven, CT.

Firby, R. J. 1995. "Lessons Learned from the Animate Agent Project (So Far)," working notes, *AAAI Spring Symposium on Lessons Learned from Implemented Software Architectures for Physical Agents*, Palo Alto, CA, March, pp. 92–96.

Firby, R. J., and Slack, M. 1995. "Task Execution: Interfacing to Reactive Skill Networks," working notes, *AAAI Spring Symposium on Lessons Learned from Implemented Software Architectures for Physical Agents*, Palo Alto, CA, March, pp. 97–111.

Fite, K. 1976. *The Amphibian Visual System: A Multidisciplinary Approach*, Academic Press, New York.

Floreano, D., and Mondada, F. 1996. "Evolution of Homing Navigation in a Real Mobile Robot," *IEEE Transactions on Systems, Man, and Cybernetics*, Vol. 26, No. 3, June, pp. 396–407.

Florence, S., and Kaas, J. 1995. "Somatotopy: Plasticity of Sensory Maps," in *The Handbook of Brain Theory and Neural Networks*, ed. M. Arbib, MIT Press, Cambridge MA, pp. 888–91.

Flynn, A. 1987. "Gnat Robots (and How They Will Change Robotics)," Working Paper No. 295, MIT AI Laboratory, Cambridge, MA, June.

Flynn, A., and Brooks, R. 1989. "Battling Reality," AI Memo No. 1148, MIT AI Laboratory, Cambridge, MA, October.

Flynn, A., Brooks, R., and Tavrow L. 1989. "Twilight Zones and Cornerstones: A Gnat Robot Double Feature," A.I. Memo No. 1126, MIT AI Laboratory, Cambridge, MA, July.

Flynn, A., Brooks, R., Wells, W., and Barrett, D. 1989. "Squirt: The Prototypical Mobile Robot for Autonomous Graduate Students," A.I. Memo No. 1120, MIT AI Laboratory, Cambridge MA, July.

Fok, K.-Y., and Kabuka, M. R. 1991. "An Automatic Navigation System for Vision Guided Vehicles Using a Double Heuristic and a Finite State Machine," *IEEE Transactions on Robotics and Automation*, Vol. 7, No. 1, February, pp. 181–88.

Franceshini, N., Pichon, J., and Blanes, C. 1992. "From Insect Vision to Robot Vision," *The Philosophical Transactions of the Royal Society of London B*, Vol. 337, pp. 283–94.

Franceshini, N., Riehle, A., and Le Nestour, A. 1989. "Directionally Selective Motion Detection by Insect Neurons," in *Facets of Vision*, eds. Slavenga and Hardie, Springer-Verlag, Berlin, pp. 360–90.

Franklin, R. F., and Harmon, L. A. 1987. Elements of Cooperative Behavior. *Internal Research and Development Final Report 655404-1-F*, Environmental Research Institute of Michigan (ERIM), Ann Arbor, MI.

Franklin, D., Kahng, A., and Lewis, M. 1995. "Distributed Sensing and Probing with Multiple Search Agents: Toward System-Level Landmine Detection Solution," in *Proceedings Detection Technologies for Mines and Minelike Targets*, SPIE Vol. 2496, pp. 698–709.

Franks, N. 1986. "Teams in Social Insects: Group Retrieval of Prey by Army Ants," *Behavioral Ecology and Sociobiology*, Vol. 18, pp. 425–29.

Fu, D., Hammond K., and Swain, M. 1994. "Vision and Navigation in Man-made Environments: Looking for Syrup in All the Right Places," *Proceedings of the IEEE Workshop on Visual Behaviors*, Seattle, WA, June, pp. 20–26.

Fukuda, T., Nakagawa, S., Kawauchi, Y., and Buss, M. 1989. "Structure Decision for Self Organising Robots Based on Cell Structures—CEBOT," *IEEE International Conference on Robotics and Automation*, Scottsdale, AZ, pp. 695–70.

Fukuda, T., and Sekiyama, K. 1994. "Communication Reduction with Risk Estimate for Multiple Robotic System," *Proceedings of the IEEE International Conference on Robotics and Automation*, pp. 2864–69.

Gachet, D., Salichs, M., Moreno, L., and Pimental, J. 1994. "Learning Emergent Tasks for an Autonomous Mobile Robot," *Proceedings of the International Conference on Intelligent Robots and Systems (IROS '94)*, Munich, Germany, September, pp. 290–97.

Gage, D. 1992. "Sensor Abstractions to Support Many-Robot Systems," *Proceedings of Mobile Robots VII*, Boston, MA, November, pp. 235–46.

Gallagher, J., and Beer, R. 1992. "A Qualitative Dynamical Analysis of Evolved Locomotion Controllers," *From Animals to Animats 2: Proceedings of the Second International Conference on Simulation of Adaptive Behavior*, Honolulu, HI, December, MIT Press, Cambridge MA, pp. 71–80.

Gallistel, C. R. 1980. *The Organization of Action: A New Synthesis*, Lawrence Erlbaum Associates, Hillsdale, NJ.

Gallistel, C. R. 1990. *The Organization of Learning*, MIT Press, Cambridge, MA.

Gardner, H. 1985. *The Mind's New Science: A History of the Cognitive Revolution*, Basic Books, New York.

Garey, M., and Johnson, D. 1979. *Computers and Intractability: A Guide to the Theory of NP-Completeness*, W.H. Freeman and Co., San Francisco, CA.

Gat, E. 1991a. "Reliable Goal-Directed Reactive Control of Autonomous Mobile Robots," Ph.D. Dissertation, Virginia Polytechnic Institute and State University, Blacksburg.

Gat, E. 1991b. "ALFA: A Language for Programming Reactive Robotic Control Systems," *Proceedings of the IEEE International Conference on Robotics and Automation*, Sacramento, CA, pp. 1116–20.

Gat, E. 1992. "Integrating Planning and Reaction in a Heterogeneous Asynchronous Architecture for Controlling Real-World Mobile Robots," *Proceedings of the AAAI*.

Gat, E. 1995, "Towards Principled Experimental Study of Autonomous Mobile Robots," *Autonomous Robots*, Vol. 2, No. 3, pp. 179–89.

Gat, E., and Dorais, G. 1994. "Robot Navigation by Conditional Sequencing," *Proceedings of the IEEE International Conference on Robotics and Automation*, pp. 1293–99.

Gaussier, P., and Zrehen, S. 1994. "A Topological Neural Map for On-Line Learning: Emergence of Obstacle Avoidance in a Mobile Robot," *Proceedings of the Third Conference on Simulation of Adaptive Behavior (From Animals to Animats 3)*, MIT Press, Cambridge, MA, pp. 282–90.

Gaussier, P., and Zrehen, S. 1995. "PerAc: A Neural Architecture to Control Artificial Animals," *Robotics and Autonomous Systems*, Vol. 16, pp. 291–320.

Georgeff, M. and Lansky, A. 1987. "Reactive Reasoning and Planning" *Proceedings of the AAAI-87*, pp. 677–82.

Georgeff, M., Lansky, A., and Schoppers, M. 1986. "Reasoning and Planning in Dynamic Domains: An Experiment with a Mobile Robot," *SRI Technical Note No. 380*, AI Center, SRI International.

Georgopoulos, A. 1986. "On Reaching," *Annual Review of Neuroscience*, Vol. 9, pp. 147–70.

Gerald, M. C. 1981. *Pharmacology: An Introduction to Drugs*, Prentice-Hall, Englewood Cliffs, NJ.

Geschwind, N. 1979. "Specializations of the Human Brain," in *The Brain*, W.H. Freeman, New York, pp. 108-17.

Gibson, J. J. 1979. *The Ecological Approach to Visual Perception*, Houghton Mifflin, Boston, MA.

Ginsberg, M. 1989. "Universal Planning: An (Almost) Universally Bad Idea," *AI Magazine*, Vol. 10, No. 4, Winter, pp. 40–44.

Giralt, G., Chatila, R., and Vaisset, M. 1984. "An Integrated Navigation and Motion Control System for Autonomous Multisensory Mobile Robots," *First International Symposium on Robotics Research*, ed. M. Brady and R. Paul, pp. 191–214.

Goel, A., Ali, K., Donnellan, M., Gomez de Silva Garza, A., and Callantine, T. 1994. "Multistrategy Adaptive Path Planning," *IEEE Expert*, Vol. 9, No. 6, December, pp. 57–65.

Goetsch, W. 1957. *The Ants*. University of Michigan Press, Ann Arbor, MI.

Goldberg, D. 1989. *Genetic Algorithms in Search, Optimization, and Machine Learning*, Addison-Wesley, Reading MA.

Goodridge, S. and Luo, R. 1994. "Fuzzy Behavior Fusion for Reactive Control of an Autonomous Mobile Robot: MARGE," *Proceedings of the IEEE International Conference on Robotics and Automation*, pp. 1622–27.

Goss, S., Beckers, R., Deneubourg, J., Aron, S., and Pasteels, J. 1990. "How Trail Laying and Trail Following Can Solve Foraging Problems," in *Behavioral Mechanisms of Food Selection*, ed. R. Hughes, Springer-Verlag, Heidelberg, Germany, pp. 661–78.

Graefe, V. 1990. "An Approach to Obstacle Recognition for Autonomous Mobile Robots," *Proceedings of the IEEE International Workshop on Intelligent Robots and Systems (IROS '90)*, pp. 151–58.

Grefenstette, J. and Schultz, A. 1994. "An Evolutionary Approach to Learning in Robots," *Machine Learning Workshop on Robot Learning*, New Brunswick, NJ, July. Also available as *NCARAI Report AIC-94-014*, Navy Center for Applied Research in Artificial Intelligence, Washington, DC.

Grupen, R., and Henderson, T. 1990. "Autochthonous Behaviors—Mapping Perception to Action," in *Traditional and Non-Traditional Robotic Sensors*, ed. T. Henderson, NATO ASI Series, Vol. F-63, Springer-Verlag, Berlin, pp. 285–311.

Guigon, E., and Burnod, Y. 1995. "Short-Term Memory," in *The Handbook of Brain Theory and Neural Networks*, ed. M. Arbib, MIT Press, Cambridge, MA, pp. 867–71.

Hartley, R., and Pipitone, F. 1991. "Experiments with the Subsumption Architecture," *Proceedings of the IEEE International Conference on Robotics and Automation*, Sacramento, CA, pp. 1652–8.

Hayes, G., and Demiris, J. 1994. "A Robot Controller Using Learning by Imitation," *Proceedings of the Second International Symposium on Intelligent Robotic Systems*, Grenoble, France, pp. 198–204.

Hayes-Roth, B. 1995. "An Architecture for Adaptive Intelligent Systems," *Artificial Intelligence*, Vol. 72, No. 1–2, January, pp. 329–65.

Hayes-Roth, B., Lalanda, P., Morignot, P., Pfleger, K., and Balabanovic, P. 1993. "Plans and Behavior in Intelligent Agents," Technical Report KSL-93-43, Knowledge Systems Laboratory, Stanford University, Stanford, CA.

Hayes-Roth, B., Pfleger, K., Morignot, P., Lalanda, P., and Balabanovic, M. 1995. "A Domain-Specific Software Architecture for Adaptive Intelligent Systems," *IEEE Transactions on Software Engineering*, Vol. 21, No. 4, April, pp. 288–301.

Hayhoe, M., Ballard, D., and Pelz, J. 1994. "Visual Representations in Natural Tasks," *Proceedings of the IEEE Workshop on Visual Behaviors*, Seattle, WA, June, pp. 1–9.

Head, H. and Holmes, G., 1911. "Sensory Disturbances from Cerebral Lesions," *Brain*, Vol. 34, p. 102.

Hebb, D. 1949. *The Organization of Behavior*, New York, Wiley.

Hexmoor, H. and Kortenkamp, D. 1995. "Issues on Building Software for Hardware Agents," *Knowledge Engineering Review*, Vol. 10, No. 3, pp. 301–04.

Hexmoor, H., Kortenkamp, D., Arkin, R., Bonasso, P., and Musliner, D., eds. 1995. Working Notes, *Lessons Learned from Implemented Software Architectures for Physical Agents*, AAAI Spring Symposium Series, March, Stanford, CA.

Hillis, D. 1988. "Intelligence as Emergent Behavior, or the Songs of Eden," in *The Artificial Intelligence Debate: False Starts, Real Foundations*, MIT Press, Cambridge, MA.

Hinton, G., and Sejnowski, T. 1986. "Learning and Relearning in Boltzmann Machines," in *Parallel Distributed Processing*, Vol. 1, eds. D. Rumelhart and J. McClellan, MIT Press, Cambridge, MA, pp. 282–317.

Hodgins, J., and Brogan, D. 1994. "Robot Herds: Group Behaviors for Systems with Significant Dynamics," *Artificial Life IV*, MIT Press, Cambridge, MA, pp. 319–24.

Hogg, D., Martin, F., and Resnick, R. 1991. "Braitenberg Creatures," MIT Epistemology and Learning Memorandum No. 13, Cambridge, MA.

Hogg, T. 1996. "Quantum Computing and Phase Transitions in Combinatorial Search," *Journal of Artificial Intelligence Research*, Vol. 4, pp. 91–128.

Holldobler, B., and Wilson, E. 1990. *The Ants*, Belknap Press, Cambridge, MA.

Horswill, I. 1993a. "Specialization of Perceptual Processes," Ph.D. Dissertation, Department of Electrical Engineering and Computer Science, Massachusetts Institute of Technology, Cambridge, MA May.

Horswill, I. 1993b. "Polly, A Vision-Based Artificial Agent," *Proceedings of the AAAI-93*, Washington, DC, pp. 824–29.

Horswill, I., and Brooks, R. A. 1988. "Situated Vision in a Dynamic Environment: Chasing Objects," *Proceedings of the Seventh National Conference on Artificial Intelligence (AAAI '88)*, St. Paul, MN, August, pp. 796–800.

Horswill, I., and Yamamoto, M. 1994. "A $1000 Active Stereo Vision System," *Proceedings of the IEEE Workshop on Visual Behaviors*, Seattle, WA, June, pp. 107–10.

Huang, H-M. 1996. "An Architecture and a Methodology for Intelligent Control," *IEEE Expert: Intelligent Systems and Their Applications*, Vol. 11, No. 2, April, pp. 46–55.

Huber, M., and Durfee, E. 1995. "Deciding When to Commit to Action During Observation-Based Coordination," *Proceedings of the First International Conference on Multiagent Systems (ICMAS '95)*, San Francisco, CA, pp. 163–69.

Hull, C. 1943. *Principles of Behavior: An Introduction to Behavior Theory*, Appleton-Century-Crofts, New York.

Ilg, W., and Berns, K. 1995. "A Learning Architecture Based on Reinforcement Learning for Adaptive Control of the Walking Machine LAURON," *Robotics and Autonomous Systems*, Vol. 15, October, pp. 321–34.

Ishiguro, A., Ichikawa, S., and Uchikawa, Y. 1994. "A Gait Acquisition of a Six-Legged Robot Using Immune Networks," *Proceedings of the International Conference on Intelligent Robotics and Systems (IROS '94)*, Munich, Germany, pp. 1034–41.

Ishiguro, H., Maeda, T., Miyashita, T., and Tsuji, S. 1994. "A Strategy for Acquiring an Environmental Model with Panoramic Sensing by a Mobile Robot," *Proceedings of the IEEE International Conference on Robotics and Automation*, San Diego, CA, pp. 724–29.

Jablonski, J., and Posey, J. 1985. "Robotics Terminology," in *Handbook of Industrial Robotics*, ed. S. Nof, J. Wiley, New York, pp. 1271–1303.

Janet, J., Schudel, D., White, M., England, A., and Snyder, W. 1996. "Global Self-Localization for Actual Mobile Robots: Generating and Sharing Topographical Knowledge Using the Region-Feature Neural Network," *Proceedings of the IEEE International Conference on Multisensor Fusion and Integration*, Washington, DC, December.

Jerne, N. 1973. "The Immune System," *Scientific American*, Vol. 229, pp. 52–60.

Johnson, P., and Bay, J. 1995. "Distributed Control of Simulated Autonomous Mobile Robot Collectives in Payload Transportation," *Autonomous Robots*, Vol. 2, No. 1, pp. 43–64.

Johnson, S. D. 1983. *Synthesis of Digital Designs from Recursion Equations*, MIT Press, Cambridge, MA.

Kaas, J., Krubitzer, L., Chino, Y., Langston, A., Polley, E., and Blair, N. 1990. "Reorganization of Retinotopic Cortical Maps in Adult Mammals after Lesions of the Retina," *Science*, Vol. 248, April, pp. 229–31.

Kaelbling, L. 1986. "An Architecture for Intelligent Reactive Systems," *SRI International Technical Note No. 400*, Menlo Park, CA, October.

Kaelbling, L. 1987. "REX: A Symbolic Language for the Design and Parallel Implementation of Embedded Systems," *Proceedings of the AIAA Conference on Computers in Aerospace* VI, Wakefield, MA, pp. 255–60.

Kaelbling, L., and Rosenschein, S. 1991. "Action and Planning in Embedded Agents," in *Designing Autonomous Agents*, ed. P. Maes, MIT Press, Cambridge, MA, pp. 35–48.

Kahn, P. 1991. "Specification and Control of Behavioral Robot Programs," *Proceedings of the SPIE Sensor Fusion IV*, Boston, MA, November.

Kaufmann, J. 1974. "Social Ethology of the Whiptail Wallaby, *Macropus Parryi*, in Northeastern New South Wales," *Animal Behavior*, Vol. 22, pp. 281–369.

Keirsey, D., Mitchell, J., Payton, D., and Preyss, E. 1984. "Multilevel Path Planning for Autonomous Vehicles," SPIE Vol. 485, *Applications of Artificial Intelligence*, pp. 133–37.

Kelly, M. and Levine, M. 1995. "Where and What: Object Perception for Autonomous Robots," *Proceedings of the IEEE International Conference on Robotics and Automation*, pp. 261–67.

Kenny, P., Bidlack, C., Kluge, K., Lee, J., Huber, M., Durfee, E., and Weymouth, T. 1994. "Implementation of a Reactive Autonomous Navigation System on an Outdoor Mobile Robot," *Proceedings of the Association of Unmanned Vehicle Systems Annual Symposium*, Detroit, MI, May, pp. 233–39.

Khatib, O. 1985. "Real-Time Obstacle Avoidance for Manipulators and Mobile Robots," *Proceedings of the IEEE International Conference on Robotics and Automation*, St. Louis, MO, pp. 500–05.

Kim, J., and Khosla, P. 1992. "Real-Time Obstacle Avoidance Using Harmonic Potential Functions," *IEEE Transactions on Robotics and Automation*, Vol. 8, No. 3, June, pp. 338–49.

Kirchner, W., and Towne, W. 1994. "The Sensory Basis of the Honeybee's Dance Language," *Scientific American*, June, pp. 74–80.

Kluge, K., and Thorpe, C. 1989. "Explicit Models for Robot Road Following," *Proceedings of the International Conference on Robotics and Automation*, Scottsdale, AZ, pp. 1148–54.

Kohler, W. 1947. *Gestalt Psychology: An Introduction to New Concepts in Modern Psychology*, Liveright Publishing Co., New York.

Kolodner, J. 1994. *Case-Based Reasoning*, Morgan-Kaufman, San Mateo, CA.

Koren, Y., and Borenstein, J. 1991. "Potential Field Methods and Their Inherent Limitations for Mobile Robot Navigation," *Proceedings of the IEEE International Conference on Robotics and Automation*, Sacramento, CA, pp. 1398–1404.

Kosecka, J., Bajcsy, R., and Mintz, M. 1993. "Control of Visually Guided Behaviors," Technical Report MS-CS-93-101, Department of Computer Science, University of Pennsylvania, Philadelphia.

Kosko, B., and Isaka, S. 1993. "Fuzzy Logic," *Scientific American*, Vol. 268, No. 1, July, pp. 76–81.

Koy-Oberthur, R. 1989. "Perception by Sensorimotor Coordination in Sensory Substitution for the Blind," in *Visuomotor Coordination: Amphibians, Comparisons, Models, and Robots*, eds. J. P. Ewert and M. A. Arbib, Plenum, New York, pp. 397–418.

Krogh, B. 1984. "A Generalized Potential Field Approach to Obstacle Avoidance Control", SME-RI Technical Paper MS84-484, Society of Manufacturing Engineers, Dearborn, Michigan.

Krogh, B. and Thorpe, C. 1986. "Integrated Path Planning and Dynamic Steering Control for Autonomous Vehicles," *Proceedings of the IEEE International Conference on Robotics and Automation*, San Francisco, CA, pp. 1664–69.

Krose, B. 1995. "Learning from Delayed Rewards," *Robotics and Autonomous Systems*, Vol. 15, No. 4, October, pp. 233–36.

Kube, C. R. and Zhang, H. 1992. "Collective Robotic Intelligence," *From Animals to Animats 2: Proceedings of the Second International Conference on Simulation of Adaptive Behavior*, Honolulu, HI, December, MIT Press, Cambridge, MA, pp. 460–68.

Kube, C. R. and Zhang, H. 1994. "Stagnation Recovery Behaviors for Collective Robotics," *Proceedings of the International Conference on Intelligent Robots and Systems (IROS '94)*, pp. 1883–90.

Kuipers, B., and Byun, Y-T. 1988. "A Robust, Qualitative Method for Robot Spatial Learning," *Proceedings of the Seventh National Conference on Artificial Intelligence*, pp. 774–79.

Kuipers, B., and Byun, Y-T. 1991. "A Robot Exploration and Mapping Strategy Based on a Semantic Hierarchy of Spatial Representations," *Robotics and Autonomous Systems*, Vol. 8, pp. 47–63.

Kuniyoshi, Y. 1995. "Behavior Matching by Observation for Multi-Robot Cooperation," *International Symposium of Robotics Research*, Herrsching am Ammersee, Germany, pp. 343–52.

Kuniyoshi, Y., Nobuyuki, K., Sugimoto, K., Nakamura, S., and Suehiro, T. 1995. "A Foveated Wide Angle Lens for Active Vision," *Proceedings of the IEEE International Conference on Robotics and Automation*, Nagoya, Japan, May, pp. 2982–88.

Kuniyoshi, Y., Rougeaux, S., Ishii, M., Kita, N., Sakane, S., and Kakikura, M. 1994. "Cooperation by Observation: The Framework and Basic Task Patterns," *Proceedings of the IEEE International Conference on Robotics and Automation*, pp. 767–73.

Kutulakos, K., Lumelsky, V., and Dyer., C. 1992. "Object Exploration by Purposive, Dynamic Viewpoint Adjustment," Technical Report No. 1124, Computer Science Department, University of Wisconsin, Madison, November.

Langer, D., Rosenblatt, J., and Hebert, M. 1994. "A Behavior-Based System for Off-Road Navigation," *IEEE Transactions on Robotics and Automation*, Vol. 10, No. 6, December, pp. 776–83.

Langton, C. (ed.) 1995. *Artificial Life: An Overview*, MIT Press, Cambridge, MA.

Latombe, J-C. 1991. *Robot Motion Planning*, Kluwer Academic Publishers, Boston.

Lawton, D., Arkin, R. C., and Cameron, J. 1990. "Qualitative Spatial Understanding and Reactive Control for Autonomous Robots," *Proceedings of the IEEE International Workshop on Intelligent Robots and Systems (IROS '90)*, Ibaraki, Japan, pp. 709–14.

Lee, D. 1978. "The Functions of Vision," *Modes of Perceiving and Processing Information*, eds. H. Pick and E. Saltzman, Wiley, New York.

Lee, J. L., Huber, M., Durfee, E., and Kenny, P. 1994. "UM-PRS: An Implementation of the Procedural Reasoning System for Multirobot Applications," *Proceedings of the Conference on Intelligent Robotics in Field, Factory, and Space (CIRFFSS '94)*, Houston, TX, March, pp. 842–49.

Lefebvre, D. and Saridis, G. 1992. "A Computer Architecture for Intelligent Machines," *Proceedings of the IEEE International Conference on Robotics and Automation*, Nice, France, May, pp. 2745–50.

Lehninger, A. 1975. *Biochemistry*, 2nd ed., Worth, New York.

Lesser, V. (ed.) 1995. *Proceedings of the International Conference on Multiagent Systems*, San Francisco, CA, June.

Levitt, T. and Lawton, D. 1990. "Qualitative Navigation for Mobile Robots," *Artificial Intelligence*, Vol. 44, No. 3, pp. 305–60.

Lewis, M., Fagg, A., and Bekey, G. 1994. "Genetic Algorithms for Gait Synthesis in a Hexapod Robot," in *Recent Trends in Mobile Robots*, ed. Y. Zheng, World Scientific, Singapore, pp. 317–31.

Lim, W. 1994. "An Agent-Based Approach for Programming Mobile Robots," *Proceedings of the IEEE International Conference on Robotics and Automation*, San Diego, CA, pp. 3584–89.

Lin, L. 1992. "Self-Improving Reactive Agents Based on Reinforcement Learning, Planning and Teaching," *Machine Learning*, Vol. 8, pp. 293–321.

Lin, F. and Hsu, J. 1995. "Cooperation and Deadlock-Handling for an Object-Sorting Task in a Multi-Agent Robotic System," *Proceedings of the IEEE International Conference on Robotics and Automation*, pp. 2580–85.

Lloyd, S. 1996. "Universal Quantum Simulators," *Science*, Vol. 273, pp. 1073–78.

Lorenz, K. 1981. *The Foundations of Ethology*, Springer-Verlag, New York.

Lorenz, K., and Leyhausen, P. 1973. *Motivation of Human and Animal Behavior: An Ethological View*, Van Nostrand Reinhold Co., New York.

Lumia, R. 1994. "Using NASREM for Real-Time Sensory Interactive Robot Control," *Robotica*, Vol. 12, pp. 127–35.

Lund, J., Wu, Q., and Levitt, J. 1995. "Visual Cortex Cell Types and Connection," in *The Handbook of Brain Theory and Neural Networks*, ed. M. Arbib, MIT Press, Cambridge, MA, pp. 344–48.

Lyons, D. 1992. "Planning, Reactive," *Encyclopedia of Artificial Intelligence*, ed. S. Shapiro, 2nd ed., John Wiley and Sons, New York, pp. 1171–82.

Lyons, D., and Arbib, M. 1989. "A Formal Model of Computation for Sensory-Based Robotics," *IEEE Transactions on Robotics and Automation*, Vol. 6, No. 3, June, pp. 280–93.

Lyons, D., and Hendriks, A. 1992. "Planning for Reactive Robot Behavior," *Proceedings of the IEEE International Conference on Robotics and Automation*, Nice, France, pp. 2675–80.

Lyons, D., and Hendriks, A. 1993. "Safely Adapting a Hierarchical Reactive System," *Proceedings of SPIE Intelligent Robots and Computer Vision XII: Active Vision and 3D Methods*, Vol. 2056, pp. 450–59.

Lyons, D., and Hendriks, A. 1994. "Planning by Adaptation: Experimental Results," *Proceedings of the IEEE International Conference on Robotics and Automation*, San Diego, CA, pp. 855–60.

Lyons, D., and Hendriks, A. 1995. "Planning as Incremental Adaptation of a Reactive System," *Robotics and Autonomous Systems*, Vol. 14, No. 4, pp. 255–88.

MacKenzie, D. 1996. "A Design Methodology for the Specification of Behavior-Based Robotic Systems," Ph.D. Dissertation, College of Computing, Georgia Institute of Technology, Atlanta.

MacKenzie, D., and Balch, T. 1993. "Making a Clean Sweep: Behavior Based Vacuuming," in working notes, AAAI Fall Symposium: Instantiating Real-world Agents, Raleigh, NC, October, pp. 93–98.

MacKenzie, D., Cameron, J., and Arkin, R. 1995. "Specification and Execution of Multiagent Missions," *Proceedings of the International Conference on Intelligent Robotics and Systems (IROS '95)*, Pittsburgh, PA, pp. 51–58.

MacLennan, B. 1991. "Synthetic Ethology: An Approach to the Study of Communication," in *Artificial Life II*, SFI Studies in the Sciences of Complexity, Vol. XI, ed. Farmer et al., Addison-Wesley, Reading, MA.

Maes, P. 1989. "The Dynamics of Action Selection" *Proceedings of the Eleventh International Joint Conference on Artificial Intelligence (IJCAI-89)*, Detroit, MI, pp. 991–97.

Maes, P. 1990. "Situated Agents Can Have Goals," *Robotics and Autonomous Systems*, Vol. 6, pp. 49–70.

Maes, P., and Brooks, R. 1990. "Learning to Coordinate Behaviors," *Proceedings of the Eighth National Conference on Artificial Intelligence (AAAI '90)*, Boston, MA, August, pp. 796–802.

Mahadevan, S., and Connell, J. 1991. "Automatic Programming of Behavior-Based Robots Using Reinforcement Learning," *Proceedings of the Ninth National Conference on Artificial Intelligence (AAAI '91)*, Anaheim, CA, July, pp. 768–73.

Malcolm, C., and Smithers, T. 1990. "Symbol Grounding via a Hybrid Architecture in an Autonomous Assembly System," in *Designing Autonomous Agents*, ed. P. Maes, MIT Press, Cambridge, MA, pp. 123–44.

Malkin, P. and Addanki, S. 1990. "LOGnets: A Hybrid Graph Spatial Representation for Robot Navigation," *Proceedings of the Eighth National Conference on Artificial Intelligence (AAAI-90)*, Boston, MA, pp. 1045–50.

Marapane, S., Holder, M., and Trivedi, M. 1994. "Coordinating Motion of Cooperative Mobile Robots through Visual Observation," *Proceedings of the IEEE International Conference on Systems, Man and Cybernetics*, San Antonio, TX, pp. 2260–65.

Marr, D. 1982. *Vision: A Computational Investigation into the Human Representation and Processing of Visual Information*, W.H. Freeman, San Francisco, CA.

Mataric, M. 1990. "Navigating with a Rat Brain: A Neurobiologically-Inspired Model for Robot Spatial Representation," *From Animals to Animats: Proceedings of the First International Conference on Simulation of Adaptive Behavior*, MIT Press, Cambridge, MA, pp. 169–75.

Mataric, M. 1992a. "Behavior-Based Control: Main Properties and Implications," *Proceedings of Workshop on Intelligent Control Systems, International Conference on Robotics and Automation*, Nice, France, May.

Mataric, M. 1992b. "Integration of Representation into Goal-Driven Behavior-Based Robots," *IEEE Transactions on Robotics and Automation*, Vol. 8, No. 3, June, pp. 304–12.

Mataric, M. 1992c. "Minimizing Complexity in Controlling a Mobile Robot Population," *IEEE International Conference on Robotics and Automation*, Nice, France, pp. 830–35.

Mataric, M. 1993a. "Synthesizing Group Behaviors," *Proceedings of the Workshop on Dynamically Interacting Robots, International Joint Conference on Artificial Intelligence (IJCAI-93)*, Chambery, France, August, pp. 1–10.

Mataric, M. 1993b. "Kin Recognition, Similarity, and Group Behavior," *Proceedings of the Fifteenth Annual Cognitive Science Conference*, Boulder, CO, June, pp. 705–10.

Mataric, M. 1994a. "Interaction and Intelligent Behavior," Ph.D. Dissertation, Department of Electrical Engineering and Computer Science, Massachusetts Institute of Technology, Cambridge, May.

Mataric, M. 1994b. "Learning to Behave Socially," *From Animals to Animats 3: Proceedings of the Third International Conference on Simulation of Adaptive Behavior*, Brighton, UK, pp. 453–62.

Matthies, L., and Elfes, A. 1988. "Integration of Sonar and Stereo Range Data Using a Grid-Based Representation," *Proceedings of the International Conference on Robotics and Automation*, Philadelphia, PA, April, pp. 727–33.

Mazokhin-Porshnyakov, G. 1969. *Insect Vision*, Plenum Press, New York.

McCarthy, J. 1995. "Making Robots Conscious of their Mental States," *Computer Science Report*, Stanford University, CA, July 24.

McCarthy, J., Minsky, M., Rochester, N., and Shannon, C. 1955. *A Proposal for the Dartmouth Summer Research Project on Artificial Intelligence*, August 31.

McCulloch, W., and Pitts, W. 1943. "A Logical Calculus of the Ideas Immanent in Nervous Activity," *Bulletin of Mathematical Biophysics*, Vol. 5, pp. 115–33.

McFarland, D. 1981. *The Oxford Companion to Animal Behavior*, Oxford University Press.

McFarland, D., and Bosser, U. 1993. *Intelligent Behavior in Animals and Robots*, MIT Press, Cambridge, MA.

McGhee, R. 1967. "Finite State Control of Quadruped Locomotion," *Simulation*, pp. 135–40, September.

McKerrow, P. 1991. *Introduction to Robotics*, Addison-Wesley, Reading, MA.

Meystel, A. 1986. "Planning in a Hierarchical Nested Controller for Autonomous Robots," *Proceedings of the Twenty-fifth Conference on Decision and Control*, Athens, Greece, pp. 1237–49.

Millan, J. 1994. "Learning Efficient Reactive Behavioral Sequences from Basic Reflexes in a Goal-Directed Autonomous Robot," *(From Animals to Animats 3), Proceedings of the Third Conference on Simulation of Adaptive Behavior*, MIT Press, Cambridge, MA, pp. 266–74.

Miller, D. 1995. "Experiences Looking into Niches," Working Notes, *1995 AAAI Spring Symposium: Lessons Learned from Implemented Software Architectures for Physical Agents*, Palo Alto, CA, March, pp. 141–45.

Miller, E., and Desimone, R. 1994. *Science*, Vol. 263, Janury, pp. 520–22.

Miller, G., Galanter, E., and Pribram, K. 1960. *Plans and the Structure of Behavior*, Holt, Rinehart, and Winston, New York.

Minsky, M. 1986. *The Society of the Mind*, Simon and Schuster, New York.

Minsky, M. 1994. "Will Robots Inherit the Earth?" *Scientific American*, Vol. 271, No. 4, October, pp. 109–13,

Minsky, M., and Papert, S. 1969. *Perceptrons: An Essay in Computational Geometry*, MIT Press, Cambridge, MA.

Mishkin, M., Ungergleider, L., and Macko, K. 1983. "Object Vision and Spatial Vision: Two Cortical Pathways," *Trends in Neurosciences*, Vol. 6, pp. 414–17.

Mitchell, T. 1990. "Becoming Increasingly Reactive," *Proceedings of the Eighth National Conference on Artificial Intelligence (AAAI-90)*, Boston, MA, pp. 1051–58.

Mitsumoto, N., Fukuda, T., Arai, F., Tadashi, H., and Idogaki, T. 1996. "Self-Organizing Multiple Robotic System," *Proceedings of the IEEE International Conference on Robotics and Automation*, Minneapolis, MN, April, pp. 1614–19.

Mittelstaedt, H. 1983. "Introduction into Cybernetics of Orientation Behavior," *Biophysics*, eds. W. Hoppe et al., Springer-Verlag, Berlin, pp. 794–801.

Mittelstaedt, H. 1985. "Analytical Cybernetics of Spider Navigation," *Neurobiology of Arachnids*, ed. F. Barth, Springer-Verlag, Berlin, pp. 298–316.

Mizessyn, F., and Ishida, Y. 1993. "Immune Networks for Cement Plants," *Proceedings of the International Symposium on Autonomous Decentralized Systems*, Kawasaki, Japan, pp. 282–88.

Mochida, T., Ishiguro, A., Aoki, T., and Uchikawa, Y. 1995. "Behavior Arbitration for Autonomous Mobile Robots Using Emotion Mechanisms," *Proceedings of the IEEE/RSJ International Conference on Intelligent Robots and Systems (IROS '95)*, Pittsburgh, PA, pp. 516–21.

Mondada, F., and Floreano, D. 1995. "Evolution and Neural Control Structures: Some Experiments on Mobile Robots," *Robotics and Autonomous Systems*, Vol. 16, No. 2-4, pp. 183–96.

Montgomery, J., Fagg, A., and Bekey, G. 1995. "The USC AFV-1: A Behavior-Based Entry in the 1994 International Aerial Robotics Competition," *IEEE Expert*, Vol. 10, No. 2, April, pp. 16–22.

Moore, A., Atkeson, C., and Schaal, S., 1995. "Memory-Based Learning for Control," CMU Robotics Institute Technical Report CMU-RI-TR-95-18, Carnegie-Mellon University, Pittsburgh, PA, April.

Morasso, P., and Sanguineti, V. 1994. "Self-Organising Body-Schema for Motor Planning," *Journal of Motor Behavior*, Vol. 26, pp. 131–48.

Moravec, H. 1977. "Towards Automatic Visual Obstacle Avoidance," *Proceedings of the Fifth International Joint Conference on Artificial Intelligence*, Cambridge, MA, August, p. 584.

Moravec, H. 1983. "The Stanford Cart and the CMU Rover," *Proceedings of the IEEE*, Vol. 71, No. 7, pp. 872–84.

Moravec, H. 1985. "Robots that Rove," in *Autonomous Mobile Robots Annual Report*, Technical Report No. CMU-RI-TR-86-4, Robotics Institute, Carnegie-Mellon University, Pittsburgh, PA, February.

Moravec, H. 1988. *Mind Children: The Future of Robot and Human Intelligence*, Harvard University Press, Cambridge, MA.

Moravec, H. Forthcoming. *Mind Age: Transcendence through Robots*, Oxford University Press.

Moravec, H., and Elfes, A. 1985. "High Resolution Maps from Wide Angle Sonar," *Proceedings of the ASME International Computers in Engineering Conference*, Boston, MA, pp. 375–80.

Moynihan, M. 1970. "Control, Suppression, Decay, Disappearance, and Replacement of Displays," *Journal of Theoretical Biology*, Vol. 29, pp. 85–112.

Murphy, R. R. 1991. "An Application of Dempster-Shafer Theory to a Novel Control Scheme for Sensor Fusion," *Proceedings of SPIE Stochastic Methods in Signal Processing, Image Processing, and Computer Vision*, San Diego, CA, July, pp. 55–68.

Murphy, R. R. 1992. "An Architecture for Intelligent Robotic Sensor Fusion," Ph.D. Dissertation, Technical Report No. GIT-ICS-92/42, College of Computing, Georgia Institute of Technology, Atlanta.

Murphy, R. R., and Arkin, R. C. 1992. "SFX: An Architecture for Action-Oriented Sensor Fusion," *Proceedings of the International Conference on Intelligent Robotics and Systems (IROS '92)*, Raleigh, NC, July, pp. 1079–86.

Murphy, T., Lyons, D., and Hendriks, A. 1993. "Visually Guided Stable Grasping with a Multi-Fingered Robot Hand: A Behavior-Based Approach," *Proceedings of the SPIE*

Intelligent Robots and Computer Vision XII: Active Vision and 3D Methods, Vol. 2056, pp. 252–63.

Nauta, W., and Feirtag, M. 1979. "The Organization of the Brain," in *The Brain*, W.H. Freeman, San Francisco, pp. 40–55.

Nehmzow, U., and McGonigle, B. 1994. "Achieving Rapid Adaptations in Robots by Means of External Tuition," *From Animals to Animats 3: Proceedings of the Third Conference on Simulation of Adaptive Behavior*, MIT Press, Cambridge, MA, pp. 301–08.

Nehmzow, U., Smithers, T. and McGonigle, B. 1993. "Increasing Behavioral Repertoire in a Mobile Robot," *From Animals to Animats 2: Proceedings of the Second International Conference on Simulation of Adaptive Behavior*, Honolulu, HI, MIT Press, Cambridge, MA, pp. 291–97.

Neisser, U. 1976. *Cognition and Reality: Principles and Implications of Cognitive Psychology*, W.H. Freeman, San Francisco.

Neisser, U. 1989. "Direct Perception and Recognition as Distinct Perceptual Systems," text of address presented to the Cognitive Science Society, August.

Neisser, U. 1993. "Without Perception, There Is No Knowledge: Implications for Artificial Intelligence," in *Natural and Artificial Minds*, ed. R. G. Burton, State University of New York Press, Albany, pp. 147–64.

Nelson, J. I. 1995. "Visual Scene Perception: Neurophysiology," in *The Handbook of Brain Theory and Neural Networks*, ed. M. Arbib, MIT Press, Cambridge, MA, pp. 1024–28.

Neumann, O., and Prinz, W. 1990. "Prologue: Historical Approaches to Perception and Action," in *Relationships between Perception and Action*, eds. O. Neumann and W. Prinz, Springer-Verlag, Berlin, pp. 5–19.

Nilsson, N. 1965. *Learning Machines: Foundations of Trainable Pattern-Classifying Systems*, McGraw-Hill, New York.

Nilsson, N. 1969. "A Mobile Automaton: An Application of Artificial Intelligence Techniques," *Proceedings of the International Joint Conference on Artificial Intelligence (IJCAI-69)*. Washington D.C., May. Reprinted in *Autonomous Mobile Robots*, Vol. 2, eds. S. Iyengar and A. Elfes, IEEE Computer Society Press, Los Alamitos, 1991, pp. 233–44.

Nilsson, N. 1980. *Principles of Artificial Intelligence*, Tioga, Palo Alto, CA.

Nilsson, N. 1984. "Shakey the Robot," Technical Note No. 323, Artificial Intelligence Center, SRI International, Menlo Park, CA.

Nilsson, N. 1994. "Teleo-Reactive Programs for Agent Control," *Journal of Artificial Intelligence Research*, Vol. 1, pp. 139–58.

Nilsson, N. 1995. "Eye on the Prize," *AI Magazine*, Vol. 16, No. 2, Summer, pp. 9–17.

Noreils, F., and Chatila, R. 1989. "Control of Mobile Robot Actions," *Proceedings of the IEEE International Conference on Robotics and Automation*, pp. 701–07.

Noreils, F., and Chatila, R. 1995. "Plan Execution Monitoring and Control Architecture for Mobile Robots," *IEEE Transactions on Robotics and Automation*, Vol. 11, No. 2, April, pp. 255–66.

Norman, D., and Shallice, T. 1986. "Attention to Action: Willed and Automatic Control of Behavior," in *Consciousness and Self-Regulation: Advances in Research and Theory*, Vol. 4, eds. R. Davidson, G. Schwartz, and D. Shapiro, Plenum Press, New York, pp. 1–17.

Noton D., and Stark, L. 1971. "Scanpaths in Saccadic Eye Movements While Viewing and Recognizing Patterns," *Vision Research*, Vol. 11, pp. 929–42.

Olshausen, B., and Koch, C. 1995. "Selective Visual Attention," in *The Handbook of Brain Theory and Neural Networks*, ed. M. Arbib, MIT Press, Cambridge, MA, pp. 837–40.

Ooka, A., Ogi, K., Wada, Y., Kida, Y., Takemoto, A., Okamoto, K., and Yoshida, K. 1985. "Intelligent Robot System II," *Robotics Research, Second International Symposium*, eds. H. Hanafusa and H. Inoue, MIT Press, Cambridge, MA, pp. 341–47.

Pahlavan, K., and Eklundh, J. 1993. "Heads, Eyes and Head-Eye Systems," in *Active Robot Vision: Camera Heads, Model-Based Navigation and Reactive Control*, eds. H. Christensen, K. Bowyer, and H. Bunke, World Scientific, Singapore, pp. 33–49.

Pahlavan, K., Uhlin, T., and Eklundh, J. 1993. "Active Vision as a Methodology," in *Active Perception*, ed. Y. Aloimonos, Lawrence Erlbaum Associates, Hillsdale, NJ, pp. 19–46.

Pani, J. 1996. Personal communication, May.

Parker, L. 1992. "Local versus Global Control Laws for Cooperative Agent Teams," *AI Memorandum No. 1357*, MIT AI Lab, Cambridge, MA, March.

Parker, L. 1994. "Heterogeneous Multi-Robot Cooperation," Ph.D. Dissertation, Department of Electrical Engineering and Computer Science, Massachusetts Institute of Technology, Cambridge, MA, February.

Parker, L. 1995. "Alliance: An Architecture for Fault Tolerant Multi-Robot Cooperation," *Oak Ridge National Laboratory Technical Memorandum No. 12920*, February.

Patel, M., Colombetti, M., and Dorigo, M. 1995. "Evolutionary Learning for Intelligent Automation: A Case Study," *Intelligent Automation and Soft Computing*, Vol. 1, No. 1, pp. 29–42.

Pau, L. 1991. "Behavioral Knowledge in Sensor/Data Fusion Systems," in *Active Perception and Robot Vision*, eds. A. Sood and H. Wechsler, Springer-Verlag, Berlin, pp. 357–72.

Pavlov, I. 1927. *Conditioned Reflexes*, Oxford University Press, London.

Payton, D. 1991. "Internalized Plans: A Representation for Action Resources," in *Designing Autonomous Agents*, ed. P. Maes, MIT Press, Cambridge, MA, pp. 89–103.

Payton, D., Keirsey, D., Kimble, D., Krozel, J., and Rosenblatt, J. 1992. "Do Whatever Works: A Robust Approach to Fault-tolerant Autonomous Control," *Applied Intelligence*, Vol. 2, No. 3, September, pp. 225–50.

Pearson, K. 1976. "The Control of Walking," *Scientific American*, Vol. 235, pp. 72–86.

Pellionisz, A., and Llinas, R. 1980. "Tensorial Approach to the Geometry of Brain Function: Cerebellar Coordination via a Metric Tensor," *Neuroscience*, Vol. 5, pp. 1125–36.

Penrose, R. 1989. *The Emperor's New Mind*, Oxford University Press, New York.

Penrose, R. 1994. *Shadows of the Mind*, Oxford University Press, New York.

Piaget, J. 1971. *Biology and Knowledge: An Essay on the Relations between Organic Regulations and Cognitive Processes*, University of Chicago Press.

Pin, F., and Watanabe, Y. 1995. "Automatic Generation of Fuzzy Rules Using the Fuzzy Behaviorist Approach: The Case of Sensor-Based Robot Navigation," *Intelligent Automation and Soft Computing*, Vol. 1, No. 2, pp. 161–78.

Pomerleau, D. 1993. *Neural Network Perception for Mobile Robot Guidance*, Kluwer Academic Publishers, Boston.

Pomerleau, D. 1995. "Ralph: Rapidly Adapting Lateral Position Handler," *Proceedings of the IEEE Symposium on Intelligent Vehicles*, Detroit, MI, September, pp. 506–11.

Premvuti, S., and Yuta, S. 1990. "Consideration on the Cooperation of Multiple Autonomous Mobile Robots," *IEEE International Workshop on Intelligent Robots and Systems (IROS '90)*, Tsuchiura, Japan pp. 59–63.

Prokopowicz, P., Swain, M., and Kahn, R. 1994. "Task and Environment-Sensitive Tracking," *Proceedings of the IEEE Workshop on Visual Behaviors*, Seattle, WA, June, pp. 73–78.

Quinn, R., and Espenschied, K. 1993. "Control of a Hexapod Robot using a Biologically Inspired Neural Network," in *Biological Neural Networks in Invertebrate Neuroethology and Robotics*, eds. R. Beer, R. Ritzmann, and T. McKenna, Academic Press, San Diego, CA, pp. 365–81.

Ram, A., Arkin, R., Boone, G., and Pearce, M. 1994. "Using Genetic Algorithms to Learn Reactive Control Parameters for Autonomous Robotic Navigation," *Journal of Adaptive Behavior*, Vol. 2, No. 3, pp. 277–305.

Ram, A., Arkin, R. C., Moorman, K., and Clark, R. 1997. "Case-Based Reactive Navigation: A Case-Based Method for On-Line Selection and Adaptation of Reactive Control Parameters in Autonomous Robotic Systems," *IEEE Transactions on Systems, Man, and Cybernetics*. Part B, Vol. 27. No. 3, pp. 376–94.

Reece, D., and Shafer, S. 1991. "Active Vision at the System Level for Robot Driving," Working Notes, *AAAI Fall Symposium on Sensory Aspects of Robotic Intelligence*, Asilomar, CA, November, pp. 70–77.

Reignier, P. 1995. "Supervised Incremental Learning of Fuzzy Rules," *Robotics and Autonomous Systems*, Vol. 16, pp. 57–71.

Reynolds, C. 1987. "Flocks, Herds, and Schools: A Distributed Behavioral Model," *Computer Graphics*, Vol. 21, No. 4, pp. 25–34.

Rimey, R. 1992. "Task-Oriented Vision with Multiple Bayes Nets," in *Active Vision*, eds. A. Blake, and A. Yuille, MIT Press, Cambridge, MA.

Riseman, E., and Hanson, A. 1987. "General Knowledge–Based Vision Systems," in *Vision, Brain and Cooperative Computation*, eds. M. Arbib and A. Hanson, MIT Press, Cambridge, MA, p. 287.

Rosenblatt, F. 1958. "The Perceptron: A Probabilistic Model for Information Storage and Organization in the Brain," *Psychological Review*, Vol. 65, pp. 386–408.

Rosenblatt, J. 1995. "DAMN: A Distributed Architecture for Mobile Navigation," Working Notes, *AAAI 1995 Spring Symposium on Lessons Learned for Implemented Software Architectures for Physical Agents*, Palo Alto, CA, March, pp. 167–78.

Rosenblatt, J., and Payton, D. 1989. "A Fine-Grained Alternative to the Subsumption Architecture for Mobile Robot Control," *Proceedings of the International Joint Conference on Neural Networks*, June, pp. 317–23.

Rosenschein, S., and Kaelbling, L. 1987. "The Synthesis of Digital Machines with Provable Epistemic Properties," *SRI International Technical Note No. 412*, Menlo Park, CA, April.

Rumelhart, D., Hinton, G., and Williams, R. 1986. "Learning Internal Representations by Error Propagation," in *Parallel Distributed Processing*, Vol. I, eds. D. Rumelhart and J. McClelland, MIT Press, Cambridge, MA, pp. 318–62.

Russell, A., Thiel, D., and Mackay-Sim, A. 1994. "Sensing Odour Trails for Mobile Robot Navigation," *Proceedings of the IEEE International Conference on Robotics and Automation*, San Diego, CA, May, pp. 2672–77.

Sacerdoti, E. 1974. "Planning in a Hierarchy of Abstraction Spaces," *Artificial Intelligence*, Vol. 5, No. 2, pp. 115–35.

Sacerdoti, E. 1975. "A Structure for Plans and Behavior," Ph.D. Dissertation, Technical Note No. 109, AI Center, SRI International, Menlo Park, CA.

Saffiotti, A., Ruspini, E., and Konolige, K. 1993a. "Blending Reactivity and Goal-Directedness in a Fuzzy Controller," *Second IEEE International Conference on Fuzzy Systems*, San Francisco, CA, March, pp. 134–39.

Saffiotti, A., Ruspini, E., and Konolige, K. 1993b. "Robust Execution of Robot Plans Using Fuzzy Logic," *Proceedings of the Workshop on Fuzzy Logic in Artificial Intelligence, International Joint Conference on Artificial Intelligence (IJCAI '93)*, Chambéry, France, pp. 24–37.

Saffiotti, A, Konolige, K., and Ruspini, E. 1995. "A Multi-Valued Logic Approach to Integrating Planning and Control," *Artificial Intelligence*, Vol. 76, No. 1-2, July, pp. 481–526.

Sahota, M. 1993. "Real-Time Intelligent Behavior in Dynamic Environments: Soccer-Playing Robots," M.S. Thesis, Department of Computer Science, University of British Columbia, Vancouver.

Saito, F., Fukuda, T., and Arai, F. 1994. "Swing and Locomotion Control for a Two-Link Brachiation Robot," *IEEE Control Systems Magazine*, Vol. 14, No. 1, February, pp. 5–11.

Sanborn, J. C. 1988. "A Model of Reaction for Planning in Dynamic Environments," M.S. Thesis, Computer Science Department, University of Maryland, College Park, May.

Sarachik, K. 1989. "Characterizing an Indoor Environment with a Mobile Robot and Uncalibrated Stereo," *Proceedings of the IEEE International Conference on Robotics and Automation*, Scottsdale, AZ, pp. 984–89.

Saridis, G. 1983. "Intelligent Robotic Control," *IEEE Transactions on Automatic Control*, Vol. 28, No. 5, May, pp. 547–56.

Saridis, G., and Valvanis, K. 1987. "On the Theory of Intelligent Controls," *Proceedings of the SPIE Conference on Advances in Intelligent Robotic Systems*, Cambridge, MA, October, pp. 488–95.

Schank, R. 1987. "What's AI, Anyway?" *AI Magazine*, Vol. 8, No. 4, Winter, pp. 59–65.

Schmajuk, N. 1995. "Cognitive Maps," in *The Handbook of Brain Theory and Neural Networks*, ed. M. Arbib, MIT Press, Cambridge, MA, pp. 197–200.

Schmidt, R. 1975. "A Schema Theory of Discrete Motor Skill Learning," *Psychological Review*, Vol. 82, pp. 225–60.

Schöner, G., and Dose, M. 1992. "A Dynamical Systems Approach to Task-Level System Integration Used to Plan and Control Autonomous Vehicle Motion," *Robotics and Autonomous Systems*, Vol. 10, pp. 253–67.

Schoppers, M. 1987. "Universal Plans for Reactive Robots in Unpredictable Environments," *Proceedings of the Tenth International Joint Conference on Artificial Intelligence (IJCAI-87)*, pp. 852–59.

Schoppers, M. 1989. "In Defense of Reaction Plans as Caches," *AI Magazine*, Vol. 10, No. 4, Winter, pp. 51–60.

Schultz, A., and Grefenstette, J. 1992. "Using a Genetic Algorithm to Learn Behaviors for Autonomous Vehicles," Naval Research Laboratory NCARAI TR #AIC-92-009, Washington, DC.

Scutt, T. 1994. "The Five Neuron Trick: Using Classical Conditioning to Learn How to Seek Light," *From Animals to Animats 3: Proceedings of the Third Conf. on Simulation of Adaptive Behavior*, MIT Press, Cambridge, MA, pp. 364–70.

Searle, J. 1980. "Minds, Brains, and Programs," *Behavioral and Brain Sciences*, Vol. 3, pp. 417–57.

Segre, A., and DeJong, G. 1985. "Explanation-Based Manipulator Learning: Acquisition of Planning Ability through Observation," Working Paper 62, AI Research Group, Coordinated Science Lab, Univerity of Illinois at Urbana-Champaign, March.

Selfridge, O., and Neisser, U. 1960. "Pattern Recognition by Machine," *Scientific American*, Vol. 203, pp. 60–68.

Shadmehr, R., and Mussa-Ivaldi, F. 1994. "Geometric Structure of the Adaptive Controller of the Human Arm," MIT AI Memo No. 1437, Cambridge, MA, March.

Shibata, T., Ohkawa, K., and Tanie, K. 1996. "Spontaneous Behavior of Robots for Cooperation—Emotionally Intelligent Robot System," *Proceedings of the IEEE International Conference on Robotics and Automation*, Minneapolis, MN, April, pp. 2426–31.

Shiffrin, R., and Schneider, W. 1977. "Controlled and Automatic Human Information Processing: II," *Psychological Review*, Vol. 84, pp. 127–90.

Shirley, D., and Matijevic, J. 1995. "Mars Pathfinder Microrover," *Autonomous Robots*, Vol. 2, pp. 283–89.

Shor, P. 1994. "Algorithms for Quantum Computation: Discrete Logarithms and Factoring," *Proceedings of the Thirty-fifth Annual Symposium on the Foundations of Computer Science*, Santa Fe, NM, November, pp. 124–34.

Simmons, R. (ed.) 1992. Working notes, *AAAI 1992 Spring Symposium on Control of Selective Perception*, Stanford University, March, pp. 138–41.

Simmons, R., and Koenig, S. 1995. "Probabilistic Robot Navigation in Partially Observable Environments," *Proceedings of the International Joint Conference on Artificial Intelligence (IJCAI-95)*, Montreal, CA, August, pp. 1080–87.

Simon, H. 1983. "Why Should Machines Learn?" in *Machine Learning: An Artificial Intelligence Approach*, Vol. 1, eds. R. Michalski, J. Carbonell, and T. Mitchell, Tioga Pubishing, Palo Alto, CA, pp. 25–39.

Sims, K. 1994. "Evolving Virtual Creatures," *Proceedings of the ACM Siggraph 94*, pp. 15–22.

Skinner, B.F. 1974. *About Behaviorism*, Alfred Knopf, New York.

Slack, M. 1990. "Situationally Driven Local Navigation for Mobile Robots," JPL Publication No. 90-17, NASA Jet Propulsion Laboratory, Pasadena, CA, April.

Smith, W. J. 1977. *The Behavior of Communicating: An Ethological Approach*, Harvard University Press, Cambridge, MA.

Soldo, M. 1990. "Reactive and Preplanned Control in a Mobile Robot," *Proceedings of the IEEE International Conference on Robotics and Automation*, Cincinnati, OH, pp. 1128–32.

Spector, L. 1992. "Supervenience in Dynamic-World Planning," Ph.D. Dissertation, UMIACS-TR-92-55, University of Maryland, College Park.

Spinelli, D. N. 1987. "A Trace of Memory: An Evolutionary Perspective on the Visual System," in *Vision, Brain and Cooperative Computation*, eds. M. Arbib and A. Hanson, MIT Press, Cambridge, MA, pp. 165–82.

Stark, L., and Bowyer, K. 1991. "Achieving Generalized Object Recognition through Reasoning about Association of Function to Structure," *IEEE Transactions on Pattern Analysis and Machine Intelligence*, Vol. 13, No. 10, October, pp. 1097–1103.

Stark, L., and Bowyer, K. 1994. "Function-Based Generic Recognition for Multiple Object Categories," *CVGIP: Image Understanding*, Vol. 59, No. 1, January, pp. 1–21.

Stark, L., and Ellis, S. 1981. "Scanpaths Revisited: Cognitive Models Direct Active Looking," in *Eye Movements: Cognition and Visual Perception*, eds. C. Fisher, R. Monty and J. Senders, Lawrence Erlbaum Associates, Mahwah, NJ, pp. 193–226.

Steels, L. 1990. "Exploiting Analogical Representations," in *Designing Autonomous Agents*, ed. P. Maes, MIT Press, Cambridge, MA, pp. 71–88.

Steels, L. 1994. "Emergent Functionality in Robotic Agents through On-Line Evolution," *Proceedings on Artificial Life IV*, MIT Press, Cambridge, MA, pp. 8–14.

Steels, L. 1995. "When Are Robots Intelligent Autonomous Agents?" *Robotics and Autonomous Systems*, Vol. 15, pp. 3–9.

Stein, L. 1994. "Imagination and Situated Cognition," *Journal of Experimental and Theoretical AI*, Vol. 6, No. 4, October–December, pp. 393–407.

Stentz, A. 1994. "Optimal and Efficient Path Planning for Partially-Known Environments," *Proceedings of the IEEE International Conference on Robotics and Automation*, May, San Diego, CA, pp. 3310–17.

Stentz, A., and Hebert, M. 1995. "A Complete Navigation System for Goal Acquisition in Unknown Environments," *Proceedings of the IEEE/RSJ International Conference on Intelligent Robots and Systems (IROS '95)*, Pittsburgh, PA, pp. 425–32.

Stone, H. (ed.), 1980. *Introduction to Computer Architecture*, 2nd ed., SRA, Chicago.

Stroulia, E. 1991. "Reflective Self-Adaptive Systems," Ph.D. Dissertation, College of Computing, Georgia Institute of Technology, Atlanta, GA.

Suga, N., and Kanwal, J. 1995. "Echolocation: Creating Computational Maps," in *The Handbook of Brain Theory and Neural Networks*, ed. M. Arbib, MIT Press, Cambridge, MA, pp. 344–48.

Sugihara, K., and Suzuki, I. 1990. "Distributed Motion Coordination of Multiple Mobile Robots," *Proceedings of the Fifth International Symposium on Intelligent Control*, Philadelphia, PA, pp. 138–43.

Sussman, G. 1975. *A Computer Model of Skill Acquisition*, American Elsevier, New York.

Sutton, R. 1988. "Learning to Predict by the Methods of Temporal Differences," *Machine Learning*, Vol. 3, pp. 9–44.

Tachi, S., and Komoriya, K. 1985. "Guide Dog Robot," *Robotics Research, Second International Symposium*, eds. H. Hanafusa and H. Inoue, MIT Press, Cambridge, MA, pp. 333–40.

Takeuchi, S. 1996. "Hybrid Insect Robot," World Wide Web URL http://scorpio.leopard.t.u-tokyo.ac.jp/takeuchi/abstract.html, University of Tokyo.

Tan, M. 1991. "Cost-Sensitive Robot Learning," Ph.D. Dissertation, Technical Report CMU-CS-91-134, School of Computer Science, Carnegie-Mellon University, Pittsburgh, PA, May.

Tanimoto, S. 1990. *The Elements of Artificial Intelligence*, Computer Science Press, New York.

Thorndike, E. 1911. *Animal Intelligence*, Hafner, Darien, CT.

Thrun, S. 1995. "An Approach to Learning Mobile Robot Navigation," *Robotics and Autonomous Systems*, Vol. 15, No. 4, pp. 301–20.

Tianmiao, W., and Bo, Z. 1992. "Time-Varying Potential Field Based on Perception-Action Behaviors of Mobile Robot," *Proceedings of the 1992 IEEE International Conference on Robotics and Automation*, Nice, France, pp. 2549–54.

Tinbergen, N. 1953. *Social Behavior in Animals*, Methuen, London.

Tsai, W., and Chen, Y. 1986. "Adaptive Navigation of Automated Vehicles by Image Analysis Techniques," *IEEE Transactions on Systems, Man and Cybernetics*, Vol. 16, No. 5, September, pp. 730–40.

Tsotsos, J. 1989. "The Complexity of Perceptual Search Tasks," *Proceedings of the Eleventh International Joint Conference on Artificial Intelligence (IJCAI '89)*, Detroit, MI, pp. 1571–77.

Tsotsos, J. 1990. "Analyzing Vision at the Complexity Level," *Behavioral and Brain Sciences*, Vol. 13, pp. 423–69.

Tsotsos, J. 1992. "On the Relative Complexity of Active versus Passive Visual Search," *International Journal of Computer Vision*, Vol. 7, No. 2, pp. 127–41.

Tsotsos, J. 1995. "Behaviorist Intelligence and the Scaling Problem," *Artificial Intelligence*, Vol. 75, No. 2, June, pp. 135–60.

Turban, E. 1992. *Expert Systems and Applied Artificial Intelligence*, MacMillan, New York.

Turing, A. 1950. "Computing Machinery and Intelligence," *Mind*, Vol. 59, pp. 433–60.

Ullman, S. 1985. "Visual Routines," in *Visual Cognition*, ed. S. Pinker, MIT Press, Cambridge, MA, pp. 97–159.

U.S. Army. 1986. *Field Manual No. 7-7J*. Department of the Army, Washington, DC.

Vershure, P., Krose, B., and Pfeifer, R. 1992. "Distributed Adaptive Control: The Self-Organization of Structured Behavior," *Robotics and Autonomous Systems*, Vol. 9, pp. 181–96.

Vershure, P., Wray, J., Sprons, O., Tononi, G., and Edelman, G. 1995. "Multilevel Analysis of Classical Conditioning in a Behaving Real World Artifact," *Robotics and Autonomous Systems*, Vol. 16, 1995, pp. 247–65.

Wallace, R. 1987. "Robot Road Following by Adaptive Color Classification and Shape Tracking," *Proceedings of the IEEE International Conference on Robotics and Automation*, Raleigh, NC, pp. 258–63.

Wallace, R., Matsuzaki, K., Crisman, J., Goto, Y., Webb, J., and Kanade, T. 1986. "Progress in Robot Road-Following," *Proceedings of the IEEE International Conference on Robotics and Automation*, San Francisco, CA, pp. 1615–21.

Wallace, R., Stentz, A., Thorpe, C., Moravec, H., Whittaker, W. and Kanade, T. 1985. "First Results in Robot Road-Following," *International Joint Conference on Artificial Intelligence (IJCAI-85)*, Vol. 2, Los Angeles, CA, pp. 1089–95.

Walter, W. G. 1953 (reprinted 1963). *The Living Brain*, Norton, New York.

Wang, J. 1994. "On Sign-Board Based Inter-Robot Communication in Distributed Robotic Systems," *Proceedings of the IEEE International Conference on Robotics and Automation*, pp. 1045–50.

Wang, J. 1995. "Operating Primitives Supporting Traffic Regulation and Control of Mobile Robots under Distributed Robotic Systems," *Proceedings of the IEEE International Conference on Robotics and Automation*, Nagoya, Japan, June, pp. 1613–18.

Wasserman, P. 1989. *Neural Computing: Theory and Practice*, Van Nostrand Reinhold, New York.

Waterman, T. 1989. *Animal Navigation*, Scientific American Books, New York.

Watkins, C., and Dayan, P. 1992. "Q-Learning," *Machine Learning*, Vol. 8, pp. 279–92.

Watson, J. B. 1925. *Behaviorism*, People's Institute Publishing Co., New York.

Waxman, A. M., LeMoigne, J., and Srinivasan, B. 1985. "Visual Navigation of Roadways," *Proceedings of the IEEE International Conference on Robotics and Automation*, St. Louis, MO, pp. 862–67.

Waxman, A., LeMoigne, J., Davis, L., Srinivasan, B., Kushner, T., Liang, E. and Siddalingaiah, T. 1987. "A Visual Navigation System for Autonomous Land Vehicles," *IEEE Journal of Robotics and Automation*, Vol. RA-3, No. 2, April, pp. 124–41.

Webster's Ninth New Collegiate Dictionary, 1984. Merriam-Webster, Springfield, MA.

Weiner, N. 1948. *Cybernetics, or Control and Communication in Animals and Machines*, Wiley, New York.

Weitzenfeld, A. 1993. "A Hierarchical Computational Model for Distributed Heterogeneous Systems," Technical Report TR-93-02, Center for Neural Engineering, University of Southern California, Los Angeles.

Werbos, P. 1995. "Backpropagation: Basics and New Developments," in *The Handbook of Brain Theory and Neural Networks*, ed. M. Arbib, MIT Press, Cambridge, MA, pp. 134–39.

Werner, G., and Dyer, M. 1990. "Evolution of Communication in Artificial Organisms," *Technical Report UCLA-AI-90-06*, AI Laboratory, University of California, Los Angeles.

Wilkes, D., and Tsotsos, J. 1994. "Integration of Camera Motion Behaviors for Active Object Recognition," *Proceedings of the IEEE Workshop on Visual Behaviors*, Seattle, WA, June, pp. 10–19.

Wilson, E. O. 1975. *Sociobiology: The New Synthesis*, Belknap Press, Cambridge, MA.

Winston, P. 1975. "Learning Structural Descriptions from Examples," in *Psychology of Computer Vision*, ed. P. Winston, MIT Press, Cambridge, MA, pp. 157–209.

Woodfill, J., and Zabih, R. 1991. "Using Motion Vision for a Simple Robotic Task," Working Notes, *1991 AAAI Fall Symposium on Sensory Aspects of Robotic Intelligence*, Asilomar, CA, November, pp. 162–65.

Yamamoto, M. 1993. "Sozzy: A Hormone Driven Autonomous Vacuum Cleaner," *Proceedings of Mobile Robots VIII*, pp. 211–23.

Yamauchi, B. 1990. "Behavioral Memory Techniques for Robot Navigation," unpublished report, Artificial Intelligence Center, Hughes Research Laboratories, Malibu, CA.

Yamauchi, B., and Nelson, Y. 1991. "A Behavior-Based Architecture for Robots Using Real-Time Vision," *Proceedings of the International Conference on Robotics and Automation*, Sacramento, CA, pp. 1822–27.

Yanco, H., and Stein, L. 1993. "An Adaptive Communication Protocol for Cooperating Mobile Robots," *From Animals to Animats: Proceedings of the Second International Conference on the Simulation of Adaptive Behavior*, Honolulu, HI, MIT Press/Bradford Books, Cambridge, MA, pp. 478–85.

Yoshida, E., Yamamoto, M., Arai, T., Ota, J., and Kurabayashi, D. 1995. "A Design Method of Local Communication Area in Multiple Mobile Robot System," *Proceedings of the IEEE International Conference on Robotics and Automation*, June, pp. 2567–72.

Yuta, S. 1993. "Cooperative Behavior of Multiple Autonomous Mobile Robots," Workshop on Needs for Research in Cooperating Robots, *IEEE International Conference on Robotics and Automation*," Atlanta, GA.

Zadeh, L. 1973. "Outline of a New Approach to the Analysis of Complex Systems and Decision Processes," *IEEE Transactions on Systems, Man, and Cybernetics*, Vol. 3, No. 1, January, pp. 28–44.

Zapata, R., Perrier, M., Lepinay, P., Thompson, P., and Jouvencal, B. 1991. "Fast Mobile Robots in Ill-Structured Environments," *Proceedings of the IEEE/RSJ International Conference on Intelligent Robotics and Systems (IROS '91)*, Osaka, Japan, pp. 793–98.

Zelinsky, A., Kuniyoshi, Y. 1996. "Learning to Coordinate Behaviors for Robot Navigation," *Advanced Robotics*, Vol. 10, No. 2, pp. 143–59.

Zelinsky, A., Kuniyoshi, Y., Suehiro, T., and Tsukune, H. 1995. "Using an Augmentable Resource to Robustly and Purposefully Navigate a Robot," *Proceedings of the IEEE International Conference on Robotics and Automation*, Nagoya, Japan, pp. 2586–92.

Zeltzer, D., and Johnson, M. 1991. "Motor Planning: An Architecture for Specifying and Controlling the Behavior of Virtual Actors," *Journal of Visualization and Computer Animation*, Vol. 2, pp. 74–80.

Zeng, N., and Crisman, J. 1995. "Categorical Color Projection for Robot Road Following," *IEEE International Conference on Robotics and Automation*, Nagoya, Japan, pp. 1080–85.

Name Index

479   Name Index

Subject Index